signposts
to criticism
of children's
literature

signposts to criticism of children's literature

robert bator

american
library
association / chicago 1983

Designed by Vladimir Reichl

Text composed by FM Typesetting Co.
 in Times Roman and Optima.
 Blippo display type composed
 by Total Typography, Inc.

Printed on 55-pound Glatfelter
 Natural, a pH-neutral stock,
 and bound in B-grade
 Holliston Roxite cloth by
 Edwards Brothers, Inc.

Library of Congress Cataloging in Publication Data
Main entry under title:

Signposts to criticism of children's literature.

 Bibliography: p.
 1. Children's literature—History and criticism—
Addresses, essays, lectures.   I. Bator, Robert.
PN1009.A1S3924   1982   809'.89282   82-18498
ISBN 0-8389-0372-X

83627

Contents

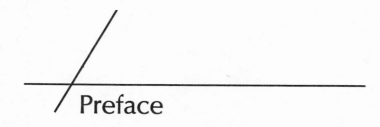

Preface

One of my colleagues pencils "criticism!" in the margins when she comes upon it in children's literature journals. In adult literature, the exclamation point would be superfluous. This book attempts to set up signposts that demarcate "criticism!" in the many regions which make up a literature for children—"Signposts which point the way toward a recognition of those qualities which are basic in good writing."[1] SIGN-POSTS TO CRITICISM OF CHILDREN'S LITERATURE is presented in the belief that juvenile literature merits not just "criticism!" but criticism, period.

Thanks to Selma Richardson, Associate Professor of the University of Illinois Graduate Library School at Urbana, Illinois, for the useful exclamation points and for generously sharing her knowledge and resources. To Gillian Avery for helpful translations from the British. To the staff, past and present, at Boys and Girls House, Toronto, for helpful and efficient library services. And to Herbert Bloom, Senior Editor, American Library Association, for his and that institution's continuing commitment to excellence in children's literature.

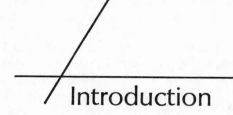

Introduction

In *Practical Education* (1798) Maria Edgeworth and Richard Lovell Edgeworth caution against tearing down literary edifices to make room for your own. In serious criticism of children's literature their advice can be dismissed, mostly because so few edifices stand. Despite the considerable heritage of literature for children and the many books about that literature, the criticism of books for children remains in the scaffolding stage.

Partly to blame is a failure to build on the reviews and critiques which were available almost from the beginning of the juvenile publishing industry. In *The Guardian of Education* (1802–5) Sarah Kirby Trimmer set out to review all that passed for children's literature in the half century after John Newbery. She did more than describe that literature; she evaluated it thoroughly, often perceptively, sometimes severely. Cinderella and other fairy tales she censured for inflaming the child's imagination, and she enjoyed *The History of Little Goody Two-Shoes* but fretted that it might "prejudice the poor against the higher orders." (Today, many who critique books for their extraliterary values are unconsciously Trimmeresque.) Nineteenth-century literary periodicals offered extensive reviews of such books for children as *Alice's Adventures in Wonderland* and *The King of the Golden River*, and as Richard Darling's *The Rise of Children's Book Reviewing in America, 1865-1881* demonstrates, mainstream American journals also seriously reviewed juvenile literature.

Twentieth-century writer-critics, such as Hilaire Belloc, W. H. Auden, and Stephen Leacock, have viewed this literature, but their observations often get crowded out by the listmakers who, trying to keep up with the 2,500 books published each year in the United States alone (and the 40,000 in print), describe on the run rather than analyze at leisure. *The New York Times* herds children's books in its seasonal "roundup reviews." Typically, one reviewer was handed twenty anthologies of poetry for children to analyze in the space normally allotted for one adult book. Only occasionally does an exceptional entry get less crowded attention.

Several of the recent anthologies about children's books are quite comprehensive, but their focus is sometimes anecdotal or embarrassingly appreciative, with principles of criticism more often assumed than voiced. "We would all rather talk about books than principles," admits John Rowe Townsend in his Arbuthnot lecture, "The Standards of Criticism."

This anthology was begun with the expectation that much suitable material would be found in newer publications: *Signal: Approaches to Children's Books, Children's Literature in Education, Phaedrus: An International Journal of Children's Literature Research, Children's Literature, The Lion and the Unicorn*, and *Children's Literature Association Quarterly,* plus even more specialized periodicals like *The ALAN Review*. The final selections did come from these publications, from the more established journals which center on juvenile literature, and, encouragingly, from those not specializing in that literature. Attention has not been paid to extraliterary concerns, including the suitability of books for particular age groups or ageism, sexism, or racism, except where these incidentally come up in the standards of literary criticism. Assertive and analytical articles were chosen over anecdotal or appreciative ones. I have had to reject some valuable explications which were signposts to narrower regions than could be covered here. Many important essays already reprinted in book form, especially the much reprinted, such as C. S. Lewis's "On Three Ways of Writing for Children" and J. R. R. Tolkien's "On Fairy Stories," are not included. This anthology represents many of those who assert that children's literature can and should be subject to serious critical scrutiny.

I am responsible for any alterations and distortions created by my transplanting and arranging of the selections to facilitate the reader's comparative analysis of a range of opinions and approaches. The selections, not equal in length nor equally valued, range from the commonplace to the unique. Inclusion of particular spokespersons is, in some cases, arbitrary; other critics could have been chosen as well to represent particular viewpoints.

I have arranged my commentary and the selections to answer three interrelated questions:

1. What is children's literature?
2. What is (and has been) the status of that literature as it affects the creator, the critic, and the consumer?

3. What critical approaches should we sanction?

Children's literature is not an island completely distanced from mainland literature, but a peninsula dependent on and emanating from the main body of literature. Those who focus on the exceptional book by Tolkien or Carroll which adults eagerly read (or the adult books which children have sometimes appropriated) earn the field some bonus acreage, but these loosened boundaries do not obviate the necessity to uncover whatever marketing considerations and artistic judgments go into what we classify as juvenile literature. Failure to define it, including the failure to separate mere books from literature, is a key element in the critical confusion.

To classify a book as a juvenile is to deprive it of many prospective readers. An almost exclusively juvenile genre—picture books—is the toughest section I have found in which to unearth criticism. This may be partly because many reviewers are not trained in art to know a halftone from a Heffalump, but when a critic can assert that one of the important reasons for the excellence of these books is simply because *adults* buy the books,[1] the problem of definition is obviously skewed with the issue of status.

Many critical questions and the existence of children's literature itself are related to the status of the child in society. In a rare book, the critical analysis of one children's writer, Neil Philip asserts that the fact that everything Alan Garner has published has been for children "has seriously distorted criticism of Garner's work."[2] Philip's solution was not to be much concerned with the problem and to treat Garner as a writer, not a children's writer. We can, like Philip and other critics, bracket distortions to give focus to the literature in question, but this should be only a temporary measure.

Unlike Philip, I am not convinced that we can separate Alan Garner the writer from Alan Garner the children's writer. Standards cannot be divorced from the status of the child and therefore the status of the children's writer. To put off those who see children as inferior beings or those who suppose that writing for children is at best apprentice work, many authors deny their work is exclusively (or even mainly) for the young. Conversely, some writers invoke children as superior savages gifted with a kinship to primitive forms not always attractive to the literary critic: folktales, myths, magic, and so on.

While demonstrating that children's books can be approached in a variety of ways, the critics offer little on the primacy of a particular method and still less on how to apply a specific method to a text. Kiddiebookland may not be quite the ghetto Sendak complains about,[3] but it is still not a very respectable place for author or critic. No wonder critics expend so much energy on apologetics and so little on actual criticism. Expository and defensive, the critics seldom move to argument. More punches are pulled than delivered, but we have at least progressed from shadowboxing.

The triple focus (is it a literature, how is that literature perceived, and how should we approach it) is also evidenced in Part 2 of this anthology, where separate genres are showcased.[4] Here also more problems than solutions are articulated, but the issues are drawn more specifically. These smaller signposts mark a more distinct territory—such as, is there a separate science fiction for children—but the questions remain familiar. And they serve the same function—to map changes and approaches. Again they reveal border disputes, for instance between fantasy and science fiction. While there has been no new genre for half a century, there are significant changes within the genres and at least one constant question: does children's literature denote a literary tag or a genuine literature?

Within that constant and changing world which marks the criticism of juvenile literature, there are many settlements but few edifices. While the region has been spared much pretentious criticism, such as the hermeneutics of *The Cat in the Hat,* even superior books sometimes are neglected for want of signposts and signposters. Instead of constantly disputing the perfect critical tools or cautiously reapplying for building permits, the critics must get on with their work if they are to move from scaffolding to the edifices they claim their territory is ready for. Whether you are a sidewalk superintendent or want to pick up hammer and nails to fashion your own signposts, you are invited to watch the master builders at their work. Just follow the signs.

part 1
the wide domain

DEFINITION
STATUS
APPROACHES

1 / Definition:
Perpetual Exception

Children's books are now almost as numerous [as adult novels].
—*The Monthly Review*, Jan. 1788

"Books for Children"—the press groans with their multitude.
—Charlotte Yonge, *Macmillan's Magazine*, July 1869

The flow of new children's books has now become a flood.
—William Lipkind, *Saturday Review*, May 12, 1962

Literature for children easily merits definition. Books have been written for them in England and America for at least 300 years, and a sizable publishing industry, almost as old, continually supplies that audience. One would expect, by now, critical consensus on what is a children's book.

One Victorian definition excluded from literature any book that "either directly or indirectly promotes any worldly or practical use." Taken literally, this directive would rule out the bulk of the juvenile books through the nineteenth century and not a few from this century. More recent criticism terms children's literature "that part of the stream that appeals to children."[1] While such a guideline would be operationally sound through the sixteenth century when books for children were those necessarily shared with adults, it is clumsily inclusive today. It would not exclude *The Amityville Horror*, the sports pages, or even cereal boxes.

To leapfrog over acceptance (what books children choose to read) to intention (what books were meant for children) is helpful. William Sloane, in his definitive study of seventeenth-century books for children, warns that "we wander far afield . . . unless we hew strictly to the line that children's books are simply books written only for children."[2] Sloane jettisoned fairy tales and all other books shared with or appropriated from adults.

The stipulative definition may be as close as one can get to the boundaries of what is children's literature. F. J. Harvey Darton offered this guide: "Printed works produced ostensibly to give children spontaneous pleasure, and not primarily to teach them, nor solely to make them good,

3

nor to keep them *profitably* quiet." Darton's history of children's books
excised textbooks but made room for pedagogic aids like Mrs. Barbauld's
Lessons for Children. Admittedly, Darton's definition was a broad principle "liable to perpetual exception." A more serviceable definition, also
by Darton, is "books originally meant to be read, or in fact habitually
read, by young persons under the age of (approximately) 15, in their
leisure hours, for enjoyment."[3] This is the best of the inclusive definitions
for the study of a particular period of literature for children. But how
is one to know at what point a contemporary book is "habitually read
by young persons"?

Intention is only one square in the hopscotch of definition, but the
easiest to mark. Obviously *The Tale of Peter Rabbit* and *The Wind in the
Willows*, which were initially intended for a specific child, can be so ear-
marked. In the absence of such a specified audience, a more generalized
intention will have to serve as a guide. To highlight the eighteenth-
century contribution, Iona and Peter Opie, updating Darton's bibliography, define by intent: "books intended to be read by children in their
leisure hours for enjoyment,"[4] with caveats of what that excludes (texts,
books adopted by or adapted for children, and so on). To include adult
works accepted by children, as does Darton, helps cover more of the
widening field of what not only is but what becomes, by annexation,
children's literature.

To define that literature of a particular era, one must be a revisionist.
A definition rejected as unsuitable for today's juvenile books fits neatly
in the sixteenth century and earlier, when children's literature *was* that
part of the stream that appealed to children, since they had no other
waters in which to fish. Today, when they have, there is some poaching
on both sides. For example, Alan Garner's *The Owl Service* is marketed
in the United States as adult science fiction and in England as "teenlit."
And *Time* complains that Maurice Sendak's *Outside over There* "has
been merchandized as *juvenilia* and is, instead, the most unusual novel
of the season."[5]

In public, anyway, many authors and artists dismiss definition as
something for publishers to puzzle over. In fact, some writers claim they
know they have penned a book for children only when a publisher classi-
fies it as such. Russell Hoban, for example, once surprised a literary
conference by asserting that he sold a manuscript as a child's book because the publisher saw it as that. He would, he vowed, just as easily have
sold it as a table or a chair, if that is what the publisher was marketing.[6]
Leg pulling or not, this is only a slight exaggeration of the public posture
of the creator of the children's book toward its audience. Some writers,
like Leon Garfield, relate shocked surprise when a manuscript they composed for adults was, with some cutting, published by their publisher's

juvenile department. John Rowe Townsend argues that the best operative definition of a book for children is whatever is issued by a publisher's juvenile division.

Critics often shun definition entirely. In a recent book of criticism of juvenile literature, the author flatly assumes "we all have a pretty good idea of what children's literature includes"[7] and lets the matter rest there. In early issues of *The Horn Book Magazine*, a leading children's journal begun in 1924, no "examination of what constitutes a book for children" was found. But, we are assured, because busy people do not waste time on questions of classification which are not giving them any trouble, this is "not a serious omission."[8] Such definition *in absentia* is condoned as well by Sheila Egoff, who believes that what is children's literature is revealed in a "unanimity . . . observable by default." Summarizing a recent international conference on juvenile literature, she, at first, seems a bit surprised over the lack of definition: "Strikingly absent is any attempt by anyone to define 'children's literature.' " But then she quickly lowers her eyebrows: "It was just assumed—and the calm assurance of the assumption is itself striking—that *children's* literature, like any other kind of literature, was simply good writing."[9]

Given such "calm assurance," it is unfashionable to hold *any* definition of children's literature. Definitions would be less crucial if it were always utterly clear which books were meant for the child and which for adults. But Victorian critics puzzled over whether Kenneth Grahame's *The Golden Age* and *Dream Days* were meant for the child or the adult.[10] And the question persists:

What is a children's book was the question being asked throughout the seventies when adults were gradually discovering that the genre so described could be the repository of fine writing as well as of the coarser bran that is part of the stuff of children's reading. Is there a line to be drawn between children's novels and adults'? If so, where does it come?[11]

Like many other critics, the questioner did not stay for an answer. Even when the question is not rhetorical, answers are seldom generated. The guidelines for the prestigious Newbery Medal, presented annually to an outstanding children's book, skirt the issue of definition. (While the books considered must display respect for a child's understanding and abilities, the award guidelines allow for any book which children ["persons under the age of fifteen"] are a potential audience. Presumably this definition embraces the book written for and the book adopted by children.) At a 1979 Modern Language Association session, children's literature experts, asked to define their own field, came up with answers "surprisingly confused and ambiguous."[12]

Such critical confusion is often condoned in preference to definition, which is invariably dismissed as "rigid." Rather than calmly assuring (or confusing themselves), the critics need to help survey the territory, however ragged its borders:

> . . . what runs between children's and adults' books is not a straight line but one as winding as the Thames on a map, if not quite so refractory a one as that of Norway's coast. It changes with tides and seasons; often it cannot be seen at all. It vanishes under flood. But there *is* a line.[13]

A line becomes many lines when distinguishing the various genres within a domain, whose limits *The British Quarterly Review* over a century ago had claimed were already "wide asunder as the poles."

Especially those who perceive juvenile literature as a single genre, as do Isabelle Jan and Perry Nodelman, would do well to plot its distinctive features if literature for children is to move from the stipulative to the qualitative. Focusing on significant characteristics, Clifton Fadiman does just that. He demonstrates that literature's lineage and its contributions.

Neither will reassurances about "good writing" alone make literature for children totally respectable. There are significant variables over time in assessing good writing and art for the young. Fashions and critics change radically. Less than a generation ago some self-appointed censors allegedly pasted paper diapers on the naked Mickey in Sendak's *In the Night Kitchen*. A contemporaneous reviewer of *Alice in Wonderland* complained that the book was stiff and overwrought. And, as the selection from *The British Quarterly Review* shows, critics can get carried away with their own enthusiasm, such as conferring greatness simultaneously on *Alice in Wonderland* and *Barefooted Birdie* (whatever that was).

As Gillian Avery illustrates, for artist and critic the final irony is that the child ultimately decides what endures in a literature mostly created and purchased *in loco juvenis*.

To avoid definition may be to flee "rigid" constraints. But what constrains, delimits. Any literature directed at a special audience is a necessarily limited literature. Literature for children will remain largely a critically uncharted and confusing territory if its limitations are not defined. For over two hundred years literature in English for children has existed in numerous varieties and techniques. For example, the school story reaches from Sarah Fielding's *The Governess* in 1749 to Robert Cormier's *The Chocolate War* in 1974, and the animal story stretches from *The Life and Perambulation of a Mouse*, 1783, to *Watership Down*, 1972. It is not sufficient to assert that children's literature has travelled a long way; signposts will be continually needed to point to where it is, how it got there, and where it is going.

The Case for a Children's Literature

Clifton Fadiman

If a children's literature is to exist as "an intelligible field of study," in Arnold Toynbee's phrase, it must justify that existence on grounds beyond its contribution to mainstream literature. It must assert some qualified claim as a sovereign state, however small. Even if a cultural sirocco were instantaneously to dry up the mainstream, a children's literature would still have to show that it is identifiable as an entity.

On the surface the literature seems to need no defense. If it is but a by-product, what is the meaning of the avalanche of children's books that annually descends upon the bookstores? What shall we say of the thousands of children's book editors, authors, artists, anthologists, librarians, professors—even critics? Is there not a gigantic, nearly world-wide industry, working away to satisfy the child's demand for something to read—or at any rate the parents' demand for something to give the child to read? Can we not, like Samuel Johnson kicking the stone to refute Bishop Berkeley's theory of the nonexistence of matter, merely point to the solid reality and say, "I refute it thus!"?

No, we must do a little better than that, just as Johnson should have known that kicks and phrases, however forcible, do not really dispose of idealism in episcopal gaiters. Let us therefore first glance briefly at the case against a children's literature.

The man-in-the-street puts it in simple terms: children's literature cannot amount to much because "it's kid stuff." The assumption here is that by nature the child is "inferior" to or less than the adult. His literature must be correspondingly inferior or less. Give the kid his comic, while I read grown-up books. But does not this amiable condescension shelter a certain insecurity? As racism is the opium of the inferior mind, as sexual chauvinism is the opium of the defective male, so child-patronage may be the opium of the immature adult. This book [the forthcoming study from which this essay is extracted], not surprisingly, admits that in

This extract, from a longer essay entitled "A Meditation on Children and Their Literature," appears by kind permission of Mr. Fadiman and Little, Brown and Company. The extract was first published in *Children's Literature* 5:9–21 (1976).

certain ways the child is patently inferior, but goes on to maintain that as an imaginative being—the being who does the reading—he is neither inferior nor superior to the adult. He must be viewed as the structural anthropologist views the "primitive"—with the same unsentimental respect, the same keen desire to penetrate his legitimate, complex symbol-system and idea-world.

There is, however, a more sophisticated case against a children's literature. Scholars have expressed it both negatively and positively.

Negatively the thing is done by omission. Literary historians leave out children's literature, as they might leave out the "literature" of pidgin-English. The English novelist Geoffrey Trease offers a key example. He refers to "Legouis and Cazamian's *History of English Literature,* in which no space is found, in 1378 pages, for any discussion of children's books and the only Thomas Hughes mentioned is not the immortal author of *Tom Brown's Schooldays,* but an obscure Elizabethan tragedian." Further examples are legion. Marc Slonim's authoritative *Modern Russian Literature from Chekhov to the Present* (1953) has no mention of Kornei Chukovsky as children's author. Hester R. Hoffman's *Reader's Adviser* (1964) finds space in its 1300 pages for a bibliography of Lithuanian literature, but not for Louisa May Alcott. C. Hugh Holman's *A Handbook to Literature* (1972) is alert to inform us about weighty literary matters from *abecedarius* to *zeugma,* but not about children's literature. That phenomenal compendium *Die Literaturen der Walt in ihrer mündlichen und schriftlichen Überlieferung,* edited by Wolfgang v. Einsiedel (1964), covers 130 assorted literatures, including the Malagasy, but from its 1400 pages you would never suspect that some writers have written for children. In Volume II of David Daiches' standard *A Critical History of English Literature* we find an otherwise excellent account of Kipling, but one from which we would never guess that he wrote masterpieces for children. While it is only fair to say that there do exist literary histories and reference manuals, notably those of recent years, that acknowledge children's books, the normal (and influential) stance of scholarship has been one of unconscious put-down by omission.

A few critics are more explicitly skeptical. In 1905 Benedetto Croce wrote: "The art of writing for children will never be a true art"; and again: "The splendid sun of pure art connot be tolerated by the as yet feeble eye of the young." He argued also that the writer's ever-present consciousness of his child public inhibited his freedom and spontaneity.

In our time, too, there have been some thoughtful students to echo Croce's negative judgment. They claim that they cannot trace a sufficiently long tradition or identify an adequate number of masterworks. Robert Coles, for instance, who has himself done much to increase our understanding of the current juvenile literary scene, cannot find in the literature "style, sensibility, vision."

As long ago as 1896, the German educationist Heinrich Wolgast aroused a storm of controversy, echoes of which are still heard, merely by his statement that "creative children's literature must be a work of art." In 1969 the French scholar Isabelle Jan felt it necessary to begin her book with the question: "Does a children's literature exist?" Three years later, in a thoughtful article, "The Classics of French Children's Literature from 1860 to 1950," she gave a cautious answer to her question, confining the issue to her own country: "French children's literature . . . does not constitute a *literature* in the strict sense. Quite unlike English children's literature it has neither continuity nor tradition."

It is apparent that the esteem in which any vocation is held affects its development. If children's literature is not generally felt to be an identifiable art, important in its own right, potentially creative minds will not be drawn to it, and it will languish or become a mere article of commerce. It is, then, worthwhile attempting to outline briefly a case which will be amplified in the book to follow. [Mr. Fadiman is currently researching and writing a book of criticism of children's literature.]

Apologists must at once concede that the children themselves couldn't care less. For them, books are to be read, not analyzed; enjoyed, not defended. They are only mildly curious as to who writes them, except insofar as a Richard Scarry, a Joan Walsh Anglund or a Maurice Sendak operates, like Wheaties, as a brand name. They do, of course, vigorously favor one book over another, but hardly on the basis of any rationale of values. Nor do they, unlike adults, show much interest in being up-to-date in their reading. The annual juvenile best-seller lists are loaded with titles first published a score of years ago. Children are proof against literary fads, literary gossip, and especially literary critics. For them books are no more literature than street play is physical exercise. The defense of their literary kingdom they cheerfully leave to their elders.

This elder rests that defense on the following grounds.

First comes the slippery concept we call tradition. A literature without a traceable history is hardly worthy of the name. If we relax our definition to the point of zero tension, children's literature may claim a foggy origin in St. Anselm's eleventh-century *Elucidarium,* possibly the first book of general information for young students. That would take our "tradition" back about 900 years. But common sense tells us that the good saint is no true source. He no more begat Lewis Carroll than the eleventh-century author of the *Ostromir Gospel* (often cited as the beginning of Russian literature) begat Dostoevsky.

Moving ahead a few hundred years we encounter an unidentifiable German who, between 1478 and 1483, issued *Der Seele Trost* ("The Soul's Consolation"), a religious tract explicitly addressed to children. Though valueless as literature, it may claim a little more legitimacy than the *Elucidarium*. One can view it as the *Urvater* of that long succession of moral tales that by this time should have turned children into paragons of virtue. If we reject *Der Seele Trost* we might accept as a point of origin Jörg Wickram's *Der jungen Knaben Spiegel* ("The Boy's Mirror"), perhaps the first "realistic" novel aimed at youth. Appearing in 1555, it would make children's literature date back over 400 years. And so we could proceed, making more and more plausible claims as we approach modern times, until we come to *A Little Book for Little Children,* by "T.W." The authority Percy Muir, dating it around 1712, considers it one of the first books designed for the entertainment of little ones. Push on a few years. In 1744 we meet John Newbery's publication *A Little Pretty Pocket-Book,* from which English children's literature is conventionally dated. But at once we recall that Perrault's fairy tales appeared almost half a century prior to this; and from the head of Perrault French children's literature may be said to spring.

Perhaps it is fair to say, then, that our field of inquiry, strictly defined, is nearly 300 years old; less strictly, perhaps 500 years old. How many mainstream literatures can claim an equally venerable tradition?

Second comes the matter of masterpieces. Here we must admit that unfortunately one word must serve two somewhat different meanings. *Oedipus Rex* is a masterpiece. But so is *Mother Goose*. Both are true to human nature. Beyond that they have little in common. It will require further discussion to determine what makes a masterpiece in our field. At this point I assert dogmatically that in its 300-plus years of history the literature has produced first-order works of art in sufficient number to support our case. I can think of about fifty that merit discussion at length. Some are already classics in the simple sense that, enduring over the decades or centuries, they are still enjoyed by large numbers of children. Indeed, are they not more naturally "classical" than many mainstream classics? It takes the whole educational machinery of the French Republic to sell its boys and girls on Corneille. But Perrault, Jules Verne, even Madame de Ségur seem to survive by their own vitality. To the nuclear core of individual high-quality works we should add the total *oeuvre* of another fifty outstanding writers whose product as a whole is impressive but of whom we cannot so confidently assert that any single book stands out. Some of these are: Lucy Boston, Colette Vivier, E. Nesbit, Arthur Ransome, William Mayne, Eleanor Farjeon, René Guillot, Paul Berna, Tove Jansson, Gianni Rodari, Joan Aiken,

Hans Baumann, José Maria Sanchez-Silva, Rosemary Sutcliff, David McCord, William Pène Du Bois, James Krüss, John Masefield, I. B. Singer, E. L. Konigsburg, Ruth Krauss, Kornei Chukovsky, Henri Bosco, Madame de Ségur, Ivan Southall.

In our view any literature worthy of the name also gains in health and variety through the nourishment supplied by writers of the second or third class, even by writers commonly scorned as purveyors of mass reading. Children's literature is rich in writers of ephemeral appeal and even richer in manufacturers of unabashed trade goods. But in a way this circumstance strengthens rather than weakens our case. The ladder theory of reading must not be swallowed whole. Yet it is true that children often normally work up from Enid Blyton or *Nancy Drew* to more challenging literature, whereas a *kitsch*-happy adult tends to stay *kitsch*-happy.

Third, our case rests also on the fact that, like science fiction, children's literature is a medium nicely adapted to the development of certain genres and themes to which mainstream media are less well suited. In "On Three Ways of Writing for Children" C. S. Lewis remarks that the only method he himself can use "consists in writing a children's story because a children's story is the best art form for something you have to say: just as a composer might write a Dead March not because there was a public funeral in view but because certain musical ideas that had occurred to him went best into that form." In the same essay, referring to E. Nesbit's Bastable trilogy, he speaks of the entire work as "a character study of Oswald, an unconsciously satiric self-portrait, which every intelligent child can fully appreciate"; and goes on to remark that "no child would sit down to read a character study *in any other form*" (italics supplied).

The major genre (perhaps nonsense verse is just as major) whose development is largely the work of children's literature is fantasy. Adult fantasies of a high order of course exist. But the form seems, for reasons we shall later examine, peculiarly suited to children; and children seem peculiarly suited to the form. Consequently we can trace a long line of fantasies, growing constantly in expressiveness and intricacy. Mac-Donald, Carroll, Collodi, Baum, de la Mare, Barrie, Lagerlöf, Grahame, Aymé, Annie Schmidt, C. S. Lewis, Tolkien, Saint-Exupéry, Rodari, Juster, Hoban—these are a few of the many writers who have found children's fantasy well fitted to statements about human life that are conveyable in no other way. While a fairy tale for grownups sounds spurious, the fairy tale for children still has successful practitioners.

There are certain experiences we have all had which, though also handleable in adult fiction, seem to take on a higher authenticity in juvenile fiction. For example, moving. For the child, moving from one neighborhood to another may be as emotionally involving as a passionate love affair is to the adult. For the adult a new neighborhood is a problem in practical adjustment; for the child, who must find a fresh peer-group to sustain him, it can be another planet.

But it is not only minor themes, such as moving, or major genres, such as fantasy, to which children's literature throws open its portals. It also offers a natural home for certain symbols frequently held to be part of our unconscious, and universally present in myth.

Take the Cave. The Cave has an eerie, backward-transporting effect on us all, a sacral mix of awe, terror, and fascination. Whether this is linked to racial recollection, to persistent memory of the womb, or to some still undiscovered kink in the psyche, we may never know. But we have all observed that the unnameable Cave-feeling is peculiarly marked in the child. With no real cave available, we will, out of a chair or a huddle of blankets, construct a reasonable facsimile. It is therefore not surprising to find in his literature a body of work ringing the changes on this "archetypal" symbol. It is no accident that Alice starts her dream life by falling through a hole in the ground; or that the most recallable episode in *Tom Sawyer* occurs in a cave. Richard Church's *Five Boys in a Cave*—an excellent suspense story—stands as the perfect type of a whole school of speleological literature, mainly for boys. France, a great land for caves, offers many examples. We can go back as far as 1864 to Jules Verne's *A Journey to the Center of the Earth,* which is really about a vast cavern. Indeed his masterpiece, *20,000 Leagues under the Sea* (1870), may be read as a vision of a watery cave. Exactly a century later Norbert Casteret's *Dans la nuit des cavernes,* extremely popular with the young, continued to exploit the theme. One of the works of nonfiction that retains its appeal is Hans Baumann's *The Caves of the Great Hunters* (German publication 1961). This deals with caves and other prehistoric sites actually discovered by boys and girls—and in one case by a dog, an animal that long ago became a first-class citizen of the republic of childhood. There is, too, Sonnleitner's vast, curious *Die Höhlenkinder,* whose first part was published as long ago as 1918 and which, despite its almost archaic tone, refuses to die. Over 300,000 copies have been sold in the German edition, and only a few years ago it was translated into English.

The Cave is but one of a group of themes, freighted with symbolic content, that find powerful development in children's literature. Related to its magical appeal is the child's affinity for the nonartificial, or for places man has abandoned to nature. A vast apparatus is needed to condition the human being to the fabricated, technological surround to which he now seems fated. But, until so conditioned, the child normally relates himself to a nontechnological world, or its nearest approximation. "The literature of childhood," remark the Opies, "abounds with evidence that the peaks of a child's experience are not visits to a cinema, or even family outings to the sea, but occasions when he escapes into places that are disused and overgrown and silent." Dozens of children's writers know and feel this, foremost among them William Mayne. Only Samuel Beckett has made grownup literature out of a dump. But in children's stories it is a familiar background, and it must be in part because such abandoned environments represent a grotesque triumph over the forces of "progress," forces the child must be *taught* to respect.

In short, any public defender of a children's literature will rest part of his case on the medium's high esthetic capacity to embody certain specific themes and symbolic structures, often more imaginatively than does the mainstream.

But the advocate must go beyond this. A body of writing ambitious to be called a literature may point to a tradition. It may claim to include a fair number of masterworks. It may make certain statements with marked effectiveness. But it must also demonstrate that it has both scope and the power to broaden that scope. A specialized, nonadaptive literature risks the fate of the dinosaur.

First, as to scope. Obviously children's literature cannot boast the range, amplitude, inclusiveness of general literature. General literature records human experience; and human experience, though not absolutely, is by and large a function of the flow of time. The child's book, though not limited to the reflection of his actual experience, is limited by what he can understand, however dimly; and understanding tends to enlarge with experience.

But we must not be too quick to pass from the dimensions of length and breadth to that of depth, and say that children's books can never be as "deep." The child's world is smaller than the grownup's; but are we so sure that it is shallower? Measured by whose plumbline? Is it not safer to say that, until the child begins to merge into the adolescent, his mental world, though of course in many respects akin to that of his elders, in many others obeys its own private laws of motion? And if this is so, it might be juster to use one plumbline to measure the depth of his literature, and a somewhat different one for that of his elders. No one will deny the depth of Dostoyevsky's Grand Inquisitor episode. But who is to say that, to a sensitive child reader, William Mayne's *A Game of Dark* does not convey an equally profound intimation of the forces of evil? Here are six lines of a "song" called *Firefly,* by Elizabeth Madox Roberts. A seven-year-old child, who happened to be a genius, might have written it; and any seven-year-old child can read it with pleasure.

> A little light is going by,
> Is going up to see the sky,
> A little light with wings.
>
> I never could have thought of it,
> To have a little bug all lit
> And made to go on wings.

The child who feels all that these six lines convey (especially the fourth) is caught up in profound reflection on the very nature of creation. The esthetic experience is for the child no less rich than would be for the adult a reading of Eliot's *Four Quartets.* The scale differs, the "thickness" does not.

To return to the matter of scope: it is clear that traditionally the child's literature has been closed (nowadays there are narrow apertures) to certain broad areas of human experience: mature sexual relationships, economic warfare in its broadest aspects, and in general the whole problematic psychic universe that turns on the axletree of religion and philosophical speculation. That vast library generated by Unamuno's "tragic sense of life" is one that—though there are certain exceptions—is not micro-reflected in the child's books. Though again one must qualify, his is a literature of hope, of solutions, of open ends. To say that is to acknowledge the limits of its scope.

But if we turn to form rather than content, the judgment becomes a little less clear-cut. Children's literature contains no epic poems, not only because it developed long after the age of the epic but because its audience is ill-suited to the epic length. As for its lyric poetry, it includes several forms—nonsense verse, nursery rhymes, street rhymes, lullabies —in which the adult lyric tradition is comparatively defective. But in general its verse forms are simple and restricted as against the variety and complexity of mainstream verse. The literature contains little drama, whether in prose or verse, worth serious attention. It has so far evolved nothing closely resembling the traditional essay, although in an acute comment Jean Karl points to its remarkable powers of mutation: "Who would have dreamed that the familiar essay, no longer popular with adults, would suddenly be found in children's books, presenting all sorts of abstract ideas in picture-book form?" The reference here is to what is often called "concept books." A first-rate example is James Krüss's *3 × 3,* pictures by Eva Johanna Rubin, which is essentially a graphic expository essay on the abstract idea of three-ness.

But almost all the other major genres, whether of fact or fiction, are represented. Some, like the ABC book and the picture book, are virtually (as would naturally be the case) unique to the literature. So, in the same way, are children's books written by children themselves: Daisy Ashford's *The Young Visiters* (1919), surely one of the dozen funniest books in English, or *The Far-Distant Oxus* by Katharine Hull and Pamela Whitlock, written when the authors were fourteen and fifteen respectively. Children's fiction can be so experimental as to be reactionary: Gillian Avery has written Victorian novels that are not parodies or pastiches, but interesting in themselves.

Most fictional forms one can think of are represented on the children's shelves. Some, such as the fairy tale, the fantasy, the fable, the animal story and the adventure yarn, can be found there in rich and highly developed profusion. The historical novel, especially in England, flourishes to a degree that makes it possible to hail Rosemary Sutcliff *tout court* as one of the best historical novelists using the language. Even the minor genre of the detective story is represented, long before Poe, in Mrs. Barbauld's *The Trial* (mid-1790s).

There are dozens of sub-genres and sub-sub-genres that are by nature given special prominence in children's literature: certain kinds of jokes and riddles; stories of toys and dolls, stuffed animals, animated objects; "bad boy" and "bad girl" stories; "career novels"; a whole school of chimney-sweep stories; children's puppet plays; "waif" novels; the school story; the vacation novel; and many others. We do not dispose of the matter when we say that these forms are simply a response to the child's natural interests, any more than we dispose of Proust when we say that his work is a response to the adult's interest in depth psychology. In both cases literature is enriched by the evolution of fresh vehicles for the imagination.

While no absolutely first-rate history or biography has been written for children, I would claim that the field has produced at least one masterly autobiography, on its own level as worthy of study as the *Confessions* of Rousseau or St. Augustine: Laura Ingalls Wilder's *Little House* series.

It is fair to say, then, that the scope of our literature, though it has its lacunae, is astonishingly broad. But it is not only broad. It has the capacity to broaden further, to invent or assimilate new forms, themes and attitudes, to devise original techniques of exposition and narration. The texts of Maurice Sendak are as "new" in their way as Joyce's *Ulysses* once was. So is the picture book itself, really a product of modern times, with its power to tell a story simultaneously in two mediums: Else Holmelund Minarik's *Little Bear* series illustrates this well. The all-picture book has evolved even more ingenious modulations: Mitsumasa

Anno's dreamlike series of gravity-defying, non-Euclidean *Jeux de Construction* is only one startling example. The trick three-dimensional book (pop-ups, for example), though hardly part of literature, is nonetheless ingenious, satisfying, and a specific response to the child's desire to manipulate, change, construct.

Finally, as we shall see, contemporary children's literature has in the last decade or so found it possible to handle, even if not always successfully, a whole constellation of themes it was formerly denied: everything from drug addiction to homosexuality. (One anticipates with confidence the announcement of *The Boy's Own Handbook of Necrophilia*.)

The contemporary "teenage" or "young adult" novel has still to prove itself as art. Yet it bears witness to the flexibility of children's literature, its power to enlarge its range, to experiment with new forms and themes. Without such power its claim to be a "literature" would be vitiated. Indeed its receptivity is now of so high an order as to blur its boundaries. "Less is more," says Browning's Andrea del Sarto, a phrase Mies van der Rohe applied perhaps too rigorously. Yet it holds profound truth. Lately the human race has become aware of the fatality lying at the heart of unchecked growth. It is possible to argue that a similar fatality inheres in the unchecked growth of any art form. We may—the returns are far from all in—be witnessing such a wild cancerous proliferation in the body we are now exploring.

To complete our case for a children's literature I offer two last considerations, one turning on the matter of scholarship, the other on the matter of institutions. Both may be debater's points. I concede that they are less persuasive than the arguments already adduced. All they do is point to the probability of the literature's existence. In themselves they do not constitute firm evidence of its high quality or organic integrity.

A literature is the sum of its *original* communications, especially its better ones, more especially its best. It is hard for us to meditate upon a literature as an intelligible field of study until the non-original communicator, the theorist and historian, have worked upon it. Had Aristotle never lived, classical Greek literature would still rank supreme. Nonetheless the *Art of Poetry* helps us to perceive its topography and distinguish its boundaries. We are trying at the moment to establish such topography and boundaries for a children's literature. Now the specific identity of any art becomes more firmly established as it develops self-consciousness. Of that self-consciousness critics, scholars, and historians are the expression.

It would seem that you cannot produce a theory without something to theorize about, nor a history without something to chronicle. Or is this always true? A. Merget's *Geschichte der deutschen Jugendliteratur*

("History of German Juvenile Literature") appeared in 1867, before the existence of any literature worthy of the name. But this striking example of German thoroughness does not completely undermine the feeling we have, when we see a signpost, that it is probably pointing to some place that is actually there.

Ten years ago, when I started this project, I thought all I had to do was read a few thousand original communications called children's books, think about them, and arrange my thoughts on paper. I knew, of course, that there were several standard histories which should probably be read too. But soon I became aware that there were almost (well, not quite) as many books *about* children's literature as there were books *of* children's literature, and that anyone who wished to do more than merely rationalize a set of impressions would have to become familiar with a learned corpus of astonishing proportions.

In one of his few transparent lines of verse Mallarmé complains

> *La chair est triste, hélas! et j'ai lu tous les livres.*
> [The flesh is sad, alas, and all the books are read.]

I can subscribe to neither half of the hexameter. Even after ten years' sampling of the scholarly literature, my flesh remains moderately cheerful; and it is a dead certainty that I have not read all the books. No one could. Few disciplines of such modest dimensions have evoked so much commentary as that associated with children's books and reading. The children themselves would be dumbfounded, perhaps exploding into hilarious laughter, could they realize what alps of research and theory have been reared since Perrault, his eye on both young and old, first set down the tale of Little Red Riding-Hood.

I intend no mockery. The body of criticism and history is not only formidable; it is valuable. It points up to the importance of what at first might seem a minor field of investigation. Though some of it, inevitably, is but dusty poking into the deservedly dead, and much of it duplicative, yet as a whole it reflects a solid tradition, of acute importance in the shaping of the minds and hearts of children.

There are few "developed" countries that have not produced a scholarly literature. It is vast in the cases of the United States, Britain, most of Europe, including Soviet Russia, and Japan. While I have not yet met with such material from Liberia, I have pored over Paul Noesen's *Geschichte der Luxemburger Jugendliteratur,* keeping in mind that the population of Luxembourg, counting every child, is 336,500.

True, the burden of our case rests on the original communications rather than on the commentaries. But it is only fair to set against such doubting Thomases as Coles and Croce the counterweight of a host of creative writers and thoughtful scholars for whom a children's literature is as much *there* as his mountain was for Malory. Among the creators of that literature who have defended its integrity are James Krüss, Eleanor Cameron, Maurice Sendak, I. B. Singer, J. R. R. Tolkien, C. S. Lewis, Kornei Chukovsky. Among the scholars who have analysed its properties, staked out its limits, and celebrated its charms are the Frenchman Paul Hazard, the Italian Enzo Petrini, the Swiss Hans Cornioley, the Englishman Brian Alderson, the Canadian Sheila Egoff, the Swede Eva von Zweigbergk, the Iberian Carmen Bravo-Villasante, the Netherlander J. Riemans-Reurslag, the Luxembourger Paul von Noesen, the Argentinian Dora Pastoriza de Etchebarna, the Mexican Blanca Lydia Trajo, the New Zealander Dorothy White, the Israeli Uriel Ofek, the Norwegian Jo Tenfjord . . . the catalogue, though not endless, is impressive.

The mere existence of institutions is, of course, no argument for the values they incorporate: the Mafia, one supposes, is as intricate and efficient an institution as one could well desire. Yet the complex world-network of children's libraries, book and record clubs, research centers, publishers, scholarly magazines, academies, book councils, "book weeks," prizes and awards, summer schools, writers' associations, radio and television programs (but switch on a red light here), illustration exhibits, book fairs—all this, while alloyed with commercialism, bureaucratization, cliqueishness, and a certain inappropriate solemnity, nevertheless demonstrates the existence of a large and lively world of children's literature.

/A Wholly Pragmatic
/Definition

/ John Rowe Townsend

What in particular is children's literature? That is quite a difficult one. There is a sense in which we don't need to define it because we know what it is. Children's literature is *Robinson Crusoe* and *Alice* and *Little Women* and *Tom Sawyer* and *Treasure Island* and *The Wind in the Willows* and *Winnie the Pooh* and *The Hobbit* and *Charlotte's Web.* That's simple; but it won't quite do. Surely *Robinson Crusoe* was not written for children, and do not the *Alice* books appeal at least as much to grownups?; if *Tom Sawyer* is children's literature, what about *Huckleberry Finn?;* if the *Jungle Books* are children's literature, what about *Kim* or *Stalky?;* and if *The Wind in the Willows* is children's literature, what about *The Golden Age?;* and so on.

Since any line-drawing must be arbitrary, one is tempted to abandon the attempt and say that there is no such thing as children's literature, there is just literature. And that, I believe, is true. Children are not a separate form of life from people; no more than children's books are a separate form of literature from just books. Children are part of mankind; children's literature is part of literature. While all this is true, it doesn't get you anywhere, because the fact that children are part of mankind doesn't save you from having to separate them from adults for certain essential purposes; nor does the fact that children's literature is part of literature save you from having to separate it for practical purposes (in the libraries and bookshops, for instance). I pondered this question for some time while working on *A Sense of Story* and came to the conclusion that in the long run children's literature could only be regarded as consisting of those books which by a consensus of adults and children were assigned to the children's shelves—a wholly pragmatic definition. In dealing with current output, I came to the conclusion that, absurd as it might seem, the only workable definition of a children's book was "a book that appeared on the children's list of a publisher."

Excerpted from "Standards of Criticism for Children's Literature" in *The Arbuthnot Lectures 1970–1979*, ed. Zena Sutherland (Chicago: American Library Assn., 1980), pp. 26–27.

This is not merely pragmatic, it is a definition that seems to hold itself up by its own bootstraps. Yet in the short run it does appear that, for better or worse, the publisher decides. If he puts a book on the children's list, it will be reviewed as a children's book and will be read by children (or young people), if it is read at all. If he puts it on the adult list, it will not—or at least not immediately.

2 / Status:
In and out of the Literary Sandbox

Creators of children's books perennially are expected to testify about their craft. Their testimony should help us map what is children's literature, yet many children's writers profess not to write consciously for children. Accepting the Newbery Medal in 1976, Susan Cooper claimed: "Most of us, mind you, have no idea whether we are writing books for children or adults. We write the book that wants to be written, and let our publishers tell us what it is."[1]

There are many precedents for Cooper's disclaimer. George MacDonald, a Victorian writer for children, denied he was such by intention: "I do not write for children, but for the childlike, whether of five or fifty, or seventy-five." MacDonald tried to hide his child audience by combining it with an adult audience. Another notable British writer for the young, Arthur Ransome, restricted his audience—to himself: "You write not for children, but for yourself, and if, by good fortune, children enjoy what you enjoy, why then you are a writer of children's books."[2]

Ransome's assertion is echoed by Meindert De Jong, Lucy Boston, Barbara Wersba, and many other children's writers. Their common cry, "I write for myself" may be shorthand for "I write for the child within me and therefore for all children." Gillian Avery, for instance, reflects that she writes to please herself without any thought of the needs or tastes of a particular age group. But she adds, "I can remember pretty well what I liked when I was ten and what I disliked, and when I come to thrash out the final shape of the book I have this in mind." Or, as William Mayne succinctly puts it, "I write for myself, but myself of long ago."[3]

The authors' claims that they write for themselves might also be what Freud termed a salutory "regression in the service of the ego."[4] (If only we could keep children's writers from ritual assemblies like cocktail parties and award banquets!) As Aidan Chambers suggests, writers should be allowed to believe what they need to believe to do their work. To maintain that one writes, initially, to please oneself may be accurate and beneficial, but, once published, the writer becomes merely the first in a succession of readers. Ursula K. Le Guin, commenting on her childhood reading, reminds us that the author comes in

like the God of the eighteenth-century deists, only at the beginning. Long ago, before you and the book met each other. The author's work is done, complete; the ongoing work, the present act of creation, is a collaboration by the words that stand on the page and the eyes that read them.[5]

Modern literary critics, whether structuralist or post structuralist, would easily concur with Le Guin.

But we should not only interpret the authors' denials, we should also account for them. Their consistency and vehemence may be explained by the perceived low status of literature for children. "It had all too easily become a habit to look at children's literature as a practice field for would-be writers, as a literary sandbox for writing housewives, grandmothers, aunts, and above all school teachers,"[6] one author laments. The fear of association with women's and children's concerns obviously causes some of the distancing of the child writer from the child audience.

Francelia Butler sees the guilt by association with the puerile and the female (the child caretaker) as one key element in juvenile literature's being excluded from serious critical consideration. Felicity Hughes reveals Henry James's plea that the novel be freed from "the presence of the ladies and children—by whom I mean, in other words, the reader irreflective and uncritical." James's assumptions demonstrate that the "adult chauvinist piggery,"[7] which Ursula K. Le Guin discovered militating against the writer for children, similarly deprecates the child reader.

No wonder children's writers sometimes use extraordinary measures to keep from being confined by and in the literary sandbox. Pamela Travers, for example, admits that she had herself listed on the title page of *Mary Poppins* as P. L. Travers because:

Children's books are looked on as a sideline of literature. . . . They are usually thought to be associated with women. I was determined not to have this label of sentimentality put on me so I signed by my initials, hoping people wouldn't bother to wonder if the books were written by a man, woman or kangaroo.[8]

Besides General Macho, "that sleaziest of dictators,"[9] the writer for children is also bedeviled by the naive belief that proximity to a specific child prompts every children's book. Arnold Lobel, recent Caldecott Medalist, answers that simplistic notion:

It's not so. Some of the greatest people in children's books, both past and present, have never been near a child. . . . Sendak, I don't think has even been within two feet of a child. You take it out of the child in yourself. It doesn't mean to write a children's book you have a special rapport with children on a social level. There's a statue in Central Park of Hans Christian Andersen with children climbing all over it. Hans Christian Andersen was a fussy, prissy, old maid of a bachelor, and I don't think he would have children anywhere within ten miles of him.[10]

Given such prevalent presumptions and prejudices, the public reluctance of the writer for children to embrace that audience and the temptation to disguise or even deny it are understandable. Some authors have reconsidered that reluctance. Like Susan Cooper, Alan Garner maintains that he is a writer, period, and a children's writer because his publisher puts his work on their children's list. Later, however, Garner rethinks his ready answer (The oh-so-familiar "I don't write for children, but entirely for myself.") with which he stops short anyone who asks him if, after "a bit more practice," he will attempt a "real book." He confesses: "Yet I do write for children and have done so from the very beginning. Only recently have I come to realize that, when writing for myself, I still am writing for children—or, rather, for adolescents."[11]

Similarly, Maurice Sendak, questioned about his claim "there is no such thing as a children's book," admits he was wrong:

There *are* books that are written, illustrated, and published as children's books, and they are good books, produced very much with children in mind: their pleasures, sorrows, and passionate interests. They are often practical and full of the pedantic details that delight children.[12]

Joseph Krumgold, in converting a film to the Newbery Award book *. . . and Now Miguel*, discovered that "if this age-old process is to be studied, in a literary way, it is the child you have to write for."[13] Such testimony is still rare enough to surprise. Ellen Raskin, accepting her Newbery Medal in 1979, acknowledged, "I do write for children consciously and proudly." This open admission prompted a cheer from at least one editor evidently wearied by previous denials from the legion of I-write-for-selfers, even though "such protestations somehow never carry a ring of sincerity or truth."[14]

Among these who readily admit to writing for the child, some writers claim too much for their young audience. To Isaac Bashevis Singer the child, no longer the "uncritical listener of stories," has become "a consumer of a great growing literature—a reader who cannot be deluded by literary and barren experiments." Many writers claim the child audience is a special challenge. When Maurice Sendak finds children "tough to work for," many of his colleagues would assent, but to claim, with him, that children are "*the* most critical audience in the world;" or to maintain with Isaac Bashevis Singer that "children are the best readers of genuine literature"; or to insist with Lloyd Alexander that "the children's book form is more mature" than the adult book seems overstated. Such idealization of the juvenile reader is expectable from authors who, like the child, have been continual victims of "oppression and inconsiderability."[15]

A more traditional attempt to raise the status of a book for children links it inextricably with the adult book. George MacDonald, we have seen, almost a century ago claimed that his readers were five, fifty-five, or seventy-five. W. H. Auden swore there were no good books written exclusively for children, but the authority most often invoked in linking the child book to adult tastes is C. S. Lewis: "I am almost inclined to set it up as a canon that a children's story which is enjoyed only by children is a bad children's story."[16] But yesterday's maxim becomes today's cliché:

An old cliché that hampers criticism of children's fiction mightily . . . is that a good children's novel is a good novel, period. That appears to claim too much for children's fiction, but it actually claims too little—like saying a good tragedy is a good play, period. Only by coming to terms with what is special about children's fiction *as* children's fiction can we come to understand its special power over us.[17]

The conflation of children's and adult literature does not simply crowd out criticism, it makes the evaluation of juvenile books impossible. Ignoring the evidence of developmental psychology (Piaget et al.), it leaves no room for the changes within the reader. Well before their children will, parents reach nausea over the sixteenth reading of Dr. Seuss's initially delightful *Green Eggs and Ham*. Should a child tucked in with *Goodnight Moon* still be babbling "goodnight socks" forty years later?

So much for the nonliterary presumptions which confine the creator of juvenile books to a literary ghetto. What are the literary constraints authors for children must assume? There are, of course, variables again across time. One eighteenth-century writer felt that writing for children required one to stifle one's imagination, a sacrifice she was certain was acceptable to the Almighty. Mrs. Trimmer worried about overheating a child's imagination; Johnson, Lamb and Coleridge thought otherwise. For decades theirs was the minority view. The twentieth-century writer, it is assumed, will have far fewer restrictions on his or her craft. In the early 1960s C. S. Lewis testified that writing for children imposed four modifications on his habits of composition: (1) a strict limit on his vocabulary; (2) the exclusion of erotic love; (3) the cutting down on reflective and analytic passages; and (4) the production of chapters of nearly equal length for convenience in reading the work aloud.[18]

Had Lewis lived to read today's young adult fiction, he could adopt fewer constraints. Some modern teen fiction does present at least mildly erotic scenes; intricate reflection and lengthy analysis can sometimes be permitted, as in Richard Adams's *Watership Down*. (Take that, Henry James!) Many writers, like E. B. White and Richard Scarry, deliberately leave in some difficult words for a child to puzzle over, so the vocabulary limits also would be less strict now than in the 1950s when Lewis put out his Chronicles of Narnia. By the late 1960s Alan Garner admitted only the laws against obscenity as a limitation on his craft. He relates one instance of "editorial inflexibility"—the excising of the word "bastards" in a novel of his printed in the early 1960s. That word would no longer be bluepencilled in a novel for adolescents this side of the Atlantic, anyway. Nat Hentoff was assured by his publisher that there were *no* limits on his vocabulary when he began his first young adult book; Jane Yolen has told would-be writers for children that there are *no* taboos in that field.[19] We are again back to dangerous overstatement. Many literary constraints still exist in writing for children. To at least one modern children's writer these are creative boundaries. To those who ask her if writing for children is constricting, Katharine Paterson answers:

William, don't you find fourteen tightly rhymed lines an absolute prison? Ah, Pablo, if you could just yank the picture off that lousy scrap of canvas! You get the point. Form is not a bar to free expression, but the boundaries within which writers and artists freely choose to work.[20]

Hugh Crago investigates the central dilemma: should an author or artist break away from or work within the constraints of the children's book world? Whichever tack the writer chooses, the critic should help shake the sand off the author. Chambers' "Reader in the Book" thesis offers one way to do this. Another would be to investigate the conscious artistry that goes into the making of so-called nursery trifles. Studying the nine separate workings of the text that became *Charlotte's Web*, Peter Neumeyer shows how E. B. White honed his prose for the sake of clarity.[21] To what extent this was done to suit a child audience is not known, but careful textual analyses like Chambers' and Neumeyer's could lead to a much needed theory of composition for the juvenile book.

If children's authors seem defensive, they have reason to be. Their chosen field is simultaneously praised and blamed for displaying simplicity, for overconcern with story, for withstanding and for escaping the claws of criticism, for ignoring and for being concerned with audience. Critical confusion keeps children's literature and its artists peripheral. Small wonder they go to the lengths Mary Stolz decries, maintaining there are no children, only younger adults, or that they utilize more subtle semantic distinctions, like Scott O'Dell who insists he is not a children's writer, rather a "writer of books that children read."[22]

If children's authors are to escape from the trap of the sandbox, the critic must move from sitting at their feet to the child readers who must reconstruct or deconstruct their texts. No less than the reader or the writer, the critic must deal with "the work itself." Critics must also discover why that literature is often relegated to a peripheral playground and what works to pen its writers in the literary sandbox.

Children's Literature: Theory and Practice, Part 1

Felicity A. Hughes

The theory of Children's Literature has been for some time in a state of confusion. That so many good and important works of literature have been produced in that time is a cheering reminder that art can survive even the worst efforts of critical theorists. There are no grounds for complacency in this state of affairs, however, because although theoretical confusion may not stifle good art, it can impose significant constraints and directions upon it.

I suggest that the origin of some confused beliefs, including the belief

Reprinted from *ELH* [English Literary History] 45:542–52 (1978) with permission from the Johns Hopkins University Press and the author. For the second half of this selection, see chapter 8 in this volume.

that there is, in some significant literary sense, such a thing as children's literature at all, is to be found in the theory of the novel. The history of children's literature coincides, more or less, with that of the novel. What historians of children's literature often call the first real children's book, Newbery's *A Little Pretty Pocket-Book* was published within a decade of Richardson's *Pamela*. It is probable that more than mere coincidence is involved since similar social conditions are conducive to both. In fact, the development of a separate body of literature addressed to children has been crucially associated with that of the novel, and the critical fortunes of the one have been strongly affected by those of the other. In this paper I shall discuss that dependence with respect to twentieth-century novels for children, and argue that it accounts for some of the many confusions which hamper attempts to construct theories of children's literature.

The crisis in the novel which occurred in the 1880s is generally agreed to have determined the development of the twentieth-century novel. In that decade a new view of the novel is held to have triumphed over an older one. David Stone writes of the eighties " . . . with the deaths of the established Victorian novelists, not only a younger group of novelists, but an entirely new set of attitudes towards fiction appeared."[1] John Goode suggests that the change involved " . . . a reappraisal of the possibilities and responsibilities of the novel which is important because it represents the beginning of the dividing line between the Victorian novel and the twentieth-century novel."[2] The emergent view is characterised by Walter Allen as "a heightened, more serious conception of the novel as art."[3] Further, it is agreed by these and other writers that this change came about at least partly in response to changing social conditions and in particular what were seen as profound changes in the readership of the novel. I propose to consider the implications of this crisis for the development of a separate literature for children.

From its inception in the eighteenth century the novel had been seen in England as at least potentially *family* reading. A glance through the material collected in Ioan Williams' *Novel and Romance 1700–1800* will amply bear this out.[4] The words "young people" or "our youth" appear in virtually every review or essay. The debate on the relative merits of Richardson and Fielding seems to have revolved around the question of which novel was more appropriate for the moral, social and literary education of British youth. In spite of occasional deprecatory murmurs, Victorian novelists also accepted the constraints that a family readership was held to impose on them. In light of this it is clear that Moore, when he protested in 1885 that "never in any age or country have writers been asked to write under such restricted conditions," was either taking a very large view of his "age" or wrong.[5] Judgement of novels had always involved a hypothetical young reader.

Moreover, throughout that same history, the status of the novel as a genre was comparable to that of the bourgeoisie it largely depicted. In spite of its rapid rise to dominance as preferred reading, it failed to gain the accolade of critical and learned opinion. Lacking the long and distinguished classical ancestry of poetry and drama, the novel was engaged in a struggle to live down the stigma of being a "low" form, not art but entertainment. Critics turned their attention to novels cursorily and with distaste, real or feigned, recommending the best novels only in the context of a general caveat against the genre.

The crisis of the eighties effected changes in both these circumstances. By the turn of the century it was clear that at least some English novelists would no longer allow themselves to be held responsible for the moral welfare of the nation's youth. By about 1910, moreover, the novel seemed to have risen above its old inferior status. It received more critical recognition; it was old enough to have something of a history; it had, as Allen Tate later put it, "caught up with poetry."[6] There was acknowledged to be an "art of fiction" and there were some novels that could be referred to as "art novels" or "serious novels."

It was also true that by the turn of the century something was emerging that might be called "children's literature." Just as D. H. Lawrence's titles seem to proclaim themselves as "M," for mature readers only, so Edith Nesbit's books equally clearly announce themselves as "C," for child readers only. Stevenson's *Treasure Island,* which had been read with pleasure by Henry James, was reclassified as a "children's classic" and the day when novels could confidently be dedicated to "boys of all ages" were over.

I doubt whether this particular development, initiating as it did a trend in fiction writing which has continued to the present, was a mere accident of literary history. I suggest that a plausible explanation for it can be found in the acceptance by writers and critics of a theory about fiction which directly attributed the low status of the novel *to* its family readership. The theory in question is that developed by Henry James in his essays. Setting aside, for the moment, the question of whether the theory is true or false, I shall argue that one major consequence of its acceptance was that novelists, in a bid for critical respectability, tried to dissociate the novel from its family readership and redirect it toward what was seen as art's traditional elite audience of educated adult males outside the home, at court, the coffee house, or the club. The "serious novel" would have to earn its laurels, or win its spurs, at the cost of being unsuitable for women and children—beyond their reach not only because it dealt with facts of life from which such people had to be "protected," but because it was too difficult, requiring not only maturity but discrimination beyond the reach of all but the highly educated. Since no one can start off life highly educated, children are *ipso facto* disqualified.

The implications of this particular aspect of the crisis in the novel can best be studied by a consideration of the controversy between James and R. L. Stevenson. It is generally agreed that James was making a bid to establish the novel as serious art in his manifesto, "The Art of Fiction."[7] In that essay, it will be remembered, he claimed that the novelist's function was "to attempt to represent life" and that the novel should not be presented by its author as "just a story" or as "make believe," but as something akin to history. Novel-writing being an art which "undertakes immediately to reproduce life," it must take itself seriously if it wishes to be taken seriously and in particular, "it must demand that it be perfectly free." "It goes without saying," he says, "that you will not write a good novel unless you possess the sense of reality." He gave *Treasure Island* only qualified praise saying that it is delightful "because it appears to me to have succeeded wonderfully in what it attempts," and compared it to its disadvantage with a story by a French writer which attempted to "trace the moral consciousness of a child." Although he acknowledged that the French story failed in what it attempted, he nevertheless preferred it to *Treasure Island* because he could measure it against his own sense of reality; "I can at successive steps . . . say Yes or No, as it may be, to what the artist puts before me." In *Treasure Island* he could not make that decision, because "I have been a child in fact, but I have been on a quest for a buried treasure only in supposition." James here suggests a criterion for critical approval which would exclude all stories except those the reader can measure against his own sense of reality. It may be inferred from this that a "sense of reality" is required of the reader as well as of the writer, so that he is actually as well as theoretically able to say "Yes or No" to what the writer offers. Writer and reader, then, are to enter into a sophisticated contract by which, although illusion is held to be the object of the exercise, no one is actually taken in, the reader having constantly to judge the merit of the novel *as illusion* by measuring it against something else.

Since James' principal criterion for the seriousness of a novel was the degree to which it gave the illusion of portraying real life, when Stevenson came to answer the essay he found himself in the position of defending the notion of the novel as "make believe." He called it "a

peculiarity of our attitude to any art" that "no art produces illusion."[8]
Yet his requirement of the reader seems to require the involuntary assent appropriate to illusion. In "A Gossip on Romance," he wrote,

In anything fit to be called by the name of reading, the process itself should
be absorbing and voluptuous; we should gloat over a book, be rapt clean out
of ourselves, and rise from the perusal, our mind filled with the busiest kaleida-
scopic dance of images, incapable of sleep or of continuous thought. . . . It
was for this pleasure that we read so closely and loved our books so dearly,
in the bright, troubled period of boyhood.[9]

Stevenson admired novels which made intense demands of sympathy
and identification, whereas James required that characters in novels be
presented "objectively" in a way that prevents the reader from entering
into any extraordinary sympathy with them. Their disagreement over
Crime and Punishment was reported by Stevenson in a letter thus:

. . . it was easily the greatest book I have read in ten years. Many find it dull.
Henry James could not finish it: all I can say is that it nearly finished me. It
was like having an illness. James did not care for it because the character of
Raskolnikov was not objective: and at that I divined a great gulf between us
and . . . a certain impotence in many minds of today which prevents them
from living *in* a book or character, and keeps them standing afar off, specta-
tors of a puppet show.[10]

While it is difficult to see the consistency of either writer's position, it is
clear enough that they were opposed on the two points under discussion.
James claimed that novels are serious in so far as they attempt to provide "the intense illusion of real life." Stevenson denied this claim.
Secondly, James required characters to be "objective" and the reader
to be detached, impartial and skeptical, whereas Stevenson saw reader
involvement and the submersion of self to be the triumph of art.

In reviewing this controversy we should also bear in mind that other
great item of discussion in the eighties and nineties—the early years of
State Education in England—the spread of literacy, which was assumed to be proceeding rapidly through the agency of universal compulsory education. By the turn of the century these two issues had come
together in James' thinking in a way that was to be widespread not
long after his death. The attitude I wish to discuss is that expressed in
an essay called "The Future of the Novel" which he published in 1899.[11]
What that essay expresses is an undisguised dismay at the galloping
popularity of the novel, the great increase in novel readers, which he
attributed to the fact that

The diffusion of the rudiments, the multiplication of the common schools, has more and more had the effect of making readers of women and of the very young. Nothing is so striking in a survey of this field . . .

and he observes the growth of writing for children in these terms:

The literature, as it may be called for convenience, of children is an industry that occupies by itself a very considerable quarter of the scene. Great fortunes, if not great reputations, are made we learn, by writing for school-boys. . . . The published statistics are extraordinary and of a sort to engender many kinds of uneasiness. The sort of taste that used to be called "good" has nothing to do with the matter: we are so demonstrably in the presence of millions for whom taste is but an obscure, confused, immediate instinct.

The distaste and even fear of the mass of women and children readers which James manifests here springs, I suggest, from his suspicion that the popularity of the novel will diminish its chances of finding the elite audience, the existence of which will justify its status as art. He thinks that being exclusive is a necessary condition for novels being serious. Popular novels cannot be good, they must be vulgar. Commercial success therefore is a sign of declining standards:

The high prosperity of our fiction has marched very directly, with another "sign of the times," the demoralisation, the vulgarisation of literature in general, the increasing familiarity of all such methods of communication, the making itself supremely felt, as it were, of the presence of the ladies and children—by whom I mean, in other words, the reader irreflective and uncritical.

So serious a menace did James take this to be that he prophesied on the brink of this century:

By what it decides to do in respect to "the young," the great prose fable will, from any serious point of view, practically see itself stand or fall.

He refrains from making any specific suggestions as to what should be done with respect to the young but his general drift is clear when he goes on to demand again "freedom" for the serious novelist. If the novelist's business is to present "life" he must be able to select his material from the whole of life: nothing must be prohibited. And he refers to the "immense omission in our fiction." It was, he claimed, "because of the presence of the ladies and children" that in novels "there came into being a mistrust of all but the most guarded treatment of the great relation between men and women, the constant world-renewal."

In fact James' solution seems to be the same as that suggested by Moore in 1885:

We must write as our poems, our histories, our biographies are written, and give up at once and forever asking that most silly of all silly questions "Can my daughter of eighteen read this book?" Let us renounce the effort to reconcile these two irreconcilable things—art and young girls. That these young people should be provided with a literature suited to their age and taste, no artist will deny; all I ask is that some means may be devised by which the novelist will be allowed to describe the moral and religious feelings of his day as he perceives it to exist, and to be forced no longer to write with a view of helping parents and guardians to bring up their charges in all the traditional beliefs.[12]

In the course of their respective essays, Moore and James both imply that keeping children in heavily guarded ignorance is not only bad for the novel but bad for the children. Neither chooses to pursue that point, however, since, unlike their eighteenth-century predecessors, they are exclusively concerned about the rights of novelists. Hence the proposed solution is not that adults should allow formerly prohibited topics to be discussed in front of the children, but that child should be excluded so that adults can discuss such matters among themselves. The children are to be sent away to play, with their mothers presumably, so that the serious novelist can be free to pursue his art and write about sex.

Within twenty years of the publication of "The Future of the Novel," the views expressed in it were widespread, in particular the view that the serious novel is one that children cannot read was generally accepted among writers and critics. The impact that this exclusion has had not only on the development of children's literature but on attitudes towards it is still overwhelming. The segregation of adult's and children's literature is rationalised, even celebrated on all sides. It has assumed the status of a fact, a piece of knowledge about the world, that children read books in a different way and have to have special books written for them.

The consequences of this de facto segregation of children's literature from the rest can be seen in general aesthetic theory, in literary theory, in the theory and criticism of children's literature and in the literature itself. I shall deal briefly with the first two and more fully with the last two.

In aesthetic theory it is a not uncommon assumption that children cannot have aesthetic satisfactions. Professor F. J. Coleman, for instance, introduces aesthetics in *Contemporary Essays in Aesthetics* by suggesting that we can rank pleasures in a sequence which "depends on the degree of intelligence and discrimination needed to experience the feelings those terms designate":

The lowest pleasures would be those that any sentient human being can feel—children, idiots, the senile; they are such pleasures that do not require any power of discrimination. To call a pleasure an "aesthetic" pleasure is to imply that it would fall on the higher end of the continuum; therefore aesthetic pleasures are those that require discrimination, intelligence and imagination to be experienced. For surely we do not speak of children or the mentally deficient as *experiencing* art, though of course they may *hear* a symphony or see a painting. . . .[13]

Professor Coleman's argument is circular and proves nothing, but it at least affords a clear view of the prejudice under discussion.

Children have also continued to figure as scapegoats in the controversy over "aesthetic distance" raised in the debate between James and Stevenson. In literary theory, the question is "what constitutes a proper attitude on the part of the reader: detachment (which James felt to be characteristic of the good reader), or involvement (which Stevenson preferred and was universally believed to characterise the child reader)?" Over the last few decades the requirement that the mature reader, qualified to be discriminating, keep his proper distance has been increasingly questioned. It is acknowledged that even the most judicious readers do become involved in the books they read. But, even so, the children have not been rescued from the scapegoat role in this debate. It seems that the prejudice against child readers is so strong that it will be the last element in the theory to be relinquished. For instance, the celebrated attack on the theory in Wayne Booth's *The Rhetoric of Fiction* turned on an analysis of Jane Austen's *Emma* in which he showed that during the course of the novel "our emotional reaction to every event concerning Emma tends to become like her own."[14] It seems then that Booth is acknowledging that even critics do identify with characters in books—that it doesn't make one an inferior reader to do so. *But,* that is only the last half of the sentence, the first half of which goes, "While only immature readers ever really identify with any character, losing all sense of distance and hence all chance of an artistic experience . . . " Even Booth feels he has to make a concession to the prejudice he is trying to overcome, and the concession he chooses to make is once again to deny "immature readers" any chance of "an artistic experience."

If the assumptions outlined here were held universally, then we would not be able to talk of children's literature but only, as James would have it, of the children's book industry. Critics and theorists who want to talk about "children's literature" have had to find a way around this pervasive prejudice. Few have been bold enough to take issue with authorities such as Professor Coleman. Many have taken a way out by arguing that children *do* have aesthetic satisfactions but that these are different in kind from those of adults. Cornelia Meigs, for example, introducing a critical history of children's literature, says:

> Just as children, in spite of having long been treated as no more than smaller and more helpless editions of their elders, have always been something apart in vigor of personality, of vision, and enterprise of mind, so has the reading of their choice, even though unrecognised as something separate, had its own characteristics, its own individuality and its own greatness.[15]

This is to make the best of a bad thing and it leads to a great deal of effort on the part of such writers to give an account of the mysteriously different way of experiencing books that children are supposed to have. Criticism, it may be noted, becomes virtually impossible in the face of this supposed fundamental difference between adults' and children's responses to the same book. Some, despairing of bridging the gap, have suggested that only children should review children's books. Such reviews are invariably disappointing to their advocates because they give no evidence whatsoever of a fundamentally different way of responding to books. Rather than explain this away on the grounds of teacher interference, we should regard the original hypothesis that children's responses are different in kind from those of adults as not proven.

The exclusion of children's literature from the class of serious literature has of course resulted in its being classed as a branch of popular literature. Just as the unsubstantiated claim that the aesthetic experiences of adults are not available to children created a need for theories of what children do experience, so the equally arbitrary categorisation of children's literature as "popular" has fostered the belief that the popularity of a children's book is a proper index of its worth which has in turn attracted the curious explanation that children, unlike adults, are possessed of natural good taste in reading, hence if they generally approve of a book it must be good. Further confusions arise from the fact that at times "popularity" is understood as a set of critical criteria rather than a function of sales and readers. Kipling, for instance, had considerable respect for Rider Haggard and tried to base a theory on Haggard's writing. In a letter, Kipling exclaimed:

> How the dickens do you do it? How do you keep and outpour the vitality and the conviction and *how* do you contrive to nail down and clinch the *interest* that keeps a man lying along one elbow till the whole arm is tone-

cramped? I don't pretend to judge the book in the least. I only know in my own person, that it held me as a drug might—but it was a good drug— . . . . You have the incommuncable gift of catching and holding. . . .[16]

Although at the time of writing Kipling was himself a top best-seller whilst Haggard's popularity was declining, Kipling still regarded Haggard as the master popular writer, indicating that for him the popularity of a novel could be determined by criteria other than its sales. What these were may be deduced from Haggard's *Autobiography* in which he tries to communicate the incommunicable gift:

. . . the story is the thing and every word in the book should be a brick to build its edifice. . . . Let the character be definite, even at the cost of a little crudeness. Tricks of style and dark allusions may please the superior critic; they do not please the average reader, and . . . a book is written to be read. The first duty of a story is to keep him who peruses it awake . . . "grip" is about everything.[17]

This passage is interesting in that, if you replace "the superior critic" by "the adult reader" and "the average reader" by "the child reader" it could be interpolated without being noticed into any textbook on children's literature. Nor is that because the audience for such textbooks are assumed to be interested in writing for children as a commercial venture. A recent critical book dealing with a handful of the best authors of books for children was called *A Sense of Story*.[18] It is thought to be the prerequisite for the good children's writer in the way that James required the "sense of reality" in the serious novelist. The source of the requirement lies in the perception of children's literature as a branch of popular literature.

This perception originated, I suggest, in the vagueness with which the group of unwelcome new readers was perceived in the eighties by those who felt threatened by them. Class, sex, and age were conflated as causes of a supposed inability to appreciate the best in art and literature, those "millions to whom taste is but an obscure, confused, immediate instinct." Walter Allen, writing in 1954, saw the class division as most important:

It was probably not accidental that this heightened, more serious conception of the novel as art should have triumphed in the eighties, for the split between the old novel and the new coincided with a cultural revolution. Forster's Education Acts of 1870 provided compulsory primary education for all, and the result, over the years, was an enormous increase in the reading public. But the gap between the best education and the worst was so great that the highbrow-lowbrow dichotomy with which we are now wearisomely familiar was inevitable. Before 1870, the poor man who strove to learn to read and, having done so, went on to read beyond the newspapers, did so because he was to some degree a superior man. To be able to read was a key to enfranchisement; it opened the door to a better position as a tradesman or to succeed in business; it was essential to the politically minded working man who dreamed of power for his class; and for a few rare disinterested spirits it offered the freedom of a culture traditionally an upper-class preserve. But whatever the motive for learning to read, the Victorian working man, by and large, accepted the cultural standards of classes higher in the social scale. After 1870 this was no longer necessarily so. The provision of reading matter for a semiliterate public became the concern of a vast industry which set its own standards, standards which had nothing to do with literary and artistic standards as normally understood. Indeed, the notion of a single standard ceased practically to exist, and perhaps this was inevitable, for when you give a semiliterate person the vote and persuade him that thereby he is an arbiter of his country's destiny, it is not easy at the same time to convince him that he is not also the arbiter of what is excellent in art: there is a natural tendency for every man to believe that what he prefers must be the best.[19]

In the closing sentences of this passage Allen echoes James, who wrote of "an industry that occupies a very considerable quarter of the scene" with which "the sort of taste that used to be called 'good' has nothing to do." Allen similarly writes of "a vast industry" setting "standards which had nothing to do with literary and artistic standards as normally understood." James had in mind the child reader, Allen the enfranchised adult male working-class reader, but from the point of view of literary theory they are treated as interchangeable.

Children's Literature: The Bad Seed

Francelia Butler

Recently I began an address at Longfellow Hall, Harvard, by calling on the audience, most of whom were prospective teachers, to picket the English department. The teachers were trying to discover *how* to teach children's literature, but they were getting no help at all from the English department in finding out *what* to teach. The English department at Harvard should be among those taking the intellectual leadership for the entire country in the study of the literature for the future generation. Yet it totally ignores the field of children's literature—for children's literature is not a genre but an entire field.

I am not alone in deploring the exclusion of children's literature from the canon of most English departments. In the February, 1977 issue of *ADE, A Journal for Administrators of Departments of English in American and Canadian Colleges and Universities,* Professor Mary Agnes Taylor deplored the "outdated snobbery" of English departments which ignore the field. In an essay, "The Case for a Children's Literature," appearing in the journal, *Children's Literature* [reprinted on page 7], Clifton Fadiman noted that "literary historians leave out children's literature, as they might leave out the 'literature' of pidgin-English":

> The English novelist Geoffrey Trease offers a key example. He refers to "Legouis and Cazamian's *History of English Literature,* in which no space is found, in 1378 pages, for any discussion of children's books and the only Thomas Hughes mentioned is not the immortal author of *Tom Brown's Schooldays,* but an obscure Elizabethan tragedian." Further examples are legion. . . . C. Hugh Holman's *A Handbook to Literature* (1972) is alert to inform us about weighty literary matters from *abecedarius* to *zeugma,* but not about children's literature.

In the same essay, Fadiman championed the validity of the field on the basis that it has a long tradition and many masterpieces, and that chil-

Reprinted from the *Virginia Quarterly Review*, Summer 1980, pp. 396–409, with permission of the author and the publisher. © 1980 *Virginia Quarterly Review.*

dren's literature is a medium nicely adapted to the development of certain genres such as fantasy to which mainstream media are less well-suited.

Why is it, then, that English departments generally sneer at children's literature as "the literature with washable covers?" Through my experiences in teaching children's literature for fifteen years in an English department, founding the initial seminar on children's literature of the Modern Language Association, and establishing a journal in the field, I think I have confronted the major objections. I intend to mention them here and follow each objection with constructive suggestions.

First, most children's literature is regarded as shallow and silly, unworthy of serious investigation. Second, it is associated with women, who bear children and are close to them at home and in schools and libraries in the early years. Third, not only scholars but other adults have subconscious resentment of those who will succeed them. Consequently, they minimize the importance of children's literature.

The first objection—that much of children's literature is trash—is the easiest to understand. Many children's books *are* trash—but so are many books for adults. I said "books" advisedly, because no real distinction is attempted yet between children's literature of high seriousness and books that are trivial—at least, no such distinction is attempted by most scholars in English departments. Books like *Alice in Wonderland, The Golden Key, The Wind in the Willows,* the Beatrix Potter books, and the more contemporary classics like *A Wrinkle in Time, Charlotte's Web,* and *Where the Wild Things Are* are considered indiscriminately with such books as *Mommy and Daddy Are Divorced* or *Sometimes I Don't Love My Mother,* that is, books that are not literature but propagandistic treatises.

Scholars of English literature are understandably confused because they see these pedagogical books reviewed in popular and semipopular journals as if they were literature. The first step, then, in gaining the respect of English departments for the field is to differentiate between literature of quality for children and mere books. Only then can clear critical judgments be made.

It might well be helpful to understand how this confusion between "literature" and "books" for children arose. Actually, the problem was generated by the Calvinists, the merchant class, in the seventeenth century. Branching out from the stories, the ballads, and the plays which children and adults had heretofore enjoyed together, the Calvinists brought out pamphlets or chapbooks designed to keep young apprentices under control. Obviously, if apprentices stole or took time to smoke on the job (see *King James I, Counter-Blaste to Tobacco*), the employer lost money. As a result, a number of books were published such as *The marchants avizo* (1589), *The apprentices warning-piece* (1641), and *A warning to young men* (1680). The books must have been effective in controlling behavior, because at about the same time a large number of similar books were directed at younger children, culminating in James Janeway's *A token for children* (1671), an account of the agonizing deaths of thirteen children. As an appendix to Janeway's famous work, Cotton Mather added accounts of seven children from New England, and this work was published in Boston in 1700. (A unique copy is now in the Antiquarian Society in Worcester, Massachusetts.)

The publication of such books continued uninterrupted through the seventeenth and eighteenth centuries and led directly into the Sunday School literature of the late eighteenth and nineteenth centuries. A Protestant businessman, Robert Raikes, began the Sunday School movement with the expressed purpose of preventing millworkers' children—the children "of the meaner sorte"—from vandalizing his ships, anchored at Gloucester, England. The children worked during the week, and Sunday was their day off. Biographers of Raikes (W. F. Lloyd, New York, 1891; J. Henry Harris, New York and Bristol, England, 1899; and Alfred Gregory, London, 1877), and other writers who praise Raikes for beginning Sunday Schools, relate how the Sunday School movement spread to the United States through the support of the business community, and sometimes regret the ingratitude of the little children of the sweat shops, who were paid a penny apiece to go to Sunday School and learn of the damnation that awaited them if they did not give their best work to their employers.

The dividing line between the Joyful Death books of the seventeenth century and the Sunday School literature of the eighteenth and nineteenth centuries and the contemporary propagandistic books is almost imperceptible. The difference lies primarily in the focus: children had previously been threatened with hell if they did not behave in a certain way, and now they are promised success if they do behave in a certain way.

A good example is *The Queen Who Couldn't Bake Gingerbread*. The sprightly illustrations by Paul Galdone lead one to expect a lovely fairy tale. Instead, one learns that it is all right to reverse sex roles: that though the Queen could not bake gingerbread, she could play the trumpet, and though the King could not play the trumpet, he could bake gingerbread. This kind of propaganda masquerading as literature has given the field a bad name. In 1968, Carmen Goldings, M.D., a child psychiatrist at Harvard, wrote an article for the *Journal of the American Academy of Child Psychiatry* (Vol. VII, pp. 377–97) in which she castigated the heavy-handedness of much modern fiction for children. In the words of Narayan Kutty, a Hindu friend of mine, "It sits on the soul."

Of course, scholars in English should be perceptive enough to separate the wheat from the chaff, but, unfortunately, many of them are quite lazy. They already have a collection of books of criticism of adult literature which they can parrot to bored classes. Digging into starkly simple children's literature and studying the theory behind it, the style, structure, and meaning, is a difficult thing when there are few helpful hints from previous critics. The simplicity of children's literature stuns, leaves them speechless. Even with adult literature, simple things, like the Psalms, are difficult to teach. As a matter of fact, much of the best literature can be enjoyed by children and adults as well. But more time needs to be spent studying the reason for this—that literature which appeals to this dual audience rises to a higher sophistication in its absolute simplicity. Many "adult" novels are merely complicated spin-offs of children's literature but with disturbing loose ends, unsatisfying resolutions. Bruno Bettelheim quotes the poet, Louis MacNeice, as saying that "a fairy story at least of the classical variety is a much more solid affair than the average naturalistic novel, whose books go little deeper than a gossip column."

Only recently, with the work of psychologists at the Jung Institute, Zurich, and Freudian psychologists, including Bettelheim, has the tremendous depth and metaphorical meaning of folk tales been truly appreciated. These tales, which have hitherto been largely discarded as attic rubbish, in Tolkien's phrase, are beginning to be studied, but an enormous amount of work remains to be done. Those who have spent a lifetime studying them find that they are not only beautiful but that they feed the soul, instead of sitting on it. Bruno Bettelheim has written on *The Uses of Enchantment,* and James Hillman of the Jung Institute, for thirty years a depth psychologist in Zurich, prescribes folk tales to sick adults. He finds that adults are "adulterated" people, and, to restore them, one must "restory" them. Somehow it helps bring the jigsaw puzzles of their minds together. Folk tales, generally regarded as children's literature, are not only satisfying but therapeutic.

So much for the negative aspects of the field. On the positive side, there are good as well as bad books, just as in adult literature, and there is a tradition of at least three hundred years—longer than that for the adult novel. Further, many famous writers of the seventeenth, eighteenth, and nineteenth centuries as well as of our own times have shown a special interest in the world of the child. Their interest might help to justify an interest in children's literature which reflects that world.

The many possible selections for a course in seventeenth-century children's literature include ballads such as "Babes in the Wood," "Tom Thumbe," "The Seven Champions of Christendom," and "Robin Good-fellow." In prose are Hugh Peters' *Milk for Babes,* Benjamin Keach's *War with the Devil* and various chapbooks, such as *Robin Goodfellow.* Then there are games in the oral tradition, such as "Ring a Ring o' Roses," while religious verse includes such books as John Bunyan's *A Book for Boys and Girls; or, Country Rhimes for Children,* Isaac Watts' *Divine Songs for Children,* and, in the Royalist tradition, a book of metaphysical poetry for children entitled *Apples of Gold in Pictures of Silver.* (The Opies, in their *Dictionary of Nursery Rhymes,* list many children's rhymes dating from the seventeenth century.) Then there are plays ranging from puppet shows to Milton's *Comus.* Selections from Sir Roger L'Estrange's two huge volumes of fables written especially for children are also to be found. Though written "only for childish eares," as the introduction (1699) to L'Estrange specifically stated, a bowdlerized edition of these fables for adults was printed in Paris in the 1930s, with Alexander Calder illustrations, and subsequently reprinted by Dover Press. It took three hundred years, but adults are finally getting old enough to hear them, if the selections are carefully screened!

The eighteenth century provides an equally rich course choice of texts ranging from the first school novel in English, Sarah Fielding's *The Governess,* to *The History of Goody Two-Shoes* (possibly by Goldsmith), *Mother Goose's Melody* (nursery rhymes), Thomas Day's *The History of Sandford and Merton,* Mary Ann Kilner's *The Adventures of a Pincushion,* Mary Wollstonecraft's *Original Stories from Real Life,* Maria Edgeworth's *The Parent's Assistant,* and Samuel Johnson's children's story, "The Fountain."

In the nineteenth century we have William Roscoe's (still reprinted) *The Butterfly's Ball,* Charles and Mary Lamb's *Mrs. Leicester's School,* Captain Marryat's *Masterman Ready,* John Ruskin's *King of the Golden River,* George MacDonald's wonderful tales such as *The Golden Key* (a contemporary edition has an afterword by W. H. Auden), *The Light Princess, At the Back of the North Wind,* and so on. Then there is Lewis Carroll's *Alice in Wonderland,* Charles Dickens' *Magic Fishbone,* William Makepeace Thackeray's *Rose and the Ring,* Louisa May Alcott's *Little Women,* Thomas Hughes' *Tom Brown's School Days,* Charles Kingsley's *Water Babies,* Mason Weems' *The Life of Washington the Great* (particularly his fifth revised edition), Jacob Abbott's *The Franconia Stories* (first important work of fiction for American children), Thomas Bailey Aldrich's *Story of a Bad Boy,* Oscar Wilde's *The Happy Prince and Other Tales,* and Eleanor Gates' *Poor Little Rich Girl,* with its interesting uses of language. These are pointed out in the Garland

Publications introduction by Marcella Spann, who co-authored with Ezra Pound *From Confucius to Cummings* (New Directions). Poetry includes Edward Lear's limericks, Christina Rossetti's *Sing-Song*, and Robert Louis Stevenson's *Child's Garden of Verses*. These are only suggestions. The list is formidable.

To the twentieth century belong Kenneth Grahame's *The Wind in the Willows,* Beatrix Potter's books, A. A. Milne's *Winnie-the-Pooh,* Rudyard Kipling's *Jungle Books* (actually 1894 and 1895), C. S. Lewis's Narnia series, P. L. Travers' *Mary Poppins,* J. R. R. Tolkien's *The Hobbit,* E. B. White's *Charlotte's Web,* Ludwig Bemelman's *Madeline,* as well as books for children by Walter de la Mare, such as *Three Royal Monkeys*, and by Ionesco, Barthelme, and other well known writers.

Not even included are classics not in English such as the seventeenth-century *Contes de ma Mère l'Oye* by Charles Perrault and the volumes of fairy tales of Madame d'Aulnoy and Madame de Beaumont, as well as Madame de Villeneuve's "Beauty and the Beast," in her *Cabinet des Fées* (1785–89). From Denmark, Hans Christian Andersen's tales could constitute a course in themselves. And from Germany, of course, there are the pervasively influential tales collected by the Brothers Grimm.

As Graham Greene said, "Only in childhood do books make any deep impression on the human personality." If this is so, then it would seem that the books children hear and read are worth study as literature. Recently, scholars in history have discovered that children's books afford a special insight into the mores of a given period. Writers tend to write in a relaxed way and in conveying information to children convey information about themselves.

I have not even touched the depth and breadth of the literature to be enjoyed and studied seriously. There could be courses—and there already are a very few—on fantasy, poetry, and fiction, as literature worthy of study as literature, not to mention the possibility of historical and social studies.

So much for the first reason why children's literature is not respected by English departments—that it is too simple.

The second objection to the field is implied rather than voiced, and not so much time need be given to considering the objection because the feminist movement has already provided the refutations. Most professors in English departments are men, and they are unreceptive to children's literature as a scholarly subject because they are unreceptive to women as scholars. Women and children go together in their minds.

My own experience is a case in point. So far as I can determine, I am the first woman to come up through the ranks to full professor in the large English department at the University of Connecticut since the school was established in 1881. In 1965, or just before the feminist movement became strong, I was flatly told at the University of Connecticut that if I wanted work, I would have to discard my years of study in the Renaissance, forget my publications, and teach children's literature, as the legislature required a course, and the men refused to teach it. The hostility to the field has abated somewhat because of its great popularity with students and the large enrollment it consequently commands at a time when English departments need students. But, in spite of a supportive chairman, the course has not yet been accepted truly on the undergraduate or graduate level.

I have taught a graduate course in the field for several years; and though there is a great need to stimulate graduate enrollment, most of the men have long refused to circulate a pamphlet indicating that if students take the traditional courses, they can, with the approval of their topic by the graduate committee, write their dissertations in the field of children's literature. They give various reasons for their attitude, but the fact remains that they are quite willing to accept such dissertations *sub rosa,* but they do not want to acknowledge it publicly, even though many schools, including Harvard, are now accepting dissertations in English departments in the field of children's literature. Harvard recently approved a dissertation on Kipling's children's stories—a real breakthrough, because, as Clifton Fadiman has noted, a history of English literature can discuss the whole of Kipling's works without noting that he was primarily a children's writer. The men in the department are willing to advertise their medieval offerings, even though much medieval literature is essentially literature for children and adults, as some medievalists freely acknowledge.

Curiously, in spite of the attitude of most male scholars toward the field, a number of the best male scholars have shown an interest in it. Oxford University furnishes the best example. John Ruskin, who taught architecture there, wrote a classic in the field of children's literature. Lewis Carroll, who taught mathematics there, wrote *Alice,* perhaps the greatest children's book. C. S. Lewis, professor of religious philosophy there, wrote a whole series of books for children and said that "a children's story is the best art form for something you have to say." W. H. Auden, who taught poetry at Oxford, wrote criticism of children's books. And J. R. R. Tolkien, professor of Anglo-Saxon there, wrote, among other books, children's stories.

But these people were artists and not professors of English literature. Because of their expansive imaginations, they may not have had the academic strictures against the field which inhibit less creative minds.

The third reason why children's literature is generally excluded from

English departments has to do with the emotional and psychological makeup of all adults, including scholars. In the April 1978 *Harper's*, the editor, Lewis Lapham wrote:

(Children) remind their parents of too much that is unpleasant—of death, time, loss and failure—and so they come to be seen as unwelcome messengers bringing bad news to the prince.

He relates this attitude to literature, in discussing the attitude of well-meaning friends:

How is it possible, they say, that I should choose to read stories to my children when I might have the chance to see Norman Mailer throw a drink at Gore Vidal?

The secret hatred and fear of children on the part of adults is reflected in such popular movies as *It's Alive, The Bad Seed, The Exorcist,* and so on, and authorities on psychohistory have related the practice of child abuse in many cases to adult envy and fear of children. Oedipus knew all about it—his father pierced his feet and gave him to shepherds to expose on a mountain. Folk tales are full of it and are metaphorical representations of a continuing psychic condition. In the Brothers Grimm tale of "The Juniper Tree," an envious stepmother shuts her stepson's head in a chest, breaking his neck. I recall a similar case in Paris in 1939 when a man, envious of his girlfriend's little boy, stuck the child's head in a door and then slammed the door, breaking the boy's neck. The man was convicted of murder. . . .

By failing to study or teach children's literature in a serious way, scholars can do the future generation considerable harm. They leave the field wide open to ignorant critics and pseudoexperts who give bad advice which is passed on to parents and teachers and ultimately affects the psyche of children. . . .

But at least the volume of criticism is increasing. People are taking more interest in the field. Even Harvard, which won't permit a course in the subject to be taught in the English department, has nevertheless yielded a little to the current interest, and a volume of literary appreciation of *Fairy Tales and After: From Snow White to E. B. White* by the eminent critic, Roger Sale, has recently been published.

Jonathan Cott, author of *Beyond the Looking Glass* and of several articles on children's literature which have appeared in of all places *Rolling Stone,* has received a Guggenheim grant to do more work in the field. His interest is forward looking. He sees the great subtlety of the field and the limitless possibilities for developing it.

"Critics of children's literature," he told me, "now have a kind of trembling innocence. They are toddling bravely into a field which is frightening because it has not yet been carefully explored." Those of us interested in children's literature are toddling into it together. Hopefully, we will make the terrain more familiar to the next round of critics—and children, too.

/ The Author Has Something to Say
/ Meindert De Jong

"What are you trying to say to your (child) readers in your books?" My goodness, after some twenty books for children that question had never presented itself to me. Now, as in confused, idle moments I pondered it for this symposium—always I came up with nothing. Then it occurred to me that that was the answer—nothing! Thank God, absolutely nothing! As a teller of tales I absolutely, resolutely believe that my sole mission is to tell the tale, and that the child as father to the man has the same inherent right as later the man to a good story and nothing but the story—without any overhang or overburden of purposed improvement or instruction. Moreover, I believe I should not even be aware of the child as audience. The only child of whom I should be aware is the child character in the book as a life-and-blood being, real and whole. If so realized and achieved, then subconsciously, inherently, inevitably, my life-and-blood book child may have something to say to the reader child—and if so, fine. But if as author I purpose and put it there, it should be a shame to me, and is an insult to the child reader.

Reprinted from "The Author Has Something to Say: A Symposium," *The New York Times Book Review*, Children's Book Section, section 7, part 2, 14 May 1961, p. 3. Reprinted by permission. © 1961 by The New York Times Company.

/ An Honorable Profession

/ Mary Stolz

What makes a children's book writer? What nourishes the imagination and the pen of the writer for young people, as distinct from other sorts of writers?

It seems that few authors of children's books are agreed upon the answer. Recently I read an article in which five of them explained what, to them, makes the breed, and I disagreed with everything they had to say. Here were men and women talking about the profession I love in terms I found oversimplified, odd, even astounding. In order to be completely unfair, I shall oversimplify in quoting from them.

They place great reliance on keeping in touch with the audience. One writer says he hangs around high schools, getting atmosphere for his stories. This is a method of research that would be absolutely closed to me; I cannot imagine how one would go about wandering through a school, and can think of few occupations that would seem less productive.

A second writer, a woman, said she bakes cookies, with which she tempts neighboring children into her house. Once they are within her purview, she becomes "as a piece of furniture" and eavesdrops, making mental notes of their conversations and attitudes. She also scouts playgrounds, supermarkets, children's rooms in libraries. Again, all this seems to me impractical. To begin with, there'd be all those cookies to make. And suppose the children came when you wanted to write about them rather than mine them. What then? Forgo what may be a good writing mood, or be abrupt with the young visitors and so risk the loss of source material? And how does a normally busy person find time to dawdle in playground, library, and market waiting for children to say or do something usable in the literary sense? I think all this would lead one into the sort of dilemma that thwarts creativity.

Still another woman offered the notion that since children are going to be the readers, children should be editors and arbiters of books in progress. She gives her manuscripts to her own children for editing and comment, strikes from the day's work anything they fail to respond to, and generally attempts to steer her course according to their lights.

I can't begin to think what a hodge-podge this must make of her approach to theme and structure, to say nothing of her self-confidence. My own belief is that no manuscript should be seen by anyone until completion. At that time an editor (a grown-up professional editor in a publishing house is what I have in mind) can be and usually is of real value in assisting a writer to stand away a bit and refocus. The best writer, even one with 20-20 vision, tends to get myopic in the presence of his own product, and I believe that few writers can dispense with an editor, meaning someone sound, literate, sensitive, tough, and grown-up. The mind and spirit boggle at the idea of delivering a day's work into the hands of children. Any day's work is the delicate, tentative product of a writer's idea, his dream, and his skill at that time in realizing it. So much conscious and subconscious planning, pruning, altering, so much growing is required to make a book, that to subject it each day to the perhaps cursory, perhaps biased, certainly unripe judgment of children seems to me like pulling up the carrots to find out if they're thriving.

A fourth writer, a man, took the astonishing position that there is no such thing as a child anyway, there are only human beings of varying size and potential. And these human beings, whom he must imagine as whittled-down adults, are capable of grasping any idea, responding to any theme, provided, he says, it is presented to them by a writer with "a supreme command of language." Presumably he means his own. For my part, I would reserve the description "supreme command of language" for a very few writers in all the history of literature. And I most definitely insist that there is a category of human being properly labeled "child." I further insist that there are facts, concepts, and ideologies totally beyond this person's grasp and completely outside his range of interest, no matter who is commanding the language.

This human being, this child, is enchanting, imaginative, flexible, sensitive, intelligent, responsive, lovable—one could go on and on with happy adjectives. This child is also, as anyone who has had even brief contact with him knows, a barbarian, an untutored, self-serving, limited creature without taste, compassion, or more than the rudiments of judgment, who must be taught, by his elders and betters, how to conduct himself with decency and civility in a complex, frustrating world.

By elders and betters I do not imply that all adults are better or, even, except in a chronological sense, older than all children. But, broadly speaking, there is an advantage accruing to age. Something is gained through the days and the years, though being educated and taught disciplines of mind and body; through loving, and sometimes losing those you love; through learning to live, for the most part, as if life were good and mankind immortal. This accumulation of courage and experience and, sometimes, wisdom is what makes an adult, what distinguishes him from the child, what gives him his quality. The most charming, the most intelligent, the most potentially valuable child does not possess this quality.

This last writer also says that he deplores the "patronizing phrase, Writing for Children." I find it a useful and accurate expression for a real and sometimes exalting profession that concerns itself with a real person—the child.

I've tried to remember what the fifth writer said, but cannot. However, since one's own type of shop talk is always interesting, I have over the years read other accounts by and about authors of children's books. Many of them seem to feel that it would be a good idea to have a college degree and helpful to have been a librarian, a social worker, a teacher, a pediatrician. Quite a few suggest that it's as well to have children of one's own; this seems practical, but it is not always practicable. In some cases, none of the foregoing is.

Now, suppose you have a person who has not finished college, perhaps not gone to one at all. Suppose he, or she, has no children of his own. Suppose, to be extreme, he doesn't even like children. Can he still write for them?

I think he can.

Now I come to my own definition of what makes a children's book writer. Assuming a talent for writing, I think what is required is that one be an ex-child, with a genuine respect for the condition and a long memory.

There is a sort of memory that does not so much recall as re-experience. This is the writer's memory, and it must be especially keen in the writer for children. If he has it, he needn't eavesdrop or bake cookies or otherwise attempt to keep in touch with his "audience." The audience, the child, is within him. There is, we all know, a child in everyone. In many if not most cases that child has receded to the outposts of one's awareness, and probably this is all to the good. But where the children's book writer is concerned, the child is an immediately available, always present being. I do not mean that such a writer *is* a child, in that distasteful sense meant by some people when they say "all men are just grown-up little boys." I mean that he always has this child with him.

I can give examples from myself. All of us remember how long it seemed, when we were children, between one birthday and the next, one Christmas and the next; how, if something glorious were going to happen on Friday and here it was only Tuesday, then Friday was simply never going to arrive. We remember it. But I find, and I imagine most children's-book writers find, that the feeling still persists. If winter comes, then spring is lost forever.

Or, again, when I see a child, especially a rebellious child, standing with his feet planted firmly, his head thrown back to eye the looming creature of authority before him, I can feel again, physically, the fury and despair of being smaller than my antagonist. The inferior stature of the child is part of his daily cup, along with other ingredients, some delicious and exhilarating, some bitter, but all sharply, intensely tasted.

The essence of childhood and youth, I think, is this intensity of the present experience. Time, taste, custom, fatigue, experience—more briefly, a sense of relativity—limit us at length so that we don't suffer (should I say rejoice in? I don't think so) these violent extremes of thought and feeling. We learn to judge, to evaluate, to measure, to restrain ourselves. This, again, is what makes us adults, and therefore able, if we try, to help children understand and cope with their situation, which is so like early man's where every thunderclap came as a threat, every night as the end, and all that mattered was to keep this particular ego and libido going somehow.

This child I have within me, with me, undergoes from time to time what might be called caveman reactions, and I sometimes suffer the consequences and sometimes rue them. Still, I wouldn't do without her, because she is my familiar, from a world I've lost but am still fascinated by.

Every writer writes as much for himself as for his readers, but some of us, it seems, are addressing not our present selves but some distant, unrelinquished part of ourselves, which part is a child.

/ I See the Child As
a Last Refuge

Isaac Bashevis Singer

Many of my readers seem amazed by the fact that I began to write for children in my late years. The desire to create for them usually manifests itself when the writer is still young himself, not far removed from his own childhood. I was driven to it by a deep disenchantment in the literary atmosphere of our epoch. I have convinced myself that while adult literature, especially fiction, is deteriorating, the literature for children is gaining in quality and stature. The child, which until the middle of the nineteenth century was nothing but a passive and uncritical listener of stories that tired mothers and nannies improvised at his bedside, in our time has become a consumer of a great growing literature—a reader who cannot be deluded by literary fads and barren experiments. No writer can bribe his way to the child's attention with false originality, literary puns and puzzles, arbitrary distortions of the order of things, or muddy streams of consciousness which often reveal nothing but a writer's boring and selfish personality. I came to the child because I see in him a last refuge from a literature gone berserk and ready for suicide.

One doesn't have to be a pessimist or a professional mourner to realize that in comparison to the nineteenth century our literature has been going downhill. The nineteenth century was an epoch of literary giants. One could cover entire pages with their illustrious names. We don't have a single writer today who can be compared to those literary geniuses. I am sure that this statement needs no elaboration. I know of no serious literary critic who believes that we have had in our century a Tolstoy, or Dostoevsky, Gogol, Chekhov, Flaubert, Balzac, Pushkin, Byron, Heine, Mickiewicz, even a Dickens, Maupassant or Edgar Allan Poe. A number of great writers who lived into the twentieth century—like Hamsun, Strindberg and others—accomplished their best work early rather than late.

Reprinted from *The New York Times Book Review,* Children's Book Section, 9 Nov. 1969, section 7, part 2, pp. 1, 66. Reprinted by permission. © 1969 by The New York Times Company.

I prefer to pause at the question: Why and how has our epoch disappointed? Even if for some biological caprice we produce only midgets, why couldn't they have stood on the shoulders of giants?

Until the end of the nineteenth century, it was almost an axiom for the prose writer, and in a way for the poet and dramatist as well, that his principal task was to tell a story. Adults, like children, want a story. The story has many functions. Like history, it does not allow time past to vanish without a trace. It creates in the listener, or the reader, a specific kind of tension which is necessary to the spirit. It describes the individual, the unique, the nonutilitarian, the incomparable and what is therefore immune to generalization. A real story is full of surprise. In a story, as in a human life, one can never foresee the end with all its variations. Writers of the nineteenth and previous centuries were not ashamed to be entertainers in the best sense of the word, for they appreciated the high value of entertainment. They knew that life without art is painful and often unbearable. Many suicides are committed because life has become boring and predictable. Homer and Cervantes created their works to entertain the people of their eras, which is why they also succeeded in teaching their own and all later generations.

Our literary century began with rebellion against the story. The writer, especially the one who emerged after World War I, imagined that to recite fables to grown-ups was beneath his dignity. I once called entertainment "the thirteen-letter word" which it is not polite to mention in society. Many writers took up social missions: to fight for peace, economic equality, and countless other causes. Others deluded themselves into thinking that literature can become a branch of psychology, or compete in any other field of science. Since literature was Freudian before Freud, they wondered why can't it be more Freudian, more Adlerian, more Jungian after Freud, Adler, and Jung? The Leninist revolution declared open war on art for art's sake. Literature had to help the revolution and strengthen the march toward Communism. A number of humanists tried to shift their own concerns to the slender shoulders of the artists. In spite of the fact that Tolstoy himself was a storyteller *par excellence,* he tried in his "What Is Art?" and in other essays of his declining years to devalue the literature of his youth. Literature had to teach morality and his particular brand of Christianity. It is in our epoch that one began to speak of bedtime literature in contrast to the literature that has to awaken the reader, shake his conscience and move him to deeds. The professors and the critics pounced upon this new use of literature. It gave them broader horizons and more action. Little could be gotten out of a story by Chekhov or Maupassant; the explicators needed more ponderous works, more complicated style and above all a kind of literature allied to one contemporary movement or another. Literature was dragged into politics.

Not everyone will agree with me, but we are living in a time when literature aspires more and more to be didactic and utilitarian. It doesn't seem to matter what lesson it teaches—a sociological, psychological, or humanistic one—as long as it teaches. There have never been more interpretations of texts or guides for readers who must be led by the hand by the critics. We are no longer allowed to enjoy a sunset without footnotes. The moral precedes the parable, and often muddles it. Even the sex literature of our time is sexless because it sets itself to reform life, change morality. It's not an exaggeration to say that the simple telling of a story is becoming a forgotten art. Narrative poetry, which was the main pillar of the literature of all previous cultures, has been liquidated almost entirely. Instead of describing character, many modern authors write essays about their heroes. Character and personality are nonrepetitive phenomena, and because of this little can be learned from them. The modern novelist prefers types and groups. It is not an accident that so many works of fiction deal with war and revolution. In Tolstoy's "War and Peace," peace made the novel. Single characters are remembered, not the multitudes driven by Napoleon and Kotuzov. Tolstoy knew too well that it is not in the power of any writer to describe masses. But the modern novelist tries it again and again—because from groups one hopes to learn about other groups.

Fifty years of Communist rule in Russia have proven that when a writer tries to teach a lesson he achieves nothing as an artist, and nothing as a propagandist. Now even Soviet critics have admitted this with regret. I don't know of a single work of fiction in our time which has contributed much to psychology or sociology, or helped the cause of pacifism. The attempt of the poet to do what no poet can do has driven readers away from poetry in the space of a generation. Few are ready to make an effort to understand the encumbered language of modern poetry, its involved rhetoric, its futile experiments, puzzles and allusions.

Thank God for the children. It's a lot easier to hypnotize grown-ups than children. It's easier to force university students to eat literary straw and clay than an infant in a kindergarten. No child can be influenced by tortured criticism or quotes from authorities. No child is altruistic enough to read a book because it might help society or progress. The child is still selfish to demand an interesting story. He wants surprises and tensions. Our children, God bless them, don't read to discover their identity, as so many wiser adults pretend to do. Young as they are, fresh from the egg, they know exactly who they are, and where they belong. Neither do they read to free themselves from guilt or to quench the thirst for rebellion. The literature of our time has torn itself from folklore, because folklore is so often superstitious and conservative, but our children are not afraid to look back. Their literature is still preoccupied with kings, princesses, devils, demons, imps, werewolves and other old-fashioned creatures. More than that, the young reader is inclined to maintain not only the spiritual truths of his own group but also those of other nations and races. With an instinct no fashion-making can destroy, the child has become the guardian of those moral and religious values which the adults have rejected in the name of an ill-conceived notion of social progress. Our children refuse to mock or subvert family life. Daddy and mommy, grandpa and grandma, brother and sister, remain for them serious and stable institutions.

I receive many letters from adult readers and from children, and I dare say that in the letters of the children there are fewer clichés and nonsense. When a child praises a book he says that it's "interesting," "pleasant," "amusing." The adults, the very refined ones, sometimes use a phraseology which embarrasses with its pretension and sheer naiveté. They ascribe to the writer qualities and intentions he never had. The psychoanalytic casuistries, the far-fetched theories of the pseudo-sociologists and the argot of those who pour out symbols from their sleeves have created a new type of adult who can no longer express himself in clear language. He doesn't talk, he quotes, paraphrases, and interprets. I sometimes suspect that this is what happened to the people of the Tower of Babel when, as the Bible tells us, God confused their tongues. Perhaps the children of Babel were the only ones who spoke clearly and helped their parents communicate with each other. If children's books inscribed on clay tablets existed in those far-off times, they were the ones that adults would read for enjoyment, their own literature having ceased to have any meaning.

One cannot say that the pedants, sociologizers and psychologizers (who are not to be confused with sociologists and psychologists) don't try to corrupt children's stories. A number of writers have taken on themselves the job of preparing children for adult literary poppycock. Stories for children are now being written without a beginning, middle or end. Their writers seem to believe that children have no head for logic. They see the child's mind as basically Kafkaesque. Actually youngsters are extremely logical. They may accept premises which don't agree with the adult image of reality, but once they have accepted a premise, the action that follows must be strictly logical. Children ask questions which adults no longer dare to ask. They demand consistency, clarity, precision and other obsolete qualities. Some illustrators try their best to accustom the child to pictures which have no connection with the text and no similarity to experience. We must put up with illustrators who have taken up writing, or writers who think they can illustrate their own works. God seldom gives two talents to one person.

One problem in literature for children is the parent who buys a children's book not because the child will like it but because of the parent's own affinity with the point of view of writer or illustrator. There is a danger that in children's literature there will arise the category of books which are bought and not read—as happens so often in literature for adults. From my own experience I know that a child wants a well-constructed story with clear language and strict logic, whose illustrations illuminate the text rather than cloud it. When a lion is drawn for children, he should look like a lion and not a hedge-hog with antlers or a Rorschach inkblot. If a child is in a mood to defy logic or to make blots, he does it himself with great charm.

I believe that if literature for adults is destined for revival it will come from literature for children. Adults will go on brooding over reader's guides, commentaries on commentaries and dissertations on incomprehensible and boring works until one day a literary Copernicus (a former child) will discover the sensational truth that a book is made to be read.

Three Fallacies about Children's Books
Aidan Chambers

I have been browsing through a clutch of recently published anthologies which draw together essays and articles about children's books, spurred on by Paul Heins's sturdy volume *Crosscurrents of Criticism* (Horn Book). There is much in all of the anthologies to admire and many ideas and points of view worth pondering. But in some of them

Reprinted from *The Horn Book Magazine* 54:322–26 (June 1978) with permission of author and publisher. Copyright © 1978 by The Horn Book, Inc. Originally titled "Letter from England: Three Fallacies about Children's Books."

there are assumptions about children's books which keep bobbing to the surface—assumptions which seem to be true but which, in fact, are fallacies. I thought I'd devote this letter to three of them.

Children's books are the only books in which you find good storytelling these days. Some writers even claim they ended up writing for children because children's editors are the only people who will publish good stories. The implication, sometimes made explicit, is that literature for adults has turned against narrative, has even given it up as redundant and outmoded.

I'm never quite sure what the authors and critics who say this can mean. For if they look about them and actually read adult literature, they will find it littered with storytelling by artists-in-narrative. Near my desk right now, for example, are new or newish books by John Fowles, Graham Greene, Kurt Vonnegut, Richard Brautigan, Ian McEwan, Robert Coover, Martin Bax, Alexander Solzhenitsyn, Patrick White, Iris Murdoch, Saul Bellow, E. L. Doctorow, Muriel Spark, John Wain, David Storey, Alan Sillitoe—just a few writers very much alive and kicking and working in narrative as "adult" storytellers. Not to mention the what-happened-next action-mongers like Alistair MacLean, Jack Higgins, Harold Robbins, Richard Adams, and the other writers who supply the racks with pop literature that often seems to me to be exactly what those who bewail the absence of story in adult literature are actually asking for.

Certainly, the nearest I can get to understanding what the bewailers mean is that they must be readers of one kind of storytelling, a kind that is worn out and little practiced, it is true, by serious writers of adult novels. Fred Inglis puts his finger on it, maybe, in an essay included in one of the anthologies. "Reading Children's Novels: Notes on the Politics of Literature" begins with the premise, now pretty widely accepted, that reading fiction is "a transaction. It involves at least the storyteller and you listening to him: but further, since a man is both himself and his history (and himself *because of* his history), it is the conversation between two histories and between two odd beings who give those histories shape and meaning."

Inglis explores this idea in relation to a certain kind of writing, which he finds strong in children's books and which adults all too often may be reading, he says, as "a disguised taste for *Kitsch*, for the thoroughgoing, rank, tasty meat and gravy of an old-fashioned bestseller." Taking as an example Rosemary Sutcliff, to whom he pays obeisance as distinguished—"a writer of undoubted grace and strength"—Inglis then tries to identify what attracts such readers, what these writers want to tell our children:

To understand the situation of a present-day, liberal-spirited teacher with a training in the humanities and a struggling sense of history is to understand the genesis of Rosemary Sutcliff's novels. . . . Rosemary Sutcliff's novels define the response of such a group to the loss of the English landscape both in itself and as a symbol of one version of Englishness; they further define a powerful and unfulfilled longing for a richer moral vocabulary and an ampler, more graceful and courteous style of living such as at the present time can only be embodied in a stylized past.

Put into crude and unflattering words, Inglis is saying that those who come to children's books for the stories they say are missing in adult literature are refugees, liberal-spirited and humanistic, who are nostalgic for a world now gone (if it ever really existed), who are confused by and unhappy with the world they see coming upon them, yet who seek by a comforting rhetoric such as Sutcliff's a way to make whatever minimal adjustments they need to make in order to survive in the world that presses around them. These writers and adult readers are often admirable in their intentions, decent-minded and altruistic. But Inglis seems to be saying, and I would agree, that they are, nevertheless, writers and readers of a conservative nature who feel oppressed, even depressed, fearful of modern times. They are often writers and readers of historical fiction and fantasy of the Tolkien kind. Because of their strong influence on children's books, literature for children, in England at least, is presently failing to respond with any energy and willingness, except in a few notable examples, to the best that is happening in adult literature. And am I right in detecting, after their complaints about the lack of storytelling in adult novels, a sigh of relief that children's books can and do offer the kind of story they want and can be made to go on doing so? Whereas we ought to be disturbed because the failure to make use of the narrative movements and styles presently explored in adult literature means that children are being plied with a literature which develops them into readers entirely unprepared for the adult novels which will face them in their adolescence—the very novels which articulate the world around them.

All this takes us into a minefield of argument—an argument which has been put off for too long, in my view. Surely we cannot argue, however, about the fact that narrative in many varied forms—storytelling as an art—is alive, and vitally so, in adult literature.

Didacticism is an old-fashioned literary weakness we have learned to expunge from children's books. Frequently suggested in writings about children's books—but never challenged. Coming as near to home as Penelope Lively's essay in the February 1978 *Horn Book,* we find it expressed like this: "It is only fairly recently that we managed to shake

off the yoke of nineteenth-century didacticism in children's literature.
. . . We do actually believe now that children's books need to be fun
and nothing else."

"We" may; I don't. For the simple reason that I have yet to be persuaded that you can write a story without an element of the didactic in
it. And far from shaking off the "yoke" of any century's didacticism, it
seems to me as plain as a popinjay that children's books are still often
overtly didactic in every way—from teaching moral lessons about life
to offering strong messages about God, sex, politics, and that oldest of
all children's book purposes, providing tips about how to behave.

All stories, as I say, carry messages. The problem lies not with the
stories or even with the messages but with our use of the word *didactic*.
We have come to abuse it. But even such an undergraduate text as *The
Nature of Narrative* by Robert Scholes and Robert Kellogg (Oxford)
can put us right on the point:

We are likely to think of a "didactic" narrative as one in which a feeble attempt is made to clothe ethical chestnuts in fictional form, resulting at best
in a spoiled story. When the term is used in this sense it effectively begs all
questions of judgment and appreciation. Our criticism may be improved if we
can strip the word of the unfortunate connotations it has acquired and allow
"didactic" simply to refer to a work which emphasizes the intellectual and
instructional potential of narrative, including all such works from the simple
fable which points an obvious moral to the great intellectual romance which
seeks to justify the ways of God to man or to present the psychological laws
which govern man's behavior in society. A didactic work may illustrate complacently a moral truism, or put to the most strenuous kind of examination
the most problematic and profound ethical and metaphysical questions. Aesop
is a didactic author, and so are Dante, Milton, Swift, George Eliot, Lawrence,
and Proust.

Which, taken to heart, saves for us Hoban's *The Mouse and His Child*
(Harper), Byars's *The Eighteenth Emergency* (Viking), Zimnik's *The
Crane* (Harper), Cormier's *The Chocolate War* (Pantheon), and a number of other valued children's books, which a charge of didacticism, dis-
paragingly intended, would banish.

Of course, what has happened is that some writers and commentators
have struggled so hard to establish the literary respectability of children's books that they have boxed themselves into a corner where worse
damage can be inflicted on the literature they seek to defend and justify.
They have thought that by denying the teaching quality of children's
books and claiming only fun as their purpose, their adult colleagues
would begin to pay respectful heed. All they'll get in reply, however, is

a brutal uppercut powered by the reply that any serious writer who is merely providing fun for his readers hardly demands anyone's attention, a child's or an adult's, for longer than the few spare moments a relaxing read requires.

There is nothing reprehensible in trying to offer, in narrative form, a gift of one's own understanding. But some authors may communicate their understandings in stories of little skill; others may fudge the issue and leave only confusion in their wakes; still others may have nothing but specious understandings to offer in the first place and so deserve scant attention no matter how skillfully they put stories together. But that is all a different matter from the one thing such authors have in common—their urgent didacticism.

Let us rescue the term *didactic* from the dustbin of dirty words.

I write for myself. In some ways this fallacy results, like the fallacy about didacticism, from a desperate need felt by some children's writers to be accorded the kind of attention they feel they deserve but do not get from those who attend seriously to adult literature. It has become, in England at least, the fashionable answer to any question that tries to probe a writer's understanding of what he is doing in relation to children as readers.

Let's acknowledge at once that writers must be allowed to believe whatever they need to believe in order to do their job. But there is another equally imperative truth to be coped with. It is a truth adult writers and certainly critics have for some time recognized and explored. Henry James is a great writer-exponent of the idea in his *Prefaces*. Wayne C. Booth has written the invaluable critic's statement of it in *The Rhetoric of Fiction* (University of Chicago). More recently, Wolfgang Iser has made an interesting attempt to deepen the foundations in *The Implied Reader* (Johns Hopkins). The idea is this:

Every time a writer puts words on paper he makes a choice. He chooses the kind of reader he wants to communicate with, no matter what he believes, consciously speaking, about what he is doing and whom he is writing for. James says an author "makes his readers, just as he makes his characters." Booth puts it, "To write one kind of book is always to some extent a repudiation of other kinds. And regardless of an author's professed indifference to the reader, every book carves out from mankind those readers for which its peculiar effects were designed."

Writing narrative is always a matter of using certain rhetorical techniques. There is no escaping this, and there is no escaping the fact that the techniques used reveal, on close study, the reader to whom the writer speaks. That is why I wished Penelope Lively, in the article I've already mentioned, had led us further into what she meant when she said: "I am writing for children as an adult, and I am clear that I am writing for children: *if I weren't I would do it differently.*" (My italics.) What would be the differences? How would they be decided upon? Those are the kinds of question we need children's writers to explore with us. It is the reality of the art to say that these choices are made, an unreality to pass them off by saying "I write for myself."

Children's books are far too important to be allowed to drift into the backwaters of literature, out of touch with the mainstream of the current. What children's books have to say to children ought to be too important to ignore or to disparage as didacticism, used in an abusive sense. And those who write and talk about children's books have too important a task on hand to allow themselves to fall into sloppy, uninformed thinking that pays little heed to what is being said and thought by our colleagues in other areas of literature or in other, usefully related disciplines.

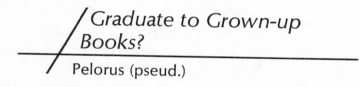

/ Graduate to Grown-up Books?

Pelorus (pseud.)

Russell Hoban, whose new book for adults has been exhaustively praised, made the following remark in a talk delivered to a joint conference of the London branches of the School Library Association and Youth Libraries Group last September, a copy of which I've just come across:

Leon Garfield is an example of what talent can do to a children's book writer: it can drive him out of children's books as he follows the development of his material wherever it takes him, and that is precisely what's happened. *The Strange Affair of Adelaide Harris,* for instance, has to be considered an adult book.

Reprinted with permission from *Signal: Approaches to Children's Books* no. 11:110 (May 1973). Published by The Thimble Press, Lockwood, Station Road, South Woodchester, Stroud, Glos. GL5 5EQ England.

I agree with Mr. Hoban's conclusion but not with his analysis, and find the implication painfully wrong. Surely he cannot mean what he seems to be saying, that "talent" is the reason why writers like Garfield, with abilities and success, stop writing for the young. Are children's books, therefore, some kind of second-best training ground for writers who, if their talents are great enough, will ultimately graduate to grown-up books?

In my view, it isn't his "talent" that is leading Garfield out of children's writing. Rather it is the fashionable expectations held out to writers for the young. Every time we allow people to talk about "writing for myself alone" when instead they ought to be talking about writing *for* children; every time we sit down, as some do at children's book conferences, and hold undergrad-like discussions for hours on end about subterranean meanings hidden beneath the artfully child-book surfaces of certain novels, uttering not a word about children and their responses; and every time we press children's writers to pretend they are anything other than what they know they are and wish deeply to be—people who speak to the young—then we help to create the results Mr. Hoban points out.

Whether we like it or not, children's writers are, unconsciously or otherwise, subject to the atmosphere generated by reviewers, critics, coterie friends. Writers tend to produce what the readers they value most look for. It is not surprising, therefore, that publishers, teachers, and those who survey the annual scene are commenting on the dearth of really good new books for children between the ages, roughly, of eight to ten. That is precisely the period which is, at present, least attended to critically, least examined and favoured.

Children's Literature: On the Cultural Periphery

Hugh Crago

"Tradition," I was told as an undergraduate, a propos of the British Empire in Australia and the culture of pagan Scandinavia as preserved in Iceland, "survives longest on the periphery." Now children's literature could be argued to be on the cultural "periphery" in several senses. First, and most obviously, because it is thus regarded by most of the people, organisations and publications which together constitute the Academy of our literature. In the eyes of the journals of literary criticism, of *The Cambridge Bibliography of English Literature,* of reviewers for national newspapers and television, children's books, if they figure at all, have a small place of their own tucked well away from "central" concerns. We may not like this, but it is true, and evidence that children's literature is slowly becoming respectable in the eyes of the Academy—witness a recent offering of four classes on the subject within the English Faculty at Oxford—has not yet mounted to a level where it seriously modifies the status quo.

What does modify it is the realisation that the potential audience for whom children's books are produced is probably considerably larger than that for which "mainstream" fiction of quality is produced, even allowing for the element of forced readership among students which must bulk large in both audiences. Of course, all "high" culture—of which children's books, simply by virtue of being hardbound and stocked by libraries, almost automatically form part—is in a way peripheral to literary culture in its broadest sense of what the majority of people in a society customarily absorb (which is magazines and newspapers more than books).

But even when seen in relation to mass culture, children's literature possesses a number of special characteristics that render it peripheral. There is, for example, that often-noted gap in age between producer and consumer: it is adults who write and review children's books, not children. Whatever we say about "writers writing for themselves" and

Reprinted with permission of Five Owls Press Ltd. from *Children's Book Review* 4, no. 4:137–38 (Winter 1974–75).

an avoidance of "talking down," the gap is bound to involve an element of displacement: one set of perceptions has to be cast in such a mould as to be apprehensible to another set. One could argue that the gap is no greater than that between the perceptions and intelligence of the average advertising copywriter and those of the public at which he aims, and hence that age is not the significant factor involved. Yet the fact remains that the adult novel (or film) is not subject to the same pressure to shape its material for audience comprehension as the children's book is.

The same shift from direct cultural communication is matched in the criticism of children's books, where critical concepts formulated in response to books for adults are applied to works which they do not necessarily fit, and where the nature of the audience enables both purely aesthetic and "educational" criteria to be employed. To some critics formally trained on the classics of adult literature, children's books offer the chance to be more in control critically than they might be in the case of an adult novel, to be able to enjoy in a more instinctive fashion the gratifications not always mentioned in formal adult criticism, and to be able to justify their enjoyment on the grounds that children will benefit. That the *dulcis et utile* criterion survives in the criticisms of children's books so long after its virtual demise elsewhere is itself a pointer to the fact that we are dealing with the preservation of "tradition" in an outlying area of culture.

There are several other clear cases of the same phenomenon. It has, for example, been recognised by John Rowe Townsend and Jill Paton Walsh that children's literature has in a sense taken over the tradition of fiction as a primarily *narrative* experience, that it carries those "strong, simple themes" which adult fiction is at present too self-conscious to express. With this could be linked the fact that children's literature preserves strong links with oral expression in that books are read to young children and that this audience responds in a direct way, acting-out in their play and "improvising" upon the story. And again related to both narrative primacy and oral tradition is the preservation in children's books of a serious, unself-conscious concern with supernatural experience, a concern lacking in mainstream literature since the gothic novel (that is, of course, until the recent Tolkien-inspired revival of interest). All these particular survivals can, on the whole, be seen as strengths, just as the growing consensus is that it is partly *because* of the displacements and constraints we have been considering that a peripheral area like children's literature has been able to develop its particular achievement. But the question which faces us now is what *sort* of a periphery is children's literature to be? Historically, peripheral cultures have acted not only as places where old values and modes were preserved, but sometimes as sources of innovation whence new, or revitalised, forms have travelled back into the centre of mainstream culture. Which way, in the case that concerns us, is the stream flowing?

To sharpen this question we could do worse than look at another area where a "peripheral" culture, long regarded as unimportant by the establishment, has in recent years developed an impressive and multifarious array of creativity within comparatively restricting formal limits. I refer to the sudden emergence of rock music out of "pop," a phenomenon which chronologically correlates not inexactly with what has been called the golden age of children's literature. Like our own cultural area, rock is in the process of moving from a phase of self-consciousness and critical evaluation from within its own camp (*Rolling Stone's* reviews are every bit as austere in their standards as those of *The Gramophone,* though naturally the standards are different), even beginning to infiltrate the musical Academy with proponents like George Melly and Leonard Bernstein.

Is there also a resemblance in terms of age range? Rock, it can safely be assumed, appeals to an age group of which the lower limit is hard to define, but which is certainly by no means confined to adolescents. The generation which grew up on, and with, the Beatles is now in its twenties. But, while many of the most outstanding and controversial books published on children's lists of the last five or so years have also been for an ill-defined twelve–thirteen–fourteen plus age group, they would seem by virtue of their being (however discreetly) stamped as "children's books" to be unable to claim the readership continuum from adolescence to early adulthood that their musical counterparts have; moreover, I am only one of many to feel that these books—Southall and Garner's later work, Mayne's *A Game of Dark*—may well be comparatively unread in the age group for which they seem most obviously fitted, even if this is compensated for by the high degree of enthusiasm they generate in adult "middlemen." With rock music, there can be no such doubt about the fact that the cultural product is consumed—to an extent which can have a significant effect on a country's balance of payments!

One could account for the greater success of rock on several obvious grounds: musicians appear to be *directly* in touch with the people who buy their records in a way authors of books for young people are not; emotional identification with the performer is possible, and practised to a high degree; music itself is a more direct medium of communication (at least of certain emotions) than words are. But what interests me are two points of more specific relevance to my theme of children's literature as a cultural phenomenon. Firstly, the sensory richness of contemporary music for adolescents. Rock is not only an auditory experience: it is also a visual experience, a quasitheatrical experience (in the case of bands like the Who), a kinetic experience—since it generates movement in the listener/spectator; it has attracted to its musical core a complex of related styles in other arts—the design of record covers and of clothes, the light show—which, while usually inferior in quality to the music itself, do render it a more all-involving cultural experience for the audience. Now this cannot, I think, be accounted for purely on the grounds that music is a more direct medium than written words. Indeed, the world of children's books does (unlike adult publishing) offer a parallel to rock's multimedia approach in its high proportion of illustrations, its cultivation of that expensive oral/visual package, the picture book (and its recent extension via Weston Woods and others into the area of film). But this great richness of creative activity is almost entirely directed at *young* children; by the time we reach the novel for adolescents, a dustjacket is all that remains of our multi-media extravaganza— just at the time when the music producers are throwing everything they've got at their audience. Similarly, children's books produce their greatest degree of audience participation and acting-out in the youngest grouping among their audience, and it declines steeply thereafter. The principle seems to be that while rock is a *unified* cultural force, children's literature is strongly compartmentalised.

Furthermore, while both cultures have absorbed influences and explored beyond their traditional limitations, the most noticeable changes in children's books—a rediscovery of the ritual/magic/terror complex and a widening of focus to include sex—are much more explicable in terms of purely literary influences than the changes in youth music are explicable in terms of purely musical ones. In going beyond its blues heritage, rock has rediscovered ethnic roots of all kinds, classical influences from the Baroque to Musique Concrete, and a whole world of extra-musical culture ranging from Bosch to Winnie the Pooh and Sri Krishna. Much of this exploration is superficial and its results ephemeral, but it points to a state of cultural excitation, to a desire for inclusiveness and unity, which children's books, sheltering behind their still conservative value-system, cannot match. It will only be by *decompartmentalising* that the children's book field will be likely to achieve a comparable effect on the culture of the country as a whole.

Examples of books that break down boundaries are already in existence. *The Golden Shadow,* for all the disappointments of its text and its faulty design, is a pointer to what may be coming *not* because it is a "new" version of Greek mythology, but because it is trying to be a non-patronising *picture book for adolescents*—a genre that could unite the visual richness and innovation of the picturebook with the literary achievement of the young adult novel.

But, on the other hand, if all categories are abandoned, if the term "children's book" becomes as meaningless in theory as many agree it has become in practice, what will happen? Will what were once children's books have become truly a mainstream culture? Or will the loss of that sense of formal limitations that characterises a peripheral art-form result in the dissipation of all that made our achievement what it was? Is it better to look backwards, with the limited perfection of Sendak and the earlier Mayne, and create art which cannot be faulted within its own terms of reference, or to look forwards, with the restless, aggressive, exploration of Keeping and Garner, risking charges of overstatement, pretentiousness and trendiness? Can we, as readers, publishers and critics, influence what happens? Should we?

3 / Approaches: The Question of What Criticism

English children's books were scarcely objects of criticism, a reviewer pointed out in 1783. A generation later, Sarah Trimmer systematically reviewed scores of books for children and young persons. Today, her opposition to fairy tales makes her seem a fussbudget, but few writers of her day sanctioned fairy stories (or any other imaginative works). On balance, this moral guardian, who urged mothers to cut out objectionable passages, also approved of nonsense rhymes and turned books for children into objects of serious criticism.

Some sixty years later, the *Quarterly Review,* marvelling at the "wide domain of juvenile literature," declared the fairy tale a "healthy amusement" and vigorously opposed the over-moralized books created by Trimmer's many disciples. The reviewer's scorn for the unreal model children shown interrupting their play to pray is set against praise for the more natural characters from the then new school of juvenile writers such as Mrs. Gatty.

In 1981 Paul Heins also found a new realism that, since the 1960s, has significantly changed the signposts, if not the boundaries, of juvenile literature. Welcoming the new freedoms, he warns against over-reliance on extrinsic as opposed to intrinsic literary analysis.

From Trimmer to Heins spans almost two centuries of critical scrutiny. Some battles have been decided. One, the fairy tale won. While literature has progressively become more realistic, one of Trimmer's considerations is still with us: what is fit for children? Note in the Heins selection the reviewer's disapproval of *The Chocolate War,* not because she found the book depressing but because she deemed it inappropriate for the young. This consideration attendant to the criticism of books for children necessarily draws us into extraliterary considerations.

Critics who agree with Paul Heins on the primacy of literary over extraliterary criticism can still disagree. The Lillian Gerhardt-Ethel Heins epistolary exchange erupted over the familiar query: where does children's literature fit adult literature? (The "literary lag" Gerhardt bemoans is also familiar. Why does it take a generation or more for some techniques and themes to move from adult to juvenile books? Monica Dickens has suggested one partial answer: that writers dip back to their own childhoods when they compose books for juveniles.)

Gerhardt maintains that current juvenile literature has yet to develop enough to affect its parent literature. Ethel Heins answers that in adult or children's literature trendy techniques or popular acclaim are not necessarily concomitant with literary superiority. To Heins those works for children created and critiqued with intellectual honesty deserve the overused but still necessary shibboleth, "mainstream."

We are constantly thrown back on the issue Crago posed: should juvenile literary practitioners labor contentedly within that stream or break through the dam to reach a wider, i.e., a more adult audience. In a literature that runs in complexity from *The Cat in the Hat* to *Watership Down*, how can any either/or dictum prevail? Whether a minor or a major tributary from adult literature, juvenile literature is vast enough to encompass the traditional and the trendy. As Paul Heins observes, for all the much vaunted realism of today's literature for children and young adults, cuddly mice and floppy bunnies are still very much with us.

Small wonder that artist and critic working the same waters can remain leagues apart. Susan Cooper's address and Lois Kuznets' rejoinder focus on criticism, but considerations of status inevitably sneak in. Remember the association of children with imbeciles that Felicity Hughes understandably decried? Note Cooper's confession that reading *The Horn Book Magazine* reassured her "that the writing of books published for children didn't necessarily mean that one was either a little old lady in tennis shoes or *retarded*" (my italics).

In "In Defense of the Artist" Cooper bemoans the quality of much criticism she found. For every critical gem, such as Lillian Smith's *The Unreluctant Years*, she dug up a dozen chunks for the slag heap. Based on my own field work, I can attest to her percentages. But in the literary seesaw between artist and critic, she overburdens the critic with psychologizers and bibliotherapeutic strawmen. The counterweight against poor criticism, she would agree, is good criticism, but Kuznets, understandably, reads Cooper's defense of the artist as an attack on literary criticism of any sort. Questioning the guilt by association with some carried-away critics, Kuznets, as critic and teacher, vows to continue to "go where the book sends me."

Striking the familiar passive pose (her publisher decides if what she wrote is destined for a child audience), Cooper distances herself from the child during the creation of her work. Yet, in pleading that nothing should come between child and artist once the work is complete, she uses the child as hostage in shielding herself from critics. Kuznets pleads for real dialogue not sermons, but literary analysis operates more out of struggles with a text than with fellow critics. There is little dialogue in children's literary criticism. Where it has been attempted (e.g., a critic taking on Roald Dahl's fiction or Walt Disney's art), debate often trickles into ad hominem defenses and other irrelevant side issues that Peter Hunt justly decries.[1]

Literary criticism of juvenile works still suffers from an identity crisis:

> Children's book people have a massive inferiority complex. . . . Critics, teachers, and librarians all expect the critical process to function like the Yellow Brick Road brightly leading the way to what is best and lasting in literature for children. This notion of criticism's role is so firmly rooted that even when the process obviously breaks down, when ruts and holes start blistering the macadam, when the road splits into a dozen forks and finally loses itself in a swamp, the travellers blame each other instead of the highway. . . . This is a dead end. What we really should do is reexamine our assumptions about children's literature and the critic's role within it.[2]

For all the heightened respectability children's literature studies have gained recently, it often runs aground on the sandbar of apologetics. The critics continually have had to maintain the necessity for and the propriety of the criticism before gaining clear passage to the actual territory. In more charted and restricted waters, as in analyzing a particular genre, less apologetics and more interchange take place.

Peter Hunt's essay gets us back to the purpose of criticism, the need to know our subject before we can know our object. His premise is that juvenile literature, sidetracked by subjective concerns, has suffered from too little, rather than too much critical discussion. Hunt insists we specify *by what standards* we assert a book is good. When he asks whether the literature is a different species and, if different, is it lesser, we are blown back to definition. Children's literature can take the weight of serious analysis, he asserts, and we can be comfortable with diverse standards so long as, ironically, the latter exclude the child. This is the standard purist position—that the child reader should be an irrelevant concern to the critic who must rely on adult standards.[3]

Children's literature is necessarily a peculiar kingdom. Modern critics have displaced the author's primacy to concentrate on the reader's experience with the text. Interpretation thus emanates from and within the act of reading. But because young children are not fully ready to articulate their reading experiences,[4] a proxy interpretive community often decides by *its* standards what is worthy of a child's attention. Thus distanced by choice or necessity from the child reader, children's literature critics turn out more commentary than criticism.

Using purely adult standards, Shelley Rubin points out, would leave us with no children's literature at all. In a literature founded on the disparity between the adults who create (and buy) it and the child who reads it, the critic has to steer between ignoring, and completely relying on, the child audience.

Aidan Chambers addresses the former danger. He counters the intentional fallacy of the legion of authors who profess they write for themselves, not children. First, he invokes an aesthetic theory that posits what readers an author has in mind as irrelevant. He concurs with F. H. Langman, whom he cites:

I do not say we need to know what readers the author had in mind. An author may write for a single person or a large public, for himself or for nobody. But the work itself implies the kind of reader to whom it is addressed and this may not coincide with the author's private view of his audience. What matters for the literary critic is to recognize the idea of the reader implied by the work.[5]

Building on this critical premise, Chambers moves from what a writer says to "the work itself," a much more reliable critical watchword. To illustrate, Chambers examines, in part, a Roald Dahl short story as written for *The New Yorker* and as rewritten for children. By textual analysis, Chambers shows how Dahl cut abstractions, chopped longer sentences and otherwise simplified his style. After analyzing how various writers (including Ransome!) create specific responses in a child reader, Chambers contrasts Lucy Boston's *The Children of Greene Knowe* with an adult novel of hers. Boston once claimed that, hearing a passage taken at random from her works, she would be unable to tell if it was meant for a child or an adult. Using textual evidence, Chambers disproves her claim and proves his case, thus moving the study of children's literature from product to process.

However, reports Peggy Whalen-Levitt, Chambers has met much resistance because attention to audience is perceived as threatening to the already shaky status of the literature. Mention of audience to an adult writer does not automatically invoke beer-swilling Babbitts, but mention of child audience to some conjures up images of drooling simpletons. Focus on audience comes off as a threat to the text's supremacy, yet Chambers rested his case on textual analysis not artistic intention.

More work is needed to clarify how an author is to take account of the indispensable "reader in the book." Will Chambers' work give more play to the empirical child studies, the parent diaries which chronicle a toddler's fear of eating apples after hearing the tale of Snow White?[6] True, a response-centered criticism is not the same as one based on reception theory, but how far will the former gravitate? Not to the measurement of galvanic response which television producers allegedly employ, one hopes.

As a student and teacher of children's literature I would vote for a democratic if not permissive approach to criticism. As children's literature is an art form that is a product of and reflection of its culture, I would agree with Hooker who asserts that "any meaning is fit that fits," so long as we do not lose sight of the text. I am not surprised if a semiotician or Jungian or deconstructionist wants to labor in the field. Whatever helps define the territory, describe the climate and/or evaluate the content is welcome. Having studied the storybook of the eighteenth century, I agree with Samuel Pickering, Jr., who claims that "the thorough study of early children's literature dispels many misconceptions and enables critics to put children's literature as a whole into cultural perspective."[7] Historical study can serve as a corrective in a field in which, taken with the noble end of the literature—the instruction and/or delight of the young—that work is often received with too much gratitude. Uncritical appreciators make literature for children as suspect as a G-rated movie. As Francelia Butler has noted, largely to blame is the failure to separate books from literature. A teen's guide to contraception or a child's guide to divorce or dental care is unlikely to be literature any more than the latest adult diet or fitness book. Kid lit and pop lit are not synonymous although there is much overlap. The Victorians have been blamed for lumping children's books as popular literature, but a recent critic has traced the separation of children's literature from serious literature as far back as the sixteenth century with the relegation of medieval romances to children.[8]

An identity problem persists to this day. Apologetics gets in the way of the real business of criticism: explication, bibliographies, biographies, etc. The adjective *children's* should function as categorization not condemnation. As C. S. Lewis, who doubted you could have a good children's story enjoyed only by children, warned: "Critics who treat *adult* as a term of approval, instead of a merely descriptive term, cannot be adult themselves."[9] Now who has the identity problem?

We have and need multicritical methods. Marilyn Kaye banks on a strength from diversity; however, in the polite arena of children's literature, critics from various disciplines seldom debate each other, much less work side by side. Like the children's author, the critic labors under an atmosphere that breeds self-consciousness, if not self-defensiveness. No wonder that more assumptions are articulated than approaches or that few approaches are tested or challenged. Still, our plural approaches represent major growth since Trimmer launched the systematic criticism of juvenile books.

The critics are, at times, understandably adrift and isolated in the vastness of the field. To see how they handle more manageable terrain, see Part 2, the territories that make up the domain that is literature for children.

The Guardian of Education
Sarah Kirby Trimmer

. . . Unhappily for us, such a rage for new publications is excited in the nation, that even children are taught to expect a daily supply of literature, and a daily supply is industriously provided for their gratification; but frequently of such a nature and tendency, as threaten the utter perversion of all principle; extraordinary care and circumspection are therefore required in selecting such publications as are proper and safe to be put into their hands; for the purchaser who is determined by the title of a book, is subject to great deception. Under the idea, therefore, that we might render acceptable service to mothers who wish to train up their children in the ways of piety and virtue, and secure them from the corruptions of the age, we have been induced to offer our assistance, as the examiners of books of education, and children's books; and we hope for the countenance and encouragement of all who are solicitous for the welfare of the rising generation.

In the course of this work there will be frequent occasion to mention the Jacobinical sect, but we wish it to be understood that it is not our

Excerpted from *The Guardian of Education* 1:15 (1802); 1:436 (1802); 2:184–5 (1803); and 4:412–14 (1805); courtesy of The Osborne Collection of Early Children's Books, Toronto Public Library.

design to bring forward subjects of a political nature any farther than as they are observed to affect the interests of religion and morality; and though we profess ourselves to be members of the Church of England, and zealous for the maintenance of its doctrines and ordinances, we have no intention to engage in questions of controversy with Christians of other religious persuasions; but having declared our own principles, we shall proceed in our examination of the books which come under our consideration, upon the supposition that these principles are established; and we shall exercise the utmost candour towards those who differ from us. It may perhaps be necessary to premise, in order to exculpate ourselves from the charge of plagiarism, that in our examination of books we shall frequently borrow the opinions of other writers, especially when by this means we have an opportunity of shewing at the same time the merits of one author, and the errors or defects of another. Indeed there would be no possibility of executing so extensive a plan, and which requires so much retrospection, without assistance from books; and though we have had considerable experience in the business of education, we are not so vain as to think our judgment ought to lead the public mind, without the support of concurrent authorities. . . .

ART. XXIX.—*The Renowned History of Primrose Pretty Face*, &c. Newbery.

This Book was originally one of Newbery's Lilliputian Library. It gives the history of a good Child, who, as she grew up, by her amiable conduct in various situations in life, became at last *Lady of the Manor*. Without such a conclusion of the story, we should think this a very proper book of amusement for children; but it certainly is very wrong to teach of girls [sic] the lower order to aspire to marriages with persons in stations so far superior to their own, or to put into the heads of young gentlemen, at an early age, an idea, that when they grow up they may, without impropriety, marry servant-maids. With a very little accommodation, *Primrose Pretty Face* might however be rendered a very instructive as well as amusing Book, for the style is pleasing, and the greatest part of it very fit for the perusal of children.

ART. XXX.—*The Prettiest Book for Children; being the history of the enchanted castle, situated in one of the fortunate isles, and governed by the giant instruction*, &c. &c. Price 6d. York. Wilson and Spence.

We think we recollect this Book also as one of Newbery's Lilliputian Library. It is a kind of allegorical work, sufficiently intelligible to interest and entertain children, as well as to convey useful instruction to their minds. What properly belongs to the History of the Enchanted Castle ends with the 5th chapter; but the Book is eked out to the sixpenny size, with some Dialogues copied from "*Le Magazine des Enfans*," of Madame le Prince de Beaumont. It would have been better if it had been printed in larger letter without this addition.

ART. XXXI.—*The Fisherman; an Interesting Tale, for Young People.* Price 6d.
Steart, Bath. Champante and Co. London.

One of the Stories, we believe, from the Arabian Nights Entertainments.
Not fit for Children.

ART. VI.—*The Life and Adventures of a Fly.* Price 6d. Newbery.

Every thing, animate or inanimate, may, by means of reflection and in-
genuity, be made subservient to moral instruction; and we here find that little
creature the Fly acting the part of a monitor to the juvenile race of mankind,
and even giving lessons of Religion well worth their attention.

In short, to speak the plain language of truth, this is a very entertaining
little book, and if the young reader is not improved by the perusal of it, he
must blame himself, not the author—A remark or two, however, we cannot
forbear making; and one of them is, that as the tale is entirely fictitious, we
think no incident in it should be imputed to the interposition of Providence.
We also think that in this book, as in many others of modern date, humanity
toward animals is carried to an extreme—not in the *act,* for we would by no
means recommend inattention to the good of the lower creatures; but to the
sentiment. Pity towards insects and brutes may be exercised without our feeling
for them as if they were of the same species with ourselves; nor do their necessities or feelings require this. A fly may be drowned even by a cruel boy without
his being chargeable with murder, or in danger of eternal punishment; and
another may be rescued from such a fate, without its awakening that powerful
sympathy, which the preservation of a fellow creature should excite; or giving
the preserver a title to the reward of benevolence. Great care, therefore, should
be taken, to teach children to make a proper discrimination, that they may
know how to proportion both their charity and restrain their revenge.

ART. VII.—*Mother Bunch's Fairy Tales.* Price 6d. Newbery.

Partial, as we confess ourselves to be, to most of the books of the old
school, we cannot approve of those which are only fit to fill the heads of
children with confused notions of wonderful and supernatural events brought
about by the agency of imaginary beings. Mother Bunch's Tales are of this
description.

ART. VII.—*Mary and Her Cat; in words not exceeding two syllables.* Price
1s. Tabart.

A little simple but interesting tale, invented to intice young children to
learn to read, for which purpose the words are divided into syllables, and the
embellishment of prints is added. We rank it with interesting and innocent
books, which is all that an author can aim at in publications for infants.

ART. VIII.—*Presents for Good Girls.* Price 1s. Tabart. 1804.

We conceive this little book to have been the production of the same
amusing pen as the preceding article. We agree with the writer in approving
of *dolls* and other toys of what may be called a *domestic nature,* as exciting
a taste for feminine employments.

ART. IX.—*Presents for Good Boys; or, the Toy Shop.* Adorned with beautiful Engravings. Price 1s. Tabart. 1804.

We have here a book of the same class as the last, but adapted to children of the other sex. The work is apparently of the same author. To these three articles no objection we think can be made but to the price of them. The expensiveness of children's books is a growing evil!

ART. X.—*The Comic Adventures of Old Mother Hubbard and Her Dog.* Price 6d. Harris. 1805.

This little book, the poetry of which is of ancient date, comes forth in this *edition* as we must call it, with uncommon attraction. In the first place it has the following dedication:

To J.B. Esq. M.P. County of _____ *at whose suggestion, and at whose house* these notable sketches were designed, *this volume is with all suitable deference* dedicated by his humble servant,

S. M. C.

We consider as a *jeu d'esprit,* the designs for the Prints in which Mrs. Hubbard and her Dog, are very respectably represented to the eye in every situation described by the poetic writer of her history. We can recollect, at this distance of time, that in our infant days the Story of this renowned woman, though full of inconsistencies we confess, afforded us much entertainment. We hope it is not a sign of our being in our second childhood, that it diverts us now. But innocent trifles may be allowed to amuse at any age; and we scruple not to recommend this little Book as one that will afford this kind of amusement.

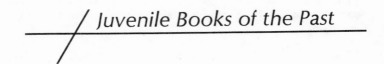

Juvenile Books of the Past

(1) *Parables from Nature.* By MRS. ALFRED GATTY. 1865.
(2) *Aunt Sally's Life.*[1] 1865.
(3) *Melchior's Dream.*

Unsigned review reprinted from *The British Quarterly Review* 47:128–49 (January 1868).

(4) *Guessing Stones.*   By the Rev. Phillip Freeman.   1864.
(5) *The Story of Papa's Wise Dogs.*   1867.
(6) *Our Four-footed Friends.*   By Mary Howitt.
(7) *Recollections of Harrow.*   1867.
(8) *Tossed on the Waves.*   By Edwin Hodder.   1864.
(9) *Walks with Mamma.*   1867.
(10) *Lightsome and the Little Golden Lady.*   1867.
(11) *Cousin Trix.*   By Georgiana Craik.   1867.
(12) *Washed Ashore.*   By William Kingston.   1866.
(13) *Silver Lake.*   By R. M. Ballantyne.   1867.
(14) *Barefooted Birdie.*   1868.
(15) *The Fairchild Family.*   3 vols.   1856.
(16) *Hans Christian Andersen's Fairy Tales.*
(17) *Aunt Judy's Christmas Volume.*   1867.
(18) *Routledge's Every Boy's Annual.*   1868.
(19) *Old Merry's Annual.*   1868.

The combination of instruction and amusement is presumably the aim and object of every writer of children's books. How difficult it is to blend these two unsympathetic elements without becoming prosy and wearisome is best known to those whose labours with the pen have lain in this particular district of the field of literature. As proof, for our own self-satisfaction, we have but to recall the long list of tedious and feeble productions of past years, which, ostensibly professing to be suited to juvenile readers, have been so overweighted and borne down at every page by the mistaken efforts of their authors to improve the occasion, no matter how inopportunely, that old as well as young have, with heavy eyes and muddled brains, thrown them down, half-read, in despair and disgust. Every character in them was utterly depraved and wicked, the good and the bad boy alike; the former little better than a whitened sepulchre, the latter a monster of iniquity and wickedness, whose fate hereafter was plainly foreshadowed in terms more forcible than elegant. Hell and the devil were dragged in at every available opportunity without the slightest regard to the context, till so much was said about them, that instead of playing the part of Bogey, as was intended, they came to be regarded quite as familiar acquaintances. Religious and secular things were jumbled up in wild and profane confusion; blind man's buff was made the occasion for a long sermon on the sin of selfishness, because one little boy wanted to be blind man all the time, to the exclusion of his companions, who also in their turn came in for a share of rebuke for being envious. Turn where you would, to the playground, to the school-room, homewards or abroad, it was always the same dreary, monotonous, never-ending dirge—"Naughty, naughty children, you are all utterly lost and wicked!" In short, the shape in which a good and merciful God was presented was not only terrifying, but repulsive; instead of inducing adoration and worship, confidence and love, the youthful imagination was disordered and affrighted by the picture of a stern and remorseless Judge, who sought rather to condemn than to save. Another grievous fault in these same books, whose titles we have no desire more particularly to mention, was the free and conversational style in which holy things were treated; Scriptural phrases were, what the authors termed, "simplified," to meet the capacities of youthful readers; and on this pretence the name of God and of Jesus Christ were dragged in amongst a string of commonplaces, which were supposed more plainly to represent the meaning of the Bible writers. It is hardly necessary to exclaim against the execrably bad taste of such a heathen course of proceeding; the brains that could contemplate, and the hands that could carry out such a work of desecration, are obviously without the limits of criticism. Comment upon such people would only amount to abuse. But enough of the shortcomings of nonentities, whose little day, if they ever had one at all, was very little indeed, and who, now buried away in the most obscure corners of their publishers' book-shelves, are forgotten by the world generally, and, as far as we are concerned, forgiven by us in particular.

It is with a genuine feeling of pleasure and satisfaction that we turn to the more modern school of juvenile literature, and find a pure and wholesome atmosphere to breathe that reinvigorates and refreshes. There is no less effort made nowadays to combine instruction and amusement; there is the same earnest endevour to adorn the tale by pointing a moral, but Bogey no longer asserts his sway: he has been slaughtered mercilessly, and hurried to an untimely end, with his long catalogue of sins and vices to keep him company in his dishonoured grave. There are good boys and naughty boys, good girls and naughty girls, as there always must be while the world goes on; but they are neither paragons of virtue nor monsters of iniquity, only very much like the real, living, breathing young people with whom we have to deal in the course of life's journey. . . .

It is high time that those who assume the responsibility of writing for the young should be careful to examine themselves as to their fitness for the work; for although it is popularly supposed that children's books are rattled off with a flowing pen and little or no effort, such is far from being the case: in those that are worthy the name, every page has cost an infinity of anxious thought and earnest consideration. To select those paragons of stories, "Little Alice's Adventures in Wonderland" and "Barefooted Birdie," it is apparent upon the face of each of them that their authors must have spent very many laborious hours over their production. There is not a single line in them that is superfluous, not a word that would not be missed if it were omitted; indeed, each picture is perfect in detail and colouring. Or again, take Mr. Freeman's "Guessing Stories," which, though they are somewhat peculiar, are none the less worthy of commendation; and mark the exceeding beauty, and yet withal simplicity of the language he uses. To quote one passage, in which, under an allegory, he describes the human eyes, as "two ample chambers placed high up in the palace, and filled with a mystic apparatus of many coloured spheres, crystal lenses, and other instruments. Into these chambers, the windows of which were flung open on purpose all day, and sometimes part of the night, were darted continually golden arrows by day, and silver arrows by night, inscribed in some way like the arrow aimed at Philip of Macedon, with information as to what was going on in the kingdom." And then in equally eloquent language he proceeds to describe the process by which the observation of the eyes feeds the brain; thus: "By means of the spheres and lenses, and other instruments before mentioned, a kind of photograph of the scenes thus described was transmitted instantaneously to the king." These characteristic quotations from two highly-finished children's books are worthy of consideration as showing the special qualifications that are required to enable man or woman to write for the young. Whether we recall "Goody Two Shoes," or "Jack the Giant Killer," or the many other multitudinous acquaintances of our childhood, over whose histories we have laughed and cried, those always were appreciated and liked the best, which in maturer years, upon reference, we find to be the most carefully and healthily written. Depend upon it, there is a great deal to be said for a book for juveniles that will bear the perusal and candid criticism of grown-up people. As we have observed, those who purpose essaying literature for the young should not rush thoughtlessly to pen, ink, and paper, and scribble down the first ideas that imagination suggests. As a model of careful composition, let them imitate Mr. Hodder in his admirable tale, "Tossed on the Waves," which any boy may read with gratification and profit to himself. It is not that there is anything very startling or very novel about it; indeed, to speak plainly, the plot is a little forced and weak, while a trifle too much of the *goody* element is introduced; but, regarding the story as a whole, it bespeaks the sound discretion and well-regulated condition of the author's mind, and the critic is fain to forget individual and isolated shortcomings in its general excellence. "Tossed on the Waves" may be considered a fair specimen of that class of children's books which are peculiarly religious in tone and character. Ordinarily speaking, works of this sort are prosy, tedious, and distasteful, simply because of the didactic, dogmatical fashion in which they are invariably written. Without doubt, marble-playing on

Sunday is wrong, and children ought to know that it is, and that for this one day in the week they must put their toys and playthings away in the cupboard, and stop their romping and shouting; but it is hardly necessary that they should be frightened into appreciating the requirements of the Sabbath by stories of how naughty little Tommy or Johnny, or whatever the young villain's name may be, nearly came to a bad end through his having begun early in life to get out his bricks on Sunday. We have a dim recollection of once reading how an abandoned and depraved monster of ten escaped being hanged at Tyburn only by the merest accident, because he had shown himself so utterly destitute of all moral principle as to model a boat out of a piece of firewood on the Sabbath. Is it right or proper to put such balderdash to children, and to imbue them with such extravagant notions of what gigantic evils may befall them if they make the smallest error? Again, it is most meet and proper that all young people should value their Bibles, and say their prayers night and morning; and nothing can be more beautiful than the picture of the young Christian on his knees, his heart and soul turned towards his heavenly Father, and his lips offering up praise and thanksgiving for all the blessings and advantages of life. But boys and girls who are perpetually stopping in the midst of their play to say prayers and sing hymns are simply nauseating, and excite contempt and disgust. Nor is it right to say that all young people are vicious, evilly disposed, untruthful, dishonest—in short, everything that is bad; and that they are always sinning and repenting, and lead an anxious and perturbed existence by reason of their frailty. We would rather believe that the more experience grown-up persons have of children, the more satisfied will they become of the purity and simplicity of their nature—

> The human blossom blows, and every day,
> Soft as it rolls along, shows some new charm.
> —Thomson

They abound in imagination and feeling; the saddest tale will amuse, and move them to laughter or tears. Moreover, their predisposition is to be good rather than naughty; they are easily susceptible of divine teachings, and full of religious feelings. When they are troublesome and disobedient, is it not generally the fault of those who are in authority over them, who have failed to "train them in the way they should go," either by indulging and spoiling too much on the one hand, or by scolding and punishing too freely on the other?

> To aid thy mind's development—to watch
> Thy dawn of little joys—to sit and see

Almost their very growth—to view thee catch
Knowledge of objects—wonders yet to thee.
                              —Byron

Such is the office of those who would mould and shape the child's character, and such the code by which children's bookmakers should be guided. There are many unnatural and unhealthy productions that have an exceedingly dangerous tendency, and do an incalculable amount of harm; for they awaken within the youthful brain thoughts and ideas that had far better be permitted to slumber on undisturbed. Young gentlemen who are brought into the drawing-room to astonish you, by way of a great intellectual treat, with their precocious and spirited recitation of "My Name is Norval," are social nuisances; and a wise discretion would keep them upstairs in their proper place—the nursery. Still, one can just tolerate them, because the poor little fellows cannot help themselves, and are to be pitied rather than blamed for the folly of their parents in making an exhibition of them. But boys and girls of Mrs. Sherwood's type, who bristle at every point with Bible texts, and quote long passages from Scripture, in the course of ordinary conversation, refreshing themselves at frequent intervals by reference to Doctor Watts, are specimens of juvenile humanity whose society would be unbearable. We say would be, because, fortunately, they exist only in the fertile imaginations of their authors, where it is sincerely to be hoped they may remain. Even an introduction to them in print is a thing to be most scrupulously avoided; for they are companions that can do no young reader any good. What a contrast, in their inflated, pretentious tone, do they present to the following simple, unaffected, but perfectly comprehensible passage from a charming little book [*Walks with Mamma*]. "How quietly, how gently flows the stream! Just as it flows now, it has flowed for long, long years. I can remember it when I was a child, and so could my mother before me. You see, my dear boy, that men and women and children pass away; but the flowers still bloom, the trees still wave to and fro their leafy branches, and the waters still ripple through the green valley." Thus, the mother instructs her child concerning man's destiny, and the inevitable death that must come, sooner or later! Taking another peep into some pleasant pages of a like description, we find a loving lecture on carelessness and disobedience:

Fanny has been told, I cannot say how many times, not to meddle with the fire, but she is a careless child, and sadly disobedient. Now you see the consequences (depicted in a prettily drawn picture at the head of the story). She has been trying to put some fresh coals on the fire. She could not lift the coal-scuttle, and she therefore filled her apron, but it slipped out of her careless fingers and emptied all the black coal and coal-dust on the drawing-room carpet. Well may she cry, for she has spoiled her apron and injured the carpet; yet I fear she does not cry because she is naughty, but because she will be punished for her carelessness. It is a very different thing, being sorry for yourself, from being sorry for your fault. The former is only selfishness; the latter is repentance. [*Peeps of Home*]

Any child that reads this will understand the lesson it conveys; he will equally well appreciate that, "if Fanny had contrived to put the coals on the fire safely, her fault would have been as great. She would still have disobeyed her parents, and run the risk of setting her clothes in a blaze." Now, although these two little books from which we have quoted are essentially "goody," they are so artistically constructed, that the sound and wholesome lessons each story is intended to convey are learnt by the young reader almost unknown to himself. At the river-side, through the valley of wild flowers, in the harvest-field, or by the garden of the dead, these are the places whither he is led to exercise his imagination, and accustom himself to reflection. "Tis thought and digestion which makes books serviceable, and gives health and vigour to the mind" [Fuller]. He sees the rushing waters sweeping onward to the sea, and wonders when those glittering ripples that, but a moment since, danced past him, and which now he beholds no more, will mingle with the green waves of the great deep. He gazes on the delicate forget-me-not, or the blushing wild rose; and his thoughts wander upwards to Him who has decked the earth with floral ornaments, that all the gold and jewels and precious stones in the world cannot equal. He watches the waving forests of yellow corn, bending with well-filled ears beneath the soft summer breeze, and feels that when the winter draws on, the blessing of plenty will soften its asperities. He stands in "God's Acre," on the green counterpane of that last bed of common humanity—the grave—and foregathers within him the fate that neither king nor peasant can avert. Here he seeks to learn that "all that nature has prescribed must be good; and as death is natural, it is absurdity to fear it. Fear loses its purpose when we are sure it cannot preserve us, and we should draw resolution to meet it from the impossibility to escape it" [Steele]. Here too he thinks of the bright and blessed hopes that change the grave-yard into a cemetery; and of His great love and grace, who is "the resurrection and the life," and who has "brought life and immortality to light by his gospel." These are the spots to lead the young mind lovingly to; these the devices by which to teach him to be good and honourable; these the scenes in which to make him learn from nature's self the mercy and greatness of nature's God. All the freshest and most vigorous stories for children are thus conceived, and are worked out upon framework such as this.

Who can paint
Like Nature? Can Imagination boast,
Amid its gay creation, hues like hers?
Or can it mix them with that matchless skill,
And lose them in each other, as appears
In every bud that blows?

—Thomson

Whether it be Little Johnny and his father out amid the great billows in
a mere cockle-shell of a boat *[Told in the Twilight]*; or Roy and Nelly
lost in the snow *[Silver Lake]*; or the yellow flower that loved the sun
[Cousin Trix, and Other Tales]; or Lightsome and the Fishes *[Lightsome
and the Little Golden Lady]* there is the same inspiration from nature to
be found busily engaged in the conduct of the tale, and whispering softly
to the young heart that

There's music in the sighing of a reed,
There's music in the gushing of a rill,
There's music in all things, if men had ears,
Then earth is but an echo of the spheres.

—Byron

Thus the budding fancy of the child finds its way, under the guidance of
fiction, to the contemplation of what is natural and true, and takes unto
itself a moral from sources the quality of which cannot be questioned.
It demands no very violent effort of imagination on a writer's part to
convince a young reader that lying is bad and vicious; there is no need
to load the picture with extravagant colouring; and he will as readily
learn it from "Lightsome's" scales as from the disobedient boy who ate
the forbidden apple, and told a falsehood to hide his fault. If there are
two roads, one bright, sunny, and cheerful, and the other dark, gloomy,
and uninviting, by which the same end may be attained, should there be
a moment's hesitation as to which to select? The young love to hear the
birds sing, to see the flowers bloom, to bask in the sun, to live in an atmosphere of universal happiness and plenty. This is the sort of realm
wherein they like to wander:

It was a village up in the sky, so far away that I cannot remember its name,
and so high up above clouds that, coming back, I forgot my way thither. But
high up and far away as it may be, it was such a fine place when you got
there! It had big trees and little houses. Such a many many birds all singing
together, and no fruit on the trees that was not as ripe as ripe could be. Boxer
tops grew on all the hedges, and cricket-bats in the wood. The outside leaves
of the summer cabbages were kites with splendid tails; and when the sweet

peas had done blossoming, they bore pods full of the most beautiful streaky marbles. There was a large holly-bush in the corner close by the pump; it never had any red berries on it, to speak of, but come round Christmas-time was so full of dolls, all dressed in muslins and silks, that, if you didn't gather them as soon as they were ripe—before breakfast-time in the morning—they were sure to tumble off, and break their pretty noses. As for the rose-bushes. . . .

But here we must stop, confessing that never before was there so beautiful and happy a place as Lightsome's beautiful village, where the roses were so large, and the people so clean, that they never wanted washing. When once Master Tom or Miss Kitty have struck up an acquaintance with a place like this, it is hard work to induce them to quit it, even for a short time, and return to the dull region of earth, where, in order to sustain life, a more generous and substantial diet than "early dew and honey from the flowers" is necessary. Entranced and spellbound, they are lost in wandering along the pleasant paths of the land of enchantment, till they regard eating and drinking as barbarous and vulgar institutions, and prefer gardens growing like Mistress Mary's—

> With silver bells and cockle shells,
> And hyacinths all of a row,

to those which produce such vulgar and material things as cabbages and potatoes. There can be no doubt that fairy stories are held in very high estimation by our young people, more so, perhaps, than any other kind of juvenile literature. The sorrows of poor, ill-used "Cinderella," the trials and troubles of "Snowdrop," the long rest of the "Sleeping Beauty," the wondrous adventures of "Tommelise," or the queer vagaries of the "Yellow Dwarf," afford an endless fund of healthy and hearty amusement. They will read each of these, and we do not know how many more into the bargain, over and over again, without a sign of impatience or weariness, even till they can repeat them by heart to an admiring circle in the nursery. Speaking of fairy tales, as a class, we can most conscientiously say that they are well worthy the affectionate favour in which they are regarded, and are instruments not only of amusement, but of instruction, that no parent need fear to employ. With some very rare exceptions, their tone is pure and refined, and in every respect suited to the freshness and innocence of the budding imagination: they transport it at once to a new world, where it is greeted with all that beauty and brightness and happiness wherein it so delights, and is fed with the daintiest fare. Nor is it surprising that children like for awhile to quit the region of tempting jam-cupboards, and weak-minded heroes and heroines who cannot resist its seductions, and to take flight to the territory of those busy, agreeable little people, the fairies, concerning whose position on the map geography is silent; though we shrewdly suspect that, if applied to, Hans Christian Andersen could inform us; for the intimate and acute knowledge he displays of their habits and customs could have been gained only by a long sojourn amongst them, and a close and careful study of their national character and institutions. We wonder what he would say to an assertion such as this about his tiny friends: "Fairies, you know, have not got hearts, but only a hollow place in their bosoms, where their hearts ought to be," when he has introduced us to so many, who have been perfect models of tenderness and love [*Down Amongst the Fairies*]. Surely this is a calumny that he would not hesitate to refute with indignation and scorn! Of course, as everywhere else, there are wicked and cruel fairies, who work all sorts of mischief and injury to deserving mortals; but they are always few and far between, and have their shameful machinations miserably exposed and defeated in the end, to the satisfaction of every right-minded reader. In fact, it is rather an advantage than otherwise that they do exist, as without them there would be no opportunity for those that are virtuous and good to counteract their evil influences, and to join the hands of the handsome and long-suffering prince and the beautiful princess, so that they may live happily together ever afterwards. And thus reaching the almost unvarying conclusion of every fairy tale, we are reminded that we ourselves must draw on to a close. Obviously, it would have been impossible for us to consider the wide domain of juvenile literature in any other than a very general way. Its limits are wide asunder as the poles, its varieties so numerous, that the space at command would have been wholly inadequate to enable us to individualise, much less to criticise them; for it must be remembered that, while the books which are written for men and women do not require that the author should consult the probable age and intelligence of those who are likely to be his readers, those which are intended for the young must be graduated according to the mental and imaginative development of that particular section of juveniles, whose vote and interest they aim at securing. Thus, the names of Kingston, Ballantyne, and Mayne Reid are associated with stirring stories of adventures by land and sea, which are dear to schoolboys; while "Tom Brown," the Rev. Mr. Adams, and a host of others *ejusdem generis,* are identified with books that are equally cherished by them. These represent a distinct class, just as Mrs. Alfred Gatty, Hans Christian Andersen, Mary Howitt, and others in their way, devote their attention to the amusement of young children. There are books and books—for boys, for girls, for young ladies, for hobbledehoys, all of which undoubtedly belong to juvenile literature; there are many of them as good as good can be, and a considerable number that deserve no better fate than to be put behind the fire. The larger proportion may be digested with pleasure and profit; the minority, if they ever happened to find a circulation, would, through their own intrinsic badness, destroy themselves. We have sought, in the course of the preceding observations, to distinguish between those kinds of children's books which are worthy the title, and those which, under a fraudulent assumption of the name, terrify the opening imagination and expanding mind of the young reader with false and sickly Bogeyisms! There are many of the former description we would gladly have mentioned; there are not a few of the latter sort we have purposely omitted. In the one case, with the increasing taste for literature among the juvenile portion of society, merit is sure to obtain a hearing; in the other, the proper criticism is, to abstain from any notice of their existence. One word, and but one word, of the periodicals for the young, of which "Aunt Judy," "Merry and Wise," and "Routledge's Magazine for Boys," stand in the front rank. It is not too much to say that each of these, in its own peculiar province, is unapproachable, and satisfies the requirements of those for whose edification it is intended. Taken together, they are highly creditable specimens of the juvenile literature of the day, and irresistible evidence of the improvement in tone and style, that has of late taken place in the writing for the young, which used too often to be done in a sadly negligent and slipshod style. Although it is a dangeous passage to quote, lest our own shortcomings may be called into account, it would be well if some authors of children's books would remember "that, when self-interest inclines a man to print, he should consider that the purchaser expects a pennyworth for his penny; and has reason to asperse his honesty if he finds himself deceived" [Shenstone].

Literary Criticism and Children's Books

Paul Heins

In *An Experiment in Criticism* C. S. Lewis made an interestingly paradoxical statement: "The truth is not that we need the critics in order to enjoy the authors, but that we need the authors in order to enjoy the critics." But being a reasonable man, he went on to admit that "criticism normally casts a retrospective light on what we have already read. It may sometimes correct an over-emphasis or a neglect in our previous reading and thus improve a future rereading."[1] Since C. S. Lewis was trying to distinguish in his experiment "between readers or types of reading,"[2] it might also be important to remember what Georg Brandes wrote to Hans Christian Andersen regarding critics: "A literary critic is someone WHO KNOWS HOW TO READ, and who teaches the art of reading."[3] Of course, if one knows how to read—in Brandes's sense of the word—one does not need critics, although what they have to say may prove interesting. Obviously, if one is seeking "a retrospective light" on what has already been read, criticism may be not only valuable but important.

The problem with children's books and with the criticism of children's books is that the endeavor is beset with ambiguities. For obviously the criticism of children's books can be meaningful to adult readers acquainted with such books; but what about people who are not extensively acquainted with them but who make audacious snap judgments about them? To cite a single example: Although Bruno Bettelheim in *The Uses of Enchantment* gave his imprimatur to the meaning and importance of fairy tales, he dismissed "the rest of so-called 'children's literature'" because "most of these books are so shallow in substance that little of significance can be gained from them."[4] The term "most" is a strange word to apply to a body of literature which in recent years has produced such works as *The Owl Service, Carrie's War, Unleaving, Petros' War, Bridge to Terabithia,* and *The Slave Dancer.* In a sense, of course, C. S. Lewis was right. The criticism of children's books will

Reprinted from *The Quarterly Journal of the Library of Congress* 38:255–63 (Fall 1981), with permission of the author.

scarcely mean anything to people completely unacquainted or—at most —only somewhat acquainted with them. At this juncture the critic can only be an apologist and suggest, "Read extensively and judiciously; discover for yourselves the children's books worthy of reading and worthy of critical scrutiny."

Actually, there has long been a symbolic relationship between books intended for adult readers and those intended for juvenile readers. It is well known that before genuinely entertaining works of fiction had been written expressly for them, children adopted *The Pilgrim's Progress, Gulliver's Travels,* and *Robinson Crusoe* for their own. And as time went on, such diverse writers as Stevenson and Kipling, Frances Hodgson Burnett and C. S. Lewis produced works for children as well as for adults. At the present time many noteworthy children's writers also write for an adult readership: Nina Bawden, Penelope Lively, Ursula Le Guin, Paula Fox—to mention only a few. Significantly, then, the development of the criticism of children's literature in recent years, especially as found in the essays of John Rowe Townsend and Eleanor Cameron, has stressed the unity of literary endeavor. Children's literature should be considered as part of all literature; the criticism of children's literature should be conducted in the same manner as the criticism of adult litera- ture. These principles may by now seem to be truisms, but they are based on a sense of justice as well as on a sense of aesthetics.

To set up an analogy for the proper literary consideration of children's books, I should like to quote a significant portion of Kenneth T. Tel- ford's analysis of Aristotle's *Poetics:*

> The supposition that art either can or ought to be examined independently of other parts of man's experience was hotly contested in Aristotle's day and is still the subject of polemical debate today. Most treatises concerned with art, in fact, do not deal with its intrinsic characteristics. That is they do not deal with the art object as such. Instead we find essays on art as the expression of various biological, sociological, political, or psychological forces operating on the artist. Or we find discussions on art as an instrument for the moral im- provement of man, or art as a technique for eliciting various emotional re- sponses in an audience. Aristotle's position does not imply that such discussions on art are meaningless or impossible. There are in fact countless references throughout his work to the relationships which can be found between art and other things which form part of man's world. But these discussions have other purposes than that of telling us what art is or what makes a poem, painting, or musical composition well or poorly made.[5]

At the risk of raising the ghost of the New Criticism, I should like to suggest a number of reasons for the importance of considering children's books as works of literature, at the same time remembering that nonliterary approaches need not be scorned or ignored. For certainly Ursula Le Guin's *A Wizard of Earthsea* is structurally as well as mythically indebted to Jung's concept of the Shadow, and Katherine Paterson's *Jacob Have I Loved* derives its ultimate meaning from Biblical allusions and from theological interpretations.

In the first place, it is necessary to keep clear the distinction between criticism and book selection. Ever since the 1880s when Caroline Hewins published her pamphlet *Books for the Young,* librarians have been motivated to offer children the best kinds of books; and although the tradition has been somewhat weakened in recent years, the principle still holds good. There are some who think the tradition elitist, but they lose sight of the fact that democracy is a political virtue and not an aesthetic one. Obviously, the desire for the best in books must lead to the search for the best; and how can that search be followed through without literary evaluation? Lillian Smith's excellent critical work *The Unreluctant Years* was obviously the result of a happy relationship between literary criticism and selection.

A second consideration of the natural and developing connection between children's books and criticism might appear to be somewhat academic. As a literary study, children's literature is coming into its own and is no longer limited to library schools or to schools of education—as adjuncts of book selection or the teaching of reading. The historical aspect of the subject has aroused interest on its own account, and the publication in recent years of such books as Richard Darling's *The Rise of Children's Book Reviewing in America, 1865–1881* and Anne MacLeod's *A Moral Tale: Children's Fiction and American Culture 1820–1860* has bolstered the scholarly reputation of the subject.

But apart from the functional and pragmatic relationships between children's books and their criticism, there exists a vital and necessary give-and-take between the two which depends upon the peculiar nature of this body of literature. Originally sporadic in production and for a long time didactic in intent, it did not—as is well-known—begin to enjoy a separate independent existence until the 1860s. Until the late 1960s children's books were following more or less the course laid out for them a hundred years before by such works as *Little Women, The Story of a Bad Boy, The Adventures of Tom Sawyer,* and *Alice's Adventures in Wonderland.* As late as 1941 Elizabeth Enright in *The Saturdays* could express in the experiences and feelings of one of her characters the spirit of what may be called the old realism in children's fiction:

Mona switched off the light, leaped into bed, and burrowed under the covers. In a few minutes she was warm and cosy. The shade flapped against the window as it always did, and far overhead tracing its lonely path across the dark she heard the hum of the airplane. She was safe in her bed, the house enclosed her in a shell of warm security and all about, on every side, were the members of her own family who loved and understood her so well. She felt calm and heppy.[6]

The 1970s saw the advent of the new realism. *The Pigman, Dinky Hocker Shoots Smack, Z for Zachariah, His Own Where, The Planet of Junior Brown, The Man without a Face* are just a few of the noteworthy books produced during the era one is tempted to call the Age of Judy Blume. Much has already been said and written about the causes of the proliferation of this new kind of realism—the social unrest, the sexual revolution, the baneful influence of television, the creation of the category "young adult fiction"—to name only a few. Suffice it to say, it is a realism unrestricted by taboos and conventions and propriety of subject matter, and it deals freely with sexual as well as with social and racial topics.

Critics are well-aware of the two kinds of realism. For example, Sheila Egoff for her 1979 May Hill Arbuthnot Honor Lecture chose as her title "Beyond the Garden Wall: Some Observations on Current Trends in Children's Literature." To her the wall represented "order, serenity, aesthetic delight." Sadly she admits that what she calls the problem novel "has vastly extended the scope of children's literature, both in content and tone. Writers are free, as never before, to attempt themes of almost any kind."[7] Admitting the influence of this new freedom on writers such as Katherine Paterson, Ursula Le Guin, and Scott O'Dell, Professor Egoff somewhat ruefully feels that "the problem novel is almost inherently inimical to the traditional values of imagination and style."[8]

If writers of children's books are "free, as never before, to attempt themes of almost any kind," it is obvious that the signposts if not the boundaries of children's literature have changed significantly. The change, of course, has been comparatively recent, even if one thinks back to such a transitional work as *Harriet the Spy,* which was published in the 1960s; and whether this new freedom will continue to be the key-note of juvenile and young adult literature for a considerable length of time is naturally unknowable. New approaches do not necessarily cancel old ones (think of the mice and bunnies that are still being glorified in new children's books); and, as Sheila Egoff suggests, the results of the new freedom are evident in the works of capable, unsensational writers.

The term "traditional values" is an important one to remember in evaluating the possibilities of the new realism. Ten years before Sheila Egoff's lecture, Eleanor Cameron in her *Horn Book* article "The Art of

Elizabeth Enright" made an ironically revealing statement: "There is traditionally more often the depiction of overt cruelty and evil [in the fairy tale] which children have taken for their own than there is in their realistic literature."[9] A perfect statement of the kind of double standard which separated the content and form of folklore presented to children from the form and content of the old realism.

In addition to critical scrutiny, the new realism has aroused caustic commentary and rebuttal. "Realism: How Realistic Is It?" by Norma Bagnall, appeared in the Winter 1980 issue of *Top of the News.* The burden of her complaint about a book like *The Chocolate War* was that its "presentation of people and events shows only the evil, the ugly, and the sordid. It is not appropriate for young people because it presents a distorted view of reality and because it lacks hope."[10] Later, in the Fall 1980 issue of *Top of the News,* in an article entitled "The New Repression," Jay Daly defended the new realism by saying that "the only excuse for writing—or reading, for that matter—is to come in contact with something real, something that expands one's experience with life. It can be a positive or a negative experience; life is full of both."[11]

Now, to judge books—works of art—by their external characteristics scarcely does justice to them. There is all the difference in the world between *Are You There, God? It's Me, Margaret* and *The Planet of Junior Brown*—two decidedly different examples of the new realism. And if we are to admit the possibility of tragic protagonists, who made their appearance in children's literature because of the freedom inaugurated by the new realism, we have to turn our attention to purely literary questions, not necessarily and entirely to the principles of tragedy as laid down in Aristotle's *Poetics* but at least to the consideration of a literary work as a work of art, as something to be grasped and understood in its own terms.

Perhaps the most uncompromising expression of tragedy in juvenile literature is to be found in *The Chocolate War.* A book inspiring—as we have already stated—violent opinions, it is worthy of careful study to ascertain what really lies below its surface, which often seems overcharged with crude, violent, cynical, and sordid details. But the author is always clear about the distinction between good and evil. As revealingly acute as he is about Archie, a twentieth-century Iago, there is never any question about the boy's villainy. If the protagonist Jerry finally tells his confidant Goober not to disturb the universe, what other statement would have been possible to him at the time? After all, Jerry is not presented as a saint. Robert Cormier was writing about a fallible young man whose actions had to correspond with the aesthetic premises of the book.

In one of her letters, Flannery O'Connor wrote: "I don't believe you can ask an artist to be affirmative any more than you can ask him to be negative. The human condition includes both states. . . . I mortally and strongly defend the right of the artist to select a negative aspect of the world to portray. . . . Of course you are only enabled to see what is black by having light to see it by."[12] If such statements can serve to illuminate what is essential to literature in general, they can also logically serve a similar function for children's literature on the special occasions which demand them.

In coping with contemporary publications, a critic may tend to be polemical, especially if he is dealing with such a controversial subject as the new realism. But fortunately not all of his efforts will be limited by the responsibility of coming to grips with current productions. Traditionally, the critic—as C. S. Lewis suggests—"casts a retrospective light on what we have already read." In *Written for Children* John Rowe Townsend did just this kind of service for English children's books published before World War I:

Robert Louis Stevenson and his successors had raised the adventure story to a higher status than it had known before or has known since. Rudyard Kipling was at the peak of his powers in the last decade of the nineteenth century and the first of the twentieth; and he was a writer of international reputation among adults, not a "mere" children's writer. E. Nesbit, also at her peak, had excelled in both family and fantasy stories. Kenneth Grahame had produced *The Wind in the Willows* in 1908, and Frances Hodgson Burnett *The Secret Garden* in 1910. Walter de la Mare's first collection of poems had appeared . . . and Beatrix Potter had already done all her best work.[13]

As adult readers of children's literature—whether for professional reasons or simply because of a certain catholicity of taste—we also play a part in casting the "retrospective light." We can admire the dramatic deftness of the characterization in *Little Women* or discern the surrealistic elements in *Alice in Wonderland*. We can discover that *The Princess and the Goblin* and *Understood Betsy* have lived not only beyond the era of our childhood but even beyond the times for which they were written.

This discussion has obviously been restricted to a literary point of view. Actually, it is possible to consider children's books from other points of view: social issues, reader response, anthropological, linguistic, or psychological significance. And literary criticism can surely glean certain insights from these nonliterary considerations. But as mathematics is considered to be the queen of the sciences, literary criticism may well be the proper topographical basis for exploring the terrain of children's literature.

An Argument Worth Opening

Lillian N. Gerhardt

Innumerable commentators on children's books plug the idea that children's books are part of " . . . the mainstream of American literature." The authors, illustrators, publishers, reviewers, and librarians who have employed or applauded that self-congratulatory tag line apparently see the children's book field from an angle completely hidden from *SLJ*'s Book Review. From where we sit, books for children are more accurately described as: the last bastion of yesterday's literary methods and standards. The Mainstreamers would be hard pressed to name one, let alone two, children's books that ever turned around writing for adults. But, there's a lot of evidence to support the Last Bastion view.

A time line of literary lag in children's books would show that an average of twenty years lapses between the time a storytelling method is generally accepted at the adult reading level and the time it is first employed and finally accepted in books for children. All of the energy in children's book selection circles, after the handed-down methods are encountered, seems to be invested in initial resistance followed by total surrender. No critical discussion relative to the usage and limitations of the methods in successful children's books ever follows.

Some examples of such literary lag in children's books are: episodic novels, first-person narration, and the unresolved plot.

Episodic novels were s.o.p. in adult fiction during the 1940s. Not until the 1960s did such books begin to appear for children. Anybody who can remember the protests against *It's Like This, Cat* (Harper, 1963) will have to concede our charge of literary lag here. The same time span and resistance to acceptance of first-person narration in novels can be observed. It was a commonplace technique in the adult fiction of the 1950s, but rarely encountered, except in historical fiction, in books for children. After initial resistance followed by critical silence, such novels have now become a depressant drug on a juvenile book market overpopulated with incredible fictional young teens gossiping with all the world-weary cynicism and end-point insights of their middle-aged au-

Reprinted from *School Library Journal*, May 1974, p. 7, with permission of R. R. Bowker Company/A Xerox Corporation.

thors. Plagues used to be called down upon authors of children's books who failed to supply a last chapter settling each and every character's hash (long after this technique ceased to be a critical factor in adult fiction). This has at last given way to a supine acceptance of participatory endings for even those juvenile novels which don't deserve five minutes of anybody's thinking time after the last pages have been turned.

All this is not Mainstream. It's the Last Bastion falling and then failing to notice.

The very latest literary time lag battle in children's books was joined in *SLJ*'s Book Review last December and has been ramping along in our Letters columns ever since. It concerns the use of blasphemy and obscenity in the dialogue of novels written for preteens. Any children's book specialist reading adult fiction in the 1950s might have predicted this conflict at this level for the 1970s. Such usage crept from our poets, to the stage, to our novels, to film in a trip that took nearly thirty years. Radio, TV, and newspapers—always more cautious—have nevertheless caught up.

Reading a great many books for children does not prepare anybody for changes or extensions of the storytelling modes that make their gradual way from adult books into novels for children. Reading too few adult books disqualifies children's book specialists from responsible criticism of any reading level. The necessarily condensed traceries above about where arguments on books for children begin, and the way they peter out, lend support to the always embarrassing suspicion that children's book specialists become immersed so far below the adult reading level that when their debates finally surface about matters literary they are all wet.

In the love/hate relationship that has developed from the overdependence of juvenile publishers on their single ready marketplace, the children's book editors and promotion personnel tend to stand aside and rejoice when librarians to children and young people publicly fall out over matters that are central to the selection of sub-adult library collections. Odd, that. In this instance, as in the others cited, they've been as slow as their library buyers in casting off, or freeing their authors from, Last Bastion dogma and have no more claim to creative credit than a caboose can get for bringing in a train.

This latest debate is the argument worth starting because it brings into clear focus for possible resolution the most divisive element in selecting books for children—the nonliterary considerations that often override the literary and block the entrance to the Mainstream.

/ Damming the Mainstream
/ Ethel Heins

When I was invited to be a speaker at a spring conference on "Children's Literature in the Literary Mainstream" sponsored by the Western Michigan University School of Librarianship, I thought—as I often have —about the well-worn metaphor *mainstream*. To link children's literature firmly with general literature was the intention of early critics like Anne Carroll Moore and Bertha Mahony Miller who were building a solid foundation of apologetics. In 1953, Lillian Smith put it squarely: "Children's books do not exist in a vacuum, unrelated to literature as a whole. They are a portion of universal literature and must be subjected to the same standards of criticism as any other form of literature."

In the *School Library Journal* of May 1974, Lillian Gerhardt disavowed the mainstream notion, sharply disagreeing with those "who have employed or applauded that self-congratulatory tag line." She continued, "From where we sit, books for children are more accurately described as: the last bastion of yesterday's literary methods and standards. The Mainstreamers would be hard pressed to name one, let alone two, children's books that ever turned around writing for adults." But is art in the mainstream only when it is cast in experimental or innovative modes? Is Verdi to be ignominiously dismissed as "last bastion" because he wrote in a traditional form long after Wagner had pushed back the frontiers of operatic convention? Moreover, many people have been preoccupied with the weakness of the adult novel in this century. Jill Paton Walsh once said that the mainstream novel has turned its back on story, and Isaac Bashevis Singer wrote, "I came to the child because I see in him a last refuge from a literature gone berserk and ready for suicide."

Last bastion or last refuge? Pigeonholing and labeling can be unfortunate—tidy, but artificial and constricting. Can we categorize, for example, someone like Virginia Hamilton—unique and daring among children's writers, black or white? Will her books prove to have "turned around writing for adults"? One way or the other, are they not in the literary mainstream?

Reprinted with permission from *The Horn Book Magazine*, August 1975, p. 335. © 1975 by the Horn Book, Inc.

/ A Letter to Ethel Heins
/ Lillian N. Gerhardt

ETHEL L. HEINS, EDITOR
The Horn Book Magazine

Dear Ethel:

The August, 1975 issue of *The Horn Book Magazine* just arrived. I read your editorial right away because I think it's the least the editor of one publication can do for another. I was pleased to see that you read my editorials, too. You quoted just enough of my editorial in *SLJ*'s May, 1974 issue to help convince your readers that I am right and that you're all wet. At any rate, when I read my quoted words I found myself just as convinced as when I wrote them that it is not only erroneous and self-congratulatory for people in children's book circles to run around claiming to each other that children's literature is in the mainstream, I think it's the sort of hogwash that induces self-defeating complacency at a time when people who care about good writing for children ought to be alarmed about the low esteem in which children's books are held in literary circles.

Now, I don't really trust myself to carry on a dignified editorial exchange with you about this. Whenever I argue, I try to be calm, logical and cool when basically what I'd rather do is pick up a chair and hit whomever I'm trying to convince over the head. The last time I employed this technique in a debate, I got sent home from kindergarten with a very stiff note. Although I never did it again, I'm always afraid I might revert.

So, logically and I hope calmly, I beg to point out that while you are trying to coax *Horn Book*'s readers that children's literature is in the literary mainstream of this country, you provide no evidence that this is so while surrounded with much evidence to the contrary. Really, Ethel, I think you should lock yourself

Reprinted from *School Library Journal*, Sept. 1975, p. 7, with permission of R. R. Bowker Company/A Xerox Corporation.

in your office, read over *The Emperor's New Clothes,* and take it to heart.

For instance, even as I write, it is still doubtful that the new sponsors of the National Book Awards will agree to restore the award in the category of children's books. The mere fact that this award has been eliminated ought to call a halt to your idea that children's literature is anywhere near mainstream status in the world of letters.

And then, please consider the implications of the actions of the newly established National Book Critics Circle. At its first general membership meeting last spring, its board of directors announced that the National Book Critics Circle would select the best essays on literary criticism each year and publish them in an anthology. The prospect this presents for in-group log-rolling and backscratching is limitless of course, but as distasteful as that may be, such an anthology can be expected to have wide influence on the types of criticism published. Now, grab for one of your horns, Ethel—essays on the criticism of children's books were specifically excluded! No apologies and no explanations in answer to the protests of those members concerned with children's literature. Children's book criticism is, for the present, outside the pale. Now, if that doesn't leave you high and dry out of the splash of the mainstream, what other evidence do you need?

I say it's time to stop invoking Anne Carroll Moore and Bertha Mahony Miller and declaring their intention to link children's literature with general literature. Nobody can doubt that the intention was and is admirable, but nobody should be led to believe that it actually happened. Making it happen now is what needs to concern us, not lulling our readers into a nonexistent security. Children's books are in trouble and are more generally recognized outside of library service as convenient vehicles for propaganda and proselytizing by every dingbat group in the country with a message to sell. Every special interest group is following the lead of the Feminists on Children's Media who provided a pattern for the analysis of children's books to make a point. Unfortunately, the others have not stopped with critical analysis, but have gone on to the creation of pressure groups insisting that publishers publish and librarians buy books that promote a given view or image. That isn't literary mainstream stuff—that's right back where it all began with the tracterians of the nineteenth century.

Finally, I thoroughly reject the notion in your editorial that children's book people can comfortably ignore without loss to themselves and to good writing for children what is going on in writing for adults. That's the sort of thing that keeps children's books and children's book people in a literary backwater far from any mainstream.

On second thought, I may fly up to Boston and hit you over the head with a chair after all.

Cordially,
Lillian N. Gerhardt

/ A Letter to Lillian N. Gerhardt
/ Ethel L. Heins

I have read your lengthy editorial letter to me (*SLJ*, September) and find it difficult to believe that my own brief August 1975 *Horn Book* editorial has elicited such a loud and illogical response. It's not that I object to the explosiveness of your remarks—I hold many passionate convictions myself and appreciate them in others. But you seem to be talking about a totally different subject, or, rather, the same subject from a totally different point of view.

To begin with, you have apparently switched horses in mainstream. In your original statement (*SLJ*, May 1974), you complained that children's books are not in the literary mainstream because of their outmoded styles, devices, or novelistic construction. "From where we sit, books for children are more accurately described as the last bastion of yesterday's literary methods and standards." But in your recent editorial, you argue that books for children are excluded from mainstream literature because of the myopic views of the sponsors of the National Book Awards and the new National Book Critics Circle—and also because

Reprinted from *School Library Journal*, Nov. 1975, pp. 4–5, with permission of R. R. Bowker Company/A Xerox Corporation.

of the stupidity and the strident insistence of pressure groups. I must point out that I never suggested that ignorance, commercialism, or didacticism are dead; all three, in fact, continue to plague adult books as well as children's. Moreover, it is difficult for me to see how the book world can be expected to take children's literature seriously when one of its professional critics uses such uncritical supports as hurling epithets or threatening to throw chairs.

The problem is not one of providing "evidence" that children's books are within the literary mainstream but of deciding on the meaning of *mainstream,* which has nothing to do with popular acclaim or even acknowledgement. Although it is unfashionable to bring the past to bear on the present, hindsight can be revealing. If public acceptance were the criterion, then doubtless Helen Hunt Jackson—and not Emily Dickinson —was a mainstream writer of her time. And surely Melville—who was neglected during his lifetime and whose *Billy Budd* was not even published for more than a quarter of a century after his death—was not contemporaneously viewed as a mainstream novelist. Children's books are part of the literary mainstream when they are produced with as much intellectual honesty as good adult books and judged by the same qualitative standards. This statement is neither "hogwash" nor "self-defeating complacency"; it is simply a definition of a term.

Actually, I am heartily tired of the imprecise, much-misused catchword *mainstream.* I discussed it in my editorial—as I indicated—because I had recently been asked to speak on the subject. Moreover, if you would read over what I said, you would see, I think, that I was not "invoking Anne Carroll Moore and Bertha Mahony Miller" but was merely ruminating on the historical development in children's book criticism of what I called the "well-worn metaphor." But if the term has any meaning at all, I am certain that the serious writers and artists who produce important children's books have a right to consider their own work within the mainstream of creativity. The burden of proving this fact to the rest of the book world rests, of course, upon people like you and me; and if we have failed so far, it is even more urgent that we keep on trying.

If you read over my editorial, you will discover also that your last statement about it is appallingly untrue. I realize that it is your suspicion and one of your favorite themes that many children's book specialists are incapable of or uninterested in reading adult books; but you should make specific charges more carefully. Nowhere in my exploration of the subject did I say or in any way imply "the notion . . . that children's book people can comfortably ignore without loss to themselves and to good writing for children what is going on in writing for adults." I find the idea and the accusation equally shocking. On the other hand, it is perfectly legitimate, in a rational discussion, to point out that many critics hold that the modern novel often wanders into eccentricity; only recently, C. P. Snow observed gloomily that "this century has produced no Tolstoy, Dostoevsky, Proust, or Balzac . . . no Dickens, Trollope, Hardy." Such book discussions can be interesting and fruitful; but no *Horn Book* editor—or reviewer—has ever made the preposterous suggestion that the world of adult literature should be ignored.

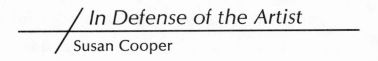

In Defense of the Artist
Susan Cooper

I must make it clear to you from the beginning that I really don't belong here. Not just because of the accent—though, mind you, as I frequently point out to American friends, *I* don't have an accent. *You* do.

I don't belong because I don't really write children's books. More accurately, I don't write books for children. Like so many authors, I simply write the book that bangs at my head asking to be written, and then my publishers tell me what it is.

Quite often they surprise me. In 1962 I wrote a straight adult novel set ahead in 1980, and to my astonishment it was published as science fiction. Later on I wrote a straight adult novel set back in World War Two, based on my own experiences at the age of eight, and to my further astonishment this was published as a children's book. What do authors know?

But I've never thought about my audience when I've been writing a book. Perhaps I had to think about them too much when I was writing stories as a journalist. My books are a reaction, a retreat—I write them for me.

And very early on, I learned that it was also unwise to listen to what the audience said. Long ago, when I first came to this country, I wrote

Reprinted from *Proceedings of the Fifth Annual Conference of the Children's Literature Association: Harvard University, March 1978* (Villanova, Pa.: Villanova University for the Association, 1979), pp. 20–28, with permission of the Children's Literature Association and the author. Copyright Susan Cooper, 1978.

a rather brash study of the United States of America entitled *Behind the Golden Curtain*. It was fairly widely reviewed—I even had my picture in *Time* magazine, which won't happen again—and, of course, being young, I gobbled up every word. It was obvious why the bad reviews were depressing, but I couldn't understand why the good ones were depressing as well. It was only later that I read something the playwright Sydney Howard once wrote to a younger colleague:

> After a while you'll learn about notices. The bad ones attack you for saying something you didn't say, and the good ones praise you for doing something you never intended to do. It comes out even in the end.

He was right. So after the America book, I retreated into a vacuum. Suitably, I work in an attic. There I sat with my typewriter for years and years, writing what my publisher now told me were children's books. I sat there refusing to look at any reviews, reading hardly anything but by own background research, and ignorant of all journals except the *Horn Book*. (That was a great comfort, since it reassured me that the writing of books published for children didn't necessarily mean that one was either a little old lady in tennis shoes or retarded.) It was a lonely but uncomplicated life. But then something unexpected happened. One of the books I had written won the Newbery Medal.

Now there is a certain fate that overcomes a prizewinning author, in this land of labels. After being obscure for years, he (or she) suddenly finds himself being asked to make speeches, and to give lectures and papers and seminars, all over the place. Suddenly he is desirable—or as they say in the theatre, "hot."

But although hot, I was terrified of audiences. So I refused to do any of these things, until my publishers began to get nervous. They knew that I would shortly have to stand up in front of 2,000 librarians and accept the Newbery Award, and they were afraid I'd make a fool of myself. So they persuaded me to make a couple of speeches, for practice, and as a result I had to come out of my attic and start finding out about children's literature.

So like everyone else conditioned by a degree in English, I began to read not just children's books, but books about children's books. Criticism. And I was appalled. It almost sent me running back to the attic right then and there.

Counterbalancing every book or paper that seemed to me wise and sensitive, like Lillian H. Smith's marvelous book *The Unreluctant Years*, there were a dozen that seemed irrelevant, picayune, pompous or just plain unnecessary. There was something peculiarly alien about them, as if they belonged to a different world from the one in which I worked.

The first that really made my hair stand on end, I remember, was a paper called "The Problem of C. S. Lewis," by the English critic David Holbrook. I couldn't think what that meant at first. I'd never thought there was any problem about C. S. Lewis. He was, for me, a brilliant English scholar who'd written some good fantasies for adults and some, shall we say, less good ones for children. Mr. Holbrook, however, had been digging deeper than that to find his problem. (And you must bear with me if I now quote something that half of you already know very well. Try to imagine yourselves inside my virgin head at the time I read it and feel the impact on an innocent author.)

I believe that C. S. Lewis's Narnia books have their origins in the fact of his life that his mother died when he was a baby. I believe that this left a psychic hunger—to be nurtured by the mother he had lost. It left him . . . needing to find his way into the other world where the mother was, the world of death. . . .

When he reached specifics of plot, Mr. Holbrook became more concerned, even shrill. He was particularly troubled by a passage in *The Voyage of the Dawn Treader* in which Eustace, a boy turned into a dragon, becomes a boy again as his dragon-skin is peeled off.

Once one recognizes its sexual-sadistic overtones, it becomes desperate and revolting. Lewis evidently relies heavily on the latency period, and on children's unconsciousness of the symbolism. At the same time, words like "bananas," "knobbly," "snaky sorts of things" press the imagery towards a clearly phallic form. . . . When Lewis spoke of adopting a children's story form "for something you have to say," there seems no doubt that one of his motives was to export his guilt into children, the guilt being that about bodily hunger, and I think, at a deeper level, masturbation. . . .

Well, this sort of thing must seem routine to many of you, but when I first read that paper, I thought it was a put-on. When I found that it was *serious,* I sat there, fresh out of my sheltered attic, and wondered what on earth had been happening to literary criticism since I left university. The paper seemed to me to tell one a great deal more about David Holbrook than about Clive Staples Lewis. I used to go to Lewis's lectures when I was an undergraduate; he was an amiable, chunky, pipe-smoking don with a splendid delivery. His reaction to this kind of analysis would have been a great roar of laughter, and he would have loved the tongue-in-cheek commentary on it which Betty Levin later wrote. I laughed too, but uneasily.

I became even more uneasy when I came across other examples of this earnest psycho-analytical approach. In volume five of your own journal, *Children's Literature,* there was, for example, an analysis of L. Frank Baum which struck a chill in my heart very early on by observing that both Carroll's *Alice* and the *Wonderful Wizard of Oz* are "packed as full as puddings of unconscious distortions and symbolizations." And off it set in that direction, describing Dorothy's three companions in Oz as "a strawstuffed scarecrow, a woodchopper who, having chopped himself to bits, is now completely artificial, and a lion afraid of his own roar (three different ways of writing Eunuch)."

Frank Baum is by autobiographical definition Dorothy, an innocent child, who through no fault of her own (but very luckily, nevertheless) kills her mother as she is born. . . . There is a great deal of fine characterization in the Woodman, who of course is Baum again at a more advanced stage. . . . The Lion is Baum again in man's conventional sexual role. . . .

It's the *confidence* of people who write like this that dazzles me. The way they say, *"of course."*
The paper went on:

Oz revenges as many old injuries as it invents fantastic fulfillments: the chief resentment apparently, next to having been brought into the world in the wrong form, is for having been brought into the world at all. . . . Baum's fondness for automata and magically constructed beings can be safely attributed to this same rejection or exclusion of natural begetting.

Safely attributed! Safely indeed—poor Frank Baum isn't around to offer any argument. When he was, all he thought he was writing was "a modernized fairy tale, in which the wonderment and joy are retained and the heart-aches and nightmares are left out." It was a terrible idea, but that's what he aimed at. And here's a critic announcing with absolute assurance that instead "his arena was the transvestite one of boy-turned-girl."

I couldn't believe it. What was this kind of pseudo-scientific parlour game doing in a periodical entitled *Children's Literature? This* was literary criticism?

Reading this sort of thing wasn't good for my blood pressure. I made my speeches and retreated again to the typewriter in the lonely attic. But there was no escape. By now the letters from graduate students and teachers had begun coming in. I've always enjoyed letters from children —if they're genuine and not part of some school project—but I didn't enjoy some of this new kind at all. Many of them, of course, were stimulating, but others (and I'm sure they didn't come from anybody here) were frankly a bit much.

They came generally from people writing theses on fantasy or on the *Dark Is Rising* books. They were full of questions I'd never thought about and false assumptions that I didn't want to think about. They would ask me in great detail for, say, the specific local and mythical derivations of my Greenwitch, a leaf-figure thrown over a Cornish cliff as a fertility sacrifice, and I would have to write back and say, "I'm terribly sorry; I made it all up." They told me I echoed Hassidic myth, which I hadn't read, and the Mormon suprastructure, which I'd never even heard of. They saw symbols and buried meanings and allegories everywhere. I'd thought I was making a clear soup, but for them it was a thick mysterious stew.

I wrote back generally, as indeed I still do, reminding them of the critic who informed C. S. Lewis that Tolkien's *Lord of the Rings* was all an allegory about the dreadful implications of the atomic bomb. Lewis had written in reply:

Tolkien's book is not allegory—a form he dislikes. . . . There could not have been an allegory about the atomic bomb when Tolkien began his romance, for he did so before it was invented. We should probably find that many particular allegories critics read into Langland and Spenser are impossible for just that sort of reason, if we knew all the facts. *I am also convinced*—now every scholar should have this written up on his wall—"*That the wit of man cannot devise a story in which the wit of some other man cannot find an allegory.*" [Cooper's italics]

I answered all my scholarly correspondents, because, I suppose, I was brainwashed when young to believe that nice, polite little girls should speak when they're spoken to. But I was growing more and more uncomfortable at being made to think about things that seemed irrelevant to my life and work as a writer. One has only so much mental energy, only so much time. I found myself believing even more strongly in the need for a creative writer—or for me, at any rate—to ignore criticism and critics. I believed, and believe, that the imagination of a reasonably self-confident artist should remain isolated, disinterested. That it should go back to the attic, and shut the door.

If I had done that, I shouldn't of course be standing here. Or if I were here, I should be making a mild-mannered speech about the nature of fantasy, or something, instead of sticking my neck out in this discourteous way. However, I didn't, because then something else happened. This was the controversy in the columns of the *Horn Book* which led me to read a book called *Children's Literature: An Issues Approach,* by Masha Krakow Rudman. That book, I'm afraid, filled me with even more despondency than the paper about C. S. Lewis's private sexual guilt. It also gave me a terrible sense of danger. And a sense of danger produces alarm—it makes me want to shout. So here I am, politely—I hope—shouting.

I think something quite dreadful has been happening to criticism in the arts, particularly in America, during the last twenty years. In an age which is so much dominated by technological advance, the methods and even the jargon of science and engineering have mistakenly been adopted not only by fringe disciplines like psychology and social studies but by many arts scholars who should have known better.

There was a time when, for instance, one thing you could reliably expect from the average scholar of English literature was a graceful use of the English language, born naturally out of his feeling for the great writers whose work is, after all, his subject. Today, the academic in any discipline who can write gracefully is rarer than rubies. Most of the papers published in *Daedalus,* the journal of the American Academy of Arts and Sciences, are written in a style which has been described as "algebra touched with *Time* and the *New English Bible.*" And the one thing you *can* expect from the English literature scholar is that any paper he writes will be full of quantitative judgments, often decorated with graphs and lists and arrows and diagrams, as if he were reporting on the result of an experiment or offering a formula.

In the field of education this tendency is even more marked, and you can also be sure that the paper will be full of words like "criteria," "value," "attitudes," "behavior," "issues," "competency," "tools," and "genres."

"Tool" seems to me a particularly doom-laden word. No country is going to breed great critics if it educates its children to regard a work of literature not as a wonderful mystery but as an implement, a thing, like an aspirin or a chainsaw.

Books like *An Issues Approach* are a natural, inevitable outgrowth of this trend. That one—written, I do realize, in all good faith and with the best of intentions—sounds the artist's death knell even in its introduction. I quote:

In keeping with the contemporary aims of education, directions in publishing for children, and societal needs, this author recommends an additional approach to the study of children's literature. A critical examination of the books in the light of how they treat contemporary social problems and conditions is as essential as are the historical and literary perspectives. Books are important influences on their readers' minds. . . . They can either help or hinder us when we attempt to construct suitable bases for attitudes or behaviors. A critical, or issues, approach should, therefore, be included in the repertoire of courses and texts available to adult learners.

Now if you can listen to that with equanimity, then you and I belong to different species. My reaction, like Ethel Heins's in the *Horn Book,* is one of distress and alarm. The assumptions made there give me an image of a growing mass of criticism which is drifting further and further away from the literature itself. It implies that literary quality is no longer *the only true measure* for judgement of a book. And there are bonfires at the end of that road.

The writer speaks often of books being "effective." "Books are most effective when they have literary merit as well as didactic intent. The best lessons are taught unobtrusively." Lessons! Didactic! Effective! What has this to do with literature? It might as well be addressed to Victorian theological students or the manufacturers of cough medicine.

The issues approach seems to entail dividing novels published for children into assorted groups with headings like Sex, War, Death and Old Age, The Female, The Black. It discusses each issue, analyzes each book, and offers "criteria" which reiterate what a book in each category *should* do.

The emphasis is always on "using" a book. John Donovan's *I'll Get There: It Better Be Worth the Trip* is, for instance, described disapprovingly as being "such a compilation of problems and afflictions that many adults have difficulty using it with young readers." There is small encouragement there for anyone hoping to teach, or "use," "The Book of Job" or *King Lear.*

There is much talk too of "power." Authors are powerful, books are powerful—so much so that perhaps, it is suggested, "labels should be printed for placing on the covers of books stating 'Caution: this book may be damaging to your mind.' " We frequently admonish ourselves and our students not to believe all that we read, but we willingly suspend disbelief when a writer is powerful, particularly when we are confronted not with facts but with fantasy. Then the messages seep into our systems without our having weighed or recognised the information.

Off we go again. Always messages, or information, or being effective, or having power. It's not that all authors are assumed to be overt megalomaniacs. The books that are analyzed in this sort of criticism are not only books that do try to teach lessons but books that are interpreted by critics as teaching lessons, whether or not the author intended to do so. Sometimes they are even taken to task for not teaching lessons, as is Paula Fox's novel *The Slave Dancer* for not including a discussion of the morality of slavery. You can't win.

The standards of this kind of approach—and bear in mind that I am concerned more with the whole trend than with this particular book—

are not aesthetic; they are moral. They would force thought on the author in an area where thought is destructive of imagination. They show a total lack of understanding of the creative process by which good novels are made. As John Rowe Townsend said in *A Sense of Story:*

It is legitimate to consider the social or moral or psychological or educational impact of a book; to consider how many children and what kind of children will like it. *But it is dangerous to do this and call it criticism.* . . . [Cooper's italics]

Literature, like all art, comes out of the subconscious. It will not be bullied. It will not be made to perform some function. And we who try to produce it are really a very uncomplicated bunch. We're like Ingmar Bergman, who once said:

I just want to get in touch with other human beings. Because of that, I make my pictures, I stage my plays. I want to communicate. Sometimes I talk about my wounds, my tensions, my problems—people might recognise something of their own in that. Sometimes it's joy. I have loved *The Magic Flute* since I was eleven years old. When I staged it, I felt wonderful. I wanted to take people by the hands and say, "Look, isn't this beautiful, this is what exists on earth, this treasure." If that helps people, it's okay. If it doesn't help, I can't blame myself. I'm an artist, not a moralist.

"I'm an artist, not a moralist." Now I could perfectly well go back to my life as an ostrich. Back to the attic, close the door, ignore the criticism. All kinds of commentary like those I have been describing are dangerous and even destructive to any artist who lets them influence his future work. But after all they aren't written for us, and nobody's forcing us to read them. Why not just go back to the desk or the easel and work as if they weren't there?

I think that's no longer enough. It seems to me that this shift in criticism, away from the basic works and towards subsidiary concerns, is not only dangerous to writers, if they're exposed to it, but it's also a threat to their readers—in children's literature, anyway, for the critics are very often involved either in teaching children or in teaching those who will teach children. And what is children's literature but a straight relationship between children and writers? Its image is the child curled up in a chair with a book. I may never think of children while I am writing, but once that story is on the page, it is a communicating link between my imagination and that of the reading child. A kind of chemical bond, like that mingling of love and friendship called *amicitia*. As Isaac Bashevis Singer once said:

I have convinced myself that when it comes to stories, little explanation is necessary. As a matter of fact, the less the better. There is a saying in Yiddish: if a story is told to you and you like it, listen to it. And if you don't like it, there is no sense in asking questions.

Of course we writers have power, if we're any good at all. But it's simply the power of spellbinding—after all, as Professor Tolkien pointed out, the old Anglo-Saxon word *spell* means both a story told and a formula of power over living men. If you attribute to us instead some more sinister kind of power over a child's attitudes and future beliefs, as both the Freudian and issues-approach kinds of criticism do, then you are doing that child a terrible disservice.

Don't meddle with the reading child's imagination. Don't restrict it or try to control its direction. It is as precious as that of the writer. More precious, because it is a new young growth and may die back if tied up or pruned. Paradoxically, you are more likely to harm it if you try to protect it.

Leave it free. It has its own built-in shield, the selectivity of skipping and forgetting. It even needs a certain amount of junk, the way chickens need grit. Six books of a kind condemned by an issues-approach critic will do the child far less harm than six minutes of television commercials—but neither is going to wreck his mind.

C. S. Lewis wrote:

The peculiarity of child readers is that they are not peculiar. It is we who are peculiar. Fashions in literary taste come and go among the adults, and every period has its own shibboleths. These, when good, do not improve the taste of children, and when bad, do not corrupt it; *for children read only to enjoy.* . . . Juvenile taste is simply human taste, going on from age to age, silly with a universal silliness or wise with a universal wisdom, regardless of modes, movements and literary revolutions.

Interfere as little as possible between the child and the book. Give the artist his chance. Let us not confuse bibliotherapy, that monstrous word, with literary criticism or with teaching the way to appreciate works of the imagination.

Teaching of course there must be. Letting the music of say, Mozart's *Jupiter Symphony* wash over you like a warm bath is a very primitive kind of listening. Your ears and imagination will find a deeper pleasure if you have been taught something about the symphony form, a little about Mozart, and can tell the difference between the oboe and the flute, the cello and the violin. Then you can not only listen—you will hear. But you must not be pushed into such an analytical state that you cease to hear the tunes.

When I was at university, long ago, I had a tutor who was a notable scholar but who gave my imagination claustrophobia. It wasn't her fault —she was concerned with training my critical faculties. For her, I dutifully peppered my essays with quotations from critics—a habit which dies hard, as you may have noticed in this speech. I even felt guilty when I expressed any opinion that wasn't backed by the opinion of somebody else. And of course it had to be the right somebody else.

I remember when I was studying Shakespeare, I got into great disfavour by quoting the works of Harley Granville-Barker. Granville-Barker was a brilliant producer-dramatist who wrote a series of Prefaces to the major plays, which have been a Bible for actors and directors ever since. But my tutor didn't approve of him at all. She felt I should have been quoting Johnson or Charlton or Bradley instead. Mr. Granville-Barker was not a scholar, not a critic from Oxford or Cambridge, or even one of the lesser universities. He worked in the *theatre*. That made him *unsound*. I never had the courage to point out that, in that case, Shakespeare was unsound too. He wasn't a scholar either; he was a working actor-dramatist earning his living in the theatre. My tutor had been enmeshed in her own academic world for so long that she had forgotten that Shakespeare didn't write Works of Literature—he wrote plays.

In the same way, those of us who write books published for children are not producing teaching aids or tools for bibliotherapy. We're telling stories. Don't forget that. Children's literature is a newly independent field of study in colleges and universities—don't let it lose sight, early on, of what it is supposed to be about. Don't, I beg you, let it get bogged down in the search for ever more recondite subjects for theses and publications; in a desperate striving after "relevance"; in a self-important categorizing of things that authors *should* write and children *should* read. Keep your perspective; keep your sense of humour. Don't forget the simple fact that if you are studying literature of any kind, then, just as if you were studying music or painting or sculpture, you are dealing with works of art. And it is your responsibility to treat the people who produce those works as artists, not as social reformers, or moralists, or teachers *manqués*.

Don't forget, for all our sakes, the story of the shoemaker and the elves. The shoemaker, you remember, did one of the little people a service one day, without knowing it, and every morning afterward he came downstairs to find that the shoes he had left unfinished the night before had been magically completed and new leather left for the next day. He and his wife enjoyed these mysterious delights for a long time, until finally curiosity got the better of them; they crept down one night, and lo, they saw several cheerful naked little elves at work.

Next day the wife made several little suits of clothes, and the shoemaker several little pairs of shoes, and they left them out at night when they went to bed. The motive was good, but the result was disastrous. The elves finished that night's work—and they never, ever, came back again. They would stay only so long as they weren't seen. Because the shoemaker hadn't been able to let well enough alone, the magic he had enjoyed was gone.

Be careful how you treat the magic of books. You have all been given a sense of it, or you wouldn't be here at this conference. But if you peer at it too hard, if you try to clothe it in suits for which nature did not intend it—or worse, try to make *us* do that—it too will vanish away. The imagination doesn't need shoes. It goes barefoot.

I work mostly in the theatre now. Adults, there, do not write theses about my use of symbolism, and children don't sit in class being made to check the derivations of my Arthurian backgrounds or write an alternative ending to Chapter Fifteen. Instead they sit in the dark theatre watching the bright stage, listening, seeing, laughing, crying, or saying, "Oooh." These days, I listen to what my audience says—and it's easy to hear. They tell me when I have bored or angered them, and they tell me if I have been lucky enough to bring them a taste of delight.

Remember, all through this conference, and remember when next you read or write about a book, that *that* kind of direct response is all the artist has ever asked.

/ *Susan Cooper, a Reply*
/ Lois R. Kuznets

For over a week, I refrained from writing about my reactions to Susan Cooper's keynote address at the Children's Literature Association Annual Conference, feeling that her speech and my reaction to it demanded some recollection in tranquility. Teaching classes and grading papers are not the most tranquil (or tranquilizing) activities, but now I feel that I can approach Cooper's speech in a reasonably contemplative mood. What she said—as well as how she said it—deserves serious contemplation and active response.

My recollections may be faulty. After some time, and with neither written notes nor a text in front of me, the following is what I remember and what I am contemplating: Cooper began with references to her own shyness in speaking and with a small joke about her British accent, to the effect that, of course, she really thought *we* were the ones with the accent. Then she presented us with an emblematic picture of herself as the writer alone in her attic, hunched over her typewriter day after day. She told us that the Newbery Award forced her to emerge from this obscurity (into which she had previously retreated after experiencing the reactions to her writing about her experience of America in *Behind the Golden Curtain).* She had now come into the limelight once more, forced to leave her attic to make speeches such as this; meanwhile, the world itself—mainly in the form of letters—attempted to invade her attic. The nature of these letters, particularly those from graduate students—in addition to some reading in scholarly journals she felt obligated to do—made her long to retreat to the attic permanently; however, she had instead chosen the harder road, to make a direct response to the attitudes epitomized in those letters and articles, attitudes that she considered mistaken and even dangerous.

Exempla of dangerous trends in criticism followed this introduction: quotations from two articles with Freudian, or at least psychoanalytic, approaches to C. S. Lewis and L. Frank Baum, respectively, and then

A letter reprinted from the *Children's Literature Association Newsletter* 3:14–16 (Spring–Summer 1978) with permission of the Children's Literature Association and the author.

excerpts from Masha Rudman's book, *Children's Literature: An Issues Approach*. The exempla and the tone in which Cooper cited them elicited some laughter, but the charges she made against them are serious. Not only did Cooper emphasize the defenselessness of authors from such ruthless personal comment as Freudian literary analysts are wont to make, but she decried what she perceived as a basically mechanistic attitude in such commentary (which she seemed to find characteristically American) as well as the utilitarianism of the issues approach (or the bibliotherapeutic approach, which she lumped together with it). Somewhere along the line were her implications that this type of criticism is usually badly written and, moreover, that the issues approach in particular leads to "the bonfire": by which I presume she meant *autos da fé* directed at either books or people.

From these particular cases, Cooper seemed to move into a more general attack on literary criticism of any sort, intimating (1) that criticism mistakenly assumes that authors have a didactic message, (2) that academic criticism tends to reject all but the pedants, who choose to listen only to each other rather than to those who are actively engaged in "producing" literature (the anecdote about her own tutor's rejection of Granville-Barker's Shakespeare criticism), (3) that critics actually interfere with the reader's enjoyment of literature, inhibiting direct response, (4) that critics drive authors back into their garrets or cause them so much pain that they can no longer write, (5) that Susan Cooper herself (if I understood her correctly) has moved into children's theater so that she can experience the direct approach of children to art, untrammeled or unsullied by intermediaries.

She finally addressed the audience with a plea to refrain from harmful criticism.

Susan Cooper, as well as any literary critic, will readily discern that my description of her speech was riddled with rhetorical devices designed to persuade my reader that Cooper herself was using rhetorical devices to deliver a sermon to the assembled multitude. Similarly discerning readers will want to suggest that I am annoyed at being told in prophetic tones (prophets are always driven from seclusion—towers, mountains, and other high places—to relay unpleasant, apocalyptical messages) to go forth and sin no more, especially since I haven't been doing the particular type of sinning that Cooper points to most directly. Yet, somehow, just by virtue of being a critic, I seem to be a sinner. Somewhere along the line, I have joined the throng that goes to the left hand of God, in company with the Freudians, the issues people, the bibliotherapists, Cooper's tutor, the hapless graduate student who wrote to ask the tradition behind one element in Cooper's book, and who knows who else?

Presumably, however, Clive Staples Lewis and J. R. R. Tolkien have gone to the right hand, their criticism and teaching of literature redeemed by some virtue. Cooper did not tell us what good critics, scholars and teachers of literature to the young and not-so-young do.

The question of what criticism can be at its best is one that Cooper did not confront and yet seems to me most worthy of contemplation. Nevertheless, since I am lumped willy-nilly with the Freudians and others, I don't want merely to slip out from under Cooper's stern gaze by claiming that they "have nothing to do with me." I, myself, have had plenty of good laughs at psychoanalytic criticism and I can also emphathize with authors who have been put down on the couch against their will. However, as Cooper read the passage about phallic symbols in C. S. Lewis, I could not help remembering how Lewis had practically forced me into such a reading by exceedingly bad writing in the following passage from *The Lion, the Witch and the Wardrobe:*

"You have forgotten to clean your sword," said Aslan. It was true. Peter blushed when he looked at the bright blade and saw it all smeared with the Wolf's hair and blood. He stooped down and wiped it quite dry on his coat.

"Hand it to me and kneel, Son of Adam," said Aslan. And when Peter had done so he struck him with the flat of the blade and said, "Rise up, Sir Peter Fenrisbane. And whatever happens, never forget to wipe your sword." (Chap. xii)

What the devil does one do with such a passage except laugh at Lewis, not with him, and say it serves him right for saying before that the girls couldn't have swords and by giving didactic remarks to Father Christmas, like "battles are ugly when women fight"? (Chap. X)

Which brings me to the fact that I have occasionally been associated with the issues approach to literature (and if I were a librarian or an elementary school teacher who knows what closet bibliotherapy I might practice?). From my experience in this line, I might say that contrary to what Cooper suggested, the issues approach to literature is not necessarily imposed on readers from outside. Reactions to racism and sexism, for instance, are direct and gut reactions to literature in members of oppressed groups who have not been conditioned by the dominant groups to repress feelings of resentment. I have had to train myself as a literary critic *not* to respond directly to the anti-Semitism in much classic English literature. Since some of my conditioning by the dominant male culture has slipped during the last ten years, I have to keep myself from responding on a wildly gut level to imagery that ranges from Milton's snide description of Eve's "wanton ringlets" to far grosser suggestions, allusions and analogies like those in a film actually cited by Cooper,

Ingmar Bergman's *The Magic Flute.* I agree that it is a minor tragedy that one set of negative reactions to the antifeminist and casually racist structure of the film must war with the other set of positive gut reactions, an aesthetic response to the glorious music and the feast of vision—but there it is. I would not give up either set of reactions, nor would I be ashamed to tell anyone of my feminist outrage, which is both strong and valid.

Let me say, however, that I would not teach a course based on the issues approach and that much of my teaching involves keeping students from making snap judgments based on issues (as a matter of fact, I think Rudman had some of this corrective literary tack in mind too, but she can certainly defend herself). What I do first in my own reading as a critic and my reading with students is to try to show them that it is worthwhile to read books—even children's books—carefully and to be aware of what Wayne Booth calls "the rhetoric of fiction," the artistic strategies and tactics that every writer uses to persuade the reader to dwell, at least temporarily, in a world of the artist's making and to see in it what the artist chooses to see. I am concerned with all the elements in the book that contribute to an effect that while not necessarily didactic is certainly influential. Moreover, I think books are fascinating primarily because they are the product of *choices* that creative human beings make, choices that readers are persuaded to accept as natural and inevitable through the sheer power that the writer exerts.

That is why I want students always to be ready to ask why: Why 1850 rather than 1960? Why New York City rather than London? Why a young woman rather than an old man? Why a dead father? Why an older brother? Why a picture of Medusa on the wall? Why "shimmering" rather than "shining"? Why an airplane crash? Why the smell of bacon and eggs? Why? Why? Why? If the book seems to send them to the dictionary, or the almanac, or the encyclopedia, or Greek mythology, or their local disco, fine, but only if the outside work illuminates the text and backs other confirmation from the book itself that we're on the right track. I use the same questioning approach for my own readings and I get up out of the armchair in which I like to curl up and read in order to go where the book sends me.

I am obviously outlining above my own predilection for close reading of texts and for moving from the text out into the world, not for taking a preconceived view of the world to the reading. That is the first principle of my idea of good criticism. But this does not suggest that the reader, child or adult, is a *tabula rasa,* rather that the reader's own experience, training, interests and needs will influence the number and kind of questions that the reader will ask of the book. It postulates that he or she has a right to ask those questions, as long as he or she is honestly trying to discover the author's answers, not trying to impose his own view of the world as the author's response. I think that Cooper and I would agree that an author has a right to depict his created world as he or she wishes to do so, but where we differ is in the question of whether the reader has the right to ask questions and penetrating ones about how and by what methods and for what reasons that world is being depicted. And we probably differ even further in that as a teacher of literature I believe that teachers should teach readers to ask questions.

I think that authors are much more powerful and influential than critics and I want to know and to understand what's happening to me when I am reading a book and how it is happening to me. I want to contemplate the aesthetic experience and I do not think that contemplation is a passive experience, but one which involves all of the faculties of the reader, implied symbolically by gut, heart and head; such contemplation is never really a danger to the writer even though it may be an uncomfortable or inconvenient experience for her or him when he or she learns of it.

Historically, the greatest danger to authors and their books has come not from intellectuals or prying critics, but from people who preferred to react first and to ask questions later (or to manipulate others' immediate response to books). In our place and time, it is probably the publishers with their estimates of the market economy that have the real intermediary power between Cooper and the child curled up in the armchair with a book: certainly more than any of the academic critics sitting in Cooper's audience and more even than the librarians or teachers who try to bring child and book together—or, as she assumes, keep them apart. In the face of that power, I would not like to see Cooper retreating to her garret, nor do I think I should retire to my ivory tower.

Sermons are not dialogues, however, and I hope that she and I can abandon them henceforth. Two human beings talking, questioning, even arguing, and hence transcending such symbolically loaded and subtly divisive differences as those of their accents, are two more fighters against the darkness.

Criticism and Children's Literature
Peter Hunt

I am almost inclined to set it up as a canon that a children's story which is enjoyed only by children is a bad children's story.—C. S. Lewis, 1947.

One examines books which children will read with the aid of all the criteria applied to books read by adults, and with one additional consideration—accessibility.—Marcus Crouch, 1972.

Now that the younger branch of literature had come to maturity, might not the grown-up sometimes find as much wisdom and entertainment on the child's bookshelf as on his own?—Mary F. Thwaite, 1963.

[Children's literature] is no-where studied in this country at a high academic level as a branch of literature.—"Aunt Judy's Christmas Volume," 1875.

The cry for proper criticism of children's literature goes back a long way; but now that there is a fair amount of space allotted to it, something seems to have gone wrong. The more I read of the increasing output of writing on children's books, the more it seems that what I read is rarely literary criticism, and that what the writers are dealing with is rarely literature. In children's books, critics have the chance, perhaps the last, of approaching and evaluating a largely virgin area of literature; but unless we decide what the purpose of criticism is, and what our subject is, then we are doomed to producing more sound than sense. There are, of course, honourable exceptions, and there have been instances of admirable scholarship—but in some respects this is getting the cart before the horse.

It will be argued that the role of the reviewer, the educationalist, the sociologist, the historian, or the librarian, is different from that of the critic; and that children's literature has been fortunate in escaping the theoretical harlequinade of "adult" criticism. This is true enough, but

Reprinted from *Signal: Approaches to Children's Books* no. 15:117–30 (Sept. 1974). Published by The Thimble Press, Lockwood, Station Road, South Woodchester, Stroud, Glos. GL5 5EQ England. Reprinted with permission of the author. Copyright © P. L. Hunt, 1974.

because the role of criticism has rarely been codified, writing on the subject is often either a blurred mixture of good intentions, or a mixture of specialist intentions, both of which contain elements of criticism but neither of which should be confused with it. If we can produce some basic theory, some sort of statement of fundamental definitions, principles, and standards, then all disciplines contributing to the subject should benefit.

Clearly, the study of children's books has suffered both in status and quality from the lack of serious critical discussion. Thus an academic approach, far from being ethereal, could have two practical results: firstly, to provide reference points in the corpus of children's books for other disciplines; secondly, to bring proper recognition to many books that have fallen into limbo. It is, perhaps, worth expanding on these two points before going further.

In order to set standards, the critic must depart from his proper role of intermediary and analyst and become, at least initially, a judge. In literature as a whole, such value judgements have been made, although they may now seem to be part of natural law; but with children's books we should begin at the beginning. Which books are "good"? Which books are "literature"? Which books may the others be judged by? The general, and usually unconsidered, assumption by the critical world is that there are few books for children which have genuine value—certainly far fewer than writers on children's books claim. This seems to me to be true, but closer critical examination suggests that the "good" books are not necessarily those which either faction would acknowledge. Thus we need to reassess our critical attitudes and apparatus, and if such a reassessment is contentious, so much the better.

The second aim, to bring books to wider notice which are good *by any standards,* but which are unread simply because they are children's books, depends on the seriousness of our critical approach. For example, it can be argued (although it very rarely is) that the best work of Kipling, or the only valuable work of Eleanor Farjeon, lies in their children's books. Gillian Avery's comment on *Rewards and Fairies* illustrates this: "The finest is the last story, 'The Tree of Justice,' incomprehensible to children, yet neglected by the adult enthusiast because it falls in what is assumed to be a children's book."[1]

I will return to Kipling, but his case raises another much debated point. Is children's literature a different species from other types of literature? Do we approach it in a different way? The attitude illustrated by the quotation from Marcus Crouch at the outset could be insidious if taken too far. In suggesting that we require additional critical weapons, there is often the implication that our subject is not just different, but *lesser,* and instead of examining where the difference lies by analysing texts, the emphasis often shifts to the intended audience.

This brings me to a central part of my argument. Whatever critical theory we produce for children's literature, it will have little or nothing to do with children. Thus we may say, Book X is literature (as opposed to reading matter), or Book Y is good literature (as opposed to not-so-good), regardless of whether children actually read it, or like it, or buy it. If this seems to make nonsense of the whole procedure, there are two answers. Most obviously, we are trying to distinguish and evaluate works of art on some sort of objective scale. That they are works of art produced for a particular audience is only significant if that audience, or the artist's conception of it, affects the nature of the work. To quote Marcus Crouch again: "I have sought the qualities which make the true novel . . . the whole presented in a style which is adapted to its purpose yet still expresses the personality of the writer."[2]

Thus the fact that Shakespeare, for example, wrote for a society, a social and educational ethos which no longer exists, only marginally affects the way in which we appreciate him. It may present problems of understanding, but the central literary value (however defined) survives. Children's books have always been peculiarly vulnerable to prescription, and while this can be seen as a strength from the point of view of historical interest, it is often taken as a literary weakness. It is as well to remember that the characteristics of work mediated by an audience do not automatically preclude the production of art.

Secondly, to ignore children is really only to regularize what is happening now. Reviewers (whether educationally or commercially orientated), educationalists, and teachers, are in an ambivalent position. Their standards and attitudes are implicitly (and not uncommonly explicitly) prescriptive; their judgement of a book is practical, and therefore involves compromise. Thus a book can only be "good" insofar as it is actually read, or actually sells. To judge a book on results, then, will involve a measure of transference of educational or commercial attitudes. The experience of a teacher of what is a useful book for particular children is of very limited value in approaching books in general. Similarly (and I say this in the knowledge that sociological method is akin to and has much the same limitations as critical method) it is irrelevant to consult children on the quality or value of their books, and positively dangerous to generalize from any findings. (Socio-educational studies, such as the Opies' *Lore and Language of Schoolchildren,* may throw oblique light on the success of an author in adapting his style to a given audience, or of interpreting his experience, but this is a different issue.) The scholar and the bibliophile, rather more extreme cases, are even less concerned with children: the less popular a book, the rarer and perhaps the more interesting it is likely to be.

None of this is, of course, intended to denigrate those who work with children's books. It is merely to say that the diversity of standards, which may be seen by a glance at almost any reviewing journal, is partly the result of immediate practical concern for children rather than literature. Equally, it is not to say that literary criticism is a higher or better activity than any other: it is simply a tool which is often neglected.

Now to some definitions. The task is The Criticism of Literature Written for Children, and it is simplest to begin with the second part of the term. If a book, in the intention of the author, was for children, then it is within our frame of reference.

There are thus three subcategories of books which we can include. Many of the "best" children's books, such as *Alice, The Wind in the Willows,* or *The Hobbit*, were initially composed for a specific child or children. The largest and most diverse group were written, for one reason or another, on Stevenson's "if this don't fetch the kids . . ." principle. In many ways, these are the most interesting to study, in that the books reflect the adult's general conception of the child, often through his own idea of his own childhood, rather than adapting his material to a specific response. Where we deal with "classic" authors who incidentially wrote for children—Dickens, Hardy, Thackeray, Wilde, and so on—this multiple undercurrent of self-revelation and perception can be revealing. A third group belongs with Arthur Ransome and C. S. Lewis, who avowedly wrote for themselves. It could be argued—but, again, rarely is—that this is a piece of sophistry on the part of these authors, and that the books are "obviously" for children. But this is to evade another central issue, the question of what exactly distinguishes a children's book. However, that question is perhaps best left until I deal with criticism itself. (On the simplest level, one might cite the decisions of publishers, but, as with the later William Mayne novels, this is an unreliable guide.)

It is courting the sort of disaster which frequently overtakes adult criticism to get bogged down in fine distinctions, but there are, of course, important marginal difficulties. *Martin Pippin in the Apple Orchard* is exactly the kind of neglected and underrated book which provoked this article, but by definition we should restrict ourselves to its sequel. While we should beware of suggesting (or ignoring the fact) that authors' opinions of their audience may be suspect, it is clear that, in this example, much would be gained from a comparison of the two books.[3]

One important purpose of the definition is to exclude many books adopted by children (or their advisers). Books frequently found on children's library shelves, such as *Jane Eyre,* or *The Moonstone,* are beyond our scope; Buchan and Hope, although mostly nowadays adolescent reading, can, like their modern counterparts, Maclean and Fleming, be put aside. So too can abridgements—especially, one might add, of *Gulliver's Travels.* It is possible to argue that abridgement can produce a new and different work of art, but the contention would be stronger if it were borne out by the actuality. However, it does raise some problems of discrimination, along with retellings such as Lambs' *Tales from Shakespeare,* and, less directly, reworkings of myths, legends, and fairy tales. This is more or less a problem peculiar to our subject. How much does the literary quality, atmosphere, and "feeling" of such books stem from the archetypes and patterns which they borrow, and for which the authors are not directly responsible? In as much as the writers are drawing from a common well, there is no valid reason for exclusion; imitation is another matter.

Next, and most knotty, Literature. Like Dr. Johnson and light, we know, severally, what it is, but it is difficult to *say* what it is. The loose usage of the word demands some sort of definition, although it is easier to say what it is not. It is not simply reading matter—educational, moral, or otherwise. It is not, for example, Enid Blyton. Attitudes to this writer are a good illustration of the critical/educational vagueness which should be cleared up—and she can be dealt with easily enough. I would as much consider including her in a study of children's literature as I would consider including, say, Mickey Spillane on a literature degree course. This is not to say that it is not enlightening, and salutary, to read both writers, but they are not literature.[4] Literature is, generally, implicitly (and perhaps not too helpfully) conceived by critics as a fusion of form and content, a crystallization of experience and meaning, and something that goes beyond these.

It may, therefore, be better to define literature in terms of the critical processes applied to it, bearing in mind that the first task is discrimination. There is, of course, formidable opposition to this approach, and one may take opinions almost at random. At one extreme there is D. H. Lawrence:

Literary criticism can be no more than a reasoned account of the feeling produced upon the critic by the book he is criticising. Criticism can never be a science; it is, in the first place, much too personal, and in the second, it is concerned with values which science ignores. The touchstone is emotion, not reason. We judge a work of art by its effect on our sincere and vital emotion, and nothing else. All the critical twiddle-twaddle about style and form, all this pseudo-scientific classifying and analysing of books in an imitation-botanical fashion, is mere impertinence and mostly dull jargon.[5]

Which seems to have put us in our place, although it has hardly dissuaded the myriad schools of criticism which take the opposite view. Erich Heller supports Lawrence to some extent, but points to a compromise:

For the ultimate concern [of the critic] is neither facts nor classifications, neither patterns of cause and effect nor technical complexities. . . . In the end . . . he is concerned with the communication of a sense of quality rather than measurable quantity, and of meaning rather than explanation.

Thus he would be ill-advised to concentrate exclusively on those aspects of his discipline which allow the calm neutrality of what is indisputably factual and 'objective.' His business is, I think, not the avoidance of subjectivity, but its purification; not the shunning of what is disputable, but the cleansing and deepening of the dispute.[6]

The obvious compromise is that of F. R. Leavis[7]—that analysis follows an immediate (and cultivated) response, although this has been attacked as "elitist" and "bourgeois intellectual,"[8] to judge from the reactions of critics, the formative role of children's literature further complicates matters.

We are, then, selecting critical tools with which to approach a fresh area of literature; on the one hand there is the Scylla of nonjudgment, on the other the Charybdis of pseudo-science. Equally, the mechanics of any art are so complex as to defy satisfactory analysis, and of such a kind, being the essence of expression themselves, as to make useless, or presumptuous, any other expression of them. In finding a compromise, we can draw a parallel with the social sciences, which share many methods and limitations with criticism.

Given the basic material—a person or a book—both disciplines operate in three phases. The first may be called the *factual*. In criticism, this is the sphere of the scholar: the establishment of the text, and the collection of contextual materials—biography, history, bibliography, and so on. Having established the "case history" the sociologist or critic moves to the *objective* phase; he applies to his materials a series of tests or theories, which by cumulative exclusion or confirmation takes him closer to the judgement or assessment aimed at. There are, of course, too many variables for truly scientific conclusions to be reached; there are dangers of predilection for one theory; no investigator or test can be absolutely objective. This process can, therefore, take us only so far, and we must apply the more disputable *subjectivity*. The problem here is not only the elitist one; literary criticism also suffers from the universality of its medium. Hence the careful application of the first two phases is essential, and for our purposes the greatest stress can be laid on the second—analysis by more or less objective tests.

Before considering these, it might be as well to look briefly at the dividing line between literature and nonliterature. Robert Liddell, in *A Treatise on the Novel,* following Q. D. Leavis, distinguishes novels which call for serious literary criticism, and those which are beneath it; in the higher category he further divides "good" novels and "those which might have been good but are not." Although one might disagree with his terminology, the classification of "nonliterary" books into "middlebrow" and "lowbrow" is worth noting. Of the middlebrow, he says that it

presents interest on account of its subject-matter, or its technical skill in managing some special device, or meeting some specific difficulty. Such reasons may make ephemeral work worth reading for some years after its publication; they do not confer on it the title of literature, which distinguishes only such reading matter as is of permanent value.[9]

It is into this category that much of the output of writers for children must fall.

In summary, then, I am suggesting a three-layer critical theory to decide, firstly, whether a book written for children is literature or not, and secondly, which parts of it are worthy of analysis and explication. We will apply several "tests," and if at least some of these produce positive results, then, objectively as may be, that book may be regarded as literature. As such, it can be taken as a standard with which to compare other (and especially, new) books, for whatever practical purpose—and with children's books, we have several. This structure of analysis is far from exclusive or exhaustive, and may seem to many to be simplistic, if not actually insulting. To these I apologise, but it seems to me that a straightforward statement of critical theory and its applicability to our subject is long overdue.[10]

Firstly, the *factual* stage. As writing for children has a comparatively short history, and literature for children an even shorter one (no one would, I hope, suggest that *A Little Pretty Pocket-Book* has anything but historical value), the establishment of a *text* is rarely a problem. Nevertheless the holographic study of, for example, Carroll can produce useful insights. The fact that little work on manuscripts has been thought necessary implies both the academic status of the subject, and the size of the first-class corpus.

With the *contextual* approach, Carroll is again a good example. Unless one is aware of the social and historical background, and the biography, character, and circumstances of the writer, then much can be lost. The terrible poignancy of Chapter VIII of *Through the Looking-*

Glass may be felt subjectively, or observed analytically through the change of pace and the intricate manipulation of sentence patterns, the selection of assonantal words, and so on. But it is contextual knowledge which enables us to understand the complex layers of symbolism and allusion; to realize the very deliberate referential structure of the nonsense.

The traditional *generic* approach may be used, as Frye observes, "not so much to classify as to clarify . . . traditions and affinities, thereby bringing out a large number of literary relationships that would not be noticed as long as there were no contexts established for them."[11] This approach, with the contextual, is particularly valuable in identifying both the particular characteristics of children's literature, and its remarkably precise reflection of the educational and social preoccupations of society. Both, however, involve further definitions, and more or less subjective filters, and it is worth bearing this in mind when considering the fourth initial approach, *moral* criticism. In the past, this has been taken to mean firstly the detection of a message within a book, and secondly (explicitly or not) a judgement of the book on the quality or character of that message. This is particularly relevant to children's literature, where the didactic element is strong, if cyclical; and it is important to point out that we should confine ourselves to the detection of aims if we are to provide material for objective assessment.

The first of the *objective* critical methods is *formal* or formalistic criticism. This, the "new criticism" of Brooks, Tate, Warren, and others, concentrates on the mechanics of a work of art: how does it work, what is its interior structure, balance and so on.[12] The emphasis is shifted to careful reading, and together with the *linguistic* and *stylistic* approaches leads us to some fascinating and revealing aspects of children's books. It is often supposed, for example, that language use is a primary (and debilitating) distinguisher between adults' and children's literature. But this is hardly true, even as a generalization.[13] Kipling, in *The Jungle Book,* consistently uses personal and present tense forms, but this is balanced and counterpointed by long, flowing, "elevated" sentence structures. In the Puck stories, the adult-to-child personal tone fades progressively and the vocabulary becomes more complex. Arthur Ransome's prose is very different, and has the appearance of spareness, simplicity, and functionalism, which matches his subject matter. But closer inspection shows that he is capable of very subtle verbal effects[14] and that his style balances larger units—paragraphs and chapters—to build up atmospheric contrasts. In a more modern novelist, William Mayne, we find verbal dexterity communicating both ambiguity and humour by such devices as the ambivalent impersonal pronoun. This random selection not only suggests possible lines of investigation, but also indicates that the material is there: writing for children and stylistic emptiness are not inevitably linked.

The *exponential* approach, perhaps that most automatically adopted by the discriminating reader, bridges the gap between the intrinsic and extrinsic. Here we are dealing with the larger patterns of expression and meaning found within a work, which will, I think, necessarily find referents outside it. Themes, symbols, motifs, imagery, patterns, may be identified and linked, either directly or by reference to context. Here we are becoming more dependent upon both the learning and perception, and the more subjective interpretative and correlative faculties of the critic. For children's literature this method is important in relation to the rich sources of folk-consciousness from which many books derive.

Similarly, another strength of children's literature is its use of the material and techniques of the folk- and fairy-tale, which are often the most direct written expressions of basic human beliefs, symbols and myths. *Mythological* and *archetypal* criticism draws on the discoveries of anthropologists and historians, and to study the recognized metaphysical elements in world cultures and their reflection in children's books can contribute to our understanding.

In its techniques, and the objections likely to be raised to it, this type of criticism has much in common with the *psychological*. It may seem singularly inappropriate to apply Freudian and post-Freudian psychoanalytical theories to our subject, but this is not so. For an author who chooses to return by proxy to his own childhood, or to his concept of "general" childhood, an examination from this point of view can show his unconscious self-revelation. Nor, as I have suggested, does any tacit limitation on the *kind* of material used by children's authors have any real bearing on this. The psychological approach has perhaps provoked more adverse reaction than any other, and when dealing with children's books seems likely to provoke even more. The implications of, say, Kingsley's or Macdonald's use of naked boys and girls in their novels could be disturbing in an educational context. Indeed, not to labour Lewis Carroll further, it seems that he has been treated with considerably more delicacy by almost all critics than an adults' novelist with similar predilections might have been.

Finally, there is the developing *sociological* criticism, useful as an interpretative tool, but also obliquely responsible for much that is prescriptive in writing on children's books.

Simply because the books which we are considering are written for a type of audience with which we have a peculiar and personal relationship, there is more to the final phase, *subjective* response, than personal and critical qualifications. We have to make a complex adjustment of our natural attitudes—to read a children's book *as a book*, in the first place, and in the second to evade our very reason for doing so. To read as an abstract exercise and to leave our practical applications for later. It is fortunate that, in practice, a good book will remove these problems —the "I couldn't put it down" approach is perhaps not a bad rule-of-thumb guide. The discriminating adult (if he can shake off both nostalgia and prejudice) is unlikely to read a great deal of W. E. Johns, the same is demonstrably not true of Tolkien, Mayne, Farjeon, or even Ransome. Sometimes, of course, the paraphernalia of the books may be a stumbling block, but, to the open-minded, only a superficial one.

Critical method is, naturally, less clear-cut than this in actuality, but I hope that I have shown that it is applicable to children's books. But has it been applied? Many of the standard works on the subject, such as those of Darton or Thwaite, do not pretend to criticism; others, such as Crouch, have other preoccupations. To find an example, we may turn to where adult criticism has to deal with writing for children. As John Rowe Townsend observes: " . . . It can be offered as a pseudo-Euclidean proposition that any line drawn between books for adults and books for children must pass through the middle of Kipling."[15] In Kipling criticism, then, we might expect to find the thesis justified. After all, a good case could be made that in the Puck stories we see the author at his best—that in them he perfects his short-story form; that his language fuses perfectly with material which he knows thoroughly, used in a context which he has genuine feeling for. Indeed, in his autobiography, he has more to say about them than about any other of his books. However, turning to a distinguished writer, J. M. S. Tompkins, we find her confronting precisely those problems mentioned above.

It is not easy to take a dispassionate view of a book to which we have been much indebted in youth. . . . If this study had aimed at a critical evaluation, I think I should not have dared to write this chapter. . . . There should be, then, some value in the testimony of a reader who was a child of the generation for which they were first written.[16]

Acknowledging the dangers of quoting out of context from a most valuable book, this view must surely give pause, especially as it is typical. Is it any easier to take a dispassionate view of a book to which we are indebted as adults? Why completely change the coinage of criticism? Such a blurring of critical acumen is less honestly expressed by other writers, and a parallel can be found, for example in Jefferies criticism.

Those whose interests lie in children's books therefore have a responsibility to their material, and, as I have said, that material can take the weight of serious analysis. This in turn leads, however, to the question—should it be expected to do so? Does one expect to find in a children's book the range and depth of emotions, situations, or verbal subtleties that one finds in books for adults? Does not, in fact, the particular audience (and the commercial demands on authors) have more than just a peripheral effect? The answer is, I hope, simple in some cases. *Alice,* or *The Wind in the Willows,* despite, or because of, their *unadult* anthropomorphism and anthropomorphitism (another singular and fascinating area for research) can stand beside any other book—different in kind, perhaps, from Henry James or Tolstoy, but not to be assessed on a different scale, or read in a significantly different way. A more direct comparison with *Sylvie and Bruno* or *Dream Days* (another edifying exercise) demonstrates their excellence.

Stepping outside this more or less undisputed ground, problems proliferate, but then so do the possibilities. The study of Pooh, for example, is encumbered by the sentimental and fashionable vogues it has suffered more than once—not to mention its use in that admirable satire on criticism, *The Pooh Perplex.*[17] But such distractions do not alter the fact of its remarkable unity (once away from the sentimental frame), its beautifully adapted and balanced style: in short, to draw on the terminology of an earlier generation—its fitness. This is not the place to make out a case for Milne, but it is as well to point out that it is irrelevant considerations that prevent its being done. Similarly, it seems to me that a book like Ransome's *The Big Six* can, and should, stand beside any other book (and higher than most) in its genre of the detective novel —whether or not it is literature *per se.* What makes it less than acceptable to the adult (and the same applies to *We Didn't Mean to Go to Sea* and sea novels) are superficialities, while such simplifications as there are, are more than compensated for by other virtues. If citing these more arguable examples seems to weaken my case I feel that the point is worth making—for some writers on children's books tend to underestimate their material, and thus do not treat it seriously.

I cannot, and would not wish to, evade the fact that in terms of content, and to a lesser extent style, children's literature has its particular problems: but it also has compensating advantages, some of which have been noted. It can acceptably deal with deep currents of myth, legend, magic, and fantasy (related to a real world or not), areas which are at best unfashionable and at worst unacceptable in writing for adults. The audience does not disbar the sexual or the religious; adult humour, often said to mar books by its archness or condescension, can equally act as a reinforcement or counterpoint to the central narrative—and this also applies to the tacit undercurrents of an author's deeper intentions. Also, if certain areas of experience are rarely found, many byways are explored, and others developed to a remarkable degree—Carroll again, or the subtlety of Mayne in dealing with natural phenomena. If books written to deal with specific social situations, or to "expand the subject matter" of children's books (from *The Family from One End Street* onwards) have been largely second-rate, this is not necessarily the fault of the children's book as a type. Certainly it is interesting to compare the general standard of contemporary writing for children with that of writing for adults.

This list begs and omits many questions, not least those of innocence and experience, the concept of the child being closer to the mystical[18] and so on, but I think that it serves to show not only the validity of applying literary criticism to children's books, but the need to do so, and some of the immense possibilities.

The state of work on children's books, admirable though much of it is, suggests that a firm foundation of academic disciplines would be valuable, and that criticism can make a contribution. It is not only children's books that would benefit, but everyone who values literature.

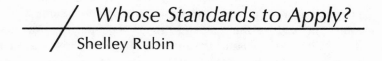

Whose Standards to Apply?
Shelley Rubin

Literary criticism rests on an uneasy balance. The literary critic must be both speculative and fastidious, building from the text without abandoning it. In attempting a critique of children's literature, Roger Sale, in his book *Fairy Tales and After* [Cambridge, Mass.: Harvard Univ. Pr., 1978], compounds the difficulties of an already precarious task. For while the author of adult literature assumes a shared level of understanding, children's literature grows out of the disparity between author and audience: it is written by and often selected by adults, but it is *for* children. In seeking to evaluate these works, then, whose standards ought one to apply?

Excerpted from *Phaedrus: An International Journal of Children's Literature Research* 6:35 (Summer 1979), with the permission of that publication.

Recognizing that many of the works of so-called children's literature are neither aimed at nor read by children, Sale sets out to share his adult enjoyment of works ranging from *Peter Rabbit* to *Alice's Adventures in Wonderland*. Rather than inferring a child's perspective, he proposes instead to "read and write about children's literature without confusing it with myself as a child, or with the study of children's habits, tastes, or ways of thinking." Taken in this spirit, Sale's commitment to the examination of children's literature from a literary standpoint opens up possibilities few others have explored. Many of the passages of analysis he offers are fresh, convincing and insightful. Yet his approach, while it indicates a willingness to take children's literature seriously, also reflects a particularly adult set of assumptions.

Sale concedes the disparity between author and audience of children's literature. However, in opposing the temptation "to make the central relation be between the teller and the audience, rather than the teller and the tale," Sale goes beyond the affirmation that art must maintain an independent integrity. He not only rejects a view of art dependent on audience standards, he contends that art should be blind to its audience. "As always," he warns, "when a writer fixes on children as the audience, a mistake is sure to follow."

Clearly, both extremes have their difficulties. Children see the world differently from adults, and grown-up attempts to assume a child's viewpoint can lead to the "superior tone" Sale decries, for example, in A. A. Milne. By dismissing the audience altogether, however, Sale risks the opposite extreme: he unnecessarily equates consideration of the audience with artistic compromise. Moreover, to assume that writing *for* children compromises a work of art is to assume that children's artistic sensibilities matter less. Although Sale's approach exposes the richness of children's literature, it ultimately means the imposition of adult standards. If the works are neither guided by the perceptions of children, nor, as Sale acknowledges, preferred by children, what becomes of *children's* literature? . . .

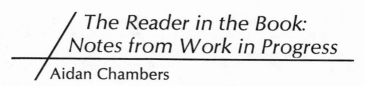

The Reader in the Book:
Notes from Work in Progress
Aidan Chambers

TWO TO SAY A THING

There is constant squabble about whether particular books are children's books or not. Indeed, some people argue that there is no such thing as books for children but only books which children happen to read. And unless one wants to be partisan and dogmatic—which I do not, having had my fill of both—one has to agree that there is some truth on both sides and the whole truth in neither.

The fact is that some books are clearly *for* children in a specific sense —they were written by their authors deliberately for children—and some books, never specifically intended for children, have qualities which attract children to them.

THE IMPLIED READER

Until we discover how to take account of the implied reader, we shall call fruitlessly for serious attention to be paid to books for children, and to children as readers by others than that small number of us who have come to recognize their importance. What has bedevilled criticism of children's books in the past is the rejection of any concept of the child-reader-in-the-book by those people who have sought most earnestly for critical respectability. And they have done this, have set aside the reader-in-the-book, in the belief that mainstream criticism requires them to do so, when in fact literary criticism has for years now been moving more and more towards a method that examines this very aspect of literature. If children's book critics look for parity with their

An edited version of a talk given in 1977 to the University of Bristol School of Education; excerpted with permission from *Signal: Approaches to Children's Books* no. 23:64 and passim (May 1977). Published by The Thimble Press, Lockwood, Station Road, South Woodchester Stroud, Glos. GL5 5EQ England. The complete essay, which is approximately three times as long as the above excerpt, has been reprinted in *The Signal Approach to Children's Books*, Nancy Chambers, ed. (Harmondsworth, Eng.: Kestrel, 1980).

colleagues outside the study of children's books, they must—if for no other more valuable reason—show how the concept of the implied reader relates to children as readers and to the books they read.

The idea of the implied reader derives from the understanding that it takes two to say a thing. In effect it suggests that in his book an author creates a relationship with a reader in order to discover the meaning of the text. Wolfgang Iser puts it this way: he says that such a critical method "is concerned primarily with the form of a work, insofar as one defines form basically as a means of communication or as a negotiation of insight."[1]

To achieve this, an author, sometimes consciously sometimes not, creates, in Wayne C. Booth's words: "an image of himself and another image of his reader; he makes his reader, as he makes his second self, and the most successful reading is one in which the created selves, author and reader, can find complete agreement."[2]

The author's second self[3] is created by his use of various techniques: by the way, for example, he puts himself into the narrator—whether that be a third-person godlike all-seer or a first-person child character; by the way he comments on the events in the story; and by the attitude he adopts towards his characters and their actions, which he communicates in various ways, both subtle and obvious.

In the same way (and let me stress again, deliberately or otherwise) the reader's second self—the reader-in-the-book—is given certain attributes, a certain persona, created by the use of techniques and devices which help form the narrative. And this persona is guided by the author towards the book's potential meanings.

Booth points out that a distinction must be made "between myself as reader and the often very different self who goes about paying bills, repairing leaky faucets, and failing in generosity and wisdom. It is only as I read that I become the self whose beliefs must coincide with the author's. Regardless of my real beliefs and practices, I must subordinate my mind and heart to the book if I am to enjoy it to the full."

THE UNYIELDING CHILD READER

Booth expresses something mature literary readers have always understood: that a requirement of fulfilled readership is a willingness to give oneself up to the book. They have learned how to do this: how to lay aside their own prejudices and take on the prejudices of the text, how to enter into the book, becoming part of it while at the same time never abandoning their own being. In C. S. Lewis's words literature allowed him "to become a thousand men and yet remain myself."

Children, of course, have not completely learned how to do this; they have not discovered how to shift the gears of their personality according to the invitations offered by the book. In this respect they are unyielding readers. They want the book to suit them, tending to expect an author to take them as he finds them rather than they taking the book as they find it. One of the valuable possibilities offered by the critical method I look for is that it would make more intelligently understandable those books which take a child as he is but then draw him into the text; the books which help the child reader to negotiate meaning, help him develop the ability to receive a text as a literary reader does rather than to make use of it for nonliterary purposes.

The concept of the implied reader and the critical method that follows from it help us to do just that. They help us establish the author's relationship with the (child) reader implied in the story, to see how he creates that relationship and to discover the meaning(s) he seeks to negotiate. Clearly, such understanding will lead us beyond a critical appreciation of the text towards that other essential activity of those concerned with children's books: how to mediate the books and their readers in such a way that individual books are not only better appreciated by children but that children are also helped to become literary readers.

We must examine one book closely in an attempt to reveal its implied reader. But before we come to that, it might be useful to consider some of the principal techniques by which an author can establish his tone—his relationship with his desired reader—and, of particular importance in children's books, by which he can draw the reader into the text in such a way that the reader accepts the role offered and enters into the demands of the book.

STYLE

Style is the term we use for the way a writer employs language to make his second self and his implied reader and to communicate his meaning. It is far too simplistic to suppose that this is just a matter of sentence structure and choice of vocabulary. It encompasses an author's use of image, his deliberate and unaware references, the assumptions he makes about what a reader will understand without explication or description, his attitude to beliefs, customs, characters in his narrative—all as revealed by the way he writes about them.

A simple example which allows a comparison between the style a writer employed when writing for adults and the alterations he made when rewriting the story for children is provided by Roald Dahl. "The Champion of the World" is a short story first published in *The New*

Yorker and now included in *Kiss Kiss,* published by Penguin. Some years afterwards Dahl rewrote the story for children under the title *Danny: The Champion of the World.* The original version could hardly be called difficult in subject or language. A ten-year-old of average reading ability could manage it without too much bother, should any child want to. Both versions are told in the first person; the adult narrator of the original is in some respects naively ingenuous, a device Dahl employs (following *New Yorker*–Thurber tradition) as a foil for the narrator's friend Claud, a worldlywise, unfazable character, and as a device to exaggerate into comic extravagance the otherwise only mildly amusing events of a fairly plain tale.

Because the original is written in this first-person, easily read narrative, which is naive even in its emotional pitch, Dahl could transfer parts with minimal alterations straight from the original into the children's version. Yet even so, he made some interesting and significant changes. Here, for example, is the original description of the entry into the story of its arch-villain, Victor Hazel (differently spelt in the two tellings), whose unforgivable snobbery and unscrupulous selfishness are justification enough in the narrator's eyes to warrant poaching his pheasants:

I wasn't sure about this, but I had a suspicion that it was none other than the famous Mr. Victor Hazel himself, the owner of the land and the pheasants. Mr. Hazel was a local brewer with an unbelievably arrogant manner. He was rich beyond words, and his property stretched for miles along either side of the valley. He was a self-made man with no charm at all and precious few virtues. He loathed all persons of humble station, having once been one of them himself, and he strove desperately to mingle with what he believed were the right kind of folk. He rode to hounds and gave shooting-parties and wore fancy waistcoats, and every weekday he drove an enormous black Rolls-Royce past the filling-station on his way to the brewery. As he flashed by, we would sometimes catch a glimpse of the great glistening brewer's face above the wheel, pink as a ham, all soft and inflamed from drinking too much beer.

Here is the recast version written for the children's telling:

I must pause here to tell you something about Mr. Victor Hazell. He was a brewer of beer and he owned a huge brewery. He was rich beyond words, and his property stretched for miles along either side of the valley. All the land around us belonged to him, everything on both sides of the road, everything except the small patch of ground on which our filling-station stood. That patch belonged to my father. It was a little island in the middle of the vast ocean of Mr. Hazell's estate.

Mr. Victor Hazell was a roaring snob and he tried desperately to get in with what he believed were the right kind of people. He hunted with the hounds

American Cancer Society, ~~~ ment of Commerce. will display ~~~ authors closest to the name you typed. If you want to see more authors, press the **UP A PAGE** (preceding screen of authors), **DOWN A PAGE** (next screen), **UP A LINE** (displays additional authors one line at a time) or **DOWN A LINE** keys.

Press **(F1) DISPLAY TITLES** to view the author's works. You may move the highlight bar using the up/down ↑ ↓ arrow keys until it illuminates the title you want. Press **(F2) DISPLAY COPIES** for call number, library and availability status.

If the same author is listed more than once,

- You can clear the screen to look for information a different way by pressing (F7) **START OVER.**

IF YOU CAN'T FIND WHAT YOU WANT:

- Check your spelling.
- Verify the author's name, a title or subject.

and gave shooting parties and wore fancy waistcoats. Every weekday he drove his enormous silver Rolls-Royce past our filling-station on his way to the brewery. As he flashed by we would sometimes catch a glimpse of the great glistening beery face above the wheel, pink as a ham, all soft and inflamed from drinking too much beer.

Dahl has simplified some of his sentences by chopping up the longer ones with full stops where commas are used in the adult version. And he does some cutting: he takes out the abstractions such as the comment about Hazel loathing people of humble station because he had once been one of them himself. Presumably Dahl felt children would not be able (or want) to cope either with the stylistic complexities of his first version or with the motivation ascribed to Hazel's behaviour. Whatever we may think about this, it certainly reveals Dahl's assumptions about his implied reader.

What he aims to achieve—and does—is a tone of voice which is clear, uncluttered, unobtrusive, not very demanding linguistically, and which sets up a sense of intimate, yet adult-controlled, relationship between his second self and his implied child reader. It is a voice often heard in children's books of the kind deliberately written for them: it is the voice of speech rather than of interior monologue or no-holds-barred private confession. It is, in fact, the tone of a friendly adult storyteller who knows how to entertain children while at the same time keeping them in their place. Even when speaking outrageously about child-adult taboo subjects (theft by poaching in *Danny* and, in this extract, harsh words about a grown-up), it does so with a kind of drawing-room politeness. At its most typical it is a style that speaks of "the children" in the tale. . . .

POINT OF VIEW

Tone of voice, style as a whole, very quickly establishes a relationship between author and reader; very quickly creates the image of the implied reader. In books where the implied reader is a child, authors tend to reinforce the relationship by adopting in their second self—giving the book, if you prefer—a very sharply focused point of view. They tend to achieve that focus by putting at the centre of the story a child through whose being everything is seen and felt.

This is more than simply a device. If literature for children is to have any meaning at all, it must primarily be concerned with the nature of childhood, not just the nature commonly shared by most children but the diversity of childhood nature too. For, like all literature, children's literature at its best attempts "to explore, recreate and seek for meanings in human experience" (the phrase is Richard Hoggart's); this attempt is made with specific reference to children and their lives through the unique relationship between language and form.

But, at the level of creating the implied reader and of an author's need to draw a child reader into his book, this narrowing of focus by the adoption of a child point of view helps keep the author's second self—himself in the book—within the perceptual scope of his child reader. And the child, finding within the book an implied author whom he can befriend because he is of the tribe of childhood as well, is thus wooed into the book. He adopts the image of the implied child reader and is then willing, may even desire, to give himself up to the author and the book and be led through whatever experience is offered.

Thus the book's point of view not only acts as a means of creating the author-reader relationship but works powerfully as a solvent, melting away a child's nonliterary approach to reading and re-forming him into the kind of reader the book demands.

Some authors, feeling constricted by a too narrowly child-focusing viewpoint, try to find ways of presenting a fuller picture of adulthood without losing the child-attracting quality of the narrower focus. A few have tried to do this directly, using adult characters and a point of view that shifts between a child-focus and an adult-focus. But very few of the few who have tried have succeeded. It remains one of the major problems for children's writers now, and is a challenge worth accepting. Nina Bawden has always been exercised by this difficulty, and has gone a long way towards finding satisfactory solutions, especially in *Carrie's War* (Gollancz/Puffin). This book is well worth critical consideration as a very fine example of how an author can deploy her craft in the creation of an implied reader, apart from her success in revealing adult characters to a remarkably complex degree without loss of definition for her young readers.

Most writers approach the problem of adult-portrayal less directly. They tend to cast their tales in the form of fantasy, usually with animal-human characters. Robert C. O'Brien's *Mrs. Frisby and the Rats of NIMH* (Gollancz/Puffin) provides a much enjoyed modern example; Kenneth Grahame's *Wind in the Willows* (Methuen) probably the best known and most affectionately regarded; and Russell Hoban's *The Mouse and His Child* (Faber/Puffin) one of the most complexly layered and handled (for which reasons, no doubt, it is finding its most responsive audience not among children but among adolescents).

But if I wanted to select, in the context of my theme, two superlative examples that encompass a possible readership of about seven years old right on to adulthood, I would choose Alan Garner's *The Stone Book*

(Collins) to demonstrate the direct approach and Ted Hughes's *The Iron Man* (Faber) as an example of the solution through fantasy. . . .

TAKING SIDES

. . . Once an author has forged an alliance and a point of view that engages a child, he can then manipulate that alliance as a device to guide the reader towards the meanings he wishes to negotiate. Wolfgang Iser provides a useful example, not from a specifically children's book, where such a manoeuvre is too rarely used, but from *Oliver Twist.* Iser cites the scene in which the hungry Oliver

has the effrontery (as the narrator sees it) to ask for another plate of soup. In the presentation of this daring exploit, Oliver's inner feelings are deliberately excluded in order to give greater emphasis to the indignation of the authorities at such an unreasonable request. The narrator comes down heavily on the side of authority, and can thus be quite sure that his hardhearted attitude will arouse a flood of sympathy in his readers for the poor starving child.

What such manipulation of the reader's expectations, allegiances, and author-guided desires leads to is the further development of the implied reader into an implicated reader: one so intellectually and emotionally given to the book, not just its plot and characters but its negotiation between author and reader of potential meanings, that the reader is totally involved. The last thing he wants is to stop reading; and what he wants above all is to milk the book dry of all it has to offer, and to do so in the kind of way the author wishes. He finally becomes a participant in the making of the book. He has become aware of the "telltale gaps."

TELLTALE GAPS

As a tale unfolds, the reader discovers its meaning. Authors can strive, as some do, to make their meaning plain, leaving little room for the reader to negotiate with them. Other authors leave gaps which the reader must fill before the meaning can be complete. A skilful author wishing to do this is somewhat like a play-leader: he structures his narrative so as to direct it in a dramatic pattern that leads the reader towards possible meaning(s); and he stage-manages the reader's involvement by bringing into play various techniques which he knows influence the reader's responses and expectations, in the way that Iser, for example, described Dickens doing in *Oliver Twist.* Literature can be studied so as to uncover the gaps an author leaves for his reader to fill, and these gaps take two general forms.

The first is the more superficial. These gaps have to do with an author's assumptions, whether knowingly made or not, about his readers. Just as we saw in the Dahl extracts how a writer's style revealed his assumptions about his implied reader's ability to cope with language any syntax, so we can also detect from a writer's references to a variety of things just what he assumes about his implied reader's beliefs, politics, social customs, and the like. Richmal Crompton in common with Enid Blyton, A. A. Milne, Edith Nesbit and many more children's authors assumed a reader who would not only be aware of housemaids and cooks, nannies and gardeners but would also be used to living in homes attended by such household servants. That assumption was as unconsciously made as the adoption of a tone of voice current among people who employed servants at the time the authors were writing.

These referential gaps, these assumptions of commonality, are relatively unimportant until they become so dominant in the text that people who do not—or do not wish to—make the same assumptions feel alienated by them as they read. And this alienation, this feeling of repugnance, affects the child just as much as the adult, once the referential gaps become significant.

Far more important, however, is another form of telltale gap: these are the ones that challenge the reader to participate in making meaning of the book. Making meaning is a vital concept in literary reading. Laurence Sterne refers to it directly in *Tristram Shandy:*

No author who understands the just boundaries of decorum and good breeding would presume to think all. The truest respect which you can pay to the reader's understanding is to halve this matter amicably, and leave him something to imagine, in his turn, as well as yourself. For my own part, I am eternally paying him compliments of this kind, and do all in my power to keep his imagination as busy as my own.

Of course, it doesn't all depend on the author; he can deploy his narrative skills brilliantly, "halving the matter amicably" with his reader. But unless a reader accepts the challenge, no relationship that seeks to discover meaning is possible. It is one of the responsibilities of children's writers, and a privileged one, so to write that children are led to understand how to read: how to accept the challenge. . . .

IN SUM

I am suggesting that the concept of the implied reader, far from unattended to by critics of literature in Germany and America, offers us a critical approach which concerns itself less with the subjects portrayed in a book than with the means of communication by which the reader is brought into contact with the reality presented by an author. That it is a method which could help us determine whether a book is for children or not, what kind of book it is, and what kind of reader (or, to put it another way, what kind of reading) it demands. Knowing this will help us to understand better how to teach not just a particular book but particular books to particular children.[4]

Pursuing "The Reader in the Book"

Peggy Whalen-Levitt

With their influential writing on the "affective" and "intentional" fallacies, Wimsatt and Beardsley[1] heralded the banishment of the reader and author from the arena of legitimate literary study and focused attention, instead, on the text. New Criticism, it is generally agreed, was thus a response to an underlying anxiety that the text, as linguistic structure, was being slighted in favor of historical, biographical, and subjective approaches. In recent years, we have seen a variety of reactions to New Criticism itself. Among these are literary theories which attempt to avoid the extremes of past approaches and argue, reasonably, for a perspective that will permit a consideration of author, text, and reader.

The children's literature field in America, with a few exceptions, has been surprisingly unaffected by these changes. At least, there appears to be considerable sentiment here for an "intrinsic" approach to the study of literature for children. Such sentiment is evident in phrases and slogans that have become fashionable in the field such as "children's literature is literature" and in the distinction drawn between "literary" and "pedagogical" approaches. This emphasis on the "literariness" of children's literature comes, I think, as a response to a concern that the children's literature text, as a linguistic structure, was being neglected by

Reprinted from the *Children's Literature Association Quarterly*, 4:10–14 (Winter 1980), with permission of the author and the Children's Literature Association.

so-called child-centered approaches. A consideration of the reader has thus been viewed as a threat to a consideration of the text.

It is ironic that the children's literature field should be so out of step with recent developments in literary theory during the very period of literary history when respected theorists have paved the way for a consideration of the reader. The time has come to realize that we can have it both ways: we can respect the aesthetic function of the text and consider the reader as well. To embrace a theoretical framework that enables us to consider author, text, *and* reader is to resolve a longstanding impasse in our field.

For let us acknowledge a dilemma peculiar to our field. We have all, no doubt, known child readers whose range of literary sensibility and experience outdistances that of many adults. It is perhaps this realization which impels us to resist the term "children's literature"; to dismiss it as "an accident of history." On the other hand, we would perhaps all agree that literary experience must begin somewhere and probably closer to the lullaby than to *Ulysses*. Implicit, but rarely explicit, in discussions of "what makes a good children's book good" is some notion of a range of literary experience considered appropriate as an initiation into the world of literature. Also, averse as some are to consider child readers, there probably lurks within most of us a curiosity about why some texts and not others nestle into a place of significance within the culture of childhood. In the past, neither a child-centered nor a text-centered approach has served us well. I believe we need a theoretical framework that will enable us to cut through this dualism and consider, at the very least, both reader and text.

We are indebted to Aidan Chambers and Reinbert Tabbert for bridging the gap between contemporary literary theory and the study of literature for children. Both in his award-winning article "The Reader in the Book,"[2] and in his address to Children's Literature Association members in Toronto last year, Aidan Chambers did an admirable job of introducing literary communication theory as a basis for the study of children's literature. Reinbert Tabbert, in his recent article "The Impact of Children's Books: Cases and Concepts" has continued the discussion by exploring the implications of "reception theory" for the children's book field.[3] Both Chambers and Tabbert, in formulating a communications approach to children's literature, have drawn upon the work of Wolfgang Iser in *The Implied Reader*. As a way of pursuing this line of inquiry further, perhaps it would be useful to take a look at two of the most recent contributions to literary communication theory: Iser's latest book, *The Act of Reading: A Theory of Aesthetic Response*[4] and Louise M. Rosenblatt's *The Reader, the Text, the Poem: The Transactional Theory of the Literary Work*.[5]

Since it is in the area of epistemology that Iser and Rosenblatt differ most markedly from the New Critics, let us begin there. Eschewing both "objectivist" and "subjectivist" approaches to the nature of knowledge, Iser and Rosenblatt develop strikingly similar "contextual" approaches. The discussion of literary meaning, they argue, must not rest with either the text or with the reader's response, but rather must center on the coming together of reader and text. This coming together, which Iser refers to as "realization" and Rosenblatt as "evocation," results in the "aesthetic object" or "poem." It is the latter, the temporal literary event, which forms the subject of inquiry. Thus, both Iser and Rosenblatt are primarily concerned with the question, "What is the nature of literary experience?"

It is not therefore surprising that they acknowledge ordinary language philosophy, as well as John Dewey's *Art as Experience,* as influential to their work. And while Rosenblatt admits some compatibility with the work of Husserl, Iser draws heavily upon the phenomenological theory of art, which, he says, "has emphatically drawn attention to the fact that the study of a literary work should concern not only the actual text but also, and in equal measure, the actions involved in responding to that text." There are at least three other important points of agreement within the epistemological realm: they both reject the Descartian mind-matter duality, and argue, instead, that the reading process is a "complex reality in which the difference between subject and object disappears";[6] this process is not viewed, however, as a linear progression wherein the reader acts upon the text, or the text upon the reader, but rather is viewed as a dynamic interrelationship of reader and text; and finally, both Iser and Rosenblatt accept, as a basic premise, the validity of diversity in interpretation.

Thus, both Iser and Rosenblatt are concerned with developing a kind of literary theory that will enable us to "look at the reality of the literary enterprise, of 'literature' as a certain kind of activity of human beings in our culture."[7] Within this overall shared outlook, however, their goals take different turns. Iser's chief concern, it would seem, is the construction of a framework designed to serve as a guide for empirical studies of reader realization. Thus, from the onset, he asserts that his "book is to be regarded as a theory of aesthetic response (Wirkungstheorie) and not as a theory of the aesthetics of reception (Rezeptionstheorie),"[8] the difference being that a theory of aesthetic response is concerned with the elucidation of *potential* rather than *real* effects. Rosenblatt, on the other hand, takes a particularized approach. Her primary goal is to encourage an appreciation for "the living work of art" in the lives of real readers.

Before proceeding further, we should perhaps inquire into Iser's and Rosenblatt's responses to the question "What is literature?" They both categorically avoid traditional functionalist and structuralist approaches, wherein literature is defined either in terms of its purpose (to instruct, please, and so on) or in terms of its distinctive characteristics (metaphor, rhythm, and so on). Iser, drawing upon the work of Ingarden, Austin, Searle, Cassirer, and B. H. Smith, regards literature "as an imitation of and not a deviation from ordinary speech." Thus, a riddle is viewed as an imitation of questioning, a novel as an imitation of reporting, and so forth. The distinguishing characteristic between fictive and natural discourse is that the former does not refer to an actual situation. Iser sums up his approach as follows: "In simple terms, we may say that fictional language provides instructions for the building of a situation and so for the production of an imaginary object."[9] Rosenblatt takes a different tack. Balking at the traditional question, "What is literature?", she turns it around and asks it another way: "We must rephrase our question and ask, 'What does the reader *do* in these different kinds of reading?' " To answer this question, Rosenblatt employs the terms "aesthetic" and "efferent" to differentiate two reading stances. In "aesthetic reading," the reader's attention is focused on the evocation itself; whereas in "efferent reading," the focus of attention is on the information to be carried away from the reading. To sum up, in Rosenblatt's view, "the essence of a work of art is precisely that a consciousness is living through a synthesizing evocation from a text which involves many—one is tempted to say all—levels of the organism."[10] By defining literature in terms of the human behaviors of speaking and reading, Iser and Rosenblatt once again encourage us to consider literature, not as an autonomous form, but rather as situated in the context of social and personal life.

This brings us to their views on the function of literature. Here, once again, they are in almost complete agreement. Literary experience, they argue, enables readers to transcend the limitations of their own experiences; to formulate themselves; and to assess cultural norms and values. All this is brought about through the complementary function of literary experience to join past experience of life and literature to present experience with a particular text. Drawing upon Dewey, Iser concludes that in the act of reading "the old conditions the form of the new, and the new selectively restructures the old."[11] Thus, literary experience, unique in the opportunity it affords the reader to employ, exercise, formulate and reformulate his or her symbolic reservoir, is viewed as central to the reader's conceptualization of reality.

Having familiarized ourselves with some of the key concepts that underlie their theories, we might now well ask what it is that Iser and Rosenblatt would have students of literature *do?* What are the implications of their theories for literary criticism? Let us begin with Rosenblatt, whose theory might alternatively be entitled "Against Impersonal Analysis," for it is this she takes as the bane of all criticism. The critic's first responsibility, according to Rosenblatt, is to adopt an aesthetic stance. Rejecting any notion of ideal reader, and stressing the affinity of all readers, Rosenblatt views the critic, above all else, as a real reader reading: "The term 'literary critic' should be reserved for one whose primary subject is his aesthetic transaction with the text; he reflects on the work of art he has evoked." As to evaluation, Rosenblatt raises the key question, "What, in fact, is being evaluated?" She concludes that it is "the quality *of the transaction* as an aesthetic event," rather than the quality of isolated texts, that merits our attention. Finally, as concerns the purpose of criticism, Rosenblatt concludes that the critic who "comes to us as a fellow reader" is in a better position to "(stimulate) us to grow in our own capacities to participate creatively and self-critically in literary ransactions."[12]

Iser envisions a somewhat different role for the critic. While Rosenblatt would have the critic report on the aesthetic event itself, Iser would have him or her report on the means by which he or she was drawn into the event. To do this, the critic needs some concept of reader. Rejecting the notions of "real reader," "ideal reader," "contemporary reader," "superreader," "informed reader," and "intended reader," Iser employs the "implied reader" as a pivotal heuristic concept. The "implied reader" is viewed as "a textual structure anticipating the presence of a recipient without necessarily defining him." Iser, it seems, would have the critic use his or her own realization of a text as a basis for considering the more general potential of the text to yield a variety of readings. The task of the interpreter, according to Iser, is "not to explain a work, but to reveal the conditions that bring about its various possible effects. If he clarifies the *potential* of a text, he will no longer fall into the fatal trap of trying to impose one meaning on his reader, as if that were the right, or at least the best interpretation."[13] To facilitate this task, Iser develops an elaborate model of the literary communication process designed to aid the critic in his or her description of the "implied reader."

The substance of this model can only be hinted at here, as it is extensive in its identification of components of the literary communication process and in its suggestions for how to consider relationships among components. Most broadly, the model covers "the formation of the text as a set of instructions" (including the social and cultural norms employed to situate the work in a referential context and the particular strategies which help to organize realizations); "the description of the reading process"; and "the spurs to interaction that are the necessary prerequisites for the reader to assemble the meaning of the text in a process of re-creative dialectics." How much of Iser's framework will survive the empirical work of the decade ahead remains to be seen. What is certain is that he has provided us with a model which offers promising heuristic schema that should help us proceed with the task of descriptive analysis. As for evaluation, Iser sides with T. S. Eliot: " 'The critic' says T. S. Eliot, 'must not coerce, and he must not make judgments of worse or better. He must simply elucidate: the reader will form the correct judgment for himself.' "[14]

In light of their approaches to interpretation and evaluation, how do Iser and Rosenblatt handle literary history? For Rosenblatt, one can safely conclude that literary history is equated with a history of personal evocations. She therefore views the literary historian as "one [who] would seek to establish the similarities, the repetitions, the variations and differences in what constituted the *Iliad* in the readings of each epoch over the centuries."[15] For Iser, not at all concerned with a history of real readers' realizations, literary history is viewed as the study of "differences in the structure of interaction" offered by texts from one historical context to another. *The Implied Reader: Patterns of Communication in Prose Fiction from Bunyan to Beckett* is a case in point.

The theories of Iser and Rosenblatt are not without their problems. For example, Iser does not adequately explain how the critic moves from the personal quality of a realization to the abstraction of the "implied reader." He himself admits that "it is extremely difficult to gauge where the signals leave off and the reader's imagination begins."[16] Rosenblatt is on safer ground advocating reports of personal evocations, but somehow we want her to provide more guidance as to how these diverse evocations are to be related, one to the other. Also, it should be pointed out that both Iser and Rosenblatt have focused their attention more fully upon the interrelationship of reader and text than on the interrelationship of reader, text, and author. Within the context of a literary communication model, the creative context deserves greater consideration.

In closing, let us consider some of the implications of Iser's and Rosenblatt's work for the study of children's literature. By defining literature in descriptive rather than evaluative terms, Iser and Rosenblatt readily admit children's literature into the realm of legitimate literary study. From there, children's literature is treated just like any other literature: for Rosenblatt, in terms of personal evocation; for Iser, in terms of the "implied reader." The value of either approach is that it provides insight into the structure of interaction evoked or implicated by a children's literature text, without putting us in the position of having to make facile assumptions about child readers. Evaluation, on the other hand, is placed squarely in the context of readers', including child readers', experience. As far as the history of children's literature is concerned, Rosenblatt's perspective would yield a history of readings of children's literature, logically including those of child readers—but limited, of course, by documentation. Following Iser's directives, we might expect a study entitled "The Implied Reader: Patterns of Communication in American Prose Fiction for Children from Goodrich to Goffstein."

Above all, the literary communication perspective encourages us to describe children's literature in terms of what a given text calls upon a reader to know and to do: to know, in terms of experience of both life and literature; to do, in terms of producing a meaning for this particular text, in time, from start to finish. Such a description should put us in a better position to introduce books to children; to respond to the plea, "I want one just like *Ramona the Pest*"; to assess a child's own selections; and to understand a child's "selective realization of the implied reader." From this perspective, the term "children's literature" refers less to a group of texts than to a range of literary experience. With the emphasis on literary experience rather than on the autonomy of texts, we are at liberty to include "first books," for example, as a legitimate topic for study. A book such as *Goodnight Moon,* considered too simple (and besides, too pictorial) to be the proper object of an "explication de texte," takes its rightful place in a "theory of aesthetic response" or a "transactional theory of the literary work." For from this vantage point, the child reader is parent of the adult reader; the evocation of a simple text a foundation for the realization of one that makes greater demands on its readers.

The Critical Front

Marilyn Kaye

Over the past few years it's been a pleasure to witness the rising interest in literary criticism of children's books. Evidence of this new direction can be found in journals devoted specifically to literature as well as in those rooted in children's librarianship or education. Conference, symposium, and seminar topics testify to a desire for more communication on the subject. It would appear that we're moving closer and closer to the recognition of children's literature as "literature," subject to the rigorous forms of analysis once reserved for adult literature and practiced chiefly among academics. Now we can go one step further toward the formation of a critical methodology, a pluralistic approach that satisfies our personal and professional needs and takes into consideration the unique nature of the literature. Very often, the established methods of English departments do not.

A number of studies that attempt an archetypal approach to children's literature have appeared in recent years. Archetypal criticism is based on the premise that certain themes or motifs in literature have a universal symbolic nature based in myth and ritual. Since many of these themes are common elements in children's books, it is not surprising to find critics turning to some form of archetypal or mythic theory. Certainly fairy tales and much of our classic fantasy offer a wealth of archetypal patterns. And in the realistic genre, themes such as the quest, journey, and initiation into adulthood are prime targets for the critic concerned with reducing a motif to its primal form. But it is a limited approach. Style, tone, and metaphor tend to fall by the wayside, and some works simply do not lend themselves to this form of analysis. This is not to dismiss the theory; there is much that can be realized in children's literature through archetypal criticism. For example, one particularly appropriate genre suitable for study is science fiction, which frequently involves mythic elements. But we cannot depend on this approach to satisfy all our needs, so we have to keep looking.

There are certain elements peculiar to children's literature. There is a didactic tradition, stronger than any that has occurred in the history

Reprinted from *Booklist* 76:769–70 (Feb. 1, 1980).

of adult literature. Children's literature has been viewed as a means of socialization, as a way to educate the young and bring them into the mainstream of values and attitudes common to a specific society. Certainly this was the intention of the authors of a century ago, and to some degree it is true today.

It is important to keep in mind the essential fact that *children do not buy books;* nor do they read reviews, peruse catalogs, or attend conference exhibits. Adults buy books *for* children; and just as the author must first convince the publisher of the potential value of a work, the publisher then must convince the book-buying adult who, hopefully, has some notion of what is appropriate for or desired by children. This is not to imply that neither the author nor the publisher knows what is appropriate; it is simply to point out the various steps that must be taken before the book reaches a child. It is only one step more than the number involved in the adult book process, but that one extra step is significant. The author/reader relationship is complicated by a third party—the buyer—who will determine availability, and the work must be made acceptable to this third party before its reception by the reader for whom it was intended.

It's a complex situation, and any real in-depth assessment of the process would require a doctoral dissertation. But the upshot is this: at some point in the process, certain social, moral, and cultural elements that must be acceptable to adults enter into the work. And since there are a number of adults involved in the process—author, editor, reviewer, librarian—one can infer that the work contains *common* acceptable sociocultural elements.

Then why not take a sociocultural approach to studying the literature? Since we can assume the elements are there, couldn't a deeper understanding of the literature result from exploring the relationships between the literature and the society that produced it, as in the current wave of books on child abuse, which has recently surfaced as a topic of awareness and concern? Certainly a study of this nature would bring to light the cultural implications of a work and would take into account the audience for which the work is intended, but what about the artistry of the work? A strict adherence to this approach could result in the neglect of aesthetic considerations; and again, while there is much to be gained from studying children's books within this framework, it is still not enough.

So now we turn to what has been called a "formalist" approach, which at first glance, may seem most suitable for our purposes. Here the focus is on the work itself in terms of the characteristics of its genre. We can study structure, technique, language—those elements of style that combine to give the work value. Yet even this is not enough, for we are, to some extent, eliminating that most peculiar element—the audience. Even if one were to ignore the audience and concentrate on the work, one has to recognize that inherent in the author/reader relationship is the fact that the author is not writing to a peer. The author is writing to an audience that comes to the work with less experience—not necessarily less intelligence, but probably with a more limited knowledge or vision of life than the author has. Thus, it is almost inevitable that the work will contain elements of the author's conception of childhood and of what a child requires in the way of literature. This can involve a self-consciousness or distance that doesn't enter into adults' writing for their own counterparts.

In weighing any and all common approaches to literary criticism, from Northrop Frye's archetypal philosophy to Wayne Booth's study of rhetoric, we don't need to accept a mold that, while useful in its own right, was not cast with any regard to unique literature for children. There is a whole universe of illuminating principles that can be plucked from various critical theories and that can be successfully utilized in the study of children's literature. But no single critical approach that now exists can satisfy our particular needs or elicit from a children's book all the subtle and underlying premises that it may contain. Therefore, it is time that we began moving toward the development of a critical approach that will combine elements of various theories and incorporate those that are particularly relevant to children's literature—the book-to-reader process, for example, and the nature of the audience.

Hopefully, many will join together in this task, and ultimately any theories that evolve will be dependent on the gradual development and refining of the work now being pursued in the journals, seminars, and classrooms. We might begin by looking at some of the problems that are apparent in our own attitude toward the literature.

1. To some degree, we all tend to view children's fiction in terms of content, with less attention devoted to form. Too frequently we classify fiction by subject—death, drugs, divorce, whatever—automatically, if unconsciously, grouping them as literature. This is okay for book talks, bibliographies, bibliotherapy, and card catalogs; but it won't do as a standard basis for criticism. It would be like grouping Saul Bellow and Jacqueline Susann because they both deal with sensual awareness. This is not to say that it is irrelevant to compare fictional works in terms of their treatment of a common subject matter, but too frequently the works have no other basis for comparison, and studies that rely on this comparative technique rarely offer insights into the deeper meanings and qualities of the works. Since we are oriented this way, it becomes that

much more difficult to go beyond "subject," to penetrate the crust of a work to discover the meat.

2. Our notion of audience has become on the one hand too vague, and on the other hand too specific. "Children" are not an audience any more than "adults" are. And while we're all too ready to group children by age, reading level, sex, and ethnic origin, we often overlook the diversity of children's intellectual capacities. We're not talking about reading ability here, although reading skill and intellectual capacity may go together. But while there are many adults who have the literal ability to read Saul Bellow, many may not be able to comprehend or enjoy his works. It is undeniably true that there are some people who are more sensitive, more perceptive, better able to deal with subtle ironies and metaphors than others—and the same goes for children.

To say "This is a good book for children" is like saying "This is a good book for people." It's a meaningless expression. And it's not enough to specify "This is a good book for a black child," or to go further and announce "This is a good book for a black child female, age ten, from a ghetto environment, with a reading level of grade four." This tells us nothing about the book. Yet we see this all the time: an attempt to identify a specific audience without realizing that it is not valid to group all black ten-year-old girls who read at a fourth-grade level. Within that group there are highly perceptive children along with others who don't have the emotional and intellectual sophistication to comprehend a work.

3. We have a tendency to judge all of children's literature, particularly fiction, by the same general criteria. In adult literature, we recognize that a distinction exists between what is considered "high" literature and what's called popular or escapist literature. We're aware that there are different standards to be utilized in evaluating them. There are good murder mysteries and bad murder mysteries, and we judge them on terms that we have come to recognize as belonging specifically to the genre. Mysteries are not judged on the same terms as Gothics. One problem in children's literature evolves from an attempt to deal with all of it as "literature," using the same set of standards with every work. Judy Blume, for example, is a good popular writer, and her work should be judged on that level. On the other hand, Virginia Hamilton writes on a whole different level, with subtle themes, complex plots, and a variety of narrative devices. We need a different set of evaluative tools in order to analyze her work.

These three examples are typical of some of the problems that we will have to confront as we work toward a critical theory specifically designed to deal with children's literature. Other problems exist, but in the course of our movement toward a unique approach we will gradually learn to deal with them in a satisfying way. We come to children's literature by way of a variety of disciplines—librarianship, education, English, psychology—and our modes of approach may vary. But this can be a strength, rather than an obstacle, for we can bring to the study of the literature a myriad of exciting ideas, goals, and motives, all of which will contribute to a sound theory that can then be adapted to our individual needs. Criticism is a tool that enables us to reach a better understanding and a deeper appreciation of literature. As we delve deeper into children's literature, our own understanding and appreciation will increase—which will in turn affect the children we influence.

part 2
the territories

PICTURE BOOKS
FAIRY TALES
POETRY
FICTION
FANTASY
HISTORICAL FICTION
SCIENCE FICTION
THE YOUNG ADULT NOVEL

4 / Picture Books

Pictures were not always provided in children's books, although they are inseparable from them today. John Comenius, a Czech educator, is credited with the first picture book for the young; *Orbis Sensualium Pictus* (1657) presented a series of numbered pictures keyed to Latin with vernacular captions, like a crude and primitive version of a Richard Scarry book. John Bunyan's *Book for Boys and Girls; or, Country Rhimes for Children,* originally issued in 1686 with no illustrations at all, became in eighteenth-century reprintings an extremely popular emblem book. And the chapbooks, shared with adults, provided occasional woodblock prints, a device Thomas Boreman and John Newbery enlarged to great advantage. By the end of the century, the illustrated children's book was commonplace. Some few, like *The Birth-day Gift; or, The Joy of a New Doll,* were true picture books, but printed color illustrations were not available for children's books before the nineteenth century, the flowering of which is seen in works by Kate Greenaway and Randolph Caldecott, the artist who first developed the picture book concept to its fullest.[1]

The picture book is not simply any book that happens to contain illustrations. When the artist merely replicates textual detail, the result is an illustrated book. If, however, the illustrator expands or interprets the text, the picture book results. It is not the number of pictures but the function of the art which creates a picture book. Here illustrations take the place of words to set up a contrapuntal relationship with the text, according to Uri Shulevitz. Brian Alderson suggests that no single definition will suffice for what is not a homogeneous group.[2] The picture book cuts through the genre groupings of nonfiction, biography, and so on.

The hard-to-define picture book, like much of the rest of children's literature, is often ignored in standard histories. Alderson found in a current history of book illustration only a few offhand paragraphs on children's picture books.[3]

The artists have been more vocal than the critics. Blair Lent, Maurice Sendak, and Uri Shulevitz all suggest an analogy with filmmaking. Shulevitz notes "the kinship between picture books and theatre or film, the silent film in particular."[4] In his selection herein Marantz echoes this view that the picture book demands an approach less like the still photographs in an illustrated book and more like what used to be known as the moving pictures. Sendak credits Mickey Mouse, Busby Berkeley, and King Kong as being more important influences on his art than William Blake.[5] So, with the artists stressing the cinemagraphic quality of their art, why then, asks Marantz, are picture books still reviewed mostly as literary texts, period? Asserting that text and pictures are equals in a literary-art symbiosis does not guarantee a proper approach to this genre.

Evidence provided by John Warren Stewig provides statistical data for Marantz's charges. Picking fifty reviews of picture books at random from four major journals in 1979, Stewig found more than seventy percent of all the reviews devoted no more and often considerably less than thirty percent of the review space to the visual qualities of books in which pictures are a major, if not the dominant, component.[6] Pictures might dominate a text, but they do not dominate the criticism of such books.

The Matthias and Italiano article demonstrates how little space reviewers devote to purely artistic considerations. Their critical corrective is to show how artists advance narrative through art. Since the literary critic is already familiar with narrative analysis, they have provided another entry point in understanding the symbiosis of pictures and text that results in a picture book.

The most obviously juvenile of the children's book field, the picture book, like the chapbooks from which it evolved, has grown to become a literature often shared with adults. Because the children's picture book is preliterature or protoliterature which an adult reads to a child, it is a necessarily shared literature. The deceptively simple picture book can contain much complexity and reveal much conscious artistry. Some fear that attention to the picture book for adolescents and adults might squeeze out attention to the picture book for the very young. Sendak's *Outside over There* seems adult-child, even a pictorial novel, as *Time* magazine suggests. Elaine Moss complains that in ignoring the audience which now includes some teens and adults, bookstores still relegate the picture book to low shelves for children.[7]

Conventional literary approaches, as Peggy Whalen-Levitt points out, fail to interpret books like *Goodnight Moon* which are only minimally texts. Familiarity with response and/or reception theory, she suggests, might help the critic approach a literary-art book better than conventional textual analysis.[8]

Whatever the approach, a dynamic picture book requires some attention to its visual dimensions. Lance Salway complains about the lack of serious consideration of an artist's work: "An artist's hobbies and the interior decoration of his home are often considered of greater significance than the success or failure of his style and interpretation."[9]

While functioning on a more dynamic level than the illustrated book, the picture book for children should be subject to the same kind of scrutiny devoted to adult artwork.[10] Often, it is not. Maurice Sendak's biographer explains why Sendak sometimes chafes at being downgraded because he produces picture books:

If there's one thing that infuriates him about his chosen battleground, it's having his books looked upon as mere nursery trifles. "When you've worked a year and more on a book, when you've put your life into it, you expect the point of view of the professionals—editors, teachers, librarians—to be somewhat larger. You certainly expect your book to be read by people of all ages.[11]

Although vocabulary level necessarily puts some adult books beyond the reach of children, there is no equivalent grade-level barrier to art. Art is art. Some children's artists are beginning to receive full-length studies; these should meet the demands of scholarship expected of any serious critical study. I am not suggesting ponderous tomes on *Curious George,* but the critical article should be no anomaly in light of the conscious artistry evidenced in the picture book for children.

The Picture Book as Art Object: A Call for Balanced Reviewing

Kenneth Marantz

What I would like to do in this article is to examine the picture book as one particular kind of "thing"—a thing that may well have singular values not currently being exploited by the book reviewers, librarians, and teachers who typically control its destiny. I share Barbara Bader's feeling that these books are a form of art and that as such they demand more knowledgeable and sympathetic treatment than they have been getting. [See Barbara Bader, *American Picturebooks from Noah's Ark to the Beast Within* (New York: Macmillan, 1976).]

From the start, it should be understood that there is a major difference between an illustrated book and a picture book. Imagine a continuum running from a novel like *Treasure Island,* with only a tipped-in frontispiece, to a totally textless book like Mayer's *Frog Goes to Dinner.* At the one extreme you have a written story that an artist has read, responded to, and chosen a single incident of which to depict. Rackham, N. C. Wyeth, and Tenniel are exemplars of artists whose vision and technical skills created appearances for us that fleshed out the more abstract prose. But Caldecott and Crane, closer to the other end of our continuum, usually produced pictures that so dominate the pages as to turn the simple texts into expandable captions. Where the former illustrations can be lifted out of context and displayed as successfully completed images, the latter are dependent upon their sequencing and association with the overall design of page and book, and so suffer a loss of meaning and significance when separated and displayed. The illustrations in the illustrated book can be viewed as still photographs, while the pictures in the picture book demand an approach more like a motion picture.

I in no way wish to suggest here any hierarchy in value or importance. There are informational, aesthetic, emotional, and other values inherent

Reprinted from *The Wilson Library Bulletin,* Oct. 1977, pp. 148–51. Reprinted by permission.

in all visual materials. My concern is that the unique potentials of a book may be obscured if we view it as if it were some other order of thing. A picture book combines some of the attributes of the illustrations in other kinds of books, but it also is a unique expressive form that gains its strength from the totality of its making, including its paper stock, typography, binding, and design. A picture book ought to be much more than some ancillary decoration or visual relief for a literary effort.

REVIEWING THE REVIEWERS

Picture books are reviewed as if they were pieces of literature. What I find in a typical review are some four or five sentences outlining the narrative, a few words of judgment, and most often at the very end, a line or two about the "illustrations." Even a wordless book like Diane de Groat's *Alligator's Toothache* receives this treatment, the review ending with: "The full-color illustrations depict with humor a problem familiar to all young children, who will probably love to 'read' this story aloud with feeling."

Am I to assume from this statement that reading words and "reading" pictures are the same kind of process? If so, then we have the basis for a major argument. But I think not. Other reviews indicate a general reticence to deal with the visual qualities of the pictures. For example, in a review of Steig's *Abel's Island,* a lengthy summary of the text concludes with: "And the delights of the text are further enhanced by his black-and-white drawings." Or again from a review of *The Little Grey Neck:* "The uninspired art work is merely stage dressing." Or from a review of a James Marshall story: "The illustrations, predominantly in yellows, greens, and maroons, provide a gentle, homey feel." Or this, of a *Hägar the Horrible* volume: ". . . with two-color illustrations that are also only so-so. . . ." Or finally from a review of Turska's *The Magician of Cracow:* "The story is beautifully illustrated. Many of the pictures—most are double-page spreads—have an intricate border and all are infused with a warm glow." You can add your own to this list of *total* comments on the look of the book from the pages of any review source.

Perhaps I misunderstand the function of these reviews. I am told and have read that librarians and others frequently make book selections based upon such comments. If so, then what fundamental help is it to tell them so much about the narrative and so very little about *why* the pictures make a difference? What can "enhance" mean, or "uninspired," or "so-so," or even "beautifully illustrated"? What qualities of the *Abel* story find enhancement through Steig's particular use of line, his manner of abstraction, his choice of detail or page layout, and his way of relating the actions on page 5 to those on page 12? In other words, what kinds of values are inherent in the total experience of the book? What can be learned by comparing Steig's drawings with Burningham's or Zemach's or Ungerer's, or even relating them to his cartoons? What is unique about the work and where are the influences? What makes certain pictures "beautiful" and others "homey"? And what characteristics must a picture book have to be called "inspired"?

WORDS AND PICTURES

Undoubtedly my bias as an "art" person is showing. Yet I am also a "word" person who respects the power of literature not only to convey meaning, but also to evoke emotion and extend experience. It is because of this respect for both the visual and the verbal modes of expression that I repeat my claim that picture books are not literature (i.e., word-dominated things), but rather a form of visual art. That they have bound pages in a cover may suggest their relationship to literary books, but it ought not establish their identity with them. What of riddle and joke books, or how-to-do-its, or toy books, or song books, or dictionaries? Do we approach each of these categories with the same appreciative criteria? While sharing some common aspects, they are nevertheless distinctive kinds of objects with particular potential values. I believe that the picture book must be experienced as a visual-verbal entity if its potential values are to be realized and that current practices in schools and the reviewing media fail to recognize these values.

Marjorie Lewis both supports and damns my position. She writes that "the 'art experience' [why the quotation marks?] does have its place, and certainly the picture book is one place for it. But children do not judge their favorites as art experiences. They value them, rightly, for the total experience of story and illustration."[1] This statement seems to me to confuse "experiencing" with "naming." Is it not possible to engage in an activity without knowing the words that have been invented to identify it? We have the delightful example of Molière's Gentleman, who discovered in middle age that he had been speaking prose all his life. Or perhaps the problem is that a verbal-visual experience is excluded from the concept of art? Would this mean that we can't appreciate a song as music because of its lyrics or a painting because of its label?

The *art* of a picture book is indeed in the totality of that book, and although far from refined, children's response to it must therefore be very much an art experience. If it were not, why would they (to use Lewis's words) "return again and again to their own favorites"? Obviously, the novelty of the plot is not as strong as at first reading. What remains is that somewhat mysterious and always personal reactivation of the book experience, each time a bit different as the metaphors grow richer. If this is not an art experience, then I don't know what is.

Lewis notes that "there is no common denominator among good picture books." Nor, would I add, is there a common denominator among children's appreciative interests or abilities. To deny youngsters Hyman's *Snow White* or Baskin's *Hosie's Alphabet* is to cut off for some children two potentially profound art experiences. Would Disney's cardboard heroine be more suitable for "young" eyes? Does picture book appreciation progress in such a structured fashion that all five-year-olds will find Baskin's work "a disappointing book"? Have you ever taken preschoolers through an art gallery and listened to their comments? Or do you steer them only to the "appropriate" age-level pieces? Does growth have to take place only in controlled, tiny stages? "Children do not have *less* taste; they have *different* taste." I prefer to think that this means children as individuals, not collectively. If so, then they deserve the artistic fruits that are now being created, whether Gorey's Victorian humor, or Sendak's cuddly beasts, or Quist's surreal images of our world.

THE DANGERS OF ABUNDANCE

If there is a danger in the increasing numbers of diverse and challenging books, it is that they push some of the older works off the shelves. As Sendak says, "Books don't go out of fashion with children; they go out of fashion with adults. So that kids are deprived of works of art which are no longer around simply because new ones keep coming out."[2]

I believe that one of the factors that motivate librarians and teachers to "grade-level" books is their essential distrust of children's capacities for idiosyncratic learning. Perhaps there is a more fundamental and practical reason for grouping literary books by the range of vocabulary and complexity of syntax—at first learning, the act of decoding words is like a demanding and impersonal science. But picture books tend to use language that can be readily broken into small pieces to fit the overall design. Much of the complexity, the use of metaphor and example, is expressed by the visual elements: the size and shape of the book, the thickness of the paper, the type, the manner in which the artist expresses his or her imagination, and the flow of the tale as the pages are turned. Responding to these qualities demands sensitivities quite different from those needed for reading words alone.

Art objects are important because they have the potential for producing a transcendental experience, a state of mind where new and personal meanings can take shape. An art object is the medium for manufacturing metaphor, for coming to see the world in a different way, for a unique sensual-intellectual experience. There is limited art and weak literature; our shelves are peppered with children's books that seem to have been designed for a single go-through. But there are others that invite repeated visits. These good picture books have the potential to pique curiosity, to extend viewpoints, to refresh wonder, to be experienced again and again, each time with a tangibly different delight.

But how can reviewers tell us about this kind of magic if they regard pictures as ancillary to the text—"and the illustrations were nice, too"? The tendency to use the pictures merely to reinforce the meaning of the words causes us to overlook the orchestration of the visual components, which, in reality, are the picture book. The game should not be looking for the meanings, but rather one of creating meanings from the clues produced by the author-illustrator-designer. Reviewers will have to learn to distinguish these clues, the better to discuss the "how" and the "why" instead of the "what" of the book. They will have to make their appraisals of the visual qualities central, rather than peripheral, to the task. Picture books are not literary works to be read. They are art objects to be experienced.

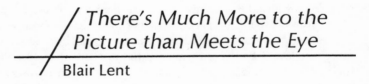

There's Much More to the Picture than Meets the Eye

Blair Lent

I first became a picture book fan as a boy. I cared about how the pictures had been made by the artist—the way colors had been used and how the colors made me feel. (I liked books without color, too, especially if the pictures had a lot of things going on in them.) I cared about how the pictures in a book had been made, but I cared just as much about

Reprinted from *The Wilson Library Bulletin*, Oct. 1977, pp. 161–64. Reprinted by permission. Copyright © 1977 by The H. W. Wilson Company.

the stories the pictures would tell—the stories they would tell *with the words.*

I have many picture books now—my shelves at home are sagging with them—and I still feel that the marriage of words and art is what makes picture books unlike any others.

APPLES AND ORANGES

First, let me say that I feel there is a difference between the picture book and the illustrated book. The former *needs* pictures, while the latter does not. A picture book is more often the artist's medium; an illustrated book, the author's.

Does this mean that Alice doesn't need Tenniel, Mole and Rat don't need Rackham, Charlotte doesn't need Garth Williams? However excellent these illustrations, they are not really vital to an understanding of the authors' words. Many picture books, on the other hand, do require artwork to tell part of the story. And some have no words at all.

Usually an illustration in an illustrated book will describe only one sentence or paragraph out of many in the text. There can be from two to one hundred pages of type between each illustration. Not only will an illustration in such a book almost repeat what a sentence in the text describes, but sometimes the sentence will itself be printed as a caption beneath the picture.

When artists create pictures for a picture book, they are *combining* pictures and words; but when they work with illustrations, the pictures appear separated from the text. Although an illustrated book can have more illustrations than a picture book (if the book has a long text, say), an artist working with this kind of book does not have to be concerned about how one drawing or painting follows another.

HOLY ALLIANCE

It is strange that picture books are cataloged and very often reviewed as though they were only *written*, instead of being understood as collaborations between artist and writer. Too often the art in picture books is considered to be mere decoration for the text. The casual reader will remain completely unaware of the part the artist has to play in the telling of the story, thinking of the pictures as *repeating*, rather than *continuing* the text.

Artists are intrigued by stories that offer them the opportunity to elaborate. Descriptions may need to be fleshed out with pictures; sentences may seem incomplete without artwork. A sentence like "Suzy went to the barn to feed the cows" can inspire picture after picture. What does

Suzy see along the way? Whom does she meet? What does she imagine as she walks along? The words may disappear while the artist, inspired by one short sentence, fills the pages, spinning out his or her own part of the tale.

Picture books can teach the beginning reader the meaning of words by placing a word or sentence beside a picture of the same thing. But they can do much more than that. A child will learn to understand even more words when the words and pictures weave in and out of one another. Take away the words and what do the pictures mean? Take away the pictures and what do the words mean?

Such a book stimulates interest in the printed word because the words must be read for the story to be understood. If the words only repeat the pictures, children may not be interested in reading them more than a few times, but if they tell a different part of the story, they will want to read them in order to enjoy and experience the story more fully.

Picture books are often read aloud, and this is when children may first become familiar with the written part of a story. They may hear new words first, then look at them, and then repeat them. Some words can be difficult and unfamiliar but still be fun to say, words like rutabaga, or aspidistra, or samovar. Pictures can suggest what the words mean.

LESS IS MORE

Since a picture book doesn't have as many words as other books, every word, every sentence becomes that much more important. A sentence appearing by itself draws more attention than if part of a paragraph. The words as well as the pictures can make the reader want to turn the page for more.

If the artist is also the writer, it becomes easier to work with the structure of the story while the pictures are being created, to substitute a picture for words, or vice versa. Obviously, this is more difficult when the writer is someone who lives hundreds of miles away, who might feel, with too many suggested changes, that the artist is trying to rewrite the story. (A well constructed tale written by someone else can be weakened by the artist—it is usually better for the book if the latter asks for very few changes. Artists who like to alter the written story as they go along should try to work only with their own words.)

All artist-authors work differently from their colleagues—and often differently from book to book. Some write the story first, others make the sketches; but many go back and forth between the two, almost writing and drawing simultaneously, entering into each medium when it is time for it to tell its part of the story.

Picture book artists usually prefer to write very spare texts, not because they can't write, but because they are able to tell so much of the story with pictures. This is not to imply that authors who work exclusively with words are unable or reluctant to write picture book stories with few words: often such books make the most delightful reading. There are many writers who have—like many artists—a special affinity for the picture book genre.

WORDS, WORDS, WORDS

Of course, a writer, who is more used to expressing things with words, will be able to create a very rich story that an artist, a visual person, could not. Many artists have never learned, either from experience or instruction, how to write well for their pictures. Even adapting a folktale or legend takes a special skill—there's more to it than just making the story shorter or longer. When adapted, it can lose its original flavor and sound, which only someone familiar with words can retain or enhance.

Even when a writer who has not thought in terms of a picture book leaves no space for pictures, there is still much that an artist can do to enhance the material, to give an added dimension to the author's words. Many stories that have been used successfully in picture books were written long before the form was even invented. Often contemporary stories and poems become effective picture books because the artist has been able to interpret them in an entirely new way, seeing something in them that not even the author had seen before.

If a picture book is a collaboration, why does the artist more often have greater influence over what the book will become? Because the picture book, dominated by the artwork, is experienced by the reader primarily through its visual images. Stories are chosen because of their "picture possibilities," almost the way a libretto is chosen by a composer for the music it might inspire.

Picture book artists often choose manuscripts because of the sequence of images they see in their minds as they read the story. What will the effect be when the page is turned? A surprise? Or an answer? *A picture book depends upon the turning of pages and how one picture follows another.* The artist thinks in terms of close-ups and long shots, movement and dialogue, almost the same way a filmmaker does. But unlike the filmmaker, a picture-book–maker has created something that readers can experience at their own pace, choosing to dwell on some pages in a different way each time the book is read.

Movement, so characteristic of picture books, is especially interesting to the artist, not only in landscapes that undulate from one page to the next, but in characters who may leap and whirl across the paper and from one page to the next. It's not at all surprising that there are some picture book artists who have been dancers. This preoccupation with movement, the continuation from page to page, and this concern that words move with the pictures, is one of the things that make picture books unique.

CREATING THE PICTURE BOOK

An artist working on a picture book is very much involved with the art director in the book's design—the book's shape, number of pages, and typography must all be determined. A picture book about a lighthouse, for example, might be vertical; a book about the desert, horizontal. Picture books come in different shapes and sizes, determined by their subject or mood. The number of pages is often determined by the number of pictures it will take to tell the story, the artist sometimes needing four pages of pictures for one short sentence of the text.

Type is chosen from catalogs that show hundreds of styles and weights, chosen as carefully as the colors the artist will use. The type must work with the picture on every page; it should not crowd it or compete with it. Good typography usually isn't noticed by readers because it is in harmony with the pictures, in its proper place in the scheme of the book.

Artists aren't necessarily interested in color and shape and line for their own sake. These are their tools, enabling them to express thoughts and ideas. If the art in a picture book is experienced only in relation to these tools and can be described only in terms of color or line, then readers will miss its full significance—much like judging a text by the number or quality of its adjectives.

Artists exaggerate for effect. They select what they feel is interesting about a subject and put that into their pictures, omitting or merely suggesting the details that do not help express their ideas. When they draw buildings, they may alter perspectives; when they draw people, they may emphasize some features and play down others. One artist may use a realistic rendering to describe a form, while another may see the same thing as something closer to abstraction, using only a few quick lines. This is the artist's language, the means of conveying experience to others, experience that so often cannot be described with words.

While making a picture book, the artist can be as curious about the details of things as the young reader will be on looking through the printed book. As a boy, I remember being disappointed by pictures that showed the inside of a house if the artist forgot to put in the stairs. But I never used to mind when other things were left out. Villages without skies, or white space around a picture that might leave a room incompletely defined didn't bother me. Why does an artist leave some things out, but fill other parts of the picture with detail? Do the details reflect the things that the artist looked for in a book when a child?

KEEPING IN TOUCH

Picture book artists are storytellers. Many seem to be in touch with their own childhood and still love the same kinds of things that fascinate children. Many people who are not artists can remember creating story-pictures when they were young. These tales would sprawl all across one big sheet of paper and off onto another as the fantasy unfolded, almost like hieroglyphics. Most good picture book artists can still remember just what they put into these early attempts at art; they remember, too, what they looked for in picture books when they were children.

The picture book is a form of art that can give readers experiences they can get in no other way. There is much more to the pictures in a picture book than meets the eye.

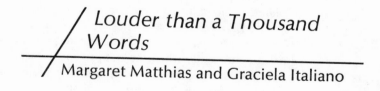

/ *Louder than a Thousand Words*

/ Margaret Matthias and Graciela Italiano

For children books begin with pictures, and the child of the eighties has much to be thankful for as thousands of picture storybooks roll off the presses each year lining the shelves of home, school, and library to await the interested reader. But, with the profusion of books comes the responsibility of making choices between what is worth sharing and what is not. Efforts to establish standards of quality for the picture storybook resulted in awarding the Caldecott Medal, established in 1938, to the artist of the most distinguished American picture storybook for children

Adapted from a talk delivered at the Association for Childhood Education International Conference, Chicago, Sept. 18, 1981.

published in the United States during the preceding year.[1] However, apparent discontent with the award process has suggested the need for a closer look at what makes a good picture storybook. There appear to be at least two prevailing and contrasting points of view.

Relatively uninformed adults often make their picture storybook purchases on the basis of the visual, aesthetic experiences of the artwork and are genuinely puzzled when youngsters cast the book aside after the first sharing. In contrast, many reviewers of picture storybooks imply that the text has more importance than the illustrations. This can be seen in the format of most reviews which consist of several sentences outlining the narrative, a few critical comments, and a very short ending sentence about the illustrations such as, "The simple drawings in orange, brown, and black stress each nuance of the childlike story,"[2] or "The simple, kindly story is illustrated with large, flat, three color drawings."[3] Neither viewpoint deals effectively with the problem of evaluating the unique literary art form of the picture storybook. The illustrator of books for young children must be concerned not only with creating a visual, aesthetic experience for the child but also with enriching the story and extending the text.

Enrichment of story and extension of text are critical roles when considered in the context of the major audience for whom the picture storybook is planned, the child under eight years of age, the relatively unproficient reader. Like others, the young child will return to favorite books time after time often without an adult to interpret the print. It is during those private moments, when the nonproficient reader wishes to relive an enjoyed experience with a book, that the picture storybook comes into its own. Compare the child's lonely return to Grahame's dawn as it breaks over ten solid pages of print in *The Wind in the Willows* to the same child's joyous reencounter with the awe-inspiring beauty of a new day's birth in Shulevitz's *Dawn*. Grahame's medium is language. Shulevitz chooses language as the seed from which the visual image of his dawn may unfold. Text and illustration combine to portray this universe of silent wonder. Both Grahame and Shulevitz are artists, each choosing a different medium to convey the same meaningful message as he describes the awesome beauty of the new day. But, for the younger child, Shulevitz provides the rich visual referents needed to bring meaning to language, and to extend the background of experiences upon which a love for literature is founded.

Compilers of picture storybooks must realize their major audience brings limited attention, verbal understanding, and experiential background to the pages of a book. The visual, aesthetic extension and enrichment of a dynamic storyline are what produce the fondly remembered picture storybook.

The good illustrator is indeed a storyteller and as such should be required to attain the same levels of excellence in his or her story development as the storyteller whose medium is words alone. The same questions of literary quality may be applied to both author and illustrator storyteller in evaluating character development, plot development, setting, theme, and style.

According to Lukens, a character can be revealed by actions, speech, appearance, others' comments, and comments the author makes about the character visually.[4] In *Lentil* by Robert McCloskey, the hero is introduced with one sentence, "In the town of Alto, Ohio, there lived a boy named Lentil." McCloskey's sketches give the additional background information we need to become better acquainted with the pleasantly untidy, happy-go-lucky, barefooted boy. We are told that Lentil could not sing. The ear-splitting truth of that statement is strongly emphasized in the pictured responses of Lentil's teacher, classmates, and animal friends. Their nonverbal reactions are visually communicative of their dismay at hearing Lentil's efforts to sing. Lentil's determination to make music is described in the text as he saves up to buy a harmonica. It is further emphasized by the text as it lists the places he practiced it. But his developing skill in playing the harmonica is defined only through the illustrations which show the changing reactions of other characters to his music as their responses progress from displays of horror to those of obvious pleasure. It therefore comes as no surprise when Lentil is able to save the town from embarrassment as he provides the musical welcome for Colonel Carter.

Solid character development is a very important element in the creation of a pleasurable and lasting story for children, as well as for adults. The role of the illustrating storyteller is to create pictures that have storytelling qualities. She or he visualizes for the child the characters of the story through their actions, appearance, his or her own comments, and comments other characters make.

"Character study alone rarely carries the child's interest, but character becomes inextricably woven into plot." A common plot in the most simple of picture storybooks is often that of presenting a familiar reality with memorable language and illustrations thus allowing the reader to experience it with a fresh perspective.[5] Eric Carle's unique rendition of the life-cycle of the butterfly in *The Very Hungry Caterpillar* is particularly effective in design. It provides the child reader a visual representation of the developing plot. The pages get larger as the caterpillar eats more and grows bigger until, after a temporary stomachache and a long sleep in his silken cocoon, the double-page spread of his emergence as a beautiful colorful butterfly concludes this excellent picture storybook. This imaginative way of visually representing the simple, repetitive text allows the child who does not read yet to "read" this book through its pictures, thus "seeing" the sequence of events laid out by the illustrator and designer of the book.

The chronological development of the plot may be visually documented more subtly as is true in J. Graham's *I Love You Mouse,* illustrated by Tomie de Paola. The black-and-white charcoal drawings are accompanied by subtle shading of the sky as the day progresses until, as the moon starts to rise, the little boy is put to bed. Never mentioned in the text, the chronological order of the developing plot is evidenced in the illustrations.

Representation of conflict is also enhanced by illustrations which may visually capture the struggle of protagonists against antagonistic forces. In his colorful book, *Hi Cat!,* Ezra Jack Keats creates a powerful scene where the major conflict of the story is revealed. Even the text is given extra visual meaning as the one word "MEEOOW!" is spelled in large black letters at the bottom of the page. In the foreground, the dark silhouettes of an adult pulling a child away from the scene add to the frightening mood of the image. Again, the illustrator has assumed the role of visual storyteller in communicating his powerful message to the child unable to decode the words alone.

The time and place of a story may be integral to its development or merely provide a backdrop for it. In *Goggles* Keats's detailed visual description of the city is integral to the action of the story and the establishment of its troubled mood, while in *A Snowy Day* his masterful composition of colorful flat geometric shapes merely evokes the concept of city as a backdrop to Peter's adventures in the snow.

As the illustrating storyteller visually develops characters and plot, the theme of the story is evidenced. Tomie de Paola's illustrations in *Charlie Needs a New Cloak* suggest a variety of themes. While the text and accompanying illustrations direct the reader's attention to the explicit theme, further examination of the illustrations will uncover the implicit theme of Charlie's harmonious relationship with his flock. The dynamic, action-filled illustrations are alive with humor and meaning, much of which is not even implied by the text.

Lukens defines style as "how an author says something as opposed to what he or she says."[6] This definition can also be applied to the artistic style of the illustrator. Robert McCloskey adjusts his artistic style to enhance the nature of the story he tells. The brown and white lithographs in *Make Way for Ducklings* are drawn in detail providing an excellent "duck's-eye-view" of Boston where Mr. and Mrs. Mallard must raise their family. This technique is particularly appropriate in creating the soft texture of the duck's plumage. In contrast, for *Time of Wonder,* McCloskey chose watercolors to paint his world of sea, bays and islands. His representation of this environment in color zones is superb. Color prevails: it delineates figures, creates setting, and establishes mood. McCloskey, as a master of visual storytelling, chooses his medium and uses it to fit the essence of the story.

In summary, the illustrator as visual developer of character and plot, as one who establishes pictorially the setting and theme of a story, is critical in providing for the young child meaningful and enjoyable experiences with books. The author's medium is language alone. The illustrator uses the simple language of the picture storybook as the seed from which his pictorial narrative may bloom. Both author and illustrator attempt to communicate the elements of a rich and lively story. Each uses his own unique medium. Words alone will not call a young child back to a story. The visual creation of lively characters and of action, humor, and pathos as accompaniment to a clever text heralds the presence of a master storyteller, a true illustrator whose work will be cherished by children of all ages.

CHILDREN'S BOOKS CITED

Carle, Eric. *The Very Hungry Caterpiller,* Cleveland: Collins/World, 1976.

de Paola, Tomie. *Charlie Needs a New Cloak.* Englewood Cliffs, N. J.: Prentice-Hall, 1974.

Graham, J. *I Love You Mouse.* Illus. by Tomie de Paola. New York: Harcourt, Brace, 1976.

Grahame, Kenneth. *The Wind in the Willows.* New York: Heritage Press, 1940.

Keats, Ezra J. *Hi Cat!* New York: Macmillan, 1970.

Keats, Ezra J. *Goggles.* New York: Macmillan, 1969.

McCloskey, Robert. *Lentil.* New York: Viking, 1940.

McCloskey, Robert. *Make Way for Ducklings.* New York: Viking, 1941.

McCloskey, Robert. *Time of Wonder.* New York: Viking, 1957.

Shulevitz, Uri. *Dawn.* New York: Farrar, Straus, 1974.

5 / Fairy Tales

Springing from the folktale, fairy tales did not start out as tales for children. For the courtiers of Louis XIV, Charles Perrault transformed oral tales to fashionable literary stories. In England the fairy story, imported or domestic, was seldom sanctioned for children before the 1800s. Thomas Boreman, who preceded John Newbery in the publishing of books for children in London, vowed that in his *Gigantick Histories* (1740–42):

> Tom Thumb shall now be thrown away
> and Jack who did the Giants slay;
> Such ill concerted artless lyes
> Our British Youth shall now despise.

A half century later, Maria Edgeworth summarily excluded fairy tales because she felt they were not much read. A climate of opinion, a holdover from the Puritans of the seventeenth century, forbade works of magic and the supernatural. Such things as "moon-leaping cows, Banbury cock-horses, booted cats . . . were the imbecilities of the peasantry."[1]

Defenders of the fairy tale appear in the later eighteenth century. Coleridge knew the case against the fairy tale, but he testified for the genre, exclaiming, "I know no other way of giving the mind a love of the Great and the Whole." Wordsworth also rose to defend the fairy tale, praising the "forgers of daring tales" and blasting the English Rousseauists who sacrificed imagination to morality.

The Wordsworth-Coleridge defense remained a minority view for at least a generation. The Grimms' *Kinder-und Haus-Märchen* (3 vols.: 1812, 1815, 1822) were in English translation in 1823. By the 1840s, one hundred years after Boreman's interdiction, the fairy tale received its long overdue general approbation for English children.

What by now has been popularly received is not always so acclaimed by the critics. Perry Nodelman shows in his article how the fairy story, reduced to its simple components (repetition, formulas, and so forth),

166

attracts the audience but confounds the critic. Nodelman demonstrates how standard critical approaches to narrative have to be modified or scrapped to meet the challenge of the peculiar fairy tale.

The limitations which repel critics often attract authors. In the fairy tale's brevity, restraints, and hostility to analysis and digression C. S. Lewis found "the ideal Form for the stuff I had to say."[2] It would be helpful then to find what distinguishes the fairy tale from other genres. In her contribution Catherine Storr shows how it differs from the folk tale. Brian Hooker discusses "the sense of the type" of fairy tales, maintaining that the presence of supernatural elements is not enough to stamp a tale a fairy tale. He categorizes the fairy tale as "a Local Color story whose controlling environment is imaginary." Note the stress on environment. In *The Classic Fairy Tales* Iona and Peter Opie also classify the genre as imaginative narrative with a strong situational focus.

Fairy tales are more concerned with situation than with character. They are the space fiction of the past. They describe events that took place when a different range of possibilities operated in the unidentified long ago; and this is part of their attraction.[3]

Because fairy tales are less fixed in meaning than allegory and are more symbolic, Hooker declares "any meaning is fit that fits." Besides the myriad interpretations possible, another complication for the critic is the establishment of a text, no easy matter (witness the one thousand "versions" of Cinderella which scholars have found). And to compound the matter, some narrative theorists would see all interpretations, even plot summaries of a fairy tale, as new "versions," each dependent on the motives of the narrator.[4]

While the term "fairy tale" dates from the mid-eighteenth century, fairy tales were told centuries before that. The Cinderella tale in some form has existed for a thousand years. Given the history of fairy tales and the countless versions of each tale, it is no surprise that they can serve many disciplines such as psychiatry. It should not be surprising that Bruno Bettelheim can demonstrate in *The Uses of Enchantment* that one can read fairy tales to a child for their Freudian bibliothera-peutic benefits.[5] In the 1920s critics like Hooker were already sanctioning such interpretations. Hooker is right about the binocularity of fairy tales. Direct and symbolic, inevitable and surprising, they manifest a perennial appeal to adult and child, if not always to the protectors of youth or the critics of literature.

Fairy Tales

Brian Hooker

The present day is exhibiting a curiously vivid interest in fairy tales; curious because that passionate self-consciousness which is always with us finds the foreground of its mirror filled with machinery, busy under a canopy of smoke; and it seems strange to discover the livid vapor shadowing forth the wings of dragons, or the faces of the little people glimmering between the wheels. Perhaps our very materialism is responsible for this new hunger after fancy. Because the world, never so bluntly actual as now, is too much with us, we spend our vacations upon the foam of perilous seas; while the scientific spirit, having charted the whole orb of fact, begins to weep the tears of Alexander. Certainly, for whatever cause, we have taken up the exploration of impossible fairyland with an instinctive eagerness which would have surprised folk of half a century ago even more than it surprises ourselves. And it is not without interesting significance that within the last few years the *Rose and the Ring* and *Alice in Wonderland* have assumed the dignity of classics; that Mr. Kipling, high priest of modernism, has revived the mediaeval beast fables; that Mr. H. G. Wells, political economist, pleases himself and us by making science the handmaid of elaborate absurdity; that the Secretary of the Bank of England is best known for his child fancies [Kenneth Grahame, author of *The Wind in the Willows*]; that a rising poet puts his wisdom into the mouth of babes; while a prominent critic and philosopher quaintly declares *Jack the Giant Killer* an epitome of the whole story of man.

Perhaps at first glance we should hardly recognize among fairy tales all of these contemporary examples; and it may therefore be the more worthwhile to trace their genealogy and point out their family resemblances. It is not strange that the type has never been defined; for fairy tales have long been relegated to the nursery; and children are well content to sense the nature of a thing without caring for analysis. But children today are possibly as indifferent to fairyland as the laws of childhood allow. It is we grown people, with our Babel tendency to orna-

Reprinted from *Forum* 40:375–84 (1908).

ment old things with new names, who have taken over the territory and with conquest brought confusion. Yet the sense of the type remains. Everyone would probably agree that if *Puss in Boots* is a fairy story *The White Seal* is another; whereas *Bob, Son of Battle,* although its hero is an animal, falls outside the category: or that *Aladdin* and *The Food of the Gods* are alike by the magic that is in them; while Poe's *Ligeia,* equally dependent upon the supernatural, is another thing. Indeed the fairy tale is of simple nature, not difficult to define; and such analysis as needs must open the door to discussion of its present popularity may conveniently be made through comparison with two kindred popular types: the supernatural story and the story of local color.

Of the many narratives wherein the supernatural plays a minor or major part, only a small portion may reasonably be called fairy tales. One would hardly so designate the *Odyssey,* for example; and indeed, so misty is the horizon of our world, that most fiction, like most life, is touched with some adumbration from beyond. That responsive cry in the night which Currer Bell intended as frankly mysterious we smugly rationalize by renaming it telepathy. At the other end of the scale such stories as *La Venus d'Ille* and Mr. Bram Stoker's *Dracula* are dominated by the supernatural, yet without being fairy tales. It is not essentially distinctive that *Markheim* is more deeply tinged with mystery than *The Ugly Duckling*. What makes the one, broadly speaking, a ghost story, and numbers the other among fairy tales, is that the first represents an incursion of the other world into human life; whereas the other at one stroke locates itself in the world of fancy by imputing human life to an existence whose actualities we can only imagine. Similarly, Scrooge may be haunted by three spirits; but it is Wonderland which is haunted by Alice. Mr. Kipling's *In the Rukh* shows the half-magical Mowgli invading ordinary India; but in the rest of the series it is Mowgli the human child who invades the extraordinary Jungle. *Hamlet* and *Macbeth* introduce a supernatural element into their account of our life; *The Tempest* lies on the borderland, a supernatural story wherein it is still enchantment which intrudes upon humanity; but the *Midsummer Night's Dream* is a typical fairy tale of human intrusion upon fairyland. So, in comparison with the *Odyssey, Paradise Lost* lies more near the border; and the *Divine Comedy* is truly a fairy tale glorified into mythology. For the fairy tale deals with natural life in the spiritual world.

And herein lies its kinship to all stories of local color. The local color story has for its theme the character of some specific environment: as in *The Outcasts of Poker Flat,* plot, persons, and tone are conditioned by the Wild West; or as capitalized society presides over *The House of*

Mirth. Stories like these happening elsewhere would happen otherwise to another kind of people. Now a fairy tale is a local color story whose controlling environment is imaginary: the Jungle, Wonderland, That Country; not of indefinite place or time like *The Mask of the Red Death*, but of some definite, highly organic Never and Nowhere; conditioned in plot, persons, and tone by a locality wholly and truly imagined. It is difficult in this connection to avoid the abominable word anthropomorphism; to suggest it is perhaps enough. For we refer our fabulous creations to humanity, not by endowing them allegorically with human qualities, but by heightening what we see of their own. Baloo is not an ursine old man, but an idealized bear; the Tin Soldier is tin first and soldierly afterwards; and Wonderland, for all its satiric symbolism, is controlled by its own laws, not by ours. This distinction becomes evident upon comparing Wonderland with the territory of *Pilgrim's Progress,* where human life is reflected. If the fairy tale is in respect of its magic the converse of the story of mystery, it is in respect of its organism the converse of allegory.

Nevertheless the element of symbolic reference to human affairs, common although inessential in the fairy tales of all times, has become exceedingly prominent in those of our own. This naturally results from the increase of adult readers; for maturity chuckles over satirical sidelights invisible to childhood. The child enjoys the chaos of the Duchess' kitchen and the Mock Turtle's lamentable reminiscences as pure narrative; while his mother blissfully perceives a reference to the servant problem, and his father smiles over the satire on literary sentimentalism. Returning after twenty years to a perusal of *The Rose and the Ring* one makes delicious discovery of the historical romance, the brimming pathos of Dickens, the middle class Briticism of the Guelph; where long before he thrilled with the gallantry of Hedzoff, wept for Rosalba desolate in her bare feet among the snowdrifts, and panted with suspense lest the deliberate eating of a muffin delay overlong Prince Bulbo's reprieve. To the nursery the Bandar-Log is simply the Monkey-People; the library recognizes a Latin republic; and I have seen a group of professors formulating with academic finality the destinies of America, thrown into confusion of tongues by the poignant quotation: "Brother, thy tail hangs down behind."

But at this point symbolism and allegory must be clearly distinguished. Confusion between the two, which is responsible for all scholarly miscomprehension of mythology, should not blur our vision of the fairy tale. The difference is merely that between metaphor and simile. Allegory explicitly compares the struggle of a traveller wading through a bog to the conflict of religion with despondency; symbolism implies a likeness between snow and purity, by speaking of the one in terms of the other. Allegory represents concrete realities by an abstraction; symbolism represents the abstract concretely. Thus, *Everyman* is an allegory of the coming of death; it means that and nothing else; its figures typify the soul, its attributes, and its last grim guests in the house of clay. Fire, on the other hand, symbolizes with equal fitness love, pestilence, ruin, religion, and life; embodying in its different aspects something of each idea. Dives is an allegorical figure; the crown of thorns is a symbol. Indeed the danger of confusing the two arises mainly from the frequent use of symbols by which allegory points its meaning; as, for example, the seed, the wind, and the weeds in the parable of the Sower. Allegory is only a crude and somewhat outworn method of narration; symbolism is the very lifeblood of all poetry.

Thus the White Rabbit symbolizes fussiness, and Artemis virginity; but the fall into the cucumber-frame is neither more nor less allegorical then the story of Endymion. For a symbolic figure is free to all acts and accidents within the law of its material nature. There are many meanings in the wrath of the goddess against Actaeon; that her method of vengeance is to set his own dogs upon him has no particular significance, but is merely beautiful narrative. It is this natural freedom of the symbol which permits the fairy tale to be at once perfect as pure art to the child and richly meaningful to maturity. If you would appreciate the Caterpillar as a bit of inspired characterization, consider the countenance of a hop-worm when it uprears itself to look horribly upon you; and in respect of his symbolism, go study literature and humanity. You will find his counterparts in the *Book of Snobs,* in *The Egoist,* in the lecture room or the police force; you will discover his relationship to Polonius, to Socrates, to your Uncle John. You will learn why he sits upon a mushroom; but not why sheer imagination depicts him smoking a hookah. Only, unless you are preparing a thesis upon folklore for the degree of Doctor of Philosophy, do not pretend that his exit after conversing with Alice represents Arrogance laying aside Authority, and descending from Conceit to crawl amid the grass of Humility after encountering the Spirit of Childhood.

Moreover, this autonomy of symbolism opens to the reader innumerable new trails of implication. Any meaning is fit that fits. It matters nothing whether the author intended it or no. Indeed the suggestiveness of the older fairy tales arises almost unconsciously from the naive concreteness of their artistry; while modern mythologers are more definitely intentional. *Cinderella* was written without reference to the dignity of labor; *The Rose and the Ring* purposely caricatures G. P. R. James. And the modern art, insofar as it is more definite, sets boundaries to its suggestion; for, indeed, the less a symbol expresses, the more it may imply. Because Cinderella is innocently and utterly herself, our wiser eyes may know her for the little sister of Jean Valjean; whereas the moiety of Count Kutasoff Hedzoff dies with the school of romanticism which he travesties. *Jack the Giant Killer* was written frankly as fable, and so contains the history of humanity for Mr. Chesterton to discover; the *Ancient Mariner,* approaching allegory, implies little else. The universe is globed in a drop of dew but not in a bowl of goldfish.

Yet however we emphasize today the critical and satiric element of our fairy tales, however eagerly we read symbolism in or into them, all this remains their least important phase. It is apparent only to the few; the mental binocularity which observes it is a faculty of age; and fairyland is the heritage of all children, regardless of the accident of years. The immortality of great phantasy is independent of reference, above intellect, rooted in the child-heart of humankind. It appeals to perception, which is older and younger than thought, more intimate, more real: as roses and rhythm please deeplier than may be disclosed by any delving of botany or metrics; for it appeals to the eternal spirit of romance. This, like the names of other great verities, such as for instance art and love, embarrasses comprehension by its rich meaning. *The Scarlet Letter* is romantic—in the perfectly clear sense that its idea is presented deductively; but so is Shelley's *Indian Serenade,* which is not narrative; so is Turner's *Ulysses and Polyphemus,* which is not literature; so at its first hearing was the Seventh Symphony, now called classical; so are such actualities as the death of Nathan Hale, the life of Lafcadio Hearn, the city of Venice, the character of Captain Kidd, the love of Dante. Now what is commonly essential of all these, and which is therefore the essence of romance, is the actualization of ideality. In other words, Nathan Hale died romantically in that he embodied the common ideal of heroic death; and Captain Kidd is romantic as a sashed and booted emblem of piracy; the *Ulysses and Polyphemus* pictures the spirit of the Odyssey; the Seventh Symphony is plangent with strains theretofore unheard but inherently musical, and latterly familiarized into classicism. Here we discover why romance implies strangeness, novelty, adventure, the contrary of the commonplace. For obviously, an ideal for better or for worse transcends any embodiment; and less obviously, every fact embodies by very actuality something of its idea. The rose of all roses never bloomed in any garden upon earth; and yet every rosebud in your own garden embodies it imperfectly and in part. Only, you are not likely to think of these ordinary flowers as incarnations of the ideal. It is the rose once given you at dusk, whose spiritual meaning is made manifest to you by association, which you find romantic. And by a quaint irony, the ultimate insistence upon the ideality of ordinary things is reserved to naturalism. Indeed, the realist's denial of romance is a thing of huge and jovial humor, like the pantheist's denial of God. For instead of leading you among enchanted islands or old unhappy far-off things, he says solemnly: "Romance is falsehood; therefore step down with me into the laundry, and behold the soul of things as they are." His worship of romance outdoes her own followers, as the Persians deified Alexander. She wings materialism to fly from her; they reckon ill who leave her out.

And of romance in this broader sense, the fairy tale is the purest narrative type. For the fairy tale makes its every reader Robinson Crusoe. In that conversion of the supernatural which represents the haunting of other worlds by humanity, it leads us upon marvellous voyages, exhaustless of satisfying mystery, wherein all fancy is fulfilled, no adventure impossible. It is difficult for the educated modern to find the pleasure of the pioneer. For we know the national debt of Ormus and of Ind; we have anchored Atlantis to a meridian, and extended the Monroe Doctrine to Eldorado; computed the facial angle of the men whose heads do grow beneath their shoulders, and knitted sanitary underwear for the Anthropophagi. We have reaped the wonder of this world; but for those of us who grow weary of gleaning with realism among the alien corn, fancy still beckons toward the Jungle, Wonderland, Crim Tartary, the Forest of Wild Thyme, the Round Table, the Lodge of Locomotives; worlds without end, that no study can outwear. For though we travel forever with Odysseus we shall not learn what song the Sirens sang.

Many, however, of our later explorations in fairyland have been confined to border provinces of the hither side, wherein we venture timidly with backward glances to see if Policeman Day pursues; fearful of the tribute these frontier States pay secretly to Oberon under cloak of a commonsensical grin. To speak in a mean, we are a trifle undecided and more unwilling to reckon among fairy tales such types as *.007, The Walking Delegate,* the pseudo-science of Mr. H. G. Wells, the child-myths of Mr. Kenneth Grahame and Josephine Daskam Bacon. Yet the first two deal with creatures no more actual than the Cheshire Cat or the Steadfast Tin Soldier; the science-magicians walk with Alice through the looking-glass; and those stories which convey us into the immemorable psychology of childhood, though lying nearer the line, work in a medium no less truly fanciful than the soul-substance of Undine. The test is that all these stories are conditioned by an environment incommensurable with fact. But in a discussion concerned, like the present, rather with content than with form, nothing is gained by rigidity of distinction. We must know precisely what a sonnet is not, lest we lose the proven form in futile variations; but we care what a problem play is, only that we may trace the type through all its varieties. It is important to the zoölogist that a bat is not a bird; what interests the observer is that it can fly. Accordingly it is more profitable to observe how far through present literature the fairy tale extends its ramifications than to examine whether *The War of the Worlds* is almost a fairy tale or almost a ghost story. Mr. Wells's luridly imaginative nightmare is undoubtedly near akin to both, without pretension to be either. But certain mythographers of the borderland, influenced possibly by that shyness toward ideality to which I have alluded above, claim tacitly or explicitly for their fables a foundation upon fact; and this claim, for the honor of franker fabulists and in justice to the doubtful narratives themselves, must be denied. Mr. Ernest Seton-Thompson, following the lead of the *Jungle Book,* has produced a number of interesting animal-stories which he expressly refers to actuality. Some of these, like *Wully* and *Johnny Bear,* are quite realistic, narrated wholly from the human point of view; others, like *Krag the Kootenai Ram,* adopting the animal view point, became evident fairy tales of the *Ugly Duckling* variety. The debated question whether the facts from which the author pretends to induce his ideas are correct has nothing to do with the case against him; nor is his plea of having only, like all novelists, combined several individuals in one character an admissible defence. You may study accurately the operation of a locomotive or combine your observations of the antics of innumerable monkeys; but you cannot induce therefrom the psychology of .007 or the race-ghost of the Bandar-Log. These can only be imagined; and to imagine them truly is a wise and worthy act. So also is the mule a wise and valuable animal, but it will not do to pretend that he is a horse. Some of Mr. Seton-Thompson's fairy tales are of considerable power; but they would touch more deeply if they were more purely imaginative; and to sentimentalize over animal emotions professedly induced from human observation insults realism and romance alike. An even greater offence against the same principle is that vivid and stirring novel *The Call of the Wild.* Mr. Jack London holds certain social and ethical beliefs with which the present is no occasion to take issue. He writes a novel upon the theme that Violence is mighty and shall prevail, and writes it from the point of view of an epic sledge-dog who is kidnapped from California to the ferocious Klondike, to end his life as a leader of wolves. Every page of this vigorous fable screams aloud Mr. London's creed; and every vehement implication refers it to the stern actualities of life. Now, to preach through parable is of course entirely legitimate; but in the same breath to insist upon the events of that parable as facts composing a demonstration is such a sophistry as to ridicule at length would savor overmuch of that savagery which Mr. London deifies. Our literature prizes the diary of Samuel Pepys and the letters of Clarissa Harlowe; but that writer who some years ago published as actual the memoirs of an imaginary defunct poet won more fame than favor.

Yet to declare the fairy tale independent of fact is by no means to abandon it to anarchy. The architecture of a castle in the clouds is less substantial, not less rigidly lawful, than the architecture of a sky-scraper. A flaw in the structure will bring down the one as surely as the other: nay more surely; for the steel tower falsely planned may cohere for a time by some casual tenacity of its material; but the enchanted palace can hope for no other support than the justice of its proportion. This is no playing with metaphor, but the statement of a profound reality. Imagination, which is the creative in man, is as infallible as the creation of God. To our finite understanding some actualities must appear exceptional; ideality, which, being manmade, we may comprehend, admits of no exceptions; and thus we demand in fiction that visible entirety of truth for which in fact all prayers have cried in vain. You must suffer in the unknowable woman you love inconsistencies whereof Cordelia blooms immaculate. The purest fiction, therefore, must be the most scrupulously real, precisely because it is irreferable to fact. Fairyland disparts from chaos as from pole to pole; between them lie the shadowlands of rational fiction and irrational fact. The ruin of Tess by the loss of the letter she pushed under Angel Claire's door we deem false tragedy; yet reference to human events obtrudes the doubt lest such cruel accidents may sometimes occur. But the false comedy in the conclusion of *The Little Mermaid* is nakedly indubitable. It was the law of her being that the winning a human love should mean for her immortality, its loss annihilation. She could not win her prince truly by her humanity; and she would not falsely by enchantment. Andersen's pretence that her honesty was rewarded by an arbitrary life of kindly deeds among the spirits of the air is a compassionate lie for which we eagerly forgive him; but the falsehood in imagination neither sympathy nor sophistry can hide. It cannot lurk among those accidents to which it cannot refer; and the innocence of a child rejects the spurious consolation as surely as the relentless wisdom of an Ibsen—as surely as Andersen's own true heart belied him while he wrote. For he knew as we all know, by a sense higher than reason, that the Little Mermaid really dissolved into the foam of the sea; and that her story is one of the rare tragedies of fairyland, almost too deeply true for tears.

And it is by this ideality of truth that the fairy tale makes its great and universal appeal. Becoming men we put away childish things: the merely marvellous we may desire or despise; we may from age to age be avid or scornful of satire; Asia may prefer her gods to our American atoms; but we alike desire to look upon Truth, inasmuch as we all have souls. It matters little under which aspect of her threefold virginity she shines in heaven, haunts the forms of earth, or lurks darkling in hell. Actaeon and Endymion, scientist and dreamer, pursue her still.

And by this the fairy tale endures and pervades, that it discloses to all people truths of which mere humanity constitutes each a judge: lesser truths perhaps, but communal; poor things, but our own. *Hamlet* is greater than *Redcoat Captain;* but we cannot carry our children to Denmark as we can join them in That Country. And the modern specialization which makes esoteric so much of our art bars no one out of these trivial heavens. Your wife may perhaps care little for Kipling, because she is not a man; she can hardly, being a woman, dislike *The Butterfly That Stamped*. It is just possible, however, that she may remain indifferent to it as a trifle, a playing with fancies, of obvious purport, silly in its language, unworthy of attention. This simply means that she is educated above its knowledge, that she has outgrown it—in a word, that she is old. Let this essay therefore, which is addressed like its theme, to youth, close as youth closes with a parable for age. Nick Bottom unquestionably left his element when he wandered from the world of fact; his negligence of material commonsense was doubtless contributory to making an ass of himself; and his return to earth was a painful disillusion. Yet his example is not altogether a warning: for only with ass's ears might he hear the melodies of fairyland; and at least for the one great hour of his life he lay transfigured in the lap of Titania.

Why Folk Tales and Fairy Stories Live Forever

Catherine Storr

When *Where* asked me to write something about fairy and folk stories, based on a collection of what is currently published in this field, I was expecting perhaps 150 representational volumes. Instead of which I must have received over a thousand. I found myself knee-deep in fairy stories, hardly able to move about the house for folk tales. Since one must presume that publishers know their business, this number of newly published books on the market implies an equal, or nearly equal, demand. The interesting question, then, is Why? What have these stories got which warrants their longevity—their immortality?

And—another fascinating point—*what* is it that survives? Because if you compare different retellings of the same story, or different illustrations, it might seem as if this was not the same, but a new, story. The story, for instance, of the beautiful girl who marries an unknown, disguised or even invisible lover, who breaks her promise not to inquire into his real nature, and who then has to win him again through suffering, is familiar to us in the myth of Psyche and Eros. But how many of us recognise it again in the more familiar Beauty and the Beast? In The Black Bull of Norroway? In East of the Sun and West of the Moon?

Difference of custom, of country, and of climate can alter any of these classic plots so that it is nearly, but not quite, unrecognisable. In this context I must record my delight in finding, in a collection of Ghanaian legends retold by Peggy Appiah (Deutsch) the Ashanti version of The Snow Maiden in which the Pineapple Child, who gives the book its name, melts in the sun like her Northern sister, but is reduced not to snow water, but to oil.

Or take the innumerable retellings of Snow White and the Seven Dwarfs. It can be told deadpan, as originally by the brothers Grimm, with all the faceless cruelty at the end; or sweetly, sentimentally; at length; or briefly; making of it a romance or a comedy at will. If you were to see only the pictures with which all the different artists have

Reprinted from *Where* no. 53:8–11 (1971), with permission of The Advisory Centre for Education, London.

decorated this one story, you'd hardly be able to perceive their common inspiration. And yet the tales, hacked about, cheapened, coarsened often both by words and pictures, do survive. In each new generation of children there are millions to whom these stories are as welcome and necessary as their daily bread. They must supply some very basic need. You could say that in the days when there were no fairy stories, it was necessary to invent them.

In an attempt to find some scholarly background for an inquiry into what this basic need is, I've been rereading J. R. R. Tolkien's essay on fairy stories. He lists the four main qualities of the fairy story as fantasy, recovery (or a fresh sight of the too familiar), escape and consolation; and he thinks that these qualities are as desirable for adults as they are for children. Professor Tolkien is familiar with a wide range of sagas, fairy stories and myths, and has also shown in *The Lord of the Rings* that he is a true "maker" or poet in the archaic sense of the word. But I think that he has, to a certain extent, fallen into a trap of which he is, nevertheless, aware.

The analytical study of fairy stories is as bad a preparation for the enjoying or the writing of them as would be the historical study of the drama of all lands and times for the enjoyment or writing of stage-plays.

In spite of this, I find this essay, with its particularising of meanings —"belief," "subcreation," "fantasy and fancy," "fairy and faery" more analytical than inspiring.

I'm confirmed in my impression that the essence of these stories is something extremely difficult to define, even more difficult to convey effectively to someone else. Where, for me, Tolkien absolutely hits the nail on the head is right at the end of the essay, when he refers to the quality of joy.

It is the mark of a good fairy story . . . that . . . it can give to the child or the man who hears it, when the turn comes, a catch of the breath, a beat and lifting of the heart. . . . This joy . . . I have selected as the mark of the true fairy story. . . .

As Tolkien points out, this "joy" is found in all sorts of other arts as well as in the art of the fairy and folk story; so I want to explore further to find out what else these stories contain which may explain their continuing appeal.

There is one element common to all of them, and this is the plot or story. In the best examples this not only has a most satisfactory beginning, middle and end; it also has that hallmark of a good plot, inevitability. The end is implicit in the beginning.

This is not to say that the end must always be the conventional one, " . . . and they lived happily ever after." Not at all; many stories end with loss, like the melting of the Snow Maiden I've already mentioned, the loss of the Seal wife, the death of the grandmother (and Red Riding Hood herself in some versions). But if the end is tragic, it is at the same time right, because the true fairy or folk story makes its own conventions and abides by them.

If the longing of the barren woman creates a child out of snow, then it is her business to guard that child against too fierce a light; if Psyche —or Pandora, or Bluebeard's wife, or Eve—disobeys a precise prohibition, she must suffer. This inevitability—if you like this way of expressing the remorseless sequence of events in nature—is an essential ingredient in the "true" fairy and folk story; it is also the one most commonly missing in the stories which are consciously invented.

Writers get carried away, particularly when they are already in the world of fantasy, by the power of creation, and they often produce what is not fantasy, but fantastick, trying to make up in gimmicks what is lost in urgency. For reasons which I shall come back to later, the "true" fairy or folk tale has an element of harshness, of ruthlessness; and this points and implements the plot.

To children particularly these stories have an almost unequalled capacity to arouse the question, "What happens next?" To stimulate this question is a vital part of the storyteller's art; it was on this that the itinerant ballad singers and narrators of epics and tales depended for their popularity; it was on this that Scheherazade counted to save the lives of her sister, herself, and countless virgins to come. I know that today it is considered rather reprehensible for adults to admit to a taste for straight narrative; and "unputdownable" is an adjective of praise only when it is applied to detective novels or, possibly, science fiction (even these are read apologetically, as it were). We really haven't progressed much since Jane Austen pointed out that the novel was undervalued.

Today, the antinovel, in which plot is of no importance, is respectable, the "story" is not. But the appetite for stories is still there, and there is an enormous attraction in the tale which engages one's attention immediately. Consider, to take three examples from widely different sources, the openings of the stories Rumpelstilzen (Tom-Tit-Tot in its English version), Cinderella, and Big Claus and Little Claus. In each we are plunged at once into a situation full of dramatic possibilities— the miller's daughter who finds herself a Queen, set to an impossible task; the lovely, gentle girl oppressed by her stepmother and sisters; the sympathetic boasting of Little Claus which lands him in such trouble. We have to read on.

As we read we find ourselves caught up in what I think is the second, but equally important feature of this kind of literature; this is the opportunity it gives to most of us to identify with the principal characters. The themes of these stories are themes with which in our daydreams we are already familiar.

We have all imagined ourselves as the virtuous protagonist, triumphing over vice—Snow White, The Wild Swans; as outwitting something larger and stronger than ourselves—The Gingerbread Man, The Gallant Little Tailor; as attaining the recognition we deserve—The Ugly Duckling, Cinderella; as succeeding where wiser men have failed—The Golden Goose, Mr. Vinegar; or, in a more romantic vein, as proving ourselves by heroic deeds—the hero sagas, The Golden Bird, The Fairy of the Dawn, and (on a more homely level) Jack and the Beanstalk.

Taking these stories at their surface value only, for the moment, they repeat to us, often with the added grandeur of their setting, the stories we would like to believe about ourselves. We are the youngest sons who have no prospect of winning the kingdom; we are the despised stepchildren (how many of us fantasied in childhood that we were adopted?); we are the small people who must learn to be clever before we can compete with the strong; we are the outcasts who will eventually receive homage; we are the generous-hearted fools who in the end marry princesses.

I must disagree with Professor Tolkien's contention that these stories are as much for adults as for children. I think that the setting of the fairy story in the far past, in a country where the laws of nature can be easily suspended or overridden by magic, or where beasts talk and behave in the manner of humans, is congenial to more children than adults. For many children the atmosphere of marvels is no hindrance to the belief, not that "this might happen to me," but that "this is the sort of person I really am." Adults in general need their wish fulfillment fantasies spelled out in rather more everyday language.

Readability. The implied promise of the granting of our heart's desire. These two qualities belong to both folk and fairy story, but the third is found almost exclusively in folk tales, and this is humour. In high romance, and in the hero legends, there is not so much scope for it. It might even be dangerous to introduce it, since humour—I don't mean wit—is apt to deflate a situation, to call into question values which must be accepted for at least as long as the story lasts. (The perfect example of this is Andersen's *The Emperor's New Clothes*.) But folk stories are about ordinary people, peasants, merchants, animals with human characteristics; and a common feature of these stories is the downfall of dignity—the lion caught in a net, the miserly patriarch robbed, the outwitting of the mighty by the underdog.

Taken to an extreme, these become the nonsense stories, the tales of simpletons who win prizes by doing everything wrong; Mr. Vinegar, the Golden Goose, Hans in Luck. Children, and adults, who find the more romantic stories too high-flown and remote from real life, are persuaded by the humour of some of the beast fables, especially when retold in an up-to-date style as in Joel Chandler Harris's *Uncle Remus,* to forget the improbability of the tale and to enjoy the situation described. There are very few of us who are impervious to the comedy of seeing our betters brought down a peg and made to look ridiculous.

So far I've dealt with what the conscious mind appreciates in folk and fairy stories, but it wouldn't be right to pretend that—much as it is—this is all they have to offer. There are many stories which are compulsive reading the first time round, which have shape and elegance and humour, and which yet are never reread. I believe that the enduring fairy stories have something beyond this, something more than immediately meets the eye.

This something is that they are concerned with the basic problems which we all share, but which are often buried deep in our unconscious minds, overlaid by the preoccupations of day to day life.

Let me illustrate what I mean. The reader, whether he be adult or child—does not think in psychologically analytical terms. He does not say to himself, "The story of the prince who has to kill a dragon and conquer the spell of the witch before he can win the princess and the kingdom, is the story of a young man who is initiated into manhood. He has to prove himself as strong as his father, the dragon, and as cunning as his mother, the witch, before he attains his identity as an adult; hence this story is important for me." He doesn't say it in these words; but he feels the importance of the story nevertheless. He recognises it as something to do with his own experience.

And here, I think, is a good place to draw a clear distinction between folk and fairy stories, often as the boundaries must overlap. It seems to me that at this deeply unconscious level—what Freud called the "latent content" when talking of dreams—folk stories deal with the problems of life at a fairly primitive level; with the need to fill one's own belly and not to become fodder for another's; with the need to keep warm and dry; to protect the young; and to keep ahead of one's neighbour. They are problems which man shares with other animals, which may be one reason why so many of these tales are expressed in terms of animal society. They are the problems connected with mere survival.

But the fairy stories are concerned with something else: the problem of identity. They are the stories of people who have to discover, each for himself, who they are, which may in part explain why so many of them open with a parent-child relationship—the old king with three sons, only one of whom can be the rightful heir; the royal pair with one daughter; the father whose newborn child threatens his own life; the magician's daughter; the widow's son.

PARENTS VERSUS CHILDREN

Almost always there is conflict between parent and child or, more obviously, between stepparent and child. The Ugly Duckling is rejected by his putative mother as soon as he emerges from the egg. Cinderella is kept at work in the kitchen. Elsa's brothers are bewitched into the form of swans. Each eventually has to make good in his own right; that is, to become the person he essentially is, to discard the character and shape imposed on him by others.

Of course these problems can be stated directly in psychological, in social, in moral, in ethical, in philosophical terms; but the strength of fairy and folk tales—and of novels, poetry, and plays—is that they present the human predicament in the terms of character and plot (symbolically is perhaps the right expression) so that while the conscious mind is employed in following the story, the unconscious is also being nourished.

And it is because this appeal is to the unconscious that it is so difficult to explain the satisfactoriness of the "true" fairy story to someone who does not also feel it. It is, perhaps, partly what Professor Tolkien means when he writes of "joy." I would call it also a feeling of recognition, but one which doesn't necessarily make it possible to say what has been recognised. We ask, sometimes, wanting to recall a name or a fact to another person's mind, "Does it ring a bell?" And by listening to the reverberations of a private belfry, deep inside, to make out whether this note or that is a harmonic which can call out an answer from one of his silent bells, the person questioned is able to say whether or not the query has meaning for him. (One of my daughters, when younger, used joyfully to cry, "It rings a very *strong* bell!" and I know exactly what she meant.)

The unconscious element in true fairy and folk stories not only makes it difficult to define their especial quality; it also makes forgeries in this line relatively easy to detect. They simply ring no bells. They are invented, on a purely conscious level. They may amuse, but they are apt to have only the trappings, the stock figures of the conventional fairy story, very little else.

In *The Magic Fishbone,* Dickens made the cardinal mistake of believing that the necessary ingredients of a fairy story were a family of King, Queen, princes and princesses, plus a fairy with magical gifts at her disposal. What he has produced is a tale of a middle-class family, archly told and with a repulsively moral streak. Thackeray's *Rose and the Ring* is a little less annoying because he at least doesn't preach and is a good deal more amusing, but it is nowhere near the real thing.

The fact that so many of the "true" stories are set in palaces and deal with exalted people is not a mere bit of snobbery, it is essential to the meaning of the stories that the events recounted should be seen to be important. What happens to a peasant is important to him, but not necessarily to anyone else, but the fate of a king or of a prince will affect a whole kingdom. The king or prince becomes, thereby, the representative of his people and so, to some extent, of mankind.

Of all the recent writers who have attempted to produce "true" fairy stories, very few have realised this. Andersen did; he never made the mistake of depreciating the value of royalty: his princesses, whether good or bad, are never belittled. If they lost their dignity by letting themselves be kissed by swineherds, they lose the more by virtue of their position. Just as the fact that it is an Emperor who recognises the worth of the real—as opposed to the artificial—nightingale emphasises the importance of the distinction.

FACING UP TO REALITY

Another mark of the real thing, is, as I mentioned earlier, a quality which could, according to one's taste, be called "realism" or "ruthlessness." By this I mean a refusal to escape into sentiment, or to sidestep into another world, when the logical consequences of the action are unpleasant. A "real" plot must follow up its issues to the end, whatever that may be, the death of the queen (both the real and the stepmother of Snow White), the slaying of the prince's faithful companion, or the second loss of Euridyce. To clap a happy ending, or the trivial explanation "It was all only a dream" on to the end of a story which has hitherto taken itself seriously, is an artistic flaw almost never made by the tellers of those stories which have survived and been handed down to us as models of their kind.

To sum up, then. Fairy and folk stories tell us, in narrative form, of the great preoccupations of man's existence. They do this both in direct and in symbolic language. Picasso said, once, about Negro masks:

Men had made those masks and other objects for a sacred purpose, a magic purpose, as a kind of mediation between themselves and the unknown hostile

forces that surrounded them, in order to overcome their fear and horror by
giving it a form and an image.

One of the characteristics which seems to distinguish man from all other
animals is this desire to impose a pattern on what mystifies and frightens
him.

It is for this, I believe, that we should value these stories, for their
beautiful form and for their message, if we can hear it. They speak in
the language of poetry, and this is a language which cannot be faked.
Either it springs from the heart—what D. H. Lawrence called "the solar
plexus"—or it is stillborn.

What Makes a Fairy Tale Good: The Queer Kindness of "The Golden Bird"

Perry M. Nodelman

Once upon a time may have been a very good time, but as Joseph
Jacobs said in "The Well of the World's End," "It wasn't in my time, nor
in your time, nor anyone else's time." The difference between the magical
world of fairy tales and the world we actually live in is so striking that to
some the difference is their most important quality. J. R. R. Tolkien
says that the tales "open a door on Other Time, and if we pass through,
though only for a moment, we stand outside our own time, outside Time
itself, maybe." Even Bruno Bettelheim, who believes the main virtue
of fairy tales to be their psychological usefulness, implies that the tales
are beneficial simply because, on the overt level at least, they "teach
little about the specific conditions of life in modern mass society; these
tales were created long before it came into being."

While there is truth in these observations, it is not the whole truth

Reprinted from *Children's Literature in Education* 8:101–8 (Autumn 1977),
with permission of Agathon Press, Inc., 15 E. 26th St., New York, N.Y.

about fairy tales. Fairy tales as we know them are literature, no longer part of the oral tradition that engendered them, but stories in books. They deserve the respect and the close attention we accord other works of literature. Bettelheim, for all his emphasis on the inner content of the tales, says that "the delight we experience when we allow ourselves to respond to a fairy tale, the enchantment we feel, comes not from the psychological meaning of the tale (although this contributes to it) but from its literary qualities—the tale itself as a work of art."

It is interesting that most commentators ignore the literary qualities of fairy tales; they do not seem easy to discuss. Unlike the other literature children are exposed to, they predate the literary conventions modern criticism was designed to accommodate and seem to confound contemporary techniques of analysis and evaluation.

Nevertheless, those techniques are surprisingly helpful in defining the special qualities of fairy tales. It should be possible to investigate the "literary qualities" mentioned by Bettelheim and to discover what the artistry of fairy tales consists of. To do this, I have chosen to investigate a tale typical of the genre, "The Golden Bird," one of the stories collected by the Brothers Grimm, Jacob and Wilhelm. It is not a tale that has seeped into the popular consciousness to the point that everybody knows it, but it is not an obscure or unusual tale either.

A literary analysis of "The Golden Bird" suggests that it has few of the virtues of good stories and most of the vices of bad ones. But the ways in which it fails to satisfy the demands of criticism turn out to be the key to its distinctiveness.

In "The Golden Bird," a king sends first one and then the other of his elder sons to find a golden bird that has been stealing his golden apples. Ignoring the good advice offered them by a fox, the elder sons give up their quest for the pleasures of a tavern. The king then sends his youngest son, who listens to the fox, avoids the tavern, and finds the bird.

But in attempting to steal the bird away, the youngest son rejects the fox's advice about not putting it in a golden cage. The bird cries out, and the son is caught. He is told that his life will be spared if he finds a golden horse. Again the fox helps him, and again he rejects the fox's advice, and puts the golden horse in a golden bridle. Captured again, the son must find a beautiful princess in order to save his life. Yet again the fox helps him, yet again he rejects the fox's advice, and yet again he is captured. This time the son is asked to move a mountain; the helpful fox does away with the mountain while the son sleeps. Joyful and obedient at last, the son now listens to the fox; as a result, he wins the princess, the horse, and the bird.

But the story is not over yet. On his way home, the youngest son discovers his brothers on the gallows and ignores the fox's advice by saving their lives. They turn against him, steal his prizes, and leave him for dead. Rescued yet once more by the fox, the youngest son regains his possessions; the older brothers are put to death, and the fox turns out to be the princess's brother, who had been under a spell. "And now there was nothing lacking to their happiness, so long as they all lived."

For all its complications, "The Golden Bird" is not much longer than my synopsis of it. That is because it is nearly all plot; the success of the story depends almost totally on our interest in the events it describes; the language it uses to communicate those events is noticeable only because it is so perfunctory.

Critical analysis thrives on linguistic subtlety; we like writing that is complex enough to require explanation. But even in the graceful version of "The Golden Bird" by Randall Jarrell, the only noticeable descriptive word is "golden"; the few other adjectives in the story merely communicate factual information. In fact, the specific words in which fairy tales are told do not seem to have much effect on our enjoyment of them. We experience the tales in translation, and at that, a translation of something that was once not written at all. And the tales seem to survive the inadequacies of all but the worst of their translators.

Furthermore, and contrary to the prejudices of criticism, the lack of stylistic ornamentation in "The Golden Bird" may be one of the sources of our enjoyment. Our delight in the mysterious otherworldliness of "once upon a time" would be spoiled if we knew that the hero's hair was auburn or that the princess's dress was an Empire-line tufted organza with a fichu and raglan sleeves. By drawing so little attention to itself, the language of "The Golden Bird" focuses our interest on the events it describes.

But those events do not seem to warrant much attention. While wonderful things happen in "The Golden Bird," anyone with even a minimal knowledge of fairy tales must admit that none of the events it describes is particularly unusual; they are clichés of the genre and not particularly entertaining in themselves. They might, however, become entertaining because of the way they are related to each other; perhaps it is the plot of the story that interests us.

Criticism asserts that a well-constructed plot is suspenseful; the way it joins events together creates interest in how they will turn out. But a perceptive reader knows soon after beginning "The Golden Bird" how the story will end. The only real question is how long it will take. After the hero has made his first wrong choice and placed the golden bird in the golden cage, the story could finish at the end of any of its episodes, without damage to its meaning or our interest in it. The story establishes a pattern, one that could be repeated indefinitely; and there is no suspense unless a pattern is broken. If "The Golden Bird" is entertaining it is not because of the excellence of its plot; that the story is little more than a plot and that it still entertains us only frustrates the manipulations of criticism.

An analysis of character as the story presents it is just as frustrating. We believe that good fiction describes complex personalities in a subtle way, and the characters in "The Golden Bird" are not complicated. The king is kingly, his sons stupid; but we learn nothing of their inner lives. In fact, the little personality the youngest son displays turns out to be a liability. The only decisions he makes for himself are bad ones, and his luck improves only when he stops acting for himself and trusts the fox.

Our critical assumptions also tell us that well-drawn characters grow and change in response to their experiences. The characters in "The Golden Bird" are static. They cannot grow because they do not change. In fact, they find it hard to respond to experience at all. At the beginning of the story, the king is convinced that his youngest son is worthless, and he does not want to send him into the garden to discover who has been stealing apples. But when the youngest son betters his brothers by discovering the thief, the king refuses to respond to experience—he sends first one, and then the other of the two brothers who have already shown their incompetence to find the golden bird.

The hero himself is just as inflexible as his father. It takes him a long time to learn his lesson and do what the fox tells him to do. And the fox, who appears to be the only wise being in the story, is just as inflexible in his unchanging evaluation of and commitment to the hero, who disappoints him continually.

Analysis suggests that the characters in "The Golden Bird" are too simple and too static to engage our interest. But that may be a virtue; since we do not have to worry about motivation or development, we can simply enjoy what happens.

In fact some commentators suggest that the simplicity of fairy tales is their main virtue, particularly because it allows the tales to make uncomplicated moral statements. Joan E. Cass says that "many of the old folk- and fairy tales provide simple, clear-cut patterns, where wrongdoing is punished and goodness justified." But investigation of "The Golden Bird" shows that its apparently clear-cut morality is not so clear-cut after all.

While "The Golden Bird" appears to be a story in which virtue triumphs, a closer look reveals that it praises vice; in particular, thievery. The hero is a successful thief, and is rewarded not only with his booty, but also with a kingdom. His brothers, who are unsuccessful thieves, are punished with death. Success seems to be more important than adherence to the Ten Commandments.

Furthermore, the story provides no evidence to justify our faith that the hero is good enough to deserve his rewards; in fact, it does the opposite. The elder brothers lose our trust when they are too proud to listen to the fox; the youngest does listen to the fox, and gains our respect. But he does so only once. On four consecutive occasions he is just as obtuse and as self-confident as his brothers were. Nevertheless, he is young, he is helped by a supernatural figure, and he does win out in the end; these things demand our faith in his goodness, and no matter what he actually does, we continue to think of him as good. In "The Golden Bird" good and evil are static, unchanging categories, quite separate from the evidence of actual behavior.

Ironically, however, its refusal to consider the implications of conduct seems to allow "The Golden Bird" to give us one of the things we want from it—a happy ending. As any student of moral philosophy knows, attempts to investigate the nature of goodness only lead to confusion. Better to ignore the subtleties, take goodness for granted, and let it triumph. "The Golden Bird" does that; but we certainly cannot admire either the clear-cut simplicity or the consistency of its morality.

The theme of the story, which seems just as simple and clear-cut as its morality, is just as inconsistent. The main idea of "The Golden Bird" is easy to discern: things are not what they seem. The king assumes his youngest son is less capable than his older brothers; but things are not what they seem. The older brothers choose a pleasant-looking inn over an unpleasant one; but things are not what they seem. The youngest brother assumes that a golden bird deserves a golden cage, and a golden horse a golden bridle; that beheading a fox is wrong; and that his brothers can be trusted. In each case, things are not what they seem.

But things are not what they seem in "The Golden Bird" as a whole either. The fox insists that the hero not trust appearances, against all the demands of logic. But he *must* trust the fox, which is the most illogical thing of all. And the story itself demands our trust as readers; if we stopped to question the existence of a golden bird or the disappearance of a mountain, the story would lose its power over us. It works only if we refuse to act on the idea it expresses.

In sum, then, critical analysis suggests that "The Golden Bird" is inadequate, its language unsubtle, its plot without suspense, its characters static, its morality and theme inconsistent. None of its literary components withstands the close attention of criticism.

But continuing the analysis does make one thing clear; the apparent failure of each of its components results from the story's refusal to engage the intelligence of its readers. The bias of criticism is that reading literature is an act of understanding—understanding events by responding to a writer's ability to describe them (style), understanding how events are tied together (plot), understanding personality (character), understanding what goodness consists of (morality), understanding ideas (theme). "The Golden Bird" does not require its readers to understand anything more than that some wonderful things happened.

Even if we have heard of similar occurrences in other fairy tales, the events described in "The Golden Bird" are beyond the pale of ordinary experience, and their magical otherworldliness is their most important quality. But the story itself expresses no excitement about the events it describes. When the fox talks to the oldest son, his reaction is, "How can a foolish animal possibly give me reasonable advice?" He might well have asked how the foolish animal could talk to him at all. But he doesn't. The story asks none of the obvious questions about the wondrous events it describes, and makes no attempt to explain them.

This lack of astonishment at the astonishing, the most surprising thing about "The Golden Bird," seems to be the key to its effect on us. If unusual occurrences are not explained, if they are not even worth getting excited about, then they seem inevitable. Things merely happen. If the story does not question them, we must accept them also.

But "The Golden Bird" does not simply suggest that unblinking acceptance is the proper attitude to the astonishing irrationality of the world it describes; it also implies that, seen properly, that world is not so irrational after all. There *is* a pattern, even if the logic of its operations is unfathomable. One will get the bird if one can get the horse. One can get the horse if one can get the princess; and so on. Once having accepted what appears to be frighteningly illogical, one learns to discern the logic in it, and to trust its operations.

In fact, that seems to be what "The Golden Bird" is all about. The hero has his happy ending when he stops thinking for himself and simply lets things happen to him. Up to that point he has only worked himself deeper into trouble. But like the characters in many fairy tales, he is rewarded as soon as he becomes passive. Just as Snow White and Sleeping Beauty triumph by going to sleep, the hero of "The Golden Bird" triumphs by sleeping while the fox removes the mountain, and by thereafter doing what he is told to do.

Furthermore, the story creates in us an urgent need for the hero to be passive. As he continues to make the same mistake again and again, the pressure builds to have him stop trying to act independently, to give in to the pattern of the mystery and accept it. Our interest in his character is created by our desire to have him be without character. Suspense is created, not by the events themselves or by their relationship to each other, but by our need to have them end the right way, and by the numerous times the story thwarts us by not yet ending the right way. Our satisfaction reaches its height when they do end that way. And our moral awareness is aroused by our understanding that it is not a rule we are dealing with, but an attitude; the point is not whether or not one is a thief, but whether or not one can be sensible enough to take the world for granted. The person who takes it most for granted is granted most of its gifts.

This profound praise of placidity runs counter to our most deeply held contemporary convictions about existence. It is no wonder that the world of fairy tales seems strikingly different from "the specific conditions of life in modern mass society."

But it may not be so different after all. Speaking of his own childhood, G. K. Chesterton once said that "the fairy tales founded in me two convictions; first that this world is a wild and startling place, which might have been quite different, but which is quite delightful; second, that before this wildness and delight one may well be modest and submit to the queerest limitations of so queer a kindness." Chesterton believed that the "wild and startling place" described in fairy tales was actually the world he lived in. He may have been right.

The world we inhabit *is* mysterious to us. If it were not, we would have no interest in reading about it. The common assumption that "literature . . . gives order and form to experience and shows life's unity and meaning" is undeniably true; but its corollary is that we spend much of our lives not understanding life's meaning. Trying to understand it is one way of coping with the mystery. In describing its own wondrous world so matter of factly, "The Golden Bird" may in fact imply another, equally satisfying response to the wonders of the real world: "before this wildness and delight one may well be modest and submit." I suspect our pleasure in fairy tales like "The Golden Bird" stems from our enjoyment of their placid acceptance of existence.

For children, the "wild and startling place" described in "The Golden Bird" may seem no more unusual than it did to Chesterton. All of us must cope with the mysterious inexplicability of the world we live in, but as any parent knows who has tried to explain to a child why the grass is green or why Cleveland isn't called Chicago, children confront it in an especially intense way. As neophytes in a complex world, children are constantly exposed to new facts and new mysteries; their cheerful willingness to broaden their horizons in order to accommodate whatever new information comes along is admirably echoed by the matter-of-fact attitude of "The Golden Bird." If a child's view of the world is always shifting in response to new, strange things, then he will find the world described in fairy tales very satisfying indeed; particularly when fairy tales insist by their very lack of astonishment that acceptance is possible, and that being shocked by experience and not understanding it can be enjoyable. Paul Hazard once said that fairy tales "date from the primeval ages of humanity. . . . In listening to them, we link ourselves to the most remote members of our race." If we do, then the theories of the psychologist Jean Piaget, who thought his investigations suggested "possible resemblances between the thought of the child and that of primitive man," are especially relevant. For children, the world of fairy tales may be an accurate image of their real world.

If this is so, then tales like "The Golden Bird" ought to be particularly entertaining for children. In fact, a calm acceptance of what ought to be astonishing, so profoundly expressed by fairy tales, may be a quality of all good literature for children; perhaps of all good literature. For if literature "gives form and order to experience," its content is the unwieldy and bewildering substance of life itself; and the order literature imposes on that bewildering substance allows us to accept and delight in it. Perhaps fairy tales accept bewildering events more complacently than most literature does; but the order any work of literature imposes on existence is more significant for the satisfaction it offers than for what it specifically consists of. The queer kindness of "The Golden Bird" is only a little queerer than the queer kindness of all good literature.

REFERENCES

Bettelheim, Bruno. *The Uses of Enchantment: The Meaning and Importance of Fairy Tales.* New York: Knopf, 1976.

Cass, Joan E. *Literature and the Young Child.* London: Longmans, 1967.

Chesterton, G. K. "The Ethics of Elfland." *G. K. Chesterton: A Selection from His Non-Fictional Prose.* W. H. Auden, ed. London: Faber & Faber, 1970.

Grimm, Jacob and Wilhelm. "The Golden Bird" in *The Juniper Tree and Other Tales from Grimm.* Lore Segal and Randall Jarrell, trans. New York: Farrar, Straus & Giroux, 1973.

Hazard, Paul. *Books, Children and Men.* Marguerite Mitchell, trans. Boston: The Horn Book, 1944.

Jacobs, Joseph. "The Well of the World's End." In *English Fairy Tales.* 1890, 1894. rpr.: Harmondsworth, Middlesex: Puffin; New York: Schocken, 1968.

Lukens, Rebecca J. *A Critical Handbook of Children's Literature.* Glenview, Ill.: Scott, Foresman, 1976.

Piaget, Jean. "The Mental Development of the Child." In *Six Psychological Studies.* Anita Tenzer, trans. New York: Vintage, 1967.

Tolkien, J. R. R. "On Fairy Stories." In *Tree and Leaf.* London: Unwin; Boston: Houghton Mifflin, 1964.

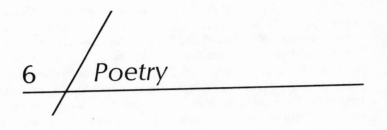

6 / Poetry

Early poetry for children was very moralistic. For example, "Manners at Table When Away from Home" (ca. 1480, reprinted in *The Oxford Book of Children's Verse*, 1973) warns its young readers, among other things:

> Eat thy meat by small morsels,
> Fill not thy mouth as doeth rascals.
> Pick not thy teeth with thy knife;
> In no company begin thou strife.

Iona and Peter Opie, the editors of *The Oxford Book of Children's Verse*, found little before 1740 for the young that was not exhortatory, and, long after, edification remained the cachet which certified a poem's respectability. For example, John Bunyan's *Book for Boys and Girls; or, Country Rhimes for Children* (1686) was obviously written for the morals like: "The Egg's no Chick by falling from the Hen; / Nor Man a Christian, till he's born agen." In 1715 Isaac Watts' *Divine Songs* served up scores of mini-sermons, like:

> Let dogs delight to bark and bite,
>   For God hath made them so:
> Let bears and lions growl and fight,
>   For 'tis their nature, too.
>
> But, children you should never let
>   Such angry passions rise:
> Your little hands were never made
>   To tear each other's eyes.

A century and a half later, Watts' verse was still available for Lewis Carroll to parody. Watts had pleaded for "some fitter pen" to follow his verse "without the solemnities of religion"; Jane and Ann Taylor were the most successful of the early secularizers of his tradition. Jane Taylor's "Twinkle, twinkle, little star" is the highlight today of *Rhymes*

192

for the Nursery, 1806, but for every twinkling star there were dozens of admonitory poems about the cruelty of fishing or the danger of climbing chairs. In moving from saving children from falls from grace to falls from ladders, children's verse remained fixed in the cautionary mold from which it sprang.

A member of Parliament and a historian, William Roscoe broke that didactic mold with his rollicking *The Butterfly's Ball* (1806), thereby setting a fad for light, nonmoralistic verse for children which even the Taylor sisters tried to imitate and which extends to a present-day spinoff of that poem. For other humorous verse besides Roscoe and his imitators, there was Edward Lear's *Book of Nonsense* (1846) and, of course, the nursery rhymes which children took over from adults.[1]

By the early twentieth century, children's verse had attracted formidable practitioners of that craft, such as Robert Louis Stevenson (*A Child's Garden of Verses,* 1885) and A. A. Milne (*When We Were Very Young,* 1924 and *Now We Are Six,* 1927). Poetry for children is one genre where many writers for adults are not disinclined to participate: Walter de la Mare, Carl Sandburg, T. S. Eliot.

But utilitarianism can thwart even the best of verse for youth. A special commission in the 1950s complained that poetry was still being taught more as a task than as a source of enjoyment, and Sir Herbert Read warned against thinking of the genre as a school subject.[2] When poems are used to teach reading or memorization skills, the deadening equation of poetry with task work is inevitable.

Myra Cohn Livingston in her article also scolds teachers, in this case college teachers, for lumping children's poetry together indiscriminately, for not distinguishing verse from poetry and the popular from the excellent. She urges sound critical standards to rescue poetry, the stepchild of literature. What Livingston asks for, Helen M. Hill demonstrates herein in her separation of the inferior from the outstanding in juvenile poetry. Without such correctives, the child reader will be stuck with deficient poetry that jingles or sentimentalizes.

The review by Naomi Lewis is presented not so much as a look at the scholarly methods of the Opies, which are, as usual, impeccable, but as an opportunity to survey the genre as it evolved. Lewis finds the problem of classification which troubles all fields of children's literature to be particularly acute in poetry. Do we mean poems written for children? About children? For adults but appealing to children?

The serious discussion of poetry for children is still minimal. Sheila Egoff reprinted no articles on poetry in her extensive anthology, *Only Connect,* because she found nothing of significance to reprint. Ten years later Alethea Helbig found some critical gaps being filled in by the newer journals, but at the same time Agnes Perkins found only a handful of articles on the subject in recent years, many of them pedagogical or appreciative in approach. Only three articles, she concludes, contributed "something new and solid" to the field,[3] one of which, the Helen M. Hill selection, is reprinted here. The Signal Poetry Award, which is supposed to be given annually, was not presented to any 1979 or 1980 books of poetry for children, an understandable situation given the relatively small number of such books and the infrequent academic criticism of that literature.[4] But the Newbery Medal for the most distinguished children's book printed in America in 1981 went to Nancy Willard's *A Visit to William Blake's Inn: Poems for Innocent and Experienced Travellers.* This, the first Newbery Medalist from the ranks of poetry (verse to be precise), augurs well for the reader and the critic of children's poetry.

Obviously poetry for children needs more attention and treatment. It has grown like the flower in the crannied wall, but it will remain fixed in the didactic cement from which it sprang unless the artists and the critics—the fairy godmothers Livingston and others plead for—rescue it.

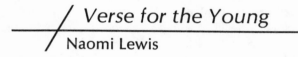

/ Verse for the Young
/ Naomi Lewis

Briskly in the wake of the two new major Oxford volumes, the basic and modern, so to speak, of British poetry, this lighter craft appears [*The Oxford Book of Children's Verse*, compiled and edited by Iona and Peter Opie; Oxford University Press, 1973]. A sort of junior *Oxford Book of English Verse*? A standard school-age anthology, Beowulf to Bunting? But no. In fact, by the particular terms of its contents, this is as curious a volume as can ever have appeared in its eminent series. Only poems explicitly written for children ("or with children prominently in mind") are admitted—verses, the compilers add, with an odd choice of alternatives, "which either were cherished in their own day, or which have stood the test of time." Out, by this reckoning, go all the traditional

Reprinted from *Children's Book Review* 3, no. 3:70–72 (June 1973), with permission of the author.

nursery rhymes, as not being meant in the first place for the young (though they are of course available in their own handsome Opie volume). Out go all the great traditional ballads—and all children's singing games and rhymes. Out too, on very much flimsier grounds, go the works of all living practitioners, however long established. Thus, the only names for the very brief twentieth-century section are Kipling, de la Mare, Grahame, (Edward) Thomas, Farjeon, Fyleman, Milne—then, on the other side of a huge unstated gap, the uneasy ones of Eliot and Ogden Nash. Of Graves, Reeves, Serraillier, Clark, Causley, Walsh—and some others who have actually qualified by not surviving—there isn't a mention.

Yet, even before we explore the contents, the problem waits about the genre itself. Verse deliberately aimed at the young—is it really an honourable literary kind, an "art-form" in the Opies' confident term? Isn't it—to all but a few writers—a desperately self-limiting field? Even major "adult" poets don't necessarily write at their best at child-level; let us hope that no one judges Tennyson, say, by the instances in this book. (One of them, in an adult collection, wrecked his reputation for years.) Nor do the greatest writers of fictional prose for children have equal luck with verse. No one can value the power of novelist George MacDonald more highly than the present critic—but "Where did you come from, baby dear?" must rank in the Top (or Nether) Ten of an affectionate list of the worst poems for children ever in print.

> Where did you get that pearly ear?
> God spoke, and it came out to hear.

Writers themselves have not always known where the line precisely lay. De la Mare admitted this in his old haphazard division of his verse into child and adult books. The best-known child-verse of Milne and Fyleman was originally meant (and published in *Punch*) for adult reading. So too, were many of Eleanor Farjeon's poems. Child and fairy stuff were enormously fashionable adult fare in the early years of this century.

And yet, the genre exists; it has, as this book makes clear, its history; it takes in writers of genius (Blake, Stevenson, Carroll, Lear, Kipling, de la Mare), and some masterworks that are increasingly welcomed into adult anthologies. But, Lear and Carroll apart (assuming that they *were* truly writing for children) do any of these major poets write as well when they have the young in mind as they do when they write for everybody? (Watts, himself, is an excellent instance.) In fact, the best child-poems are often by lesser hands. A quick choice of durable works from the present book (major items apart) could take in Allingham's "Up the

Airy Mountain," Field's "Wynken, Blynken and Nod," Mrs. Ewing's "The Dolls' Wash" (less known than most in the list), Mary Lamb's "The Boy and the Snake," Mrs. Alexander's hymns, Howitt's "The Migration of the Grey Squirrels," Southey's "The Cataract of Lodore"— and one unknown to me: Celia Thaxter's beautiful poem "The Sandpiper." (It should be read with the note on the poet's own strange history. Much of her life was spent in a lighthouse out at sea, to which her disappointed politician father had withdrawn.) Coleridge's rhyme about metres, firmly lodged in my head as are, since childhood, about seventy-five per cent of the contents of this book, has always served as a useful reference; others should find it so. All these are worth being kept alive in print. But much else here is of lower imaginative temperature and much more casual craftsmanship. The old sense of mute distaste at the lines

> You are more than the Earth, though you are such a
> dot:
> You can love and think, and the Earth cannot.

comes back to me now after years as my glance is caught by them. Would a modern child think otherwise?

What makes a writer succeed in this field? Different one from another as they may be, the best of them share a quality which is hard to define in a single word: something unconfused and direct—sophistication might be its opposite. All have a streak of childlike nature, which need not equate with innocence. The main successes appear to be of several kinds. The most reverberating, and perhaps most valued today, are the surreal or nonsense poems—supremely by Carroll and Lear. Both are verbally brilliant; both invest the sheerest nonsense not only with logic but with haunting drama and pathos. A first experience of "Jabberwocky" can draw tears. Both writers are well represented in this book. Nobody else included here comes near enough in this field for a mention.

A second kind, popular too in the post-moral years, but perilous in an unskilled or whimsical hand, is the child-voice poem—one where the writer speaks as, or identifies himself with the child. The master hand here is of course Stevenson's. Time doesn't blur his brilliant economy and poignant precision of detail in *A Child's Garden of Verses*—though to be sure, like Nesbit, Andersen, and most of the great writers for the young, their author was not observing, but re-animating his own child-life.

A third kind, the magical (witches, fairies, phantoms, Grimm-born forests, elves, and brownies), has areas in common with the first, the surreal-fantastic. It has some sturdy Elizabethan antecedents, and an occasional superb variation turns up here and there (but mostly, alas, in

adults' poetry). But it is something of a surprise to realise that its pro-
liferating time belongs to the earlier years of this century. De la Mare,
the prince of this region in children's verse, is so powerful an influence
that he has left his mark on almost every child-verse writer of the roman-
tic-necromantic sort for the past sixty years or so. His is not the only
influence, though. The Irish fairy group (belonging to about the same
period) ought not to be overlooked, but they aren't represented in the
Opie volume. Though you will find a familiar forerunner in Allingham's
"Up the Airy Mountain" (1840), I suspect that the exploding elf and fay
population in the lower reaches of child-verse during the first half of our
century has a Celtic origin. In a later edition, the Opies may give more
evidence.

These are not the only forms. A few poets can still speak convincingly in the traditional way of an adult addressing the young. "Lollocks,"
by Graves (not in this volume), is in its own style as moral-admonitory
as any of the Polonius pieces at the start of the volume. The didactic
verse—the poem with a contained or pendant moral (the main kind
until the mid-nineteenth century) is indeed a study in itself. As we see
from this book, the mediaeval and sixteenth-century child was offered
little more than versified admonition to a kind of blend of social and
spiritual behaviour (though in "The Unhappy Schoolboy" [Anon, sixteenth century] we suddenly hear the other side—the silent scream of
the rebellious child). Few of these early Polonius-utterers can have had
much insight into what we might now call human psychology.

> The Devil's children sin all day,
> But you must not do so.

wrote Abraham Chear. The lines sound more like a wild cry of frus-
tration at missing a pleasure than the sober reverse. It is a sad thought
that fays and goblins abounded in "adult" poetry of these seemingly
joyless days. Or it would be sad if children were kept, as this book might
suggest, to nothing but children's verse.

Later, in the seventeenth, eighteenth, and early nineteenth centuries,
when counsels come to be more happily contained in stories and parables, the reader could, after all, reject the pill and enjoy the drama,
especially when it came from the Taylors, or Adelaide O'Keeffe. Southey
did better still; it isn't always appreciated how skilfully this top narrator involved the moral thread with the whole so that readers of "After
Blenheim," or "Bishop Hatto," or "The Inchcape Rock" (none of them
in this book) swallowed it with the rest and, if they noticed, would not
have found it offensive, either.

But what the bygone moralists could not have guessed was their fate. Demolished and remade through brilliant parody and pastiche, they become the base of some of Carroll's most triumphant nonsense verses for the young. It took the clear, nostalgic gaze of de la Mare (the fashion has been taken up later by modern anthologists) to turn again to the originals, such as "Twinkle, Twinkle Little Star"; or "'Tis the Voice of the Sluggard" (a more interesting poem in itself than Watts ever knew). Both are in this book. Belloc's *Cautionary Tales,* undeniably moral in their way, are based on the same agreeable plan. Here is an author who well understood the young child's ruthless appetite for black comedy.

What must be kept in mind, however, is that the contents of this book were never at any time the only diet of the poetry-liking child. What did Marjory Fleming turn to at the age of seven or so (pierced by the very word Helvellyn) but Scott? What ravishing book did young Clare walk miles to buy but Thomson's *Seasons?* What nourished little Pope and many another child in or out of the Age of Reason but Spenser's *Faerie Queene,* the Tolkien-saga, so to speak, of at least two centuries of post-Elizabethan readers? Can anyone doubt that the boy in *Alton Locke,* who devoured *Paradise Lost* as a weekly treat, was founded on genuine evidence? Open any anthology for the young— those of Bell, Read, Grigson, de la Mare, Reeves, Ireson, Holbrook, Causley, Clark, Shannon, and Dickinson come (literally) to hand—not one of them draws entirely, or mainly, or even much on verse specifically written in this genre. It isn't, in short, the best that's going, or, with a few exceptions, the best that each poet can offer.

There is, however, a good enough case for gathering it together, as the Opies have done (and not only to gratify the nostalgia of adults lacking other poetry volumes). It does, to be sure, turn up the occasional lost item. More to the point, it does illustrate a changing series of moods and manners. But if this is an honest historical survey, why is the "rich man in his castle" verse omitted from the main text of Mrs. Alexander's hymn? What has become of Macaulay, and a whole school of "noble" nineteenth-century ballads? Where is "After Blenheim" with its unexpectedly modern content—a real child's classic if ever there was one? Why is Longfellow, another superb narrator, so feebly represented? What about Newbolt? Surely "Vitae Lampada" rates a place. And if the compilers flinch at that (one can see their point) why is there not a line of James Stephens, intrinsically sympathetic and rewarding as a writer for the young? Indeed, the whole of the early twentieth-century Irish contingent seems to be lost. The omission of all living writers is not made more explicable by the Opies' explanation that they include no writer "whose work cannot be seen as a whole." Several of those noted above have been busily in print for over thirty years. They point to as many paths and reflect as many poetic antecedents as the Opies could wish.

But these things, perhaps, are details. The key to what is troubling in this book can be found, I think, in the compilers' introduction. What is absent from it is a genuine critical look at what they are offering and a clear idea of whom it is offered to. They cite Sir Arthur Quiller-Couch [editor of *The Oxford Book of English Verse*] about not omitting the best, however familiar (a claim that cannot hold water); they describe their aim, in a passage of mounting euphoria, as "to make available in one place the classics of children's poetry: that small satchelful of verse whose existence constitutes one of the pleasing advantages of being born to the English tongue." Well, one need not go to a court of law to query the claim.

It is hard to say *exactly* why the volume leaves one unsatisfied. There *are* good items here. And it is no bad thing today to acquaint the young with what is delightful in verse which has a technically skilful form. Technique has more to do with keeping Milne and Fyleman (yes!) alive than is generally realised. (Why do I still recall every word of "Elfin Town" and "Grown-up Land"—also unknown—neither of them, sadly, in this book?) But the good lasts anyhow, valid anew for every generation. The best in the volume—nearly all of it out of copyright—is being reprinted again and again, in picture books and anthologies, anywhere you look. Much of the rest is by its nature sub-poetry, to be apprehended (or savoured) only by understanding the context of its time. And does the child know what isn't in this survey? Too many children used to pass into adult life thinking that Kipling stood for admonitory "If" and "The Camelious Hump," and Browning for no more than that loved but worn "Pied Piper." Younger readers may leave with a similar block. One could wish that the enjoyable Opie notes had sometimes suggested what *else* a child might read. Meanwhile, the Clarendon imprint and the Opies' name will ensure the volume a place on shelves or in hands where it doesn't quite belong. Would not *The Oxford Book of Verses Written for Children* have been a fairer name?

How to Tell a Sheep from a Goat—and Why It Matters

Helen M. Hill

It is always risky for a teacher to claim that he or she has the divine insight it takes to understand the true meaning of a poem or that he knows how to tell a good poem from a bad one. And when students ask, "Why isn't my opinion just as good as yours?" it is hard to answer tactfully. The honest answer lies in the fact that an opinion is only as good as the evidence it is based on, and many readers of poetry are not very good at gathering the evidence. It is necessary to read a great many poems and read them attentively in order to develop a discriminating taste. If we start life by listening to bad poems instead of to good ones, we are handicapped from the very beginning. But how do we learn to tell the difference?

Poetry needs to be read as if it were read aloud. Even when reading silently, a person must listen for the sounds of words, for the way they fit together or strike against one another. We need to read slowly enough so that there is time for the images to take shape in the mind and— equally important—time to catch the implications of words that have been scrupulously chosen. The reader should not just watch the words go by, like pictures on a screen with some background music that doesn't matter. A good poem deserves a good listener; and it is only by listening that we can learn how to tell a good poem when we find one.

People who have studied poetry have learned what to listen for. There may be rhyme, though of course there doesn't have to be, nor does it have to come only at the end of a line. Rhyme, as Eve Merriam has said, may be

> the repeat of a beat, somewhere
> an inner chime that makes you want to
> tap your feet or swerve in a curve.[1]

This selection was presented at the 1978 Midwest Modern Language Association meeting in Minneapolis. Reprinted from *The Horn Book Magazine* (Feb. 1979), pp. 100–10. © 1979 by The Horn Book, Inc.

There may or may not be a definite meter, but at least there must be something that can be recognized as rhythm, even though it is not identifiable as regular iambics or anapests or pentameters. These techniques are easy to learn about and to recognize if one is interested and wants to talk about them, though what really matters is the whole poem and the effect it has on the listener. The bat-poet was understandably appalled when the mockingbird, whose technical skill he admired so much, responded to his poem about the owl by telling him that he liked the rhyme scheme, that it was written in iambic pentameter, and that it was clever of him to make the last line two feet short to produce the effect of holding one's breath. " 'I didn't know that,' the bat said. 'I just made it like holding your breath.' " Later the bat thought bitterly to himself, " "Why, I might as well have said it to the bats. What do I care how many feet it has? The owl nearly kills me, and he says he likes the rhyme-scheme!' " And yet, both poet and reader have to have some knowledge of technique and a sense of the full value of words, of their sound and meaning—the poet, in order to choose his words scrupulously; the reader, in order to appreciate fully what the poet has written.

Looking at many of the poems that are written or collected for children, I wonder if the bat was right after all in objecting to the mockingbird's analysis. Too many people who write or collect poems for children seem to assume that if the subject might appeal to a child, the technique doesn't matter. They seem to assume that the child, with an uneducated ear and mind, won't notice inadequacies in concept or language; that it is all right to force rhymes, to pad lines, to use images that are merely cute, and to let the poem run down at the end like an old Victrola record. Too many anthologists begin with the wrong premise. They look for poems children will sit still for, poems children can read by themselves, poems about subjects children "can relate to," and above all, poems that are light or nonsensical—because serious poems, by definition, must be too difficult and uninteresting. I would like to argue, along with Frost and de la Mare, that even an uneducated child deserves the best and that no poem is good enough for children that is not good enough for adults. Nor should any poem be acceptable to adults if it does not have integrity. By integrity I mean wholeness or soundness of thought, perfection of technique, and sincerity of tone.

Most of the poems I am using as examples of bad poetry come from widely used anthologies which include much good work. Most, though not all, of the poems were written by people with good ears—that is, with a strong sense of rhythm—who find pleasure in the lilt or the jingle of lines and rhymes. Sometimes too strong a sense. Sometimes the writers are so inflexible about their rhythms that they strain the language, invert the word order, or use archaic forms just so the meter will come out right. One such poem is "New Shoes" by Marjorie Seymour Watts.

> When I am walking down the street
> I do so like to watch my feet.
> Perhaps you do not know the news,
> Mother has bought me fine new shoes!
> When the left one steps I do not speak,
> I listen for its happy squeak.[2]

Children don't talk like that, nor do they think that way. They love new shoes, and when they walk down the street, they may like to watch their feet. Certainly a child would not be so stiff and formal; instead, he would blurt out his excitement. A child might be amused by the squeak, but "happy squeak"? The word *happy,* like "do so" in the second line and the whole of the third line, is there for padding and to make the rhyme and the meter come out right.

In "Unsatisfied Yearning," the poet Richard Munkittrick has an amusing enough idea about the irony or the orneriness of the dog who wants to come back in as soon as he is let out. But Munkittrick, too, is so conscious of his scansion that he pads his lines, unnaturally inverts the word order, and fails to think hard enough about his language.

> Down in the silent hallway
>   Scampers the dog about,
> And whines, and barks, and scratches,
>   In order to get out.
>
> Once in the glittering starlight,
>   He straightway doth begin
> To set up a doleful howling
>   In order to get in![3]

"Doth" is obviously padding; "[s]campers the dog about" is strained and unidiomatic. And how silent can a hallway be when a dog is scampering, whining, barking, and scratching to get out of it?

A good poem needs to have more than regular rhythm and natural idiom. It needs images that work—that is, images that make sense when you stop to think about them after the echoes of sound have died away. "On a Snowy Day" by Dorothy Aldis starts with an acceptable image in the first stanza. Though I find the first line rather a mouthful of syllables, I can see and accept

> Fence posts wear marshmallow hats
> On a winter's day.

The next stanza

> Bushes in their nightgowns
> Are kneeling down to pray

is rhythmically smoother, but I have reservations about the kneeling and praying. Kneeling takes hinges in the knees. The bushes are bowing under the weight of the snow, but they can hardly be kneeling. Why not bowing down to pray? Furthermore, what are they praying for? What train of thought connects the two images of marshmallow hats and praying bushes? How is the poet going to follow through with whatever it is the bushes might be praying for? Do they desire marshmallow hats to wear with their nightgowns? Or, more likely, do they desire to have the burden of snow lifted from their backs? It is neither. In the last stanza the author writes,

> And trees spread out their snowy skirts
> Before they dance away.[4]

I believe in Tolkien's walking trees. They were heavy and slow to move, and it took them a long time to uproot themselves; but once roused by their anger they did move with rugged determination, and I have no trouble imagining their movement. Yet I can visualize Dorothy Aldis' trees only as standing on their heads with their snow-covered branches spread out like skirts. How could they possibly dance away?

Another poem about snow for children, which appears in several anthologies, is "First Snow" by Marie Louis Allen. It starts with a similar effort to compare snow to something that a child knows and would be amused to consider:

> Snow makes whiteness where it falls.
> The bushes look like popcorn-balls.

Though "[s]now makes whiteness" is dull, the popcorn balls—like the marshmallow hats—are vivid and appealing. But how lamely the poet goes on:

> And places where I always play
> Look like somewhere else today.[5]

Aside from the mechanical rhythms, how disappointing it is to be left with a picture as vague as "somewhere else." It goes dead. De la Mare's "The Snowflake," on the other hand, stays alive to the very last word, both in sound and image.

Before I melt,
Come, look at me!
This lovely icy filigree!
Of a great forest
In one night
I make a wilderness
Of white:
By skyey cold
Of crystals made,
All softly, on
Your finger laid,
I pause, that you
My beauty see:
Breathe, and I vanish
Instantly.[6]

Whatever one thinks of the inversion in "[m]y beauty see," every word and every line say something. One sees the snowflake in the icy filigree and the crystals made of "skyey cold." The rhythm is controlled yet varied, and the whole poem moves so swiftly that one rushes along with it to see the snowflake before it vanishes.

Rhythm and imagery are elementary yet important considerations in judging poems. Equally important, however, once the poet has these techniques under control, is a skillful control of thought and tone. The effort to think and talk like a child is what most often causes a failure in tone, because few poets are successful at both overhearing a child's language and using it sensitively, without condescension, to express a child's point of view. De la Mare and Milne are notable exceptions. Sometimes the condescension appears not so much in the language itself as in the failure of the poet to take his craft or his audience seriously. "New Shoes" is condescending because it is an artificial attempt to think like a child. Shel Silverstein's "Beware, My Child" is condescending because it assumes that nothing matters but the nonsensical idea and the rhyme and rhythm of the poem. It is true that sometimes children like to be scared by harmless monsters. It is also true that children often play with ideas without knitting them together, but this does not justify a lack of logical coherence in a poem written by an adult, even when he is writing for children.

Beware, my child,
Of the snaggle-toothed beast.
He sleeps till noon,
then makes his feast
on Hershey bars

> and cakes of yeast
> and anyone around—o.

So far it's plausible, perhaps, though any beast who eats Hershey bars sounds more companionable than frightening if he is snaggle-toothed. And I think the yeast is in his diet only because it rhymes with *feast*. But let us grant that a child might be deliciously frightened by such a creature. How can he protect himself or fend off the beast? If he is going to triumph over it, he must confront it, as Carroll's hero confronted and vanquished the Jabberwock. Yet Silverstein offers the child three unrelated options, none of them prepared for in the first stanza and none of them appropriate. When you see him, says Silverstein, you must

> sneeze three times
> and say three loud
> and senseless rhymes
> and give him all your
> saved-up dimes,
> or else you'll ne'er be found—o.[7]

Not only do these random measures sound ineffectual. The last line is ambiguous—does the child want to be found by the beast?—and obviously padded with an archaic *ne'er* for the sake of the meter.

Aileen Fisher's "Raccoons" is more of a poem than Silverstein's; her intention is more serious, yet it, too, fails at the end. Though its strong rhythm and vivid imagery help to conceal its other weaknesses, I think the poem fails also in tone and in point of view.

> Did you ever look
> near a wildish brook
> or a green-eyed pond
> with a wood beyond
> and see (on the bank
> where the grass grows rank)
> a five-toed track?
> Hands in front
> and feet in back
> like an all-four child
> in a place so wild?
> There a raccoon
> on a late afternoon
> or under the light
> of a lantern moon

> went looking for frogs
> and mice to eat . . .
> in his barefoot feet.
> That's where he walked
> in the thick black ooze
> without any shoes.
>
> And so will I
> when the sun is high
> in the wide June sky![8]

The poem starts with an adult asking the child a question but using childish words and phrases—"wildish" and "in his barefoot feet"—on the pretense of getting down to the child's level and adding the redundant "without any shoes" to rhyme with "ooze." But in addition to being condescending in tone, the whole poem is not soundly thought through. Fisher sets a trap for herself in the first six lines by asking a question that can only be answered by yes or no. Before the child can answer, however, she starts to describe the raccoon, and she gradually shifts the reader's attention from the raccoon to the childlike pleasure of squishing about barefoot in the mud. She remembers then that she started with a question for the child to answer; yet when the child does speak, he responds not to the question asked but to the implied one, Wouldn't you like to go barefoot in the ooze, too? When the child answers, "And so will I," the poet is trapped again, for now she needs a rhyme for *I;* and forgetting all about the nocturnal habits of raccoons, forgetting, too, that the poem is called "Raccoons" and so presumably should make its point about them, she concludes with this pointless rhyme:

> When the sun is high
> in the wide June sky!

Though Fisher fails to pull her poem together at the end, one can see rather easily what associations led her from the idea she began with to the one that took over at the end of the poem. Karla Kuskin's "The Witches' Ride" fails in quite a different way. She, too, has an ear for rhyme and rhythm, but she uses sounds and images so ebulliently for their own sakes that she doesn't stop to think about their meanings and relationships to one another.

> Over the hills
> Where the edge of the light
> Deepens and darkens
> To ebony night,

Narrow hats high
Above yellow bead eyes,
The tatter-haired witches
Ride through the skies.
Over the seas
Where the flat fishes sleep
Wrapped in the slap of the slippery deep,
Over the peaks
Where the black trees are bare,
Where boney birds quiver
They glide through the air.
Silently humming
A horrible tune,
They sweep through the stillness
To sit on the moon.[9]

At first sight the poem may seem vivid and pleasing. It has an easy, swingy rhythm; its imagery is specific and appropriate to witches. They are "tatter-haired" and wear their high narrow hats "above yellow bead eyes." We have no idea how the witches are traveling; we have to assume that it is by broomstick, for the writer doesn't tell us. But the witches remain close to the earth. Although the night is black with no moonlight to help us see objects, we are supposed to see their journey over the hills and through the skies; then "Over the seas/ Where the flat fishes sleep"; and finally over the peaks, still close enough to earth to see the black trees and "boney birds" quivering in the dark. At last, "Silently humming/ A horrible tune,/ They sweep through the stillness/ To sit on the moon." *Silently* humming? And what does a "horrible tune" sound like? Are they humming for any other reason than that *tune* rhymes with *moon*?

This is a poem which has possibilities, both in its rhythm and in some of its imagery, but the poet has compiled images without imagining fully and coherently how they are going to work together. She does not keep our attention on the witches, nor does she keep their destination clearly enough in mind; and she fails to use sounds and images thoughtfully. We are even distracted by them. "[F]lat fishes sleep" is an impossible tongue twister, and our attention is drawn noisily away from the witches when the fish are described as sleeping "[w]rapped in the slap of the slippery deep."

It is tempting to compare "The Witches' Ride" with Walter de la Mare's "The Ride-by-Nights"—another poem describing a witches' ride. De la Mare always knows where he, and the witches, are going, and he keeps our attention clearly focused. Not only do we see the witches more clearly—we never lose track of them as, "bearded, cloaked, and cowled," they ride through the air on their brooms; swarm in and out among the constellations; "surge pell-mell down the Milky Way"; swoop between the legs of Cassiopeia's Chair; and then wheel around "[u]nder the silver, and home again."

Enough of the poet's not thinking hard enough about using language responsibly—for not, as Dante Gabriel Rossetti said, doing the fundamental brainwork necessary to the writing of a good poem. The reader, the teacher, and the anthologist have some responsibility, too. If they are to read poems intelligently and choose poems wisely for children, they also need to know how to do the fundamental brainwork. It is a rewarding experience to learn to distinguish good poems from poor ones, to discover rewards in the depths and delights of language when it is discriminatingly used. One discovers also that the best poems for children are very often written by poets who do not write only for children or who were not thinking of children at the time they wrote particular poems. They were thinking only of writing good poems. They were concerned about technique, but having mastered it, they were able to do what the bat-poet did: use their knowledge of technique to create a whole poem that moves us as often as we read it.

It is true, of course, that poets can make technically good poems that fail to move us or that move some of us and not others. It is here that we get into the matter of personal taste, where the evaluation of the poem depends upon more than what is demonstrably bad from a technical point of view, where we have to make judgments about the poet's imaginative use of language, and where our own responsiveness to language may make a difference that we have no clear way of measuring. Though I think sensitivity to language is something that can be cultivated, the cultivation does take time and thought. Compare, for instance, the effectiveness of these two poems about a child on a merry-go-round.

Merry-Go-Round

I climbed up on the Merry-go-round,
And it went round and round.
I climbed up on a big brown horse
And it went up and down.
    Around and round
    And up and down,
    Around and round
    And up and down,
    I sat high up

On a big brown horse
And rode around
On the merry-go-round
And rode around
On the merry-go-round
I rode around
On the merry-go-round
Around
And round.
And
Round.[10]

Though Dorothy Baruch's poem lacks imagery, I can't quarrel about its rhythm or the sincerity of its tone. It is admired by May Hill Arbuthnot because "[t]he words and lines of this poem go round and round like the carrousel itself. From the fifth line on, the merry-go-round and words seem to move faster and faster until shortly after the 'big brown horse' they run down, slower and slower until they stop with the last word."[11] Though I think one may choose to slow down after the "big brown horse," it is only the spacing at the end, not the language, which suggests that one should.

Aside from that question, however, I find the poem dull and unimaginative beside Mark Van Doren's "Merry-Go-Round," which catches not only the rise and fall of the horses on the carrousel but the dreamy imaginings, the idyllic happiness of the child as he rides his own horse, the best one of all.

Horses in front of me,
Horses behind,
But mine is the best one,
He never looks down.
He rises and falls
As if there were waves,
But he never goes under,
Oh, music, oh, mine.

He is steady and strong,
And he knows I am here,
He says he is glad
That I picked him to ride.
But he hasn't a name,
I told him my own,
And he only went faster,
Oh, music, oh, mine.

>Around and around,
>And the people out there
>Don't notice how happy
>I am, I am.
>The others are too,
>But I am the most,
>The most, the most
>Oh, music, oh, mine.[12]

Van Doren was not writing a poem for a child so much as he was re-membering his own experience and recreating it so vividly, in rhythm as well as in mood, that anyone—child or adult—could share the ex-perience with him and gain both pleasure and understanding from it.

Poems for children must be good enough for adults because children have the same need that we have for what is genuine. Inexperienced though they are, they deserve the same authenticity, the same respect for craft and language that we expect for ourselves. Children's poetry should be good enough for adults because it is rarely read only by chil-dren. The poem is an experience shared by the adult who is reading and the child who is listening. The better the poem, the better the experience for both of them. An adult who loves poetry doesn't want to waste time reading poor poems to a child any more than he wants the child to waste time listening to them. He wants the child to grow up hearing the best so that the child will become a discriminating reader. There is more likelihood for this to happen if the poet, the anthologist, and the teacher all learn to become discriminating, too.

Some Afterthoughts on Poetry, Verse, and Criticism

Myra Cohn Livingston

The recognition that children's literature deserves only the best in criticism was spelled out by Francelia Butler in the first volume of *Children's Literature,* published in 1972. Dr. Butler's assessment as to why "clear critical standards" had not been implemented by humanists and critics, up to that time, struck me as valid. Her challenge, reflected in the essays which appeared in that volume, "to stimulate the writing, teaching and study of children's literature by humanists—to encourage humanists with the best (and open) minds to enter the field"[1] has met with response through subsequent issues of *Children's Literature* and through the Children's Literature Association *Newsletter* by those interested in fiction, myth, history, folk tales, fantasy, and illustration. To a much lesser degree, however, has poetry been included. A quick glance through the publications concerning themselves with literature for children, including both the *Newsletter* and *Children's Literature,* corroborates the fact that attention to original poetry, to major poetry anthologies, and to serious study and critique of this genre has yet, from my point of view, to be cultivated and achieved.

The reasons for this lack are somewhat understandable. It is no secret that most critics, humanists or no, are frightened by the very word Poetry. It seems to bespeak some mysterious, esoteric branch of literature comprehensible to the very few. In spite of a burgeoning interest in adult poetry, in spite of what can be called a Golden Age for poetry, written for and anthologized for young people during the past twenty-five years, poetry is, in comparison to other areas of literature, neglected.

Reviewing does appear at times. Occasional articles have been written, but tend to focus more on historical research rather than interest in poetics. Many lean toward a vehicle for what A. E. Housman called the

Reprinted from the *Children's Literature Association Quarterly* 5:16–21 (Summer 1980), with the permission of Myra Cohn Livingston. No part of this article may be reprinted in any form or by any mechanical or visual means without permission in writing from the author.

"rawness of personal opinion."[2] Still others juxtapose the work of established poets with children's writing, serious anthologies with slapdash minor collections of verse built around a popular theme. With few exceptions, there is a lack of the ability to differentiate among light verse, nonsense and serious poetry, between the poet's craft and what John Ciardi labels as "spillage of raw emotion."[3] Little attention is paid to important new voices, while large amounts of space and effort are apportioned to minor work. Liberties are taken with books of poetry that would never be tolerated in other fields of literature. The closest analogy I can dream up in to imagine a scholarly and thoughtful piece on the importance of beautiful prose as found in the work of George MacDonald, Judy Blume, Eleanor Cameron, the Walt Disney *Cinderella,* and the writers of the Nancy Drew books. To say that all of these authors write prose is true, but to compare them in terms of literary merit is plainly ridiculous. Yet this has been done often in the field of poetry and light verse.

During the Seventh Annual Conference of the Children's Literature Association in Waco, I directed an appeal to those who attended to become more aware of—and to take seriously—the field of poetry; to become familiar with the wealth of contemporary poets writing for children, and while not neglecting poets of the past who still speak of the universals of childhood, to view their work in a reasonable perspective. This request was precipitated by my growing concern with various newspapers and periodicals where the level of reviewers' knowledge is patently preposterous. To call a book by a single poet "an anthology," to compare Valerie Worth with Marchette Chute, to be totally unaware of the work of Eve Merriam, to recognize "Someone" by Walter de la Mare as a new poem, to criticize an anthology on the basis of how many of the selections start with the words "A" or "The," or to judge by illustration rather than the merit of the book is only a beginning of a list of grievances I can cite.

I am enough of a realist, however, to understand that poetry is a stepchild—a Cinderella, if you will—who needs a Fairy Godmother to intervene and show her worth. As an idealist, I look to the members of the Children's Literature Association to raise the level of reviewing and criticism, to become *many* godmothers! I went to the conference in Waco, with two minds about response to a *Newsletter* survey as it pertained to poetry choices. My delight in finding David McCord, John Ciardi and Eve Merriam on the list, as well as the predictably popular Shel Silverstein, was sobered by the high ratings for A. A. Milne, Robert Louis Stevenson, Walter de la Mare and Edward Lear. Lear happens to be a passion of mine. I could not do without some poems by de la Mare or a good dozen from *A Child's Garden of Verses*. I was raised on Milne. But to see Milne, who was self-admittedly a writer of light verse, head the list with Stevenson and de la Mare close behind made me keenly aware that even among the most receptive—those who are dedicated to children's literature—who live and breathe it (as opposed to those who write reviews for more commercial publications)—a return to the past, to the familiar and well-worn verse of childhood is easier, more comfortable. This was *not* true of response to other categories in the survey where those who replied seemed vitally up-to-date on contemporary fiction, picture books, fantasy, animal stories, and others.

I think I might make a guess, although I have not seen the list of poets or poems chosen as most popular, that the work is charged with levity, easily read and understood, and probably without any emotional demands upon the reader. It would be written with a largely anapestic beat and elicit immediate and vocal response from children. This is always a good beginning when introducing poetry, but it does fail to probe the deeper aspects of what poetry—real poetry in contrast to light verse—can do if one thinks of literature as a humanizing force.

To further this point I choose to refer to materials given out in Waco for the "Panel on Developing a Canon for Children's Literature." I was unable to attend this session, but I have read the material to be covered by the panel. I like to think that someone pointed out an error in the list of "Some Great and/or Historically Important Pre-1920 Books and Authors for Children." . . . In the interests of scholarship, it seems incorrect to me to pit Blake against the Taylor sisters. Blake's quarrel was with the originator of didactic verse, Dr. Isaac Watts. Jane and Ann Taylor only furthered the precepts of Watts, whose high-handed moralism and invectives against idleness, dreaming, and the pleasures of childhood were countered directly by Blake, complete to the "briar" and "thorn" of the sluggard's garden.[4] Lest this seem picayunish, I return to the points raised by Dr. Butler who asked for "careful study"—a care most certainly respected and nourished by members of the Children's Literature Association in other areas of inquiry, and one that should be exercised for poetry.

Just as important, it seems to me, is an examination of the list contained within this "Canon" material for "Creators of Poetry Worthy of Study" after 1920. There are thirty-six names on this list, writers both living and dead, and I quarrel with this list for two specific reasons.

In the first place, not all of the thirty-six mentioned are poets in the true sense of poetics. If one takes poetry to mean anything written to *look* like poetry, or any words that have either meter and rhyme, or some combination thereof, one might include all the names with the

exception of Christina Rossetti who lived during the nineteenth century
and was, therefore, published before 1920. But such a listing of versi-
fiers and poets seems to me not only simplistic, but inaccurate. As
Rebecca J. Lukens points out in *A Critical Handbook of Children's
Literature:*

Verses can be pleasant and entertaining; they can remind us of sentiments and
ideas with which we agree, but often their expression is trite and awkward,
with rigid metrical structure, ordinary images, obvious rhymes, or phrases
twisted to produce rhyme. They are not poetry as T. S. Eliot has described
it—the distilled and imaginative expression of feeling. Available to children
are large quantities of both verse and poetry. With exposure, children grow in
awareness of the pleasure that artful poetry can bring. Greater experience
with imaginative poetry can lead children to an awareness and appreciation
of Walter de la Mare's "rarest of the best."[5]

As Rebecca Lukens views it, there is a "whole range from rhyme to
nonsense to imaginative poetry,"[6] and it is within this framework that
I feel those who would wish to study and criticize must work. It is impossible to judge A. A. Milne by the same criteria as apply to Randall
Jarrell. To take this a step further, I have taken the liberty of breaking
up the thirty-six names into three distinct categories. In the first group
are those who write merely verse: Dorothy Aldis, Richard Armour, Hilaire Belloc, Marchette Chute, Rose Fyleman, A. A. Milne, Ogden Nash,
Laura Richards, and James Tippett. Those who write poetry and who
avoid versifying or light verse number nine: Mary Austin, Padraic
Colum, Hilda Conkling, Nikki Giovanni, Langston Hughes, Randall
Jarrell, Elizabeth Madox Roberts, Carl Sandburg, and Sara Teasdale.
The longest list is of those who write both in rhyme and light verse as
well as poetry and includes Harry Behn, Stephen Vincent Benet, John
Ciardi, Lucille Clifton, Walter de la Mare, Mary Ann Hoberman, Karla
Kuskin, Vachel Lindsay, Myra Cohn Livingston, David McCord, Phyllis
McGinley, Eve Merriam, James Reeves, Beatrice Schenk de Regniers,
and William Jay Smith.

In many instances, however, it is impossible to classify a poet or versifier. I am aware that such an arbitrary assignment may be a matter of
taste, or merely a matter of determining form. Hilda Conkling, for example, never used the tool of rhyme; Langston Hughes wrote in both
traditional and free forms. I offer this grouping, however, as some guide
to those interested in verse and poetry to examine their own ideas of
what makes a verse and what makes a poem! A versifier may occasionally
write a piece of "artful poetry" just as a poet may wish to play with
light verse. One must always remember that rhyme and metrics are

merely tools; some use them well and others less skillfully. The difficulties arise, in my mind, when the critic or reviewer judges a poet by the same set of standards as one who writes light or humorous verse. I have read many reviews in which a reviewer will moan the lack of "vitality" or bounciness in a poem, as opposed to a piece of light verse, when what is meant is not what the poem says, what the strength of the voice or image may be, what power it may have to stretch the reader's imagination, but rather that it is not written in a running, happy, tripping meter, that is, anapests.

Many critics assume that because children are young and physically active they will respond only to active rhythm. This is often true. But it is no excuse for a putdown of poets whose work is not primarily playful or whimsical or funny. The reviewer who compared the artful metaphors of Valerie Worth to the verse of Marchette Chute, James Tippett, and Bobbi Katz reveals ignorance of the difference between meter and rhyme and poetry. The critic (and even reviewer) of poetry, it seems to me, must understand the craft of the poet and the tools which are used. Had Shakespeare written, in the strict iambic pentameter of blank verse, "To be or not to be is what I ask," he would be a far lesser poet. The break from the traditional iambic beat to the use of the dactyl and trochee emphasizes Hamlet's doubting, perplexed condition and mood: "that is the question."

Here, heaviness of mood is strengthened by heavy and falling metrical feet. It is no accident that one of the most parodied poems in the English language is Edgar Allan Poe's "Annabel Lee," for the subject matter, supposedly tragic, is presented in the light-hearted anapestic line beginning "It was many and many a year ago," and continuing throughout in meter diametrically opposed to the sadness Poe wishes to convey. A Shakespeare would have begun the poem, "Many and many a year ago," thereby restructuring the meter to match the sadness of subject with the falling dactyls.

Just so would David McCord's poem about "Castor Oil" be weak and ineffective if he had started it, "Oh, I hate Castor Oil, it's bitter and bad," for a reader will scarcely believe by the bouncing rhythm that it is nasty stuff. Rather does McCord wisely choose the falling trochee and dactyls for the opening lines:

> Ever, ever, not ever so terrible
> Stuff as unbearable castor oil[7]

Such explication may seem superfluous to many, but to those who take poetry and light verse seriously it is of the greatest importance, and should be familiar to anyone who wishes to establish some measure of standards in the field of criticism. If one is unaware of the craft of poetry, how can it be reviewed credibly and with scholarship?

My second disappointment with the list of poets deemed worthy of study is the omission of about twenty-four poets currently writing for children whose work is every bit as important as those who are listed—and in a number of instances, far more important. It strikes me as nescient that the same group who is aware of contemporary writers like Mildred Taylor, Virginia Hamilton, and Paul Zindel, to mention but three, would not put on the list of poets such accomplished light verse writers as N. M. Bodecker, Charles Causley, Dennis Lee, Shel Silverstein, and Clyde Watson. They have given children laughter and pleasure just as surely as have Lear, Milne, and Richards—and perhaps more!

Insofar as poets are concerned there are glaring omissions: Arnold Adoff, Elizabeth Coatsworth, Norma Farber, Siv Cedering Fox, Ted Hughes, Leslie Norris, Judith Thurman, Richard Wilbur, and Valerie Worth. We might add to this list Gwendolyn Brooks, Eloise Greenfield, and Joan Aiken, who might only be judged by one book—yet others who appear on the original list have written no more than one.

Those writing both poetry and light verse who are omitted deserve consideration as well: Conrad Aiken, Countee Cullen, Felice Holman, Patricia Hubbell, X. J. Kennedy, Lilian Moore, Bonnie Nims, Jack Prelutsky, E. V. Rieu, Mary O'Neill, Ian Serraillier, Kaye Starbird, and John Updike, as well as Robert Froman writing in open forms.

And certainly Maurice Sendak, Dr. Seuss, and Ludwig Bemelmans might spill over from the picture book category into that of light verse.

Of course, one could go on, choosing for worthiness adult poets whose work is enjoyed by children; E. E. Cummings, T. S. Eliot, Theodore Roethke, and many others come to mind who write in a diction which the young understand and of emotional matters or subjects to which children respond. One could end up with a list of a hundred or so light verse and poetry writers, all in tune with the sensitivities, rhythms, and interests of young people.

I am not unaware of the process of selection. I realize that those who were chosen must have met some specific criteria of the panel. Yet, I must continue to wonder what critical standards are involved! I do not, as a reader of light verse, nonsense verse, and poetry, respond equally and wholeheartedly to the work of those selected for this list—not even to those I have added.

But, if we speak of a "canon," then surely we must establish some guiding principles by which we separate the mediocre from the outstanding. I remember touching on the matter of selection of anthologies in Waco, attempting briefly to point out that there is a marked difference between a slim volume of somewhere between eighteen to twenty-four poems and verses, illustrated with at least some color on the dustjacket (if not within the book itself) to attract the reader, and the anthology of from eighty to one hundred poems, less brilliantly decorated, perhaps, but with meat and bone to the selections. Few people seem to be aware that anthologists may pay for use of poems not in public domain—that an anthology may cost many thousands of dollars. The price one pays for books today seems high, and reviewers are eager to equate the number of poems to the price when it comes to books of one poet who is presenting new and fresh work. Yet they voice no protest if there are colored illustrations for an anthology which contains no more than several dozen selections, most of which can be found elsewhere.

I fear, alas, that many are led too far astray by illustration. There seems no protest about price or mediocrity of selection, if the pictures are pleasing. It is at this point that the poetry or verse is always a second consideration, and this should not be so. I think of one book of original poetry that has received much praise for the illustrations and wonder how many reviewers and critics have read the poems, carefully crafted to be sure, but so opposed in content to the spirit of childhood that it is frightening to me. We must all be aware of the hopelessness and fear and pessimism that permeate other genres of literature. We speak out against it, if we so wish—but not so with poetry.

I mention this now, because most of us are cognizant that without critical standards, the mediocre will triumph over the excellent. It takes vigilance and wide reading to be aware of what is happening in poetry, the contribution that is being made by poets and anthologists. It is up to those who are in touch daily with the literature published for children to make themselves aware of the new, as well as the old, and a framework in which both may be judged.

A year or so after the Children's Literature Association was formed and I had seen the first *Newsletter* I became uncommonly excited about the organization. Some of its supporters were known to me through their writing. I had met very few. I sent in the application blank and dues because I wished to support those who took children's literature seriously. I felt honored to be invited to Waco; I am equally pleased to contribute to this Poetry Supplement, and my criticism is offered as constructive. It is through saying or writing what we feel, I believe, that all of us grow.

If the Children's Literature Association establishes criteria of excellence and continues to re-evaluate what makes for excellence, continues to publish papers and essays with regard for humanism as well as for scholarship, and continues to exchange ideas through publications and conferences, it might well happen that the inferior reviewing of many other publications will feel some impact. This may well be another idealistic viewpoint, but I strongly believe that those I spoke with in Waco and those whose work I have previously read have the vitality, interest, and ability to make this happen.

Ours is an age where the lowest common denominator prevails. It would seem to me to be the credo and task (and not an easy one) of the Children's Literature Association to continue to set high standards in all genres of children's literature.

Let poetry be one of these.

7 / Fiction

The children's novel has been around almost as long as the adult novel. Sarah Fielding, Henry Fielding's sister, presented a series of stories in a boarding-school setting in *The Governess* (1749), the first of the much-imitated school stories. But *The History of Little Goody Two-Shoes* (1765) has much more of the continuity one expects from a novel, as Mary Thwaite observes.[1] Margery Meanwell, like Samuel Richardson's Pamela, rises in Cinderella fashion from peasant to lady. Hundreds of such storybooks were available in the eighteenth century, not to mention abridgements of adult classics like *Tom Jones* and even *Pamela*.

The changing fortunes of this literature are revealed here by Gillian Avery, who shows that not the critics nor the educators but the child ultimately decides what endures in fiction for children. But as Mrs. Piozzi told Samuel Johnson when he protested that babies do not want to read about babies, the adult buys the books, not the child. For the artist, the sobering conclusion Avery makes is that, whoever the author writes for, chances are slender indeed if his or her work lasts beyond a generation.

Over two centuries after the first child novel, Margery Fisher's article asks whether fiction is educational; primarily, it is not, she answers. One could conceivably learn the care and feeding of a pig by reading *Charlotte's Web,* but the experience of the book is what matters; otherwise we are back to the "Pray, Papa, what is a camel?" books of the English Rousseauists that Avery criticizes. While the child novel can be an educational tool misused, Fisher notes, there is no danger in a proper study of the child novel.

A century after *Goody Two-Shoes,* another landmark of juvenile fiction was printed, Lewis Carroll's *Alice in Wonderland,* the most scrutinized book for children ever. But the novel of fantasy has evolved its own genre or subgenre. The adventure story was also a Victorian specialization, along with an attendant bifurcation of the boy-girl audience begun, in part, a century earlier. Although Henry James deplored the female and the child audience, some of his contemporaries, like Robert Louis Stevenson deliberately wrote adventure yarns "to fetch the kids." And Mark Twain intended *Tom Sawyer* for boys and girls.

In some ways children's fiction has been penalized for its own growth. The child novel, no longer a simple storybook, has been broken up into the regions of fantasy, science fiction, and the young adult novel, and so on. Some critics see a neglect of younger children's needs:

It seems that commentators enjoy talking about picture books—all that lovely art work—and about novels for the older child—all those lovely complexities and near-adult themes. But talking about what pleases children of 7 or so to 9 or so lacks the fashionable taste for obscurity, psychological dilemma, and social disenchantment.[2]

Natalie Babbitt made a special plea for "the great American novel for children," noting the classics of children's books which belong to this genre.[3] And Isaac Bashevis Singer sees the child as the natural audience for the story. Where then are the novels for young children?

We need yet another boundary survey. Myles McDowell has pointed out some essential differences between fiction for children and adults. He finds the former generally are briefer and feature child protagonists and contain more dialogue and incident than description and introspection. In essence, he finds "a good children's book makes complex experience available to its readers; a good adult book draws attention to the inescapable complexity of experience."[4] Two books on children's fiction also attempt to show differences between juvenile and adult fiction. Wallace Hildick in *Children and Fiction* sees an abundance of concrete detail, an element of surprise, logical conclusions, and an appeal to curiosity along with verbal dexterity as signal qualities of fiction for the young. Of the critics of that genre Hildick expects more than "blurb regurgitation" or "thin unsubstantiated comments as: 'What child could resist the following pen-picture?' or 'This is a masterly piece of writing.' . . ."

What we wish to know is *why* the critic thinks a piece of writing is "masterly" or "fine" or "characteristic" or "irresistible to a child." We need closely pursued investigations and closely argued conclusions. We need, in fact, studies of children's fiction of the same calibre as such classics in the adult field as *Seven Types of Ambiguity . . . The Liberal Imagination, The Craft of Fiction*.[5]

Until we find out where children's fiction stops and adult fiction begins and what is necessarily shared, the studies Hildick asks for will be hopelessly muddled. Nicholas Tucker's *The Child and the Book* does investigate why certain themes and approaches are popular with the young. He admits that there may be no real difference between the two forms other than the artificial and commercial habit of separating the audience by age group, but he finds a distinctive difference between the needs of adult and child "and therefore between the types of literature they get." Tucker finds children's fiction less complex than adult fiction and more selective as contrasted with the endless paragraphs of Proust or James. And the child's imaginative responses to words and their sounds he finds "probably the single most unpredictable topic to try to understand in the whole field of children's literature."[6] The complication is children are not sophisticated in explaining why they like or dislike a book. One critic observed that asking a child to review a juvenile novel is like asking a gamekeeper to review *Lady Chatterley's Lover*.

For all the seeming neglect of the young reader in today's fiction, only in fiction for the young has there been a series of attempts to analyze literature for a child in terms of what the artist must do to relate to that audience. Contrasting various versions of the ballads he edited, Francis Child saw three different kinds of person responsible for changes to them: the blind beggar who modified his story to suit a particular audience, the nursery maid who edited or appended moral elements, and the clerk who modified them to please himself. Up through at least the early nineteenth century, the nursery maid held sway over the child story; then the learned clerk stepped in who wrote to please himself. Thanks to the work of Chambers, Hildick, and Tucker we can see how blind we have been to the extent to which a teller, consciously or unconsciously, suits the story to the primary audience—the child.

Fashions in Children's Fiction

Gillian Avery

For an author it is sobering to study the history of children's books. You realize then that though you may have thought you were original— that you were writing what you really thought and what you really wanted to say, you are no more original than the people who call their daughters Sarah and Emma and think that the names are their own idiosyncratic choice. You are dancing, as like as not, to the tune of the age; you are under the spell of the Zeitgeist. And most specially does this apply to those of us who hope to win the approval of the adults: of educationists, literary critics, child psychologists, moralists. For fashions in education for children change rapidly, and the child-hero that pleases one generation of pundits seems dismally out of date to the next, and usually completely incomprehensible to later child readers.

The heroes of the children's story show the qualities that the elders of any given time have considered desirable, attractive, or interesting in the young. Sometimes they have wanted the obedient, diligent, miniature adult, sometimes the evangelical child, or perhaps they have had a penchant for sprightly mischief, or sought to inculcate self-knowledge and independence. The surprise lies not in the swings of fashion in the pattern child, but in the unanimity of opinion at any given time about his qualities. But the melancholy fact is that the higher the reputation of the book with the educationists and moralists of the time, the flatter it falls with the children of succeeding generations. To the social historian it may be valuable; as literature it is moribund. One might even say that to be acclaimed by the pedagogues and pundits of the moment is to receive the kiss of death.

But there has never been a lack of authors willing to be so kissed. At the beginning of the last century flocks of docile sheep were crowding to provide little conversational treatises of the "Pray, Papa, what is a camel?" sort, and to urge diligence, dutifulness and prudence. Fashion then demanded a rational and well-informed young person, free from

Reprinted with minor corrections from *Children's Literature in Education* no. 12:10–19 (Sept. 1973), with permission of Agathon Press, Inc., 15 E. 26th St., New York, N.Y., and the author.

distressing childish traits. No responsible person dreamed of writing a fairy tale; they were a reminder of the bad old days when children's reading was not taken seriously, when the young were exposed to the malign influence of chapbook versions of *Jack the Giant-Killer*. Besides, how could you expect rational thought from a child whose mind was tainted by works of imagination? And those who desired an evangelical child entirely agreed on that point at least with the utilitarians: fairy tales were dangerously corrupting.

The enlightened went further. They saw that by providing the right sort of books they could reason a child into sensible, good behaviour. If correctly written, a book need not only inform or issue warnings; you could produce a form of fiction that did not pervert the character or inflame the imagination, that would exert a positively beneficial effect. We get an example of this in "William and his Story Books," an episode in *Rich Boys and Poor Boys* where little Charles, the child of up-to-date parents, bravely confronts Mr. Maynard who represents the old-fashioned way of thinking. They are disputing over the reading of William, a farmer's son. Mr. Maynard says to provide him with anything other than copybooks and manuals of accountancy would be a wicked error. Little Charles (with great courtesy and modesty, of course) says that storybooks play a part in education too. His own want of moral courage had been corrected by one such, and he asserts that modern books "are very different things from the fairy tales, and Jack the Giant-Killer stories boys used to read when you and [my father] were young." Two years go by and then William himself is asked which books have proved the more valuable—Mr. Maynard's accounting books or Charles' stories. William is in no doubt about the matter; the storybooks are the winners every time.

Why, sir many's the time they kept father at home when he would have gone out, and that made my mother happy: my sister Sally, who was once proud and pettish, was taught by *them* to be humble and obedient; and Nancy, who was indolent, became industrious; and as for myself, why. . . .

The list of the improvements in William are as predictable as they are tedious. Charles and his father do not think so, however, and the latter is so delighted that he presents the boy's father with the tenancy of one of his farms and the boy with a supply of reading matter suitable for his station in life. In those days writers believed in material rewards.

The succeeding generation however desired more spiritual things. The knowledge of a good deed well done, a quiet conscience, and perhaps a holy death was more likely to be the reward. The threats of fire and brimstone and everlasting punishment which the evangelical writers used towards the transgressing child diminished as the Victorian era advanced, and the tone became gentle and affectionate. Standards were high; it was not enough to do the right thing, you should do it for the right reason, to please God, not merely to curry favour with your schoolteacher or your fellows. But death more often than not was the reward. "Good young people are not allowed to see many years of life," lamented Edward Salmon referring to the fashion in girls' stories still current.

By 1900 the taste in children had changed entirely; the little friend of all the world was the new ideal, the innocent child who might do deliciously naughty things, but who was sound at heart, since he looked up at scolding elders with brave, fearless eyes and never flinched for an instant from the truth. "Madcaps," "scamps," "pickles," these children were variously called by their creators; they are essentially a product of a generation who handed their offspring over to nurses and nurserymaids, and did not have to deal with the dirt, confusion, and torn clothes that resulted from these heartwarming pranks. We can see how much attitudes have changed by comparing *The Child's Companion* (a publication of the Religious Tract Society for Sunday Schools) of 1844 and the same magazine in 1923. In 1844 we are shown the dreadful consequences of a Sabbath scholar who, though spoken of by his teacher "with peculiar pleasure as a hopeful character," is tempted to stroll in the fields one Sunday when school is done. He breaks his leg and suffers great mental anguish as well as physical pain. In 1923 there is virtually no attempt to improve, and very little to inform, and the magazine carries a serial about two children known by their mother as the "torments" and their cat Torrid (because he is "hot stuff"), whose various desperate deeds result in stolen diamonds being restored to their owner.

We have now reached the era when the child is emancipated from his elders, when the Enid Blyton heroes roam the Devon moors in happy freedom, encountering adults only in the form of international criminals on the run, or welcoming, rosy-cheeked farmers' wives eager to provide cream teas. On a more sophisticated plane we have the cool, level-headed children of the Arthur Ransome and M. E. Atkinson type, intent on enjoying themselves without the burden of parents and interfering adults. After about thirty years of this the teachers and critics rebel; enough of this middle-class ascendancy, why not books about secondary modern school children *for* secondary modern children. The authors oblige; they fall over themselves to show Mum with her hair in rollers eating fish and chips at the launderette while her offspring roam the streets with latchkeys round their necks, and some of those who had been writing about grooming the pony for the gymkhana now turn their attention to the coster-monger's nag.

Stretch the child's imagination, plead the pundits of the late sixties, expand his horizons. A flood of sombre pseudo-mythology and sub-Tolkien follows, kingdoms where the rats and the rabbits reign, where the powers of darkness wrestle with the powers of light. They wrestle on still, and have been joined by the child of the seventies, the child who "comes to terms with himself" and achieves catharsis through violence. Rufus, in Catherine Storr's story of that name, is not fulfilled until he has knocked down Mickey at the orphanage. Ivan Southall's Josh is not a whole person until he has been lynched and nearly drowned by the juveniles at Ryan Creek. And in the same writer's *Finn's Folly* the two adolescent central characters realize themselves in a swirling fog in which three parents have been killed, a mentally retarded brother lost, and enough cyanide unleashed to poison the whole of Australia.

Thus the history of children's books is fascinating to the social historian for the picture of the pattern child that emerges at any given time; the virtues that elders have vigorously sought to inculcate; the dangers that have seemed most potent; the taboos of the period. But those of us who write for children realize that our chances of survival beyond this generation are slender indeed, and beyond the next, minimal.

To grasp just how minimal they are we have only to consider the case of those two experts on children's reading, Mrs. Trimmer and Charlotte Yonge. They were both women who shared very much the same outlook. They stood for the same Christian ideals. They passionately supported the established church and felt that this should be the overriding influence in educational matters. In one of Charlotte Yonge's novels, for instance, we are shown girls busily working for a bazaar whose purpose is to raise money to suppress a National School which might threaten the existing parish school. Mrs. Trimmer, in the Lancaster versus Bell battle that raged in her lifetime, took up cudgels for Bell and whacked away at Lancaster because she believed the Church of England must control all schools. Both ladies were deeply and practically involved with the education of the poorer classes. But when they came to recommend books for children's reading there is hardly a title which they have in common.

From the engraving at the front of the work *Some Account of the Life and Writings of Mrs. Trimmer,* which was published in 1814, four years after her death, we get the impression of a round-faced, middle-aged lady, with a pleasant, fresh English complexion. She looks good, and she was good. You have only to read her meditations, which make up the bulk of the book, to know that she was God-loving and dutiful and very serious about her responsibilities. She was also enviably certain that what she stood for was right; what she opposed was wrong, and there was no middle way. Life would be so simple and pleasant, she seems to be saying, if only everybody did what they were told, and feared God and honoured the king and loved their neighbour (only you must first be sure that the neighbour held the right opinion).

Her interest in education came with the birth of her children. At first she was wholly occupied with their upbringing (there were twelve of them), but by 1786 she was sufficiently unencumbered to occupy herself with the promoting of a Sunday School in Brentford, and in 1802 she founded *The Guardian of Education*, with which her name nowadays is chiefly linked.

Before we can really understand the strictures and comments in it we have to know the background. It was the time of the French wars; revolution was in the air, plenty of intellectuals had been dangerously excited by the happenings in France earlier on—it had then seemed like the start of a wonderful new era. And now the French philosophers were infecting the minds of men: Diderot, Voltaire, Rousseau. Mrs. Trimmer thought their influence unutterably evil, and she wanted to protect the new generation from them. The way to achieve this was to see that no books reached children that were tainted by the Jacobin or atheistic notions so distressingly prevalent.

Just as critics of today have disclosed all sorts of dangers arising from the reading of Enid Blyton, so Mrs. Trimmer could find threats to the social order in the most unexpected places. *John Gilpin* should be barred because "it places an honest, industrious tradesman, worthy to be held out as an example of prudence and economy to men of his rank, in a ridiculous situation, and provokes a laugh at the expense of conjugal affection." A riddle in a joke book called *Mince Pies for Christmas* was so obviously detestable that she needed to make no comment herself. It was "What is Majesty deprived of its Externals?" The answer is "A Jest" (Majesty without the M and Y), and this of course is Jacobinism of the direst sort. Nor did she like jokes about courtiers or great men, because these too threatened the social order as did *The Renowned History of Primrose Prettyface*, because it suggested to girls of the lower order that they might aspire to marriage with persons so far superior to their own, and put into the heads of young gentlemen at an early age an idea that they might, when they grew up, marry servant maids.

Harvey Darton has given an account of her stern line with fairy stories. At first she was tender towards them, remembering how she had been delighted in her own childhood by Mother Goose, Aesop, and Gay's Fables. She did not think they did any positive good but at this stage she did not realize their potential harm. As far as I can see, the hardening of her attitude dates from a review which she wrote of Bible stories retold by a certain William Scolfield. Mr. Scolfield was not content to let the Bible stories stand on their own merit; he had to write a foolish preface in which he recommended them as a way in which children's imaginations might be exercised: "without imagination . . . we can neither ourselves love, or be fitted to excite the love of others. . . . It is the heart which must be cultivated."

Mrs. Trimmer was outraged. "How the heart is to be cultivated by the force of imagination only, is to us inconceivable. We are told by God himself, that the imagination of the heart of man is evil from his youth, and we are persuaded that will be fully exemplified in those who have been accustomed in their earliest days to be led by it." And having said this, she had, to be logical, to condemn anything that she felt was tainted by imagination. Fairy stories, she could hardly bear to think of them now; she lamented every time that Tabart or Newbery put out a little volume of the tales she had loved when she was a child, though it was one of her correspondents who pointed out to her just what a force for evil *Cinderella* was, and how it painted "some of the worst passions that can enter into the human breast."

What books did she approve of? Very few names mean anything to us nowadays. There is John Aikin and Mrs. Barbauld's *Evenings at Home,* whose popularity lasted into Victorian times. There are Isaac Watts's *Divine and Moral Songs,* remembered chiefly because of Carroll's parodies. She liked Jane and Ann Taylor's *Original Poems,* and though she had criticism to offer as to the moral content she thought that the young authors would improve in subsequent works. She gave much space to the educational works of Richard Lovell Edgeworth (of whose Rousseauist theories she disapproved) and the stories of his daughter Maria which she recommended though she felt their lack of religious teaching. Otherwise, the authors she recommends are totally forgotten— people like Mrs. Pilkington, Mrs. Pinchard, Priscilla Wakefield, Mrs. Hofland, Miss Sandham; schoolmistresses, most of them, who made a little extra money through their books, and vented some of their irritation with girl-nature at the same time.

And so we come to the story that Mrs. Trimmer herself wrote for children in 1786, *Fabulous Histories,* on which the children of all right-minded parents were reared for two generations. Nothing could be done to revive this book now. It is entombed in its period, slain partly by its didacticism, partly by its literary style—considered so mellifluous in its time. There are two interwoven sets of characters, the human family and the robin family; and the author aimed to teach kindness to animals while at the same time presenting in the person of the robins human qualities that she wished either to encourage or to discourage. Highly didactic though it is, it was popular among children of the more educated sort in the first half of the last century. After all, it was the nearest approach to imaginative literature that responsible elders allowed them at the time, and the theme of kindness to animals was a more palatable moral than most. The portentous title, *Fabulous Histories, Designed for the instruction of children, respecting their treatment of animals,* was later discarded in favour of the more tempting *The History of the Robins.*

From the modern point of view the interest lies in the picture that is given of the pattern Georgian child. There are four robin young: Robin, Dicky, Pecksy, and Flapsy. (These rather endearing names seem un-Trimmeresque, and that is correct—she took over Flapsy and Pecksy from a Newbery publication.) Pecksy is the shining light of the family, the ideal daughter. She is dutiful, grateful, submissive to the will of her parents, plentifully endowed with sensibility. (Sensibility was a quality that exercised the Georgians; they desired a young person to show feeling, but not extravagant feeling, and deprecated the sort of false sensibility that sent a girl into hysterics, for instance, when her parrot died.) She obediently accepts the necessity of acquiring accomplishments, though a little doubtful of her ability to sing. "I would apply to music with all my heart," she says to her father, "but I do not believe it is possible to learn it." "Perhaps not," says Mr. Robin, "but I do not doubt that you will apply yourself to what your mother requires of you: and she is an excellent judge both of your talents and of what is suitable to your station in life."

Protected and observed by the human family, Mr. and Mrs. Benson and their children, the robins grow to maturity, and take leave of their parents. "Oh! delightful sentiments of maternal love, how can I part with you? Let me, my nestlings, give you a last embrace," says Mrs. Robin, folding them to her bosom with her wings. On their own, Dicky and Flapsy, who are rather giddy and heedless, get trapped and imprisoned in an aviary. (Imprudence and overboldness was a favourite theme of the Georgian moral tale.) Pecksy cannot bear to live very far from her parents; Robin makes himself dependent upon the bounty of the Bensons since he is something of an invalid—having also been incautious and imprudent in his time. The older robins, with exquisite tact, move on to another human benefactor since they wish to be a burden to the Bensons no longer. Seldom can even a children's book have been written with so little sense of the ludicrous.

Certainly when Charlotte Yonge came to compile in 1887 a choice of books for the parish library and for reward books she did not include *The*

History of the Robins. In fact, a comparison of this pamphlet, *What Books to Give and What to Lend*, with *The Guardian of Education* recommendations of eighty years earlier drives home the hard fact of how transitory are the fashions in children's books. Miss Yonge, as we have seen, wrote from just the same sort of background and the same viewpoint as Mrs. Trimmer. She had had fifty-five years of experience in running a parish Sunday School by the time she came to draw up her booklist. She was thoroughly acquainted with the books available at the time, and knew what was in the various readers used in the classrooms, and where these needed supplementing. She was a person of great cultivation, and though her outlook was rather limited by the restricted circle in which she had spent her life, she had a shrewd good sense when it came to selecting books with which to amuse and instruct children.

A library is an almost indispensible adjunct to a school, if children are to be lured to stay at home instead of playing questionable games in the dark, or by gaslight, out of doors; and an amusing story is the best chance of their not exasperating the weary father with a noise. If the boy is not to betake himself to "Jack Sheppard" literature, he must be beguiled by wholesome adventure. . . . If the girl is not to study the "penny dreadful" her notions must be refined by the tale of high romance or pure pathos.

Only eighty years have gone by, but the attitude to children's reading has been completely changed. Charlotte Yonge talks about "beguiling" and "amusing," and, furthermore, deplores the ignorance that she has found in the cottages on the subject of fairy stories. A knowledge of them is absolutely necessary, she says stoutly, if only to understand common allusions, and she includes a whole section devoted not only to the Arabian Nights, Hans Andersen, Grimm, and legends, but to literary fairy tales such as the Alices, *The Water Babies, The Light Princess* and *Four-Winds Farm*.

The 955 titles that she lists are of great interest, not only to show what was available and acceptable in 1887, but in comparison with what had gone before and what was to come. Miss Yonge herself was struck by how few children's books remained from an older epoch. "It is curious to find how many stories have become obsolete. Not only have the tales where vanity is displayed by wearing white stockings . . . become archaic; but the stories of the good children who are household supports and little nurses, picking up chance crumbs of instruction, have lost all present reality."

Certainly the pattern for the cottage child had changed, even in Miss Yonge's lifetime. Her first books for the parish school children in the

1850s had stressed such sins as vanity and trying to move out of one's station in life. We have Clementina, who tries to emulate the dress of the young ladies who teach her, thereby showing too much white drawers below her dress, and too much fringe on her spencer. Such homilies were out of date in 1887. The pattern daughter of the upper class home was different in the 1850s too. In *Henrietta's Wish,* which Miss Yonge wrote in 1850, we are shown the strong-willed Henrietta who expresses a wish that her widowed mother might consider moving back to her old home in Sussex. Neurotic, feeble, and frail, Henrietta's mother does this. Nothing but disaster follows, for all of which Henrietta is held responsible. Commenting on this book from the distance of the Edwardian epoch, Ethel Romanes, one of Miss Yonge's biographers, remarked that nowadays this mother's children would be pitied not blamed. She also remarked on how different children of 1908 were from those of sixty years before; "decidedly younger than they used to be, and we are not sure that this is a change altogether for the worse."

Thus in 1887 the Victorian child hero was so completely different from the Georgian child hero that Charlotte Yonge could include almost nothing from that period. Certainly not *The Robins* nor that other Georgian classic, *Sandford and Merton.* From the scores of books that Mrs. Trimmer had recommended she took only one author, Maria Edgeworth. Mrs. Trimmer had been doubtful about the lack of moral content in her writings; Charlotte Yonge had no such reservations. *The Parent's Assistant,* the Harry and Lucy stories, the Frank and Rosamond stories were of an excellence, she considered, that could carry them over to Victorian times even though all their contemporaries were obsolescent.

And if we move on another eighty years, to 1957, when the *Sunday Times* in consultation with Kathleen Lines produced a list of ninety-nine best books for children, we cannot find a single title on which all three authorities are agreed. *Robinson Crusoe* is on all the lists, but then far from recommending him, Mrs. Trimmer had warned that he was dangerous reading; "it might lead children into an early taste for a rambling life, and a desire of adventure," and she gave a sombre warning about the lady who had been led into a fatal illness through fright at her little boys trying to emulate the hero.

The curious thing is that while at the time it seems to be adult standards and adult taste that dictate the nature and the form of the children's book that is in favour at any given time, in the end it is the children who get their own way. They had their own way about the fairy stories; Mrs. Trimmer and her contemporaries proscribed them, but these were the books which the Victorians had to welcome back, and which the lists of 1887 and 1957 agreed were unfailingly popular. And in the various surveys of children's reading, such as the poll in the Pall Mall Gazette of 1898, they have appeared at the top of the list.

The child's own pattern hero has in fact varied far less than the adult's notion of it. Victor Neuburg in his introduction to *The Penny Histories* has pointed out how there seem to have been always two kinds of archetypal figures in children's literature—the "serious" type like Jack the Giant-killer or Robin Hood, and the comic such as Simple Simon. And all through the history of popular children's literature one finds them: on the one hand Dick Turpin, Spring-heeled Jack, Sexton Blake, Batman, Tarzan, on the other Billy Bunter, Just William, or Jennings—all deprecated, if not downright denounced by the educationists. But it is these who have the unfortunate knack of lingering in the memory long after the moral and the lesson and the immaculate literary style of the "good" book has been forgotten.

Perhaps the best example of how the lesson in a children's book can misfire is given by Angela Brazil:

When I was just able to read, my aunt sent me a delightful little book by R. M. Ballantyne, entitled *The Robber Kitten*. The hero ran away, after proclaiming "I'll never more be good," and lived the life of a bandit in a gloomy wood. Of course he came to sad grief and finally limped home with a bandaged head, in deep repentance, but I completely missed the point of the story! I only concerned myself with his magnificent and fascinating independence. I tried it on too, refusing point-blank to do what I was told, and chanting airily "I'll never more be good." [*My Own Schooldays,* 1925]

It should come as a solemn warning to us well-meaning authors that if we are remembered at all, it may well be for some point we never intended to make.

REFERENCES

Brazil, Angela. *My Own Schooldays.* London: Blackie, 1925.

Neuburg, Victor. *The Penny Histories.* London: Oxford Univ. Pr., 1968.

Southall, Ivan. *Finn's Folly.* London: Augus & Robertson, Penguin; New York: Macmillan, 1969.

Southall, Ivan. *Josh.* London: Angus & Robertson; New York: Macmillan, 1971.

Storr, Catherine. *Rufus.* London: Faber; Boston: Gambit, 1969.

Is Fiction Educational?

Margery Fisher

What do we mean by stories being educational? A child who has just finished *King Solomon's Mines* will have a vague idea of what the landscape of central Africa is like, but he won't be able to recite the chief products and river systems of the country. What he will carry to his grave (at any rate I know I shall) is a mental image, not always the same in detail with each reading but always the same in essence, of that mysterious, rocky, hot, exciting land. This image in my mind has always been altered by later impressions of Africa, but I know it won't be wholly blotted out even if I go there, and I wouldn't want to lose this image, although I have now added many which are far truer in the literal sense. This is what fiction does. It educates in a way, not necessarily more valuable, but quite different from the education in geography of film strips or lectures or visits or books of direct information.

If I can give another example, the child who reads that story by Esther Hautzig, *The Endless Steppe,* is not going to be able to reconstruct the political situation of eastern Europe from it. He will take from it perhaps his first and possibly his strongest impression of the Siberian Steppes from the author's descriptions, but the most important lesson he will learn will be more directly relevant to him. He will have learnt something about people, the way they laugh and suffer and work and contrive, and he will never entirely forget this lesson.

The Endless Steppe was not primarily written as a book for children, and its British editor has put it on record that she had to be very persistent before she succeeded in getting the book for her children's list. I have not heard any protests about this and I do not expect to, but I do foresee that there may be incidental protests from some list makers and card indexers, because this book won't fit into separate categories. It isn't a teenage novel. It isn't an adventure story with a foreign setting. It does not suit the headings World War Two and Its Aftermath or

---

Reprinted from *Children's Literature in Education* no. 1:11–18 (March 1970), with permission of Agathon Press, Inc., 15 E. 26th St., New York, N.Y. Originally given as an address at the Exeter Conference, "Recent Children's Fiction and Its Role in Education," August 1969 at St. Luke's College, Exeter, England.

Family Story, and this I think is going to worry people who like to have books neatly docketed in pigeonholes like brands of soap powder. I can think of other works of fiction published in recent years which have bothered the orderly minded: *The Owl Service* for one; Philippa Pearce's *A Dog So Small*—perhaps few books have been so variously classified, and of course it belongs everywhere; Ivan Southall's electrifying story *Finn's Folly*. We can all think of many more. Certainly we have to put books like this somewhere on some list. There must be lists to help those who work with the young and have not the time or opportunity to read all the hundreds of books published each year for children. We are here this week to demonstrate the need to do more work, not less, in classifying and studying children's books, examining them in relation to this kind of child or that kind of child. We are all of us, directly or indirectly, looking for the perfect system of education. I don't believe we shall ever find it. But as we look for it and legislate for it and argue about it we do turn up interesting ideas and methods of work by the way, and we find out a great deal about the way children feel and think and behave. We also find out, if we are lucky, how little we know about them as individuals. In all this activity we necessarily examine books as one of the great tools of education, and a great deal of time and typewriter ink is spent discussing the response of children to stories. What do they remember best in a story? Do they want to read about children older or younger than themselves? What are they frightened by? We even remember to ask sometimes what kind of stories they enjoy.

In all our queries we put the children first, because they are our first responsibility. But the book was there before the child, and it will be there after him. I think there's a danger in the remarkable acceleration of work on children's books in the past few years. I think it has brought increased and unjustified pressure on writers. An author writes of course in order to communicate something to other people. He can never be completely unaware of his audience. He calls upon his craftsmanship to shape an original impulse, so as to bring it out of the depths of himself and make it accessible to other people. But it is still his book—it is part of himself. Something inside him has forced him to manipulate it into independent life. Once he has done this (in other words, once his book has been published), he has exposed it to criticism and analysis and categorizing. He has given us the right to consider it closely in relation to accepted literary principles and to decide what we think of it and what kind of child might read it. But he hasn't given us the right to meddle with his writing of the book. He has not given us the right to say, "Please accept this or that formula. Please avoid violence, because we don't think it's good for children. Please don't use any words they don't understand.

It might bother them." As they say of television programmes, we can always switch off. We have the right to put a book aside if we object to it, but we have not the right to try to dictate to the author in the first place. We must accept his book as an entity. We must approach it without prejudice or prejudgment and make it our first business to try to find out why the author wrote it, what he is aiming at.

A book is *not* primarily educational. It is an experience for the reader. It is an individual creation existing in its own right made by the individual who, in the long run, makes his own rules. Now every art is susceptible to fashion and to public demand. Johann Sebastian Bach was criticized by his employers at Arnstadt because he extended and elaborated the preambles to the hymns so that the congregation did not know when to start singing. His answer was to stop preambling altogether. Now I would hate to start a writer's strike. Music of course has seldom been as susceptible to direction from outside as it was for Bach. The medium of painting is not so direct and universal that it could be easily controlled by the customers, except perhaps in the sphere of illustration. I hope very much that Charles Keeping will have something to say on this subject. I am sure that any discussion of censorship will have to concern itself with the surprising agitations aroused in adults (not in children) by Sendak's picture book *Where the Wild Things Are*. But I think it will be admitted that words, which are the easiest and most universal means of communication, are unusually vulnerable. A writer may choose to work within specified limits. He may on the other hand offer something entirely original, but whatever he writes, the germ of the book is his own and it is for him to choose his theme and his attitude and the words he will use. I think the writer of children's books is probably the most often harried and impeded of all writers in this matter of vocabulary. We are all familiar with the attempts of the late Miss Blyton to have Beatrix Potter rewritten so that the kiddies can understand her. We all express pious horror at the very idea. But there are more ways of killing the cat than choking it with butter, and we are just as guilty if we ask that a book of personal vision should be carried out within word limits, or if we provide a difficult future for a writer by suggesting that he has used words too difficult for his supposed readership. The words the writer chooses are part of himself. He chooses partly from a practical point of view because they are suitable to his dialogue or his narrative or his description, but to some extent the words choose themselves as an expression of his personality. In their identity and their arrangement they make up that intangible that we call style.

I should like to illustrate this with examples from two very individual writers. The first passage comes from a book I have already mentioned,

Finn's Folly by Ivan Southall. The situation is this: a boy of fourteen is climbing down a steep hillside in Australia to confirm what he is trying not to know, that his parents have been killed in a motor accident. The time is a cold after-midnight with a clearing fog.

He fought against everything that held him to the ground. Again and again he felt himself turn, felt his feet lift, felt the wild slide, the slipping and the scramble into a steep place of stones and sticks and cloud, but then looked back with shock and saw himself as before, unmoving, still drooping on the road. It was a sensation so weird that it began to hurt, as though something inside him was forcing its way out of his body then fleeing in dismay back into it. He tried with all the strength he had to stop it and suddenly the wild slide, the slipping and the scramble were real. He was clawing with feet and hands in a shower of pebbles and twigs; rocks were hard, undergrowth was rough, the slope was like a steeple.

He crashed against a tree trunk and it felled him. There was the stink of fungus and decomposing leaves, a deep, wet softness with sharp fragments like thorns that penetrated his clothes. He lay stunned by the force of impact, aching to his teeth.

In a while he groped out of the mould and pulled himself upright beside the tree and clung to it, spitting dirt from his mouth, rubbing creepy things like spider webs from his eyes and ears and hair.

Where was the road? Somewhere up in the cloud. For how long had he slid and scrambled? He didn't know; he could draw no line of time between the real event and the others he had imagined. It was an effort of comprehension to accept the tree and the slope and the ankle-deep humus, to accept that everything had suddenly changed, that the mood of sadness up there had gone forever, had belonged to a time that might as well have been years ago. Wreckage lay up there, deadly poisoned, solitude, and a half-dream world of imaginings. Up there the window dressing; down here the things that were real.

The second extract comes from Meindert De Jong's *Journey from Peppermint Street*. Here is a little boy travelling across a marsh with his grandfather, again at night, and he has to wait alone until his aunt rows back with her boat to take him out of a flooded area to her farmhouse.

He settled himself on the hump in the middle of the waggon path between the deep wheel ruts. He hugged his knees to his chest. He squeezed the cane between his knees. The ball lay tight against him; the lantern stood—warm with its light—close to his other side. It wasn't good, though, to be quiet; he sang his one-line song again. If he didn't sing, he could hear the watery muck . . . still making dark ugly noises. There were filthy plopping sounds when great welling black bubbles broke—it was just as if a giant were breathing under the muck. A giant . . . he hastily started to sing again.

An owl, or something fierce and horrible, cried far across the swamp. Horror rose higher and higher in its screeching call, then the calls went low and weepy and spooky. Siebren's song stopped in his mouth. The owl, or whatever awfulness, also stopped. Now everything was unnaturally still, and clouds swept low. He sat very small.

The horrible owl started up again. Suddenly Siebren sang out fiercely at the owl—for his little aunt's sake. . . . He made his one-line song go up and down the way the owl screeched high and low.

It made it fun; it made it brave. It was a little nothing song, but it was brave. When his throat felt tired from singing the one-line song up and down, he began to sing the naked-frog song over and over. He kept count. And it was when he had sung the silly song thirty-eight times that suddenly—near—his aunt began singing along.

In each of these pieces the writer is getting to the roots of fear, describing the child alone, responsible for himself in a situation full of terror. The first passage, and quite possibly also the second, will be objected to by people who believe that children should not meet fear in their books, but that is not the point that concerns me at the moment. The point I want to make here is that there is an individual voice in each of these passages. There is the rough, abrupt, deliberately crowded sequence of words from Ivan Southall, containing difficult emotional changes and mixing abstract and concrete words; and there is the artless, child-like sequence of words in which Meindert De Jong calls back his own childhood. Each author has chosen his words not for children but for the whole impact of the prose. Which came first, the chicken or the egg? Was the kind of style chosen to suit the subject? Not really, because this is the typical style of Southall and of De Jong. The subjects were chosen, but the style is the man himself.

I do not mean to suggest that anyone's ideas of what children can or can't understand are likely to influence these writers or indeed any of the writers present at this conference, but I do suggest that any attempt to restrict words and the use of words is an impertinence on our part and suggests that we expect books to exist primarily to serve our own ends. Any attempt to erode the individuality of a writer's style is a disservice to children, because they need books of integrity and strength and not books written to rule.

Now another way in which we serve children badly in serving them too well is by being dogmatic about the age range of a book. On the face of it Meindert De Jong's artless books might seem perfectly suited to readers around eight or so, but if we try to restrict books to this age group it would be to deprive other children older and occasionally younger who could enjoy De Jong's innocent shrewdness. I notice that in the lists of books sent out in connection with this conference, Ted Hughes' fantasy *The Iron Man* appears on one page under a primary heading for children of 5–7 and on another list it is suggested for a range of 6–8. Most of us would agree that this fantasy really belongs to that age range which is sometimes rather coyly rendered as 7–70. To take another example, Philippa Pearce's *A Dog So Small* has been put in the 10–12 category for the purpose of this week's discussion. I am sure many people here today have read this book to children as young as seven with great success and no adult could fail to fall under its spell. Obviously we shall often find it convenient to group books under age headings, but this mustn't be more than a convenience. An author who is pressed to write within a very strict age range is bound to cripple his original conception, and we shall get fewer books like the two I have just mentioned—books that are expandable and have something to offer children at many stages and to adults as well. This isn't to say that an author does not often find the space he needs within an apparently restricted length or subject. The point is that the author finds his ideal form. It hasn't been wished on him because of the needs of some particular readership. I'd recommend you to consider two books in particular in which a picture-book length and format have mysteriously expanded to contain wit, a perceptive study of character, and a wonderfully rounded story with a beginning and end and a middle and a humour that reaches out to adults as well as children. The two stories are William Mayne's *House on Farmont* and Barbara Willard's recently published story *The Pocket Mouse*. Incidentally, although these two books are technically picture storybooks, they are going to bother some classifiers quite a bit. They are originals and not altogether classifiable.

Life would be frustrating for the writer of stories if we insisted on being dogmatic about age groups. Also of course we should do a great deal of harm to young readers. The books that affect us most are often those that we find ourselves. Children are more likely to discover the full pleasures of reading if they are left to skirmish through a broadly based collection of books, many of which may in theory not be for their age group at all. Well-meaning suggestions to children can be very chancy, as I am sure you all know. I thought I was a fair judge of what was suitable after noticing the peculiarities of my six children's taste in books. Evidently I hadn't learnt my lesson thoroughly enough. The other day I was picking out books for my eldest granddaughter, who is a late reader of nearly eight. I was thinking in theoretical terms. I thought, "Ah, yes, reluctant reader, repetition to help her along," and I found an easy book with a repetitive pattern. When she came to the fourth repetition of words and situations she heaved a great sigh and said,

"Not again." So I left her by the bookshelf. It is obvious that we can't think in terms of groups of children but only in terms of individuals. When John Masefield was a child of five he was made free of his grandfather's library; and, as far as I know, nobody told him that he wasn't old enough for Chambers Journal; and it was in the pages of Chambers Journal a year or two later that he found the adventure stories of Mayne Reid. That, of course, led to books like *Odtaa* and *Live and Kicking Ned*. Incidentally, if we work to rule we shall never give these books to the young, because they are not children's books. It seems a pity.

An expandable book, a book that offers something to everyone, has surely a rather special value for that very difficult age group, the group of young people of eighteen to twenty-two who are training to be teachers and studying children's books as a curriculum subject. Many students like this have poor reading backgrounds through no fault of their own, and they have to approach the field of children's literature, as it were, in cold blood. On the face of it no category can be directly relevant to them but of course there are stories in every category very relevant to their stage of development if they read properly. They can find something of much more than academic interest in a great many picture books, in some fantasies, in farces, in adventure stories, in these books which offer them a complete experience and not just an example of one kind of story or another. If these young students are going to introduce books to children they must be able to believe in them and they must be able to enjoy them. Storytelling and reading aloud are I suppose accepted as an essential part of teaching in almost every school nowadays, but is it regarded as essential that there must be shared pleasure? I don't mean to suggest that students may be allowed to regard children's literature as a soft option, though I believe that in some colleges in the United States the subject is known as "Kiddy Lit." If there are dangers in being too strictly occupied with children's books as a part of childhood there is no danger in a proper study of them.

I am proud to be among the people currently discussing the possibility of a centre for children's literature, and I am proud that *Growing Point* provided John Townsend with a medium for the two articles on the subject [v. 6, no. 6, Dec. 1967; v. 7, no. 1, May 1968] that have been circulated among you. One of the possible functions of such a centre is the encouragement of the study of individual writers and their work. Obviously the best way to enjoy a writer is to look closely at his work as a whole, with respect and with intelligence. As I have already said a great deal of work is being done on the responses of children to books, especially to story books. This needn't mean, as some people seem to think, that less work must consequently be done on the books themselves. There are far too few places, for instance, where properly considered articles on writers for children can be published. One of the advantages of literary articles is that they may help students in training who are too old and yet too young to enjoy children's books to see some point in them and to recognize them as part of the mainstream of literature and to see that they are a real force in education, but only in their own right and in their own way. All those of us who are working with children must learn to fit the child to the book and not the book to the child. This way I think we shall get the books we deserve and we might perhaps deserve the books that we get.

8 / Fantasy

How did children acquire ownership to the fields of fantasy? Felicity Hughes here sees it as another relegation to children of that which adult writers no longer favored. This seems surprising given the flood of fantasy begun in the nineteenth century by Ruskin, Carroll, Grahame, and so on—suddenly there were many able practitioners of the illogical logic that is fantasy. It should not be surprising that children picked up what adults abandoned or neglected. Children have lived, Ruth-like, on literary leavings for centuries. Earlier, they took over romances and biographies of talking objects, and so they could just as easily have appropriated fantasy or, as Isaac Bashevis Singer claims, even all of "story."

Attempts are often made to separate fantasy fiction from other strands of speculative fiction. Fantasy fiction has been classified as those works dependent on a fantastic focus in a form which utilizes particular elements and conventions. Jane Mobley here defines pure (not technological) magic as that which separates fantasy from science fiction, another branch of speculative fiction. Not a technique so much as a focus and a form, fantasy to Mobley is an internally consistent genre, characterized by multidimensionality, extravagance, and the creation of effective secondary worlds, among other things. Because the real world should not obtrude into the secondary world, many critics would exclude all dream fiction. As this leaves out *Alice's Adventures in Wonderland,* some critics and many readers might object.

Some distinction is often made between high and low fantasy. The former would be any works that create seamless secondary worlds; this would include Le Guin's Earthsea, Lloyd Alexander's Prydain and Tolkien's Middle Earth. Low fantasy is at least partially based in the real world. Obviously for the child there can be high and low fantasy. To create an artificial category "all ages fantasy," as some critics have done, creates the implication that no excellent fantasy is meant exclusively for children:

Whether they intend to do so or not, the authors imply that excellent fantasy written for children is "all ages fantasy" and poorly written fantasy for children is "children's fantasy." The larger issue here, of course, is "What is children's literature?"[1]

Note that in dealing with the specific categories of juvenile literature we are constantly thrown back on the need to define or at least distinguish the child's share from the adult's and the attendant presumptions about what is suitable for a child. In their article Bingham and Scholt agree with Hughes that fantasy is often relegated to children, but they stress the price any audience must pay to enter the world of fantasy, which they insist can and must be taught as literature, period. Neil Philip sees many writers turning to fantasy because it enables them to express symbolically what could not be comprehended by a child in a realistic form, but this symbolic shorthand attracts excellent writers as well as second-rate hacks.[2]

For all the fanciful's flirtation with the exotic, Jane Yolen insists that its rules "have to work as surely as gravity works on our own world." As Lloyd Alexander observed, "In the algebra of fantasy, A times B doesn't have to equal B times A. But, once established, the equation must hold throughout the story."[3] However unbelievable fantasy becomes, it must maintain an internal consistency to be believable to its audience. Fantasy's distinguishing quality—magic—creates not merely illusion but also a world with shape and substance, however ethereal, for child or adult who will consent to pay the extra price of attention to see its wonders.

Children's Literature: Theory and Practice, Part 2

Felicity A. Hughes

It was claimed at the beginning of this paper that theoretical confusion can impose significant constraints on art. One of the most striking features of English children's literature is the amount and quality of fantasy offered to children, especially in the last quarter century. The prominence and excellence of fantasy in children's literature have often been remarked on, yet the criticism of those works has been confused and superficial. I believe that both of these phenomena can be explained in terms of the theory I have offered in this paper.

I have shown that the exclusion of children from the readership of the serious novel was associated with the acceptance of a version of realism. One consequence of the acceptance of realism was that fantasy was immediately déclassé. Since fantasy can be seen as the antithesis of realism, it seemed to follow to those who espoused the realist cause that fantasy was also the opposite of serious, that is, trivial or frivolous. That is precisely how Forster used the term in *Aspects of the Novel*.[1] In that book, he devoted two chapters to non-realistic aspects of the novel, one called "Fantasy" and one called "Prophecy," characterising both by what they require of the reader. Fantasy, he says, "asks us to pay something extra." It is, he suggests, "like a sideshow in an exhibition where you pay sixpence as well as the original entrance fee." The analogy is damaging, raising the question as to whether the show is worth even sixpence. He divides the potential audience into two groups. Of the first group, those who "pay with delight" (enjoy fantasy), Forster claims "it is only for the sideshows that they entered the exhibition" (a taste for fantasy precludes a taste for other literature); to the second group who "refuse with indignation" (detest fantasy), he offers "our sincere regards, for to dislike the fantastic in literature is not to dislike literature. It does not even imply poverty of imagination, only a disinclination to meet certain demands that are made on it." So, while a taste for fantasy

Reprinted from *ELH [English Literary History]* 45:552–561 (1978), with permission from the Johns Hopkins University Press and the author. For the first part of this selection, see this volume's chapter 2, page 26.

is said to be incompatible with a taste for any other literature, a distaste for fantasy is said to be quite compatible and, not surprisingly, wins Forster's regard. Although he finds the demands made by fantasy unfulfillable, he admits that he cannot show that they are unreasonable:

No doubt this approach is not critically sound. We all know that a work of art is an entity, etc. etc.; it has its own laws which are not those of daily life, anything that suits it is true, so why should any question arise about the angel etc. except whether it is suitable to its book? Why place an angel on a different basis from a stockbroker—once in the realm of the fictitious what difference is there between an apparition and a mortgage? I see the soundness of this argument, but my heart refuses to assent. The general tone of novels is so literal that when the fantastic is introduced it produces a special effect.

In comparison with fantasy, prophecy is, according to Forster, a much more serious affair and demands to be taken seriously. Fantasy and prophecy are said to be "alike in having gods, and unlike in the gods they have." In comparison with the gods of prophecy, those of fantasy are "small." "I would call them fairies if the word were not consecrated to imbecility." He suggests that fantasies should be saved from "the claws of critical apparatus," that "their appeal is specially personal—they are sideshows inside the main show." The implication here is that the appeal of fantasy is so ephemeral that critical inspection would destroy it—show it to be a trick, an illusion, a device. In fact, he suggests that fantasy can be identified by its "devices" and "the fact that their number is strictly limited is of interest." Prophecy, on the other hand, demands of the reader "humility and a suspension of the sense of humour." It is interesting to note that, in this case Forster feels that *refusal* to submit is childish:

Humility is a quality for which I have only a limited admiration. In many phases of life it is a great mistake and degenerates into defensiveness and hypocrisy. But humility is in place just now. Without its help we shall not hear the voice of the prophet, and our eyes will behold a figure of fun instead of his glory. And the sense of humour—that is out of place: that estimable adjunct of the educated man must be laid aside. Like the school-children in the Bible, one cannot help laughing at the prophet—his bald head is so absurd—but one can discount the laughter and realise that it has no critical value and is merely food for bears.

In *Aspects of the Novel,* "Fantasy" and "Prophecy" together represent a byway in Forster's train of thought on the novel—he calls them interludes "gay and grave." Neither can be dealt with properly by his critical equipment, which was designed for novels that are "literal in tone," though prophetic novels induce him to consider the possibility that this critical equipment is not the best, or that there may be no such thing as critical equipment at all. Such doubts are momentary, however, and characteristically, brushed off with a sigh. "It is a pity that Man cannot be at the same time impressive and truthful."

In those 1927 lectures Forster reflected and helped disseminate a widespread prejudice against fantasy. A consequence of the prejudice that fantasy is childish has been that the writer of fantasy has been directed into writing for children no matter how good he or she might be. The realistic writer has had a choice and indeed been encouraged to regard writing for adults as more satisfying. In writing for children the realistic writer has been conscious of taking second best since realism was defined in terms which excluded children as readers hence "real" realism was impossible in a children's book. The fantasist has written under no such shadow—has had no such option—all fantasy goes on the children's list. Some excellent writers have found themselves writing for children for this reason, which partially explains the high amount and quality of fantasy in children's literature this century.

Moreover, writers of children's literature have been able to turn to advantage the fact that a work which announces itself as fantasy is deemed frivolous, childish, and not worth critical attention. Edith Nesbit referred to this situation at the beginning of *Five Children—and It:*

I could go on and make this into a most interesting story about all the ordinary things that the children did—just the kind of things you do yourself you know—and you would believe every word of it; and when I told you about the children being tiresome, as you are sometimes, your aunts would perhaps write in the margin of the story with a pencil, "How true!" or "how like life!" And you would see it and very likely be annoyed. So I will only tell you about the really astonishing things that happened, and you may leave the book about quite safely, for no aunts and uncles either are likely to write "How true!" on the edge of the story.[2]

Using fantasy thus as a protective cover to save the work from prying adult eyes, writers having managed to extend considerably the range of subjects dealt with in children's literature.

An inevitable consequence of the way that children's literature came into being was that a certain restraint has been imposed on children's writers in the realist tradition when it comes to topics such as terror, politics and sex. That such censorship has been found too restrictive by some writers is clear from books like William Mayne's *A Game of Dark* (1971) and Philippa Pearce's *A Dog So Small* (1962). The protagonist of the former is schizoid, of the latter, obsessive, which enables the writers to present intense fears and resentments. But such shifts are of limited use: one can't write about deranged people all the time, nor is it true that only the mad get frightened. What is clear is that these devices will never accommodate what are, after all, incompatible demands made on the writer in this tradition, that he be true to life and also that he avoid certain topics. Moore's solution was to exclude the children; the children's writer's solution is to turn to fantasy.[3] Even Mayne, who is inventive enough to write a highly schematic book like *Sand* (1970) or a mythopoeic book like *The Jersey Shore* (1973) and remain, technically, within the conventions of realism-for-children, found it necessary, in order to deal with the more terrifying aspects of his earlier preoccupation, the alien time-scheme of the earth, to resort to fantasy, in *Earthfasts* (1966).

The so-called "new realism" in children's books proves, on inspection, to be an attempt to introduce adolescent sex into children's books. In fact the acclaimed writers of the "new realism" have a long way to go before they can deal with the range of sexual feelings including jealousy, possessiveness, despair, and the desire for liberation that Alan Garner dealt with in *The Owl Service* (1967) by using fantasy.

Political topics such as class and race have recently been self-consciously injected into children's realistic fiction, but again the fantasists have set the standard to be met. Those writers who are attempting accurate description of working class life in realistic terms are only attempting what Mary Norton did so brilliantly in the Borrowers series (1953 *et seq.*) in which, by one fantastic stroke, she invented a way of presenting the experience of being small and propertyless in a society in which that entails constant vulnerability. Accounts of dispossession and exploitation given in fantasy by Norton and by Russell Hoban in *The Mouse and His Child* (1969) are much more penetrating than those given in books like Serrailler's *Silver Sword* (1956) and Rutgers Van der Loeff's *Children on the Oregon Trail (Oregon at Last)* (1961) though the latter make the strongest claim to verisimilitude—that of being based on the real experiences of real children. Similarly, in *A Stranger at Green Knowe* (1961) Lucy Boston depicts the relationship between a Chinese boy and an escaped gorilla in a way that makes the self-consciously antiracist realistic literature look crass.

A preoccupation with the role of the imagination in relation to time would appear unduly sophisticated in a realistic children's book as is suggested by the reaction of reviewers to Mayne's *The Jersey Shore*. So Pearce was able to contribute to that immemorial topic only by writing fantasy in *Tom's Midnight Garden* (1958). Finally and by a just revenge, fantasy gives cover to parody, the children's own traditional weapon, to mount attacks on the pretensions of adult art and artists in Randolph Stow's *Midnite* (1967) and Hoban's *The Mouse and His Child*.

These admirable novels have not received the critical appreciation they deserve. I suggest this also stems from the fact that the rejection of the child reader by influential critics and writers was accompanied by the rejection of fantasy and the associated claim that fantasy does not appeal to the mature mind. Scholes and Kellogg's *The Nature of Narrative* is often cited as a work which challenges the domination of realism in the novel. In so far as they champion Romance, however, it is with a reservation (similar to that made by Booth) concerning reader-involvement and identification:

Romance, the only narrative form which is ineluctably artistic since it is the product of the story telling impulse at its purest, diminishes in interest as its perfection carries it too far from the world of ideas or from the actual world. A pure story, without ideas or imitation of actuality to tie it to human concerns and experiences would be, if such a possibility were realized, totally uninteresting to adult readers. In some children's stories this infinitude of inanity is approached. But in general, narrative artists have sensed the dangers of purity in their art and shied away from it consciously or not.[4]

The use of the term "inanity" here is reminiscent of Forster's identification of fairies with "imbecility" and Coleman's association of "children, idiots, the senile." A tendency to class children with the mentally defective seems to have supplanted the older prejudices which classed children with women or with working-class men. From the point of view of thinking clearly about children as readers this can hardly be counted progress.

The first and major impediment to useful criticism, then, lies in the acceptance by critics of the idea that fantasy is peculiarly suitable for children, not for adults. In order to interpret this supposed fact in a way that attributes no inferiority to children (a considerable feat) many critics rely on some version of the "culture epoch" theory which states that individual human development recapitulates the development of the race. According to this view children are primitives and are most appropriately served by primitive literature—myths, fables, folk tales and fairy tales. It should be remembered that until recently, fantasies were called "invented fairy tales" or "modern fairy tales." Thus Lillian Smith writes, in *The Unreluctant Years:*

A child of today asks "why" and "how" as he wonders about the natural world which he does not understand. So, in the childhood of the race, without knowledge of the discoveries with which science has enlarged our understanding, primitive peoples made their own explanations of the physical world in terms of themselves.[5]

And Elizabeth Cook documents the "natural afinity between the child-hood of the race and the childhood of the individual human being" in matters of taste:

They expect a story to be a good yarn, in which the action is swift and the characters are clearly and simply defined. And legends and fairy tales are just like that. Playground games show that children like catastrophes and exhibi-tions of speed and power, and a clear differentiation between cowboys, cops, and spacemen who are good, and Indians, robbers and space-monsters who are bad.[6]

This "natural afinity" is brought forward to explain why fantasy appeals to children, but it is not taken as a sufficient explanation as to why fantasy is *good* for children. The Romantic version of the recapitulation theory was inclined to rate the child's and primitive's view of the world highly and to regard growing up as a process of losing touch with essen-tials. Since that time other theories of development have prevailed, the one most in point here being that which views growing up as a progress towards maturity and that people, as part of that process, gradually ac-quire a grip of reality in the course of their childhood; that to do so is a vital advance in child development, and that anything which interferes with a child's acquisition of a sense of reality is harmful to his develop-ment. Fantasy might, according to this theory, constitute just such a hazard to a child's healthy acquisition of a sense of reality. Indeed, the eighteenth-century Rousseauists who held an analogous theory about the acquisition of reason, acted consistently with it in banning all fairy tales (thus annoying Lamb and Coleridge). Mrs. Barbauld, for instance, sup-ported a programme almost the reverse of the modern, namely that children should be offered informative, factual material about the actual world and that only the most highly educated and developed tastes would reach the "pure poetry" of, say, Collins, the literature least concerned with actuality.

The inconsistencies in our position lead to an anxiety about children reading "too much" fantasy and the advocacy of a "balanced diet." The range of critical opinion on the issue includes those who, like W. J. Scott, are inclined to place severe limits on the reading of fantasy:

An acceptance with such enthusiasm of a representation of human beings in action that is so patently false must tend to create some misunderstanding in the mind of the young reader of the nature and motives of human behaviour. Further it compels him to lead a dual existence, using part of his energy in an excessive emotional participation in a life of fantasy at a time when he needs so much to grapple with the real world. Granted that it is still necessary for him to withdraw sometimes from the real world into one of fantasy, it is of great importance that the experience given in fantasy should be of good quality, indirectly extending his understanding of reality.[7]

and those who, like Lillian Smith, are prepared to adopt the Romantic position:

A child's ready acceptance of fantasy is based on imagination and wonder. An adult lacking these universal attributes of childhood is often at a loss when he is asked to consider seriously a work of purely imaginative content, far removed from the reality of his experience of life. Before the adult can feel at ease in this different world of fantasy he must discover a means of approach. There is an interesting discussion of fantasy by E. M. Forster in his *Aspects of the Novel,* in which he says "What does fantasy ask us? It asks us to pay something extra." That is to say that over and above what we ordinarily bring to the reading of a story, fantasy demands something extra, perhaps a kind of sixth sense. All children have it, but most adults leave it behind with their cast off childhood.[8]

Lillian Smith's misinterpretation of Forster's remarks is a clear example of the way that such apologists for fantasy have had to close their eyes to the manifest change in the critical climate, in order to feel justified in what they are doing.

Obviously, the whole issue is distorted by the almost universal assumption that fantasy appeals to children because they believe it is true or at least don't know that it is false, and that adults reject it because they know it is not true. The question as to whether any art produces belief in any reader of any age is too big to go into here. I merely point out that confusions and disagreements on that question add to the confusions on this one. The issue of belief is introduced in an attempt to answer an irrelevant question on to which critics have allowed themselves to be diverted, namely, "Why does fantasy appeal to children and not to adults?" They have discussed that question because they were unwilling to face the fact that fantasy had been merely abandoned to the child reader. Even where critics have avoided the distracting question, they have found themselves ill-equipped to deal with fantasy properly, perhaps because they have only second-hand equipment of the Forster design.

The theory of children's literature has been for some time in a state of confusion. The achievements of the writers, in particular the fantasists, in spite of the lack of critical and theoretical support has been remarkable and provided a challenge to the critic which should be taken up.

Toward a Definition of Fantasy Fiction

Jane Mobley

As speculative fiction develops a steadily increasing following of readers and critics, the necessity for categories and distinctions becomes more pressing. This paper represents an attempt to separate fantasy fiction from other genres within the mode of speculative fiction, operating on the premise that fantasy depends on a conjunction of focus and form peculiar to itself and not readily applicable to other types of speculative fiction, particularly science fiction. The tendency to lump all speculative fiction under the term "science fiction" does not recognize that fantasy is not scientific in either its subject or treatment. By the same token, the term "fantasy" should not include science fiction proper since science fiction is not magical, as fantasy must be, in either subject or treatment. The term "speculative fiction" seems to me best to describe a mode of narrative that may include science fiction, dream literature, horror tales, and fantasy. The term "fantasy fiction" should be reserved for those works which depend on a fantastic focus, or world view, actualized in a form which utilizes certain structural elements and conventions.

The fantasy fiction[1] which this paper examines is essentially a non-rational form (although a reasonable form in that it has an internal logic of its own) which arises from a world view essentially magical in its orientation. As a fiction, it requires the reader's entering an Other World and following a hero whose adventures take place in a reality far removed from the mundane reality of the reader's waking experience. This world is informed by Magic, and the reader must be willing to accept Magic as the central force without demanding or expecting mundane explanations.

It can be said that all fiction creates worlds peculiar to the fiction itself, but in realistic narratives the worlds are still dependent for their focus on the world the reader knows. This sort of fiction stands in recog-

A paper presented at the Seminar on Speculative Fiction at the Midwest Modern Language Association meeting in Chicago, November 3, 1973, this article was first published in *Extrapolation* 15 (May 1974). Reprinted with permission.

nizable relation to life; it creates an illusion of life and the effect on the reader depends on its "convincing reading of life," to borrow Austin Warren's phrase.[2] In other words, the fiction depends on a norm grounded in the details and standards of mundane reality and it derives its validity, at least in part, from its relation to this norm. Fantasy fiction, however, is not conditional in this way. It creates an absolute reality which is not contingent upon everyday reality, but is instead self-sustaining. Fantasy fiction, like symbolic logic, operates on givens. Logic is valid when it is internally consistent whether that consistency relates to physical reality or not. The perfect syllogism of Lewis Carroll's *Jabberwocky* illustrates this sort of self-validating consistency, for despite its working in language and image which do not directly reflect things we know, it makes logical sense.

Fantasy fiction depends on just such self-validation. It is intrinsically meaningful and is distinct from other sorts of fiction which require a "real life" norm from which some or all meaning may be derived. This norm might be called a frame of explicability; no matter how bizarre the narrative may be in some respect, it is always held within a framework of explanation based on recognizable daily realities.

I exclude dream fiction from fantasy fiction since dream literature suggests the Other World is one from which we can wake. The dreamer's sleep may give him fantastic visions, but his arousal to the Real World cancels the absolute validity of the Other World. *Alice in Wonderland* would be an ideal example of fantasy fiction if Alice simply existed in Wonderland; that she wakes from it returns us to the norm and frames her Wonderland travels in recognizably ordinary experience.

Without such a normative frame, fantasy fiction forces the reader into the Other World irrevocably since for the fiction's duration it is the only world. Therefore, I exclude from this study those fantasies which are psychological constructs on the part of the narrator himself, for in such narratives the reader may choose to remain outside the fantasies. The reader has the option of seeing the narrator's fantasy as an aberration of normative consciousness. In fantasy fiction proper, the world of Magic is not a disortentation of our own world; rather, it is a formative orientation within a wholly different world. In other words, in fantasy proper the forms are there but the frame is absent. In fantasies which are purely psychological constructs on the part of a narrator who is presented as having a consciousness like our own, we can call his fantasies disorientations and refuse to accept them as real. For instance, in Kurt Vonnegut's *Slaughterhouse-Five,* Billy Pilgrim's visits to Tralfamadore may be viewed as mere "mind tripping"—other characters in the novel certainly regard them as such. The reader may or may not believe Billy visits the planet; the point is that the reader has an explicable "out." The frame of Billy's life allows the reader not to enter Billy's fantasy world, but to tag him instead as psychotic. Fantasy fiction proper does not allow such choices within the work. The fantasy world *is* the Real World. The reader may accept or reject the fiction as a whole, but if it is internally consistent, he cannot choose to accept or reject incidents only.

Horror fiction may or may not be fantasy fiction depending on its frame. Some fantasy fiction is admittedly horrific within its own world. More often, however, horror fiction requires a norm drawn from our everyday apprehension of natural form. Psychologists have shown that people and animals most fear what is similar but discrepant,[3] and much horror fiction rests on a norm of similarity to the known for its effect. H. P. Lovecraft is explicit about this use of a frame in his monograph *Supernatural Horror in Literature.*

To make a fictional marvel wear the momentary aspect of existing fact, we must give it the most elaborate possible approach—building it up insiduously and gradually out of apparently realistic material, realistically handled. The time is past when adults can accept marvelous conditions for granted. Every energy must be bent toward the weaving of a frame of mind which shall make the story's single departure from nature seem credible—and in the weaving of this mood the utmost subtlety and verisimilitude is required. In every detail *except* the chosen marvel, the story should be accurately true to nature. The keynote should be that of scientific exposition—since that is the normal way of presenting a "fact" new to existing knowledge—and should not change as the story gradually slides off from the possible into the impossible.[4]

Horror tales which demand this sort of frame are not truly fantasy fiction. Indeed, fantasy may have elements of horror but always within its own created norms. In addition, in horror fiction, horror is the end-in-itself, whereas horror in fantasy is subordinate to the total, magical effect.

Finally, from fantasy fiction I exclude science fiction which secures the reader's belief by offering rational (if sometimes bizarre) scientific explanations. Scientific exposition provides the narrative frame for this type of fiction. Sometimes credulity is built by the mere use of scientific jargon or physical detail, as in *Frankenstein,* for instance, where surgical and electrical information provide norms. In science fiction where consciousness is confronted by an intrusion from another reality, the reader still has the methodology of technological consciousness to provide him a working reference for dealing with the intruder. Fantasy fiction borrows no such methodology from daily experience.

To sum up then, fantasy fiction develops its own frame released from what we usually consider probable reality. The reader and the hero alike must confront the passing strange and wondrous fair without any of the standards or norms applicable to physical reality. Perhaps this partially explains the frequent occurrence of guiding figures and testing situations in fantasy, since there the old boundaries do not apply, and as the narrative creates new ones, both reader and hero must be guided within them. Both must be continually testing and tested by the new norms.

Fantasy narratives are essentially books of changes. Reality is changed at the outset so that, once over the "threshhold of adventure" into the Other World, the reader and hero must necessarily face accommodating changes. The thrust of fantasy might be expressed as a "crossing over" into new realms. For the reader, this means a change of mind, a willful redirection of consciousness and perception, and an acceptance of normative reality as it exists within the fantasy itself, independent of explicable or "normal" frames. As a narrative type, fantasy is evocative rather than explanatory. This evocation set apart from explanation is perhaps the chief distinction in fantasy and other forms of speculative fiction, for the world evoked is magical and therefore not bound by our usual modes of discursive explanations, be they those of dreams, psychosis, physical nature, or science.

Magic is the key informing principle in fantasy and delineates both the focus (subject) and form (treatment) of the genre. Magic power is the subject of fantasy and shapes the landscape, the hero, his quest, and his discovery. The form of fantasy fiction might be said to be magically derived as well, since the basic assumption of Magic is that consciousness creates form, and magical consciousness can work out its forms in a variety of dimensions and guises. At the level of treatment, the narrative must be magical, acting upon the reader to enchant, to draw him into the magic circle which includes the paradoxical, the ecstatic, the awe-ful, —and excludes the safely mundane.

Before going further, it would be well to attempt a working definition of Magic. Magic has engaged the human mind so variously for so long that it is impossible to synthesize the implications of the term. Paradoxically, the most adequate definition of Magic is its indefinability. Even J. R. R. Tolkien, whose understanding of Magic is indisputable, says of the realm of Faërie that it may not be described, "for it is one of its qualities to be indescribable, though not imperceptible. It has many ingredients, but analysis will not necessarily discover the secret of the whole."[5] However, there are some distinctions to be made which may be helpful.

Perhaps Magic is best described in terms of power: Magic is an elemental creative power capable of actualizing itself in form (these forms are actual—not "illusions" which are the function of humans' cloaking magic in forms they can understand in ordinary ways). This actualization appears to our consciousness as essentially transformational; Magic changes or reshapes the appearance of things. Ariel, for instance, is an air spirit who assumes different forms as suit the functions of the Magic directing him and the perceptions of those to whom he must appear. Magic may also mean a willed participatory power brought into play by a magus or gifted hero figure.

If we can agree with Ernst Cassirer that language operates in two modes, discursive (logical) and mythical (creatively imaginative), the term "Magic" must belong to the mythic conception. To quote Cassirer, discursive reflection "is characterized by the fact that even in apparently immediately 'given' data, it recognizes an element of mental creation and stresses the active ingredient."[6] Mythic conception, on the other hand, shows all spontaneous action as receptive, and all human achievement as something bestowed. "Magic" is a term generated in this mode of thought, for it means a bestowal of power, not a construct of human consciousness. In the realm of Magic human consciousness is seen as receptive to the constructs of Magic. The magician is one who employs a power which is given.

For the purpose of discussing fantasy fiction, then, let us say that Magic is an effective power which can be brought to bear on everything we know, even what is usually considered the realm of ordinary nature. It is a condition of life, and it works on or through persons and things, manifesting itself in results which can only be ascribed to its working. As a power it is impersonal, but it is often connected with some person who controls or embodies it. Of the terms employed in various languages to describe the magical perhaps the one closest to the force we find in fantasy fiction is the Latin *numen:* the vague sense of mysterious power which may be benevolent or dangerous.[7]

Though the term "Magic" may mean this undirected mysterious power, it can also be used to define a certain human willfulness in the face of the unknown. Anthropological and sociological studies suggest that the fundamental aim of practiced magic is to impose the human will on nature, man, or on the suprasensual world in order to master them. Magic in fantasy fiction, then, has two basic manifestations: it may be a power which imposes itself on man capriciously (or is imposed through spirits or divine beings); or it may be a power which can be utilized, induced, or controlled by man to his own purposes. In its first form it is a force paradoxically dualistic, appearing creative/destructive, moral/immoral, benevolent/malevolent, eternal/incarnate simultaneously. In its form it works in human affairs largely by chance; that is, the hero (landscape or other elements of the narrative) may be cursed or blessed by Magic according to luck rather than to worth or skill.

In the second form, personal or directed Magic is a power called out by a gifted one, an initiate in the arts or discipline of magic usage, skilled in effective magic. His skill is the end of study, not luck, and he functions in special roles in the community. In fantasy fiction, his is most often the role of guide or tester, the arbiter of change and purveyor of new wisdom in the narrative.

To simplify enormously, we could say that the first sort of Magic, effective elemental power, delineates the focus of fantasy fiction, and the second, the willed use of that power, determines at least some elements of the narrative form. Because the focus and form of fantasy are so integral to each other, the structural feeling and form create an organic whole. Working from fantasy's focus, we can distinguish six elements of form necessary to fantasy fiction. Certainly some of these appear in other fictional forms, but perhaps not in the exclusive conjunction that fantasy affords. In this space, this list can only be provocative, not definitive, and hopefully suggestive of directions in fantasy criticism. These elements of fantasy fiction are:

1. *Poetic quality.* Fantasy is by nature incantational as poetry must be in its oldest forms. Incantation is calling up Magic through words, and the effectiveness of the incantation rests on the occult power of the word itself as well as associations and method of delivery. Cassirer points out that when the linguistic and mythico-religious consciousness is linked (early in man's conceptualizing history) all verbal structures are also mythical entities, endowed with certain mythical powers, so that the Word becomes a primary force in which all being and doing originate.[8] In fantasy the sheer arrangement of words is creative, calling up (rather than describing) a world dependent on the words themselves for its reality. It is a world which has its own meaning actualized in forms internal to itself. It can project meaning into the everyday world (as can any fiction), but it projects only meaning, not the forms themselves. For example, from *The Last Unicorn,* the meaning of the unicorn herself—purity, truth, light, beauty—can be projected into our world, but the unicorn cannot.[9]

The incantatory nature of the narrative also works on the reader, seeking to enchant, not merely to suspend disbelief (as any art must do), but to promote new belief. Fantasy depends, as does incantation, upon compression, image, and poetic language to create and maintain its reality, and on feeling rather than discursive logic to dispense its "meaning." This spell-casting quality of fantasy can be seen in the formulaic language units it recurrently employs. For instance, certain characteristic opening and closing formulas set the timeless, placeless realm of Faërie apart from the common world: "Once upon a time"; "A thousand years ago tomorrow"; "And they lived happily ever after."[10] These units are very old, as are many devices that even contemporary fantasy uses, but older still is the incantational quality, hearkening to a time when man believed in the physico-magical power comprised in the Word. Incantation assumes the word does not just symbolize; it actually transforms. Fantasy fiction, like poetry at its roots, utilizes this assumption.

2. *Creation of secondary magical worlds.* Fantasy creates virtual life or the feeling of directly experienced reality, but in another world from the one we know. Magic is central both to the working of this world and to the reader's acceptance of it, for fantasy does not seek to build a bridge from primary to secondary worlds; rather, it gives the reader faith to leap the gap.

This "faith" is not a suspension of disbelief so much as a willingness to accept or discover new belief, a process Tolkien calls "enchantment." It is a process of subcreation, as Tolkien says, "rather than representation or symbolic interpretation of the beauties and terrors of the world."[11] To venture into this world the reader does not give up his experience of the primary world entirely, for his own imagination participates in the subcreation utilizing sensual experience and associations to make incarnate the words which create the Other World. The reader carries to this Other World his own understanding of the primary world but without an insistence that the Other World be restricted to that understanding. The reader must have an image of sea foam to appreciate the ocean's froth which becomes a wave of captured unicorns in *The Last Unicorn,* but he must allow his primary image to be thus transformed. In other words, meaning is transferred from primary world into secondary (and vice versa), but the forms or shapes that meaning takes belong to the secondary world and operate by its rules, not the rules of ordinary nature. These forms may not be recognizable in ordinary vision (transferable in that shape to the primary world), but they are conceivable, bodying forth the forms of things unknown. The secondary world, then, is a magical blending of the known and the unknown, a subcreative process which accepts and discovers shapes expressive of itself which also have meaning (if not form) in the primary world. This process, perhaps more than any of the other structural devices we discuss, must be wholly consistent in its unfolding, for the other world is the foundation of fantasy, and it must not crack open at any point and drop us to the ground beneath.

3. *Multidimensionality.* Though the Other World is in a sense within a magic circle which needs remain unbroken for the duration of the narrative, the line of encirclement is broad and worlds overlap. Fantasy

does not force us to make distinctions between the real and the not-real on the basis of empirical evidence which may not have validity in the realm of feeling. It cheerfully overlaps dimensions that mundane cognition would separate and fosters the growth of wonder.

In the everyday world, categories such as space and time seem to us static but in fantasy they are fluid, subject to change as the necessities of feeling dictate. Time and space in such narratives are simply ways of expressing intensity and association. Places far distant from each other are associationally different: [in *The Last Unicorn*] Hagsgate and Haggard's castle are many weary days' travel from the unicorn's green forests, the distance expressing less about the topography of the country than about the difference between Haggard's realm, where the unicorn is miserably mortal, and her own forest, where she is happily untouched by time. In Evangeline Walton's *The Island of the Mighty,* the hosts of Bran, returning from war, bring with them the severed head of their leader which still gives orders from a golden platter. Eighty years they feast with the magical Head, but when they return to their loved ones, the babies they left are still infants, and their wives are young and strong enough to bear children to replace the men slain in battle. The eighty-year feast is not an expression of time as we conceive it, but of the devotion the men had for their leader. So it is in fantasy that dimensions of existence stretch and change to become expressions rather than regulations of existence.

Yet fantasy fiction has internal consistency, and despite a commitment to the nonrational, fantasy has rules. Chief among these rules is one that it must be faithful to the "truth" it has chosen. It is not correct that "anything can happen" in a fantasy. Only those things can happen which are true to the conception of that fantasy and to the forms it works through. Consistency must be maintained, not only for the sake of the reader's belief, but for the maintenance of the secondary world itself. New dimensions of the fantastic may be constantly opening within the narrative; but if the taleteller allows primary reality to intrude in ways which violate the integrity of the secondary world, it will shatter like a dropped prism into glittering shards that not even the most ingenious craftsman can put back together so that it will again break light into colors.

4. *Essential extravagance.* A fantastic world view is by nature extravagant, and in treatment this means the forms employ marvelous description and often baroque plotlines. In its essence, fantasy deliberately dissociates itself from our network of expectations, from sameness, and from consistency with everyday life. To achieve this dissociation, fantasy strives for the wonderful, the flamboyant, the exotic. The characters are

often larger-than-life, their exploits complicated, their retinues gaudy. Treasure hoards are too vast to be counted, mountains too high for the crest to be seen much less to be scaled. Recurrently extravagance is conveyed by stylistic formulas which report the events, as "more horrible than can be imagined," or describe the ladies as "more beautiful than tongue can tell." The language of fantasy is itself extravagant, creating oftentimes by the mere unpronounceability of names the wonder and greatness of it all.

5. *Spirit of carnival.* Fantasy fiction is essentially a playful form, kin in its structures to ritual and dance. Like all imaginative forms of play it encourages the growth of man's creative capacity. It is a form of play which extends man's frontiers; it allows him to cross the boundaries that notions of space and time have set up, to press past the border guards of propriety and civic responsibility, to venture on into uncharted realms of imagination.

Fantasy, like carnival, is essentially a comic life-celebration, but this does not mean it must be gaily festive. It incorporates the grotesque, the terrible, and the dark as well as the light, the joyful, and the beauteous. Ishmael Reed's contention in *Yellow Back Radio Broke Down* that he writes circuses not novels, Charles G. Finney's *The Circus of Dr. Lao,* and Peter Beagle's Mommy Fortuna's circus (in *The Last Unicorn*) are all metaphoric statements of the carnival element in fantasy.

6. *Mythic dimension.* Fantasy fiction is drawn from a well of imagery which springs not in the mind of a single teller of tales but in the hidden emotional life of the people. This well of immemorial and traditional material we call myth, and from this material the writer of fantasy fiction forms character, motif, and plot. In literature myth may be said to provide the essential intuitive subject of the narrative, while the craft of the writer determines the form. This is possible since the material of myth is substantial but not static, and can be transformed so that the essential power of the myth may work through a variety of shapes or guises. This can easily be seen in many modern writers whom we regard as mythic: Joyce, for example, has crafted in Stephen Daedalus a character who derives power from a number of myths yet whose form is distinctively Daedalus' own. In fantasy fiction, however, the conjunction of mythic material and the form it takes is less distanced by the craft of a particular writer. In fantasy, the forms more nearly approximate the mythic narrative from which their substance is drawn.

The world of fantasy is a primitive mythic world peopled with gods and heroes and magicians mingling freely with ordinary men. The action deals with the elemental confrontation between human consciousness and its physical and spiritual environment: the basic action of myth. Bronislaw Malinowski, in *Myth and Primitive Psychology,* says that the serious myth "is a narrative resurrection of primeval reality." The primeval reality is for the moment more important to human problems than the reality of the ordinary world, and myths are told to gain perspective, meaning, and purposefulness. With regard to the sense of primitive reality myth conveys, Andrew Lytle remarks, "The seeming tone of the far past is the announcement of the timeless held within the point of the moment. To emphasize this there is little or no natural landscape, no recognizable cities, in myth or fairy tale. This is a crucial distinguishing feature between myth and fiction which deals with myth. They have the archetypes in common, but in fiction the action must be put in a recognizable place and society."[12] Fantasy fiction seems to lie somewhere between the polarities of myth and fiction Lytle mentions, for fantasy retains the sense of placelessness and distant past by giving us places which are names but not known to us. Fantasy fiction hearkens back to a literature perhaps more "primitive" than the sort which we have grown used to in an attempt to revitalize the mythic conception in our time, both for the material that conception grants the fantasist and for the emotional power it shares with the reader.

Some of this power is garnered from the close tie myth has with magic, a tie particularly integral to fantasy fiction. Here fantasy is again like primitive literature, for as Richard Chase points out, "Primitive literature is shot through with magic and we may regard it as mythical when it fortifies the magical view of things, when it reaffirms the vibrant dynamism of the world, when it fortifies the ego with the impression that there is a magically potent brilliancy in the world."[13] This "potent brilliancy" is a share of that numenous, elemental power we earlier ascribed to magic, it is the play of that power, the clash and ring of magic forces as they interact, and the struggle of man to interpret or use them. Myth, therefore, must always accept and reveal the preternatural, myth always goes beyond ordinary nature. The preternatural forces which concern myth have *mana,* a Melanesian term which is applied to whatever has impersonal magic force or power and is therefore uncanny, wondrous, terrible, threatening, and beautifully strange. It is this same magic power that is the focus of fantasy fiction, and the fantasists consequently become conscious mythmakers as they turn old narratives to their own uses. Fantasy fiction, like myth, preserves and gives significance in the present reality to the sensation of *mana* or magic. And because fantasy, like myth, does not describe but reveals, it may also create this feeling in the reader (Tolkien's "enchantment"), catapulting him however briefly into a realm that only works of a visionary nature can build.

Because fantasy fiction is informed so directly by magic, the fantasist uses most often those myths which have overtly magical elements. The chief narrative pattern of fantasy, the quest and discovery motif, gives ample opportunity for the intervention of magic at nearly every turn. Early mythmakers invoked magic to express the possibilities of freedom and power and man's struggle with these possibilities, and this remains a dominant concern in contemporary fantasy fiction. Magic rings and magic swords, talents in shape-shifting, war, and song recurrently raise the pressing questions about power and its uses. In the narrative it is the magical force which most often brings up these questions, but it is the human consciousness which must answer them. So it is in *The Last Unicorn* that magic gives Schmendrick the power to make the unicorn woman, but it is his human conscience which must decide how to bear that responsibility.

It quickly becomes evident in even so brief a discussion of myth, that in such narratives the vision or theme is of principal importance. Ernst Cassirer says that the mythic conception grasps great fundamental experiences and then differentiates characters out of them to stand for parts of what the mythmakers see as whole. He says " . . . mythmaking genius 'has' separate and individualized forms only in so far as it 'posits' them, as it carves them out of the undifferentiated whole of its pristine vision."[14] The use of such "mythic" characters in fantasy means that characters may become stiffly stylized. In aesthetic terms, a work might be judged "good" or "bad" with regard to such characterization, but in mythic terms the stylization does not hamper the efficacy of the myth, indeed increases it, for it is the power of the myth that is to be communicated, not the nuance of individual character. In fantasy fiction this distinction really should be drawn. In some contemporary fantasy the craft of the fantasist is sufficiently great that the essential power of the material is retained and the character also assumes "a life of its own" in ways that realistic fiction has taught us to expect. But in terms of the myth/magic, fantasy fiction which has stylized characters may well be effective as fantasy; that is, as an evocation of the kind of reality we have earlier discussed, and should be judged such, the aesthetic consideration for the moment aside. Granted, the most complete integration of all elements of a fiction is desirable, but the fantasy of the "pulps," the sword-and-sorcery fantasy, still "works" for its readers, and in mythic terms that is the most important thing. The craft is secondary to the material here, for myth has always a practical element; it is intended to project a certain potency, a certain meaning and emotional import into ordinary reality, and it can do that on the strength of the material. The sturdy ability of myth to survive even mediocre retelling is a part of fantasy fiction and should be considered in criticism of fantasy. Perhaps our aesthetic standards must be altered somewhat to allow the inclusion of "function." In fantasy fiction, the characters could often go nameless, and they sometimes speak in the worst grade-B Hollywood fashion, yet they act out the elements of plot necessary to reveal the essential *mana,* or magic and that is what fantasy and myth demand.

The mythic dimension is a characteristic fantasy shares with many other forms of art, but unlike some, fantasy could not operate without it. It is perhaps this dimension which gives fantasy its lasting quality. Myths cannot be fabricated; they occur and take forms that are always familiar even when most strange. Even H. P. Lovecraft, who called his work an "artificial pantheon," was really using artifice only in names and specific development of situations. The forms were there before him.

Fantasy fiction, then, is a genre which depends on a magical orientation for both focus and form. Fantasy is not just a technique; it is a mode of thinking. To write and to read fantasy demand a magical conception, a willingness to be enchanted and to give up the maps or norms that chart our consciousness in favor of unexplored territories of imagination. It is this very lack of "maps" that is the chief obstacle to criticism of fantasy fiction, for by giving up even partially terms we apply to other fiction, we are left without a critical vocabulary comprehensive enough to fantasy's needs. Those critics who have seen fantasy fiction chiefly as a minor form of speculative fiction often wind up naming its parts but missing the whole. Other critics who "do" fantasy as a habit of mind find themselves facing critical barriers and escape on the wings of metaphor, deserting us earth-bound and still without a concrete vocabulary. This paper has attempted to delineate some areas where vocabulary for criticism is vague or lacking and to suggest the need for a criticism that can approach fantasy fiction as both feeling and form.

Enchantment Revisited: Or, Why Teach Fantasy?

Jane M. Bingham with Grayce Scholt

While there will always be those persons who simply do not enjoy fantasy (H. L. Mencken said that even as a grown man he skipped large sections of *Alice*), others are devotees. To a non-partaker fantasy is hard to describe. Any description must incorporate the notion that fantasy creates a sense of wonder or amazement and that it must have at least one element that takes the reader beyond the observable, physical world. While all fiction, realistic or fanciful, requires that the reader use his imagination to form mental images that might occur in his life, fantasy demands that the reader accept things that could not occur, that are extraordinary. Fantasy as we use the word usually means capricious, unearthly, "out of this world!" (Even our overused slang exclamation "Fantastic!" indicates something beyond belief, but the meaning is so diffused that it can also indicate "I agree," or "How nice," or "Right on!" or "Neat!") In spite of the "beyond belief" nature of fantasy, it must be equally believable. The weaving together of dissimilar qualities is the main work of the fantastic. Virginia Woolf in *Granite and Rainbow* says fantasy is the work of those writers who have a

sense of the unseen. . . . Such a sense may bring visions of fairies or phantoms, or it may lead to a quickened perception of the relations existing between men and plants, or houses and their inhabitants, or any of those innumerable alliances which somehow or other we spin between ourselves and other objects in our passage.[1]

Unfortunately some adults miss these ephemeral alliances simply because they are adults, as the reading of fanciful literature is today largely relegated to children. In addition, fantasy demands, as E. M. Forster points out in *Aspects of the Novel*, that we "pay something extra" which adults often cannot or feel they should not pay. Children, on the other hand, are eager to put forth the "kind of sixth sense" that Lillian Smith in *The Unreluctant Years* says fantasy requires:

Reprinted with permission from *The CEA Critic* 39:11–15 (Jan. 1978). Copyright The College English Association, Inc., 1978.

All children have it, but most adults leave it behind with their cast-off child-hood. . . . (T)his ability to see further through a stone wall . . . requires what many (adults) are unwilling to give. It asks of the reader what Coleridge calls "the willing suspension of disbelief." . . . (F)antasy constitutes a barrier for many people. They think their intelligence incapable of accepting the premise of suspended reality. Yet in fantasy are found perhaps the most subtle and profound ideas in books written for children.[2]

A child or any reader, continues Ms. Smith, must "listen with sympathy. . . . If one has no desire to listen, no pleasure can result whatever the creative power of the writer or the intellectual content of the book." Children, the sympathetic listeners who have not as yet put away "childish things," are obviously the audience for whom fantasies are most frequently recommended. But should they be the only audience?

The world of fairies, gnomes, phantoms was for many centuries the domain of children and adults, peasants and royalty alike; indeed the entire world of epic, myth, folk tale, and legend has only in recent times been thought of as "children's literature." Today there are even those who think of children's literature and fantasy as synonyms, not realizing that many other types of literature are read by children—biography, contemporary realistic fiction, poetry, historical fiction, informational books. But for most readers, adult and fantasy do not go together. C. S. Lewis says he knows that a man who "admits that dwarfs and giants and talking beasts and witches are still dear to him in his fifty-third year" is not likely to be praised for his youthful spirit but is more likely to be abused for "arrested development." But Lewis goes on to defend his right to partake of his "childish" world:

Critics who treat *adult* as a term of approval, instead of as a merely descriptive term, cannot be adult themselves. To be concerned about being grown up . . . to blush at the suspicion of being childish . . . are the marks of childhood and adolescence. . . . When I became a man I put away childish things, including the fear of childishness and the desire to be very grown up.[3]

He points out quite rightly that one does not have to dispose of "old things" in order to add to the new. He tells us that it is perfectly possible to enjoy Tolstoy, Austen, and Trollope along with fairy tales; that real growth is not rejecting one parcel for another but acquiring, changing, developing, and incorporating new experiences as they come to us. Lewis also points to Tolkien's statement that the appeal and importance of the fairy tale is not that it comments on real life, but that it creates a whole new world—a new experience—that comes to us in proportion to our ability and willingness to enter into it. The great writers of fantasy, not the popular ones who create "cute" characters and tired plots in lackluster style and condescending tones, have the same kind of creative power as the great poets. They are able to go, as Lillian Smith says, to the "heart of the unseen" and shed the "clear light of understanding, or at least . . . partial understanding . . . (on the) inexpressible. According to their varying capacities, they are able to evoke ideas and clothe them in symbols, allegory, and dream."[4]

Is this then the stuff that should remain the province of children only? Is fantasy exclusively for the young? Precious as children are, they do not need to keep such wonders all to themselves. And we need not deprive ourselves or our college students of such works of art. C. S. Lewis says we "must meet children as equals in that area of our nature where we are their equals."[5] When we share the world of fantasy with anyone, we share important feelings of meditation and reaching for "beyondness," all marked, as James E. Higgins says in *Beyond Words* "by an atmosphere of joyful sadness" stemming from a note of "neverendingness" on which fantasies most often conclude.[6]

We should share fantasy with college and university undergraduates as part of our regular English curriculum offerings. We know that the fanciful played an important part in our students' lives when they were children; we know that for some students it plays an important part in their personal lives even now. The best fantasy deserves to be taught in English departments as *literature*. To present it in children's literature courses only, or to think of it only as escape fiction, or "pop culture stuff" is to do a large segment of important, even great, writing a serious injustice.

James Higgins points out that great fantasy appeals to the "inner selves" of all people; that it deals with questions of reality and values in objective and significant ways that realistic literature simply cannot manage; that it fosters a sense of wonder about the world and its creatures in an age when "wonder" is old-fashioned, even quaint; that it frees the partakers from earthly limitations in a way that is almost "religious" and at the same time fosters a sense of humility as one stands in the shadow of great visions, great dreams, great symbols. "The literature of fantasy," says John S. Morris in "Fantasy in a Mythless Age"

inasmuch as it is "unearthly," "extra-ordinary," and "supernatural," is a creative attempt to re-experience the fundamental lifegiving forces. . . . Human life is not easily lived without the active powers of the imagination which catch on to the symbols of the Absolute, which are presented in myth and fantasy.[7]

Even if one were to discount all of the above, the literary elements alone (intriguing plots and characters and often soul-searching themes) make these writings appropriate pieces for critical study. The following books are usually classified as "children's literature," but as with most classification, the label is arbitrary. Given close readings, they lend themselves to discussion, thought-provoking argument, and genuine literary analysis: Carroll's *Alice in Wonderland* and *Through the Looking Glass,* Andersen's *Fairy Tales,* Tolkien's *Lord of the Rings,* Lewis's *Chronicles of Narnia,* Thurber's *The White Deer,* Kipling's *Just-So Stories* and *The Jungle Books,* Juster's *The Phantom Tollbooth,* Grahame's *The Wind in the Willows,* Godden's *The Dolls' House,* Jarrell's *The Animal Family* and *The Bat Poet,* Saint-Exupéry's *The Little Prince,* Kingsley's *The Water-Babies,* MacDonald's *At the Back of the North Wind* and *The Princess and the Goblin,* Mayne's *Earthfasts,* Sandburg's *The Rootabaga Stories,* and Wilde's *The Happy Prince* and *The Selfish Giant.*

Readers of fantasy on the level that these books and others represent will be in the good company of countless devotees who know its power. G. K. Chesterton, who thoroughly enjoyed fantasy, tells us in his essay "The Dragon's Grandmother" that although the universe is wild and full of marvels, the inner self of man is sane. In the fairy tales the cosmos goes mad; but the hero does not go mad.[8] Perhaps this appeal to man's sanity of soul is after all the greatest attraction of fantasy; it helps us to believe that at least within the world of the fairy tale, man is safe, in charge of the present, and looking forward bravely to a happy "ever after."

9 / *Historical Fiction*

Historical fiction, yet another state carved out of the republic of fiction, owes its independence to Walter Scott's historical novels. Later in the same century, "to fetch the kids," Stevenson and Henty set historical characters in adventure-laden plots.

Walter Scott is credited with originating the historical romance. Although not written for children, some of his novels (e.g., *Ivanhoe*, 1820) by 1870 were relegated to children's consumption. Placing his major characters in an historical setting, Scott created a type of novel that, in lesser hands, became mere costume drama. To Robert Louis Stevenson, a Scot influenced by Scott, his mentor should have been more conscious in his artistry. Beginning with a tale spun to entertain his twelve-year-old stepson, Stevenson came up with *Treasure Island,* a serialized psychological adventure story about an adolescent coming to terms with an adult world.[1]

The most prolific of the nineteenth-century adventure writers for boys wrote over ninety volumes. Addressing them to "my dear lads," George Alfred Henty created a "you are there" feeling, due to his experience as war correspondent and world traveller, hinted at in titles like *With Clive in India* (1894) or *With Wolfe in Canada* (1896). Not only did Henty direct these books to boys, but he told his biographer that he prided himself on the fact there was no love interest shown and that his "essentially manly books helped make his boy readers resistant to "weak emotion."[2] It is ironic that Stevenson and Henty, both sickly when young, should be largely responsible for the virile boys' (and men's) book, an audience and thematic division still with us a century later.

In the 1930s Geoffrey Trease found the Scott-Stevenson-Henty legacy still strong but clogged by third-rate imitators and heavy-handed dialogue, not to mention a highly romanticized view of history. From such abuse Trease rescued the historical tale for children. In the selections reprinted here, he relates the difficulties he faced and the solutions he devised for working in the tricky terrain of historical fiction. Evidently he succeeded; Robert Leeson credits him with revitalizing and injecting new credibility into the juvenile historical tale.[3]

To Trease a good historical novel is simply "a good novel, neither more nor less, whose story happens to be laid outside the time limits of living memory."[4] However recent or dated the period covered, Belloc's warning against "reading history backwards" must be heeded. To illustrate, Mollie Hunter, writing about her native Scottish history, first presents some popular myths about Bonnie Prince Charlie, then destroys them with the historical realities she has assembled for her children's books. She finds that writing for children demands, in addition to painstaking scholarship, special care in opening up the story for an audience which may bring to it no historical background. Historical fiction for children, she insists, requires absolute truth.[5]

Mark Cohen also deals with the pitfalls that await the historical-fiction practitioner. As he points out in his essay, what is still inside the living memory of an adult is outside the memory of a child. (Thanks to the musical *Evita*, my temporarily teen-aged daughter knows Juan Peron as Eva Person's spouse, not vice versa.) Besides facing linguistic difficulties and copious research, the writer in this genre must have not only a passion for history but also an equally strong fictive purpose.

Thanks to Trease and others who worked against the romanticizing of such fiction, by 1976 Leeson could find two to three hundred examples of acceptable juvenile historical fiction, in contrast to the genre's "prehistory," up to the 1930s. Among today's better juvenile historical-fiction practitioners, he includes Rosemary Sutcliff, Leon Garfield, and Gillian Avery.[6] Leland Jacobs confirms Leeson's observations about the maturation of the genre and the renewal of interest that occurred just after World War II.

The growth in seriousness and scholarship has earned the critics' attention and approval. Over thirty percent of all the Newbery Awards granted up through 1981 have gone to historical fiction, the most for any single category. Popular though the form has been (some would say more with adult readers and educators than with children), by the mid-1970s, authors faced additional difficulties. These Trease takes up in his article, in which he maintains the continued relevance of the historical novel, even to the reluctant reader. The child's backhand compliment to Scott's novels, which Trease cites, sums up the challenge as well as the reward of the genre: "though they are rather painful to read they always give benefit." Like the adult novel from which it sprang, the juvenile historical novel is less burdened today with stagey archaisms, a "forsooth" here and a "verily" there, and is less sanitized for a young audience than it was before the 1930s.

Ironically, the genre, for all its growth in technique and quality, is shrinking in popular and critical acceptance. Historical fiction dominated the Newbery Awards in the 1930s, when it emerged from its pre-history. By the 1960s, there were only one-fourth as many titles from this category honored as Newbery Award medalists or honor books. Two-thirds of the books so honored through 1951 are no longer in print,[7] a high figure considering the durability of exceptional children's books and the efficacy of the Newbery Awards.

Why? Partly the vocabulary level and the complexity of the double balancing act: history and story. The young adult novel may also be siphoning off some of the traditional readers of juvenile historical fiction. Possibly, too, the defection from historical fiction may be more apparent than real. Research may only now be confirming what has been long known: that this challenging medium for author and reader has never been the most popular literary form for adults or children.

Never an extensive part of the publishing kingdom, children's historical fiction is now no bigger than a duchy. Nonetheless, Sheila Egoff maintains that the quality of the writers attracted to this genre, predominantly British writers, "account to a large extent for a feeling of substance in the genre."[8] Although possessing the least acreage and being extremely demanding of author and reader in the re-creation of what has become a secondary world—the past, historical fiction remains an important principality.

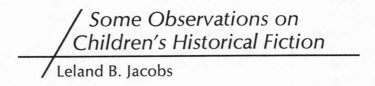

Some Observations on Children's Historical Fiction

Leland B. Jacobs

In children's literature one type of prose fiction that is currently developing apace is the historical story of American life. Careful perusal of the chronology of American literature for children reveals that previous to the twentieth century there was no significant body of historical fiction.

Reprinted from *Elementary English* 29:185–86 (April 1952), with permission.

There are, from the writings of Peter Parley and Jacob Abbott, from the famous writers of the latter half of the ninetenth century, children's stories that take on historical significance but which are, in reality, stories of the contemporary life of their day rather than of historical intent. It is also true that children early took for their own some of America's adult literature: Cooper's Indian stories, Helen Hunt Jackson's *Ramona*, and Paul Leicester Ford's *Janice Meredith*, for example. But, factually, such novels became children's stories only by adoption. Only within the last half century have worthy authors consciously turned their attention to America's past as a very rich source of story material for children's books.

It is not at all surprising that parents and teachers have readily accepted this genre as highly desirable reading fare for children. The historical novel has long been popularly rooted in the American literary tradition. The elementary school has long assumed responsibility for acquainting American children with national backgrounds as a significant educative experience. And current concerns for the preservation of a democratic way of life in the world give rise to beliefs that to comprehend the historical growth of the democratic ideal in our country helps to reinforce faith in that ideal.

Whatever the motivation, historical fiction has become, presently, very prominent in children's literature. On several occasions the Newbery Award has been given to distinctive works in this genre: *Caddie Woodlawn* in 1936; *Roller Skates* in 1937; *The Matchlock Gun* in 1942; and *Johnny Tremain* in 1947. Every publishing season sees important new titles added to an impressive list of books of prose fiction which deal significantly with America's past. The historical story is undoubtedly here to stay. It is more than a fashion. It is one of the most promising fields of story-writing being explored in our day.

Historical fiction has been variously defined. Alfred Tresidder Shepherd, English novelist and essayist, says that "Historical fiction deals imaginatively with the past and can follow paths where Trespass Boards confront the pedestrian historian. . . . The historical novel must of necessity be a story of the past in which imagination comes to the aid of facts."[1] John Buchan is quoted as having said that the historical novel is one that portrays a time in which the light of the living generation's memory does not fall any longer in its full force.[2] Herbert Butterfield believes that "historical fiction fuses the past into a picture and makes it live."[3] And Brander Matthews, eminent American critic, asserts:

If we were to go down the list of so-called historical novels one by one, we might discover that those which were most solidly rooted in our regard and affections are to be included in the subdivision wherein history itself is only a casual framework for a searching study of human character.[4]

Looked at broadly, historical fiction for children can be rather well defined. It reconstructs the life of an age, period, or moment other than that of the present generation. It recaptures realistically the spirit, atmosphere, and feelings of such an age, as that time was experienced by children as well as adults. It deals imaginatively with the reconstruction of life, with verisimilitude. It utilizes historical settings, events, and personages not for their own sakes but as a framework for the creation of a picture of the past that comes to life in a significant study of a child character's realization of life. It creates by the method of fiction such settings, characters, social groups, events, or homely workaday occurrences as are realistically typical of the age or moment being reconstructed. And, above all else, there must be, in historical fiction that will endure, genuinely fine storytelling, so graphically impelling that the historical elements find their necessary bearings deep within the plot pattern as it is artistically developed by a sensitive writer.

Problems of the Historical Storyteller

Geoffrey Trease

To the critic, historical fiction must seem one of the easiest branches of the author's craft. Plots and characters are ready-made, adventures abound, colours are richer, language and sentiments nobler than today's. . . . Set against such advantages, what are a few hours spent browsing in the Quennell's useful volumes, to "get the costumes right"?

When I wrote my first historical story for children, eighteen years ago, I was as confident as a critic. I would write, I privately resolved, exactly as I would have written for adults, but leaving out the sex. Now

Reprinted from *The Junior Bookshelf*, 15:259–64 (Dec. 1951), reproduced by permission.

I know where I was wrong. If I had left out almost everything *but* sex, I might now be a best-selling novelist for adults. And that is about all I do know. After the tenth story I am rather more aware of the special problems confronting the writer in this deceptive field, and much less sure of the answers to them.

Is an overloaded, old-fashioned style the main reason why modern children are so often prejudiced against historical stories? In particular, should we avoid the Wardour Street [Pseudo-archaic, by association with the mock antique furniture that used to be sold there.] dialogue which was long considered essential? In preferring to write conversations in more or less standard English, avoiding both archaisms and anachronisms, I have felt that the most important thing was to establish the distance between them and the suspicious young reader. I believe this choice of style can equally well be justified on historical grounds. A recent correspondence in the *Times* about the "period voice" affected by the B.B.C. in nineteenth-century plays brought out the point that the Victorians, though more precise and artificial in their public delivery, spoke in private life very much more like ourselves than actors would have us believe. So, too, if the historical-fiction writer were to reconstruct his dialogue from the less affected private letters and diaries of the past, and above all from the verbatim records of State Trials and similar proceedings, he would be even less inclined to write, with Stevenson in *The Black Arrow*, "Shalt have a quarrel in thine inwards, boy!" or "Alack, I am shent!" or (with an eminent living writer) "Wot you what?" The plain English of Raleigh (who could turn a phrase if he cared to, as when he spoke of the dead queen as a "lady whom Time hath surprised") suggests that one can go back at least as far as the Elizabethans without finding everyday conversation so very different from that of today. As for remoter periods, surely we must take refuge in the convention which permits foreigners, whether Roman gladiators or Gestapo agents, to converse in English? Either Robin Hood must speak standard modern English or he must use some pre-Chaucerian variety which no normal child will understand. There is no logical justification for anything between.

But—and this is where experience brings doubt—*is* the young reader logical? Is there not within him perhaps a natural and admirable thirst for the colour and music of wild words? Does he not prefer, in his private games, to scream: "Down, varlet, or by my halidom—!" rather than: "Stop it, you fool, or else—"? May it be that, triumphing over all considerations of History and English, Wardour Street tushery appeals on entertainment grounds, because it gives the reader something he wants and which we have not yet learnt to provide otherwise?

In the same way I now find myself asking a question which would never have occurred to me in the old days: does historical accuracy matter? Then (as now) I believed that the writer should work with, rather than against, the classroom teacher. It has always seemed to me regrettable that Victor Hugo, after claiming in an introduction that "all the details of erudition are scrupulously exact," should go on to describe James II as a "jovial monarch" and to imply that a "wapentake" was a kind of English policeman. But does it matter all that much? Which in the long run has done most for a child—a painstakingly accurate reconstruction, in which all the evidence is so well balanced that neither heroes nor villains can be distinguished as such, or a turgid, swashbuckling narrative which, while possibly leaving some minor misconceptions, has certainly left one abiding impression, that History after all is fun? There seems no clear reason why vitality should spring from falsehood rather than from truth, but it seems to happen more often than it should. Perhaps the sanest word on this was said by Margaret Irwin in a recent lecture, when she declared that she would not for one moment wish Dumas' novels unwritten but that personally she had always found the truth so exciting in itself that she saw no point in deliberate falsification.

Suppose then that accuracy is desirable but not the prime essential. What *is* it, anyway? In one's first books one is delighted to get one's material details right—to check on a boy's underwear (if any) in 1400, on the time taken by the Exeter to London coach in 1686, on the possibilities of laburnum overhanging an Oxford wall in 1643. Then, with reflection, come questions harder to answer than what the characters ate and wore. What did they feel and think? Can their psychological processes be reconstructed with any confidence? Is it not just as wild guesswork as Henry Williamson's attempts to imagine the life of an otter or a salmon?

Years ago, before the war, I remember meeting Naomi Mitchison at a party and congratulating her on *The Conquered, Cloud Cuckoo Land,* and her other stories of the ancient world. To my disappointment she told me she would write no more in that style; nor has she, I believe, to this day. "You see," she said, "I'm no longer sure that the Greeks and Romans and Gauls were *like* that." I could hardly understand her scruples then. I do now.

Lesser writers than Miss Mitchison have usually bypassed this obstacle by presenting characters who are little more than modern persons in fancy dress. However scornfully we may dismiss such an expedient as an insult to the adult reader's intelligence, we may feel that it is sometimes hard to avoid it in juvenile literature. It is still our national policy to bring up boys and girls with an absolute standard of ethical values. At the age when they are reading historical adventure stories they can hardly be expected to grasp more sophisticated conceptions of relativity. How then can we present them with "authentic" historical heroes, who combine admirable feats of daring with acts of repellent cruelty? The temptation to endow one's medieval or Renaissance heroes with additional modern virtues, such as kindness to animals, consideration for servants, modesty in dress, and reluctance to commit private homicide, is extremely hard to resist. After all, the first requisite of a hero is that he can be admired.

A special—but a specially frequent—example of this dilemma is presented by heroines. If they are to appeal to the modern young reader, they must possess much of that spirit and independence which characterise the girl of today. In some historical periods this can be squared with the facts: too often, it cannot. If our heroine is to be mobile, if she is to be available for adventures, we are all too often driven to the expedient used (for a different reason) by the Elizabethan dramatists: once again the tresses must be snipped and the delicate limbs encased in boyish hose. So convincingly indeed, that in *The Black Arrow* Dick Shelton can spend over fifty pages with Joanna, including a night in the woods, without noticing the disguise. Whether or not this is equally convincing to the adolescent reader today, the repetition of the device becomes wearisome to the writer, yet hard to avoid. The most difficult problem of this kind I have personally met was in a story of classical Athens. How—without suppressing the almost Oriental attitude of the ordinary Athenian to women—could I introduce a girl with sufficient liberty of action even to meet the boy-hero, let alone have any adventures? Add that, for the sake of a happy ending to their friendship, she must be the lawful daughter of a citizen, not a disreputable alien or slave, and the problem is almost insoluble. It is fun solving such puzzles, but, if one writes with a respect for the facts of social history, they are uncomfortably common.

One final question: how far can, and should, the storyteller work against the rooted prejudices of the young reader? My own instinct is to answer, "just as far as his conscience prompts him," but he should be warned that it is an uphill task. "I'm awfully sorry," I was once told by a B.B.C. producer who had serialised several of my books in Children's Hour, "but I daren't do your new one. All the listeners would be up in arms. You see it's anti-Cavalier!" It was hardly that, actually; it was an attempt to present my own belief that, in every ten people during the Civil War, there were approximately one Cavalier, one Roundhead, and eight others just longing for it to stop. I suspect that children are almost equally prejudiced in favour of Jacobites and French aristocrats, but I have not yet had the chance to prod them and find out. . . .

What Shall We Tell the Children?

Mark Cohen

"The past is a foreign country: they do things differently there," as L. P. Hartley warns us. But if we are travellers by inclination or education, a number of different guides offer their services to us and to our children: archives and architecture, books and museum displays, the stage and screens, large and small.

As children's curiosity grows, we long desperately for the moment when the questions of the "Why did God do that?" type will dwindle into "What's a pyramid?" and "Who was Norman Conquest?" Then we reach gratefully for our education system and our work of reference. Britannica Rules, O.K.? But children *will* go on being ontological and the "Is it true?" refrain echoes on for several years. In the past when this question was asked *about* the past, it was reasonably straightforward for the adult to differentiate between the truth of fact—institutionalized in the textbook and the history lesson—and the untruth of fiction which was beautiful and happened in the English lesson. So we could say apologetically of *Kidnapped*, "No, but it's a marvellous story, isn't it?" But this satisfactory distinction was too good to last, for fact and fiction ceased to be so conveniently categorized. Literary critics confusingly emphasized the truthfulness of our greatest novelists. Was Tolstoy's Napoleon less truthful than Rose's or than his Natasha Rostov? What were we to make of the new label: faction? Or of barely fictionalized autobiography? Where did this leave the historical novel as a guide to the "foreign country"? What were we to tell the children?

One of the first complications is the frontiers of foreignness. When do children's (or indeed adults') novels start being historical? In one sense all fiction is historical. "Once upon a time, there was . . ." links chronology and narrative from the start. Unlike a television newsreel, every story is about the past, has already happened. Since children don't develop a very strong sense of chronology in the crèche (the "Were you alive" or "What

Reprinted from *History Today*, 29:845–46 (Dec. 1979), with permission of author and publisher.

did you do in the Wars of the Roses?" stage), such categorization is more real to parents, teachers and librarians. For the writer who wishes to evoke the past this is the first of several problems.

The most recent setting in the group of books under review is 1947, and the India of Partition. The thirty-year gap will make it quite as remote to the eight- or ten-year-old as Ancient Greece, so Anita Desai's *The Peacock Garden* does not belie the title of the series in which it appears: the "Long Ago Children Books," aimed at that age range. But perhaps a children's novel can count as historical, simply by taking place at a period just *beyond* the reader's memory.

There seem to be two main approaches to the problem of temporal location. Penelope Lively in *Fanny and the Monsters*, her contribution to the "Long Ago Children Books," holds her breath and plunges straight in, "For her tenth birthday, in 1866, Fanny received as presents. . . ." Yet how much will the date mean to her readers? Her chronological demands do not stop there, for Fanny is a somewhat precocious paleontologist who within the book's forty-two pages is introduced, along with us, to Darwin's Theory of Evolution. Others are less uncompromising with their readers. Jennifer Burnap in her rather limp *Obediah's Flag*—a story of the American Civil War—does not show her colours until page fourteen: "Folks reckon there's bin some big arguments ever since Lincoln got to be President. I don't rightly understand it but it's got something to do with Virginia and some of the other states not wantin' to belong to the Union no more."

A second major problem is inherent in that of chronology: that of language. Whereas an adult reader can cope with archaisms in the establishment of atmosphere, a young reader can easily be put off. Henry Treece, whose *Swords from the North* has just been reprinted in paperback, opts for a directness of tone that is never arch, and sweeps us straight into his breakneck story of Harald Hardrada at the Court of Byzantium. Geoffrey Kilner in his story of nineteenth-century mining, *Joe Burkinshaw's Progress*, gives us on his second page: "William Lamb was just putting the motty on the last of the corves"—a sentence that is hardly brillig. The compromise is the rich evocative word glossed, as in June Oldham's retelling of the Beowulf legend, *The Raven Waits:* "One night when I was three winters and the lords celebrated the birth of my brother Hrothmund, he burst into the hall and slaughtered thirty of the duguth, the tired warriors." A trying device, if used too often.

The strain between authenticity and comprehensibility is at its fiercest in dialogue, of course. " 'But Hrethic! Your scramasax! Why is this?' She was surprised and charmed." On the evidence of the present selection, the Vikings are the least fluent conversationalists (though with a swing!). Mary Ray's *Spring Tide*, a story of Roman Britain, flows far better. Iona

McGregor's *The Snake and the Olive*, a horrendously ambitious attempt to bring to life Hippocrates and the origins of medical ethics, uses a simple and timeless language that serves her purposes well. Unless you go to the dangerous and triumphant lengths of, say, Joan Aiken's *The Cuckoo Tree* with its intoxicating mix of thief's cant and old Welsh (that demands great sophistication in her reader and a glossary), it seems authenticity (and how often do we know how they would really have spoken anyway?) is far less important than transparency.

Transparency is required so that the historical novelist's characters show through as clearly and as credibly as those of a contemporary chronicler. But here again his difficulties are far greater. People take a recognizable shape when we see them responding to recognizable situations, so that the most successfully drawn among these books are the most ordinary and at the other extreme, the blatantly larger than life—the hero. The children and adults in these stories who come alive often do so through their very ordinariness, yet Treece's Hardrada is unashamedly the eleventh century's Norse superman. But then Treece based his hero not on history but on the Heimskringla. The introduction's disclaimer is significant: "A saga is first and foremost a story to be enjoyed for its own sake and so, in retelling this one, I have not tried to correct Snorri's history but instead have attempted to interpret and to set down in more modern terms his picture of those heroic and sad times." The old spellbinders knew what they were doing—both Sturluson and Treece—and this recipe is as potent as ever. The strength of Treece and, say, Mollie Hunter is that they start with people. This Hardrada is in no strict sense historical, perhaps that is why he is so much more real than many of the other protagonists in these books. There appears to be an overemphasis on the sadness of "the sad times," a belief that history is smile-resistant. For the majority of the tales are ones of daring-dour. Solemn adolescents work their way unsmilingly to maturity, through the American Civil War, the Battle of the Gauges, the Industrial Revolution.

It is back to authenticity again. Almost without exception the authors have researched their books, gone back to the primary sources, based their fiction on an actual incident. The spidery script of the archives is invisible through even the palest of rose-tinted spectacles. Treece can still swash a buckle because his source is literature, and laugh at his hero, who however deflated will be still larger than life. But the sacredness of the facts on which the majority of these stories are based, the very fidelity, betrays their authors. For the centre of the book becomes the *event*, rather than the participants. They are puppets, and remain wooden. In putting down the books we can say what happened, but this is not the same as saying what happened *to* our heroes and heroines. They tend to be terribly preoccupied with their age and growing up.

276 / *Historical Fiction*

"Matthew, her eldest son, would be fifteen now, three years older than Obe [this is *Obediah's Flag* again]. It took him beyond the realms of childhood into the higher plane of manhood where hard work and responsibility replaced the fun and dreams of his youth."

It is clear what is happening. This is not Obediah internalizing, but the author externalizing; the twentieth-century novelist reminding the nineteenth-century hero he had to grow up quickly in them thar days. Since she has not been able to get inside the characters, we cannot hope to.

This brings us to the final pitfall awaiting the children's historical novelist. In the search for *significance*, an event in the past is seen in an unmistakably modern way, a child character of yesterday is given an adult thought of today.

All this sounds horribly negative, as though all these novelists had been put through impossible hoops. It is because at its best the form can have such an immense imaginative impact on children, widening their range, engaging their sympathies, sending them scurrying off to the "other sort" of history, that the critic needs to be so exacting. Children will *learn* from all these stories. None are less than craftsmanly, but they are historical before they are fictive. The writer must have a real story that demands the telling, about real people no matter how imaginary, if the historical novel is to work and move. Otherwise it will stay parked in one of the many cul-de-sacs off Wardour Street.

CHILDREN'S BOOKS MENTIONED

The Peacock Garden, Anita Desai, Long Ago Children Books, Heinemann.
Fanny and the Monsters, Penelope Lively, Heinemann.
Swords from the North, Henry Treece, Puffin.
The Snake and the Olive, Iona McGregor, Puffin.
The Cuckoo Tree, Joan Aiken, Puffin.
Spring Tide, Mary Ray, Faber Fanfares.
The Raven Waits, June Oldham, Abelard.
Joe Burkinshaw's Progress, Geoffrey Kilner, Methuen.
Obediah's Flag, Jennifer Burnap, Blackie.
Lightning Boy (the Battle of the Gauges), Fred Richens, Blackie.
Mollie Hunter: various titles, Hamish Hamilton, Piccolo and Puffin.

The Historical Story—
Is It Relevant Today?
Geoffrey Trease

"The trouble is," said my friend gloomily, "a lot of Americans are convinced that the historical novel is dead. They won't even consider a book in that field." My friend is herself American but with wide experience in children's book publishing in Britain, too. "It's maddening," she went on, "and clearly a passing phase. But it's difficult to argue with this kind of received dogma."

A few weeks earlier I had encountered similar views voiced by Americans attending the 1976 International Seminar on Children's Literature, held again in England at its original venue, Loughborough University. A school librarian of long experience lamented the decline of interest in historical fiction, even among good readers. "Back home," she told me, "history isn't taught to children and young teenagers as straightforward history. It's brought into the social studies curriculum along with other disciplines, like anthropology or archaeology, to teach certain concepts."

"Is that necessarily bad?" I said. . . .

"No, not necessarily bad," agreed the librarian, "except insofar as the continuity of straight history is lost. Our children learn even American history in a spotty fashion. English and European history suffer still more. The ordinary social studies curriculum leaves many children with only vague generalities."

"A number of teachers," she continued, "are willing enough for children to read historical fiction." . . . But more than approval is needed. There must be knowledge of the stories available to complement a particular study. Children require guidance."

A well-known New York editor, Ann Durell of E. P. Dutton, recently warned British writers in *The Author*, the journal of our Society of Authors, about the American children "who do not have the guidance now to be lured into a 'special' book." The specialist who might have guided them, she explained sadly, "has been done away with in the last salary budget cut." Among the "special" books that have suffered from this economy we may suppose that historical fiction looms large.

Reprinted from *The Horn Book Magazine*, 53:21–8 (Feb. 1977), by permission of the author. Copyright © Geoffrey Trease, 1977.

278 / *Historical Fiction*

It seems worth asking the questions: Do we need it? Is the historical story relevant today?

For the writer of such stories—indeed, for all lovers of the genre, these questions pose fresh challenges. Mere unpopularity—some children's instinctive resistance due to reading difficulties and lack of background—is nothing new. When I myself, over forty years ago, began writing historical fiction, it was in the doldrums. It was long-winded, its vocabulary unfamiliar and unreal. Even in 1934 children had begun to groan at all the tushery, the "varlets" and "quothas" and the rest of it. The schools approved of Scott. As a schoolgirl of those days once wrote, "Though the details of Scott's novels are not always correct, they give one a very good idea of the period, and though they are rather painful to read they always give benefit." However, most of the stories children were reading were not by Scott, but by his third-rate imitators with none of the northern wizardry that infused his massive volumes with a compensating vitality. Historical fiction had got stuck at G. A. Henty, and even he had died in 1902. Those of us who began to write it in the nineteen-thirties had to overcome plenty of prejudice among children, but at least we could usually count on the good will of teachers.

Can we always, now? There must be many—especially younger teachers—who, in common with others of their generation, are in passionate or cynical revolt against existing institutions in our society. It has ever been so. But among some people today this disenchantment with tradition, this impatience with evolutionary change, has developed into an anarchic rage. They have no use for historical thinking, even less for historical fiction.

I feel some sympathy with their rebellious emotion. I, too, was once an angry young man, long before that phrase was coined. But in my case rebellion drove me not into contempt for history but into a determination to rewrite it. My first book, *Bows against the Barons*, was born of a wish to retell the Robin Hood story in grimly realistic rather than romantic terms. My second dealt with the Chartist disorders in South Wales and Birmingham in 1839. Both stories were regarded as unacceptably controversial at the time. Only the boldest teachers dared to take them into schools. It gives me some wry amusement to see that today one of the books has achieved the ultimate respectability of a special school edition, while the other, recently translated into French, was at once put on the recommended list by a religious organization, *L'Office Chrétien du Livre*. The whirligig of Time does indeed bring his revenges.

No, far from being irrelevant to our current ills, historical fiction can be supremely relevant. It was certainly that conviction, not romantic nostalgia for bygone ages, that set me on my own path all those years ago.

The conviction remains as powerful today, though the brash partisan dogmas of the nineteen-thirties are forgotten. When I am casting round for a new theme, it is contemporary relevance that aids my choice and provides the emotional drive. Most often, two things come together like flint and steel to produce the initial spark. One is the historical period or person or event that is for the moment exciting me. The other is the immediate modern significance.

The latter should not be obtrusive. Ideas can be presented more objectively if removed from the realm of current controversy and prejudice. I am glad when the adult book-selector perceives what I am trying to say, but I am content that the young reader get as much, or as little, out of the story as he is equipped to do. It is pleasant to know that sometimes one's point has been taken. "I wondered," wrote a boy from Western Springs, Illinois, "if you might have injected any part or experiences of your personal life into this book. Although in a different time and place I can see how it is possible to do so."

How right he was! *The Red Towers of Granada*, for instance, is, on the superficial level, a thirteenth-century adventure, with a quest leading from Nottingham Castle to the Alhambra. That book, I well remember, sprang from a desire to tell children about the wonderful Moorish civilization of southern Spain. I have a brief notebook entry, dated May 2, 1960, ending, "these characters might wander southwards to Granada or Cordova and be astonished at the culture of the infidel." Over the next five years, as I can still trace in my notebooks, the idea slowly evolved, nourished not only by reading and by a tour of the cities concerned but also by the emotional impact of what was happening in my own world of the nineteen-sixties. To my cultured Muslims were added equally sympathetic Jewish characters and, since my central figure was, like myself, an English Gentile, the story that finally emerged was an implicit plea for racial and religious toleration. Could anything today be much more relevant?

That is not, needless to say, why children read the book. Nor, equally, was it my sole motive in writing it. The main thing must always be the story itself; the joy in action and suspense and mystery; the interest in human relationships (far beyond mere "toleration"!), in colorful settings and, above all, in language. But the contemporary relevance is not just an extra, tacked on. It lies at the heart of the theme. It is the quality that, however little noticed by the young reader, gives the writer an additional dynamic for his work.

Web of Traitors, originally published in England as *Crown of Violet* but renamed for America when I was assured that "no red-blooded American boy would open a book with a flower in the title," was inspired partly by my lifelong passion for classical Athens, Pindar's "shining city with violet crown," and partly by my very contemporary (1952) concern at the way democracies could be overthrown by minorities. As in Athens, 411 B.C. That was the underlying message of the book.

Popinjay Stairs: An Historical Adventure about Samuel Pepys is, on the face of it, a picturesque thriller, a tale of murder, blackmail, and general skullduggery in Restoration London, a setting that has always fascinated me and about which I had previously written an adult book, *Samuel Pepys and His World*. The plot deals with corruption in naval contracts and the pressures applied to force an honest public servant into slipping it past his committee. A perceptive adult reader may notice that this tale was written in the early seventies, during a period of sensational exposures on both sides of the Atlantic. I felt that young people would need, as they grew up, to know about such things.

One of my most recent stories, *The Iron Tsar* (not yet published in the United States), was set in 1831 in the repressive era of Nicholas I. He, it will be remembered, was the Russian emperor who liked to conduct his own browbeating interrogations of political prisoners far into the night, dazzling them with massed candelabra (the arc light being yet unavailable) and clapping dissident intellectuals such as Peter Chaadayev into mental homes. I felt that even a quite young reader would find no difficulty in seeing modern parallels.

Such books involve long research. I have rewritten whole chapters to correct a slight inaccuracy, belatedly discovered. It might make no difference to the story whether a certain morning at Versailles in 1789 was wet or sunny. Perhaps not a single reader would ever notice. But once I had detected the slip myself—in this case from an entry in Thomas Jefferson's diary—I was miserable until I had put it right and got the picture "like it was." If I introduce historical personages into fictitious episodes, I can only justify it if all they say and do is consistent with their recorded behavior on real occasions. And the purely fictitious characters and incidents must similarly accord with the circumstances of the period.

This can raise problems—notably, that of giving girls a fair share of the action in many bygone societies. I was amused when a Canadian girl wrote to me about *Word to Caesar*, which in the United States is titled *Message to Hadrian*: "I liked the way you described Tonia as a Women's Libber." I had not, of course, depicted—much less "described"—my heroine as any such thing, but I saw what had pleased young Wendy out in British Columbia. I had certainly ransacked the social history of the Roman Empire to find how much independence I could justifiably allow a high-spirited teenage girl in the second century A.D.

It was in *Web of Traitors* that I ran into my major obstacle. I wanted boy to meet girl and form a friendship which, I would imply in the closing pages, would lead to marriage in later years. Research showed, however, that in Athens the citizens kept their daughters in almost Oriental seclusion. Alexis could never have run into Corinna outside the home unless she were the daughter of a resident "alien," Greek enough but not Athenian and, therefore, freer to move about. Unfortunately—and here seemed the insoluble difficulty—a purebred Athenian like Alexis would not be allowed to marry a noncitizen's child. I had to rack my brains for a long time before I found a twist I could give to the plot that would resolve my dilemma.

Some historical liberties have always been allowed the imaginative writer if the literary result proves worthwhile. "One can violate History," said Dumas in his earthy Gallic way, "only if one has a child by her." Today, perhaps, our standards of scholarship are more strict. We shrink from faking, even to make a better story. I have never thought much of that excuse, anyhow. History has all the raw material the novelist needs. If he knows his job, he will not require to alter the facts.

The modern writer has resources denied to Dumas and Scott and must face a far better informed public. It is not just the professional critic or the historian; I treasure a letter from an English plowman who, having detected a slip in my enumeration of Charles I's family, wrote bluntly: "I like my facts straight, same as my furrows." So today we storytellers must take infinite pains, prowling through museums, plodding through the mud of ancient battlefields, and filling our shelves with books on costume, transport, and everyday life in all their aspects and in every period. The danger is that we fall in love with all our discoveries and allow our plots to get bogged down in the authentic detail we cannot bear to leave out. The reward comes in the response, like a girl's letter from Whitehorse, Yukon: "We all think this novel was fascinating, because it has helped us a lot in our Social Studies course on Rome."

Doubtless her class had plenty of other aids. The nonfiction reference book, beautifully and lavishly illustrated, researched and written by a small team of editors and consultants, often produced and marketed as an international venture, is one of the most impressive phenomena of juvenile publishing in recent years. But while such volumes excel in the depiction of material things, they are not able to convey psychological truth. They can show us the probable equipment of Cleopatra's dressing table, each unguent-pot and pair of tweezers authenticated by a museum exhibit, but they cannot bring Cleopatra and her maids to life as the novelist can.

So, even in the context of social studies, the historical story has an important part to play, and it would be wasteful not to utilize all that the writer has so painstakingly researched and made available to children in attractive form. No less importantly, in schools where (as my librarian friend complained) concentration on social history alone has left children vague about the continuity of events, the historical story can help to fill the gap.

Children—and this is a truism which we neglect at our peril—love a story, a chronological sequence of incidents and situations ending in a climax. It is interesting to learn what people wore in days gone by, what their houses were like, and what they ate. But it is only moderately exciting. Children more often want to know about individual, named people—and what happened to them.

When the children of the twenty-second century turn their minds back to the twentieth, will they confine their interest to our primitive television sets, our quaint automobiles, and the way we heated our homes before solar energy? Or will they want to hear about Hitler and Stalin and all the hundreds of other fantastic characters and dramatic conflicts that filled our era? If these aspects of the past are out of fashion in some schools today, then the historical novel is even more badly needed to make up for the omission.

Are such stories relevant? Let another schoolgirl, writing to me from the Pacific coast, have the last word: "The setting of *Message to Hadrian* is old, but the story relates to battles of today."

10 / Science Fiction

Science fiction, like a moon recently ripped from the planet of fantasy, veers off into space but sometimes orbits close to its home planet. Booksellers often merge the two entities, fantasy and science fiction; fewer subdivide the latter to unearth children's science fiction. There have been books with a technological cast for centuries, for example, Thomas More's *Utopia* (1516) or Mary Shelley's *Frankenstein* (1817), but as a publishing category science or space fiction dates at least from the pulp magazines of the mid-1920s, like *Amazing Stories*.

Clearly it is a subgenre of fabulation, but what form? Robert Heinlein sees science fiction as one subclass of "speculative fiction" which combines fantasy and adventure stories with exotic locales, sociological speculation (as in H. G. Wells), and pseudo-scientific fantasy. Beyond this helpful classification, science fiction has been defined as "the genre of literature that imaginatively depicts plausible events that are logical extrapolations of known facts and are descriptive of the social impact of science and technology." Darko Suvin sees this "misshapen genre" as one "distinguished by the narrative dominance of a fictional novelty (novum, innovation) validated both by being continuous with a body of already existing cognitions and by being a 'mental experiment' based on cognitive logic."[1]

But even a validated novum might seem merely wondrous to child or adult not up-to-date on the latest products of metallurgic engineering. Thomas J. Roberts, in his article, asks, "How different, after all, is a wizard with a magic wand from a scientist with a micro miniaturized matter-transformer?" And once the latest scientific advance becomes commonplace, it is easy to see why, according to Jane Yolen, today's SF becomes tomorrow's folklore. But, because the core of fantasy is magic, it is important to attempt some distinction between speculation and extrapolation. The bond between science fiction and fantasy is illustrated by Eleanor Cameron who relates her struggles with and within that genre. A few generations after *Frankenstein*, Francis Molson has pointed out, children's writers from Frances Hodgson Burnett on to

Frank Baum and up through the Tom Swift series dabbled with the equipment of science.[2] Defending the distinction between teenage and adult science fiction, Thomas J. Roberts herein sees both as modes not forms. Adolescent science fiction, he insists, can serve that age group without necessarily appealing to adults.

Extrapolating from studies of children's fiction, one assumes that science fiction for children will be simpler, more action dominated and less sophisticated than its adult counterpart. Robert Heinlein has written many science fiction novels for adolescents and for adults, but it would be no easy task to discern on internal evidence which were intended for teenagers. Textual analysis of the sort Aidan Chambers applied to the child novel would be needed. While science fiction journals differentiate between that genre for youth and for adults, and some recent bibliographies of science fiction have featured such books for children, a comprehensive guidebook is needed for that which appeals to the nonadult in a misshapen but wide-ranging genre.[3]

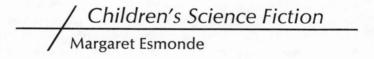

/ Children's Science Fiction
/ Margaret Esmonde

With children running around wielding light sabres like Luke Skywalker, or zapping Space Invaders on their Atari Video Consoles, or watching the ubiquitous Star Trek reruns, who could deny that science fiction is an important part of their life.

Science fiction—the literary response to the technological explosion—has become an increasingly significant subgenre of children's literature as well. It is a curiously ambivalent literature. Its supporters look back to such distinguished writers as Thomas More, claiming that his *Utopia* is science fiction. (Imaginary lands and imaginary lunar voyages were the earliest forerunners of modern science fiction.) Its detractors cite the seemingly endless supply of Grade Z "monster" movies, the science fic-

Reprinted from the *Children's Literature Association Quarterly* 6:1–4 (Winter 1981), with permission of the author and the Children's Literature Association.

tion pulp magazines, and the old Flash Gordon serials as representative of the genre they unhesitatingly label "trash."

It is difficult to pinpoint *the* first real science fiction story, but many critics argue for Mary Godwin Shelley's *Frankenstein* (1817). Although it is basically a Gothic novel, Shelley did introduce as her protagonist a scientist, not a wizard, who revivifies a corpse through "galvanics" rather than incantations; she also introduces one of the central themes of science fiction, the proper use of knowledge and the moral responsibility of the scientist for his discovery—a theme often expressed in later "mad scientist" movies by the hushed statement at the end of the film: "There are some things man was not meant to know!"

Throughout the nineteenth century, various authors such as Hawthorne, Melville, and Poe produced stories which could be classified as science fiction according to modern definitions. But it was the work of Jules Verne and H. G. Wells that is considered the most significant predecessor of twentieth-century science fiction. Wells styled these novels "scientific romances," and they are still highly popular with young readers. But Wells and Verne were not alone in producing literature which extrapolated on scientific possibilities. In the children's literature of the same period, authors reflected the increased interest in science. In his essay, "Juvenile Science Fiction,"[1] Francis J. Molson notes that as early as 1879, Lu Senarens turned out the first of his 180 Frank Reade, Jr. stories "which chronicled the adventures of a boy genius responsible for many remarkable inventions." Frank Reade, Jr. was followed by other well-known teen protagonists such as Tom Edison, Jr. and Tom Swift, a series inaugurated in 1910 and continued through the 30s. . . .

In addition to the juvenile series books the children's magazines occasionally offered stories based on the growing interest in science. But these magazines were overshadowed by the emergence of the science fiction pulp magazines in the 1920s. The first magazine devoted solely to stories which its editor, Hugo Gernsbach, labeled "scientifiction" initially, later changing the term to "science fiction," was *Amazing Stories,* which first appeared in 1926. Depending heavily on reprints of authors such as Wells and Verne, the magazine attracted teenage male readers chiefly. (Girls weren't encouraged to be interested in science, and relatively few were attracted by these magazines.) The original material which appeared in Gernsbach's publication was seldom (if ever) of significant literary quality, but the teenage reader could overlook an enormous amount of bad writing if the action or the idea held his interest. There emerged in this first flowering of science fiction two main types of plots: "space opera," the action-adventure oriented story with a strong young hero in conflict with an evil villain. The young hero is usually associated with a good scientist who practically always has a beautiful daughter whose function, in addition to decorating the cover of the magazine in the clutches of a tentacled monster, robot or other unspeakable horror, was to ask questions so that information could be conveyed to the reader, and to be captured (screaming shrilly) so that the hero could act heroically. It is, of course, a plot familiar to children's literature. Substitute a sword for the hero's laser gun, call the scientist a wizard, make his daughter a princess, the despot a sorcerer, the assorted aliens enchanted animals, and the structure is apparent. In *Star Wars*, George Lucas capitalized on this rich fantasy vein which underlies so much science fiction, even opening the film with the familiar fairy tale beginning: "Long, long ago in a galaxy far, far away."

The second basic plot in this period was nicknamed "gadget" science fiction because the chief feature of this type of story was the description of the invention. Again, the scientist (often eccentric but with the mandatory beautiful daughter), aided by the young lab assistant (the galactic hero thinly disguised in a lab coat), is asked by the daughter the all-important question: "What is that thing you're working on, Father?" The rest of the story consists of the answer to that question.

Though subliterature, these "thrilling wonder" tales exerted considerable influence on young readers, and many of today's leading scientists have credited these magazines with encouraging them to pursue careers in various scientific disciplines.

The first American juvenile science fiction novel to be admitted to library shelves was Robert A. Heinlein's *Rocket Ship Galileo,* published in 1947 by Scribner's. The plot is naive by today's standards: three teenagers and their scientist uncle build a rocketship in the backyard, journey to the moon, disrupt a Nazi plot to conquer the earth, discover a lost lunar civilization, and return home, but Heinlein proceeded to dominate adolescent science fiction, publishing twelve novels between 1947 and 1958. Critic Alexei Panshin is of the opinion that it is by these novels, rather than his adult science fiction, that Heinlein's reputation will be sustained.

Another significant writer who contributed to the rapidly expanding field of the adolescent science fiction novel was Andre Norton, whose *Star Man's Son* (1952) introduced the post-catastrophe science fiction story, less "engineer-oriented" than Heinlein's work. Isaac Asimov contributed the Lucky Starr series, and many other magazine science fiction writers tried their hand at juvenile science fiction, with varying degrees of success. The Winston Science Fiction Series, begun in 1952, was perhaps the most ambitious attempt to provide adolescent readers with science fiction novels.

In addition to the Winston Series, there was the predictable assortment of "tentacled monster" novels and alien invasion novels; there were any number of space exploration novels in which the young cadet saved the galaxy by courageous and timely action. Even Lassie was translated into science fiction in William Morrison's *Mel Oliver and Space Rover on Mars,* the saga of a super collie.

At the same time that science fiction writers were discovering the juvenile market, children's authors who had no connection with the science fiction magazines began to respond to youth's expanding scientific interests. Ellen MacGregor's *Miss Pickerell Goes to Mars* appeared in 1951. Ruthven Todd introduced *Space Cat* in 1952, and in 1954, "middle-aged" children were delighted to make *The Wonderful Flight to the Mushroom Planet* courtesy of Eleanor Cameron. *Wonderful Flight,* the first of a series of five imaginative space fantasies, followed in the long tradition of stories written for the author's own child. Written for her son David, Mrs. Cameron's series has proved an enduring favorite. . . .

Like its parent, children's science fiction has diversified considerably since the 1950s. Two science fiction novels—Madeline L'Engle's *A Wrinkle in Time* and Robert C. O'Brien's *Mrs. Frisby and the Rats of NIMH*—have won the Newbery Medal. Sylvia L. Engdahl has provided a series of novels, including *Enchantress from the Stars* and *The Far Side of Evil,* which feature a resourceful female protagonist.

Throughout the last two decades, science fiction continued to gain acceptance as a legitimate literary genre, suitable for classroom use. In the 1970s, courses in science fiction began to proliferate on college and university campuses, and serious literary criticism appeared. . . .

Science fiction has come a very long way from the days of the boys' series books and the pulp magazines. It has emerged as a significant subgenre of children's literature. Blending the realism of today's technology with the magic of future possibilities, it is particularly suited to fire the youthful imagination "to boldly go where no man has gone before."

Science Fiction and the Adolescent

Thomas J. Roberts

> It's a poor sort of memory that only works backwards.
> —*Through the Looking Glass*

"The phases of being a science fiction reader can be traced and charted," says Donald A. Wolheim in *The Universe Makers:*

So many read it for one year, so many for two, so many for life. For instance, reading it exclusively can be as compulsive as a narcotic for a period of an intelligent teen-ager's life. The length of time as I see it—and I have seen and talked with and corresponded with hundreds and hundreds of such readers in my lifetime—is about four or five years of the most intense reading—usually exclusive, all other literature being shoved aside. After that a falling off, rather rapid (often due to college entry or military life or the hard stuff of getting a job for the first time). There is, I suspect, something like an 80 percent turnover in the mass of readers of science fiction every five years.

Science fiction has many shapes. It is a mode, not a genre, which is to say that its traditions and content vary with the media in which it appears. The science fiction television series (*Star Trek*) is governed by different conditions than the feature film (*2001: A Space Odyssey*). Just as science fiction radio (*X-One*) is beginning to fade from human memory, a new oral tradition is beginning to emerge on records with The Firesign Theatre's *Don't Crush That Dwarf* and *I Think We're All Bozos on This Bus*. Even the lowly comic strip (Alex Raymond's *Flash Gordon*) is actually rather different from both the old comic books and the new underground comics (*Planet Stories: Fantagor*). But it is science fiction prose—by far the most sophisticated and demanding of all these genres—that is capturing that adolescent reader. We seriously underestimate him if we suppose we understand science fiction prose merely because we have watched *The Creature from the Black Lagoon* and read

Reprinted from *Children's Literature*, 2:87–91 (1973), with permission of The Children's Literature Foundation, Box 370, Windham Center, Conn. 06280, and the author.

Flash Gordon when we were younger. It would be like supposing we know *Moby Dick* because we have seen John Huston's film. The science fiction film may be lovable, but it is stupid. Science fiction prose is often clumsily written but it is intelligent.

It may surprise some nonreaders to learn that within science fiction prose itself there is a tangle of conflicting traditions. Samuel J. Lundwall in his study, *Science Fiction,* identifies five strands: pure adventure (e.g., Edgar Rice Burroughs, *The Moons of Mars*); horror (the stories of H. P. Lovecraft); sword and sorcery (Tolkien, *Lord of the Rings*); social satire (Huxley's *Brave New World;* Pohl and Kornbluth's *Gravy Planet*); scientific speculation (Hal Clement's *Mission of Gravity*); and literary experiment (Harlan Ellison's anthology *Dangerous Visions*). One of the leading magazines makes this mixture of subgenres explicit; it calls itself *The Magazine of Fantasy and Science Fiction.* The truth is that a large part of science fiction is not about science at all; it is about the supernatural. And much of the rest of it is either covertly or quite openly doubtful about scientific values: we all think of Ray Bradbury as a writer of science fiction, but he knows very little about modern science and is blatantly antagonistic to it. The adolescent who likes Isaac Asimov's stories about robots (*Caves of Steel; I, Robot*) probably also likes Tolkien's *Lord of the Rings.* In some of the best stories, magic and science are deliberately intertwined. There is nothing quite like Jack Vance's *Dying Earth* and Roger Zelazny's *Jack of Shadows* in the motion picture, or in any of the classic literary genres. Science fiction stories are often simple, but the genre itself is not simple.

Finally, some science fiction is written for adults and some for adolescents. This is so well recognized by readers of the genre that *Luna Monthly,* which is devoted to news about science fiction, has a special section of reviews titled "Lilliputia." There are some good novels which only the exceptional adolescent will find absorbing: Stapleton's *Last and First Men* and *Star Maker,* and Frank Herbert's *Dune,* and John Brunner's *Stand on Zanzibar,* and the oeuvre of H. G. Wells (when read as anything more than gadget-stories). He feels more at ease with simpler books like Arthur C. Clarke's *Childhood's End* and E. E. Smith's *Gray Lensman* than with, say, Walter Miller's *Canticle for Leibowitz.* It is wrong—inaccurate to say the least—to defend adolescent interest in the genre by citing books that will sustain the serious attention of adults.

C. S. Lewis once observed that it is the mark of the serious reader that he returns to certain important books again and again; but I think this is not (or only rarely) true of the serious reader in adolescence. He reads voraciously, drunkenly. He does not return to a book he loved. As soon as he has finished one book he reaches hungrily for something new. In a sense, he is not reading the books, he is reading the genre itself. Only later, and only if he continues to read, will he develop a private canon of books that have earned his continuing attention. Reading by genre is a different style of reading. It has its own logic, its own rationale, its own satisfactions.

Adolescent science fiction is a fictional analogue of those Jacques Cousteau films I suppose everyone has seen. Cousteau is giving us an exotic world invaded by men equipped with exotic devices for survival. Make some of those strange creatures Cousteau finds under the sea intelligent and make that equipment even more exotic and we have the world of technological science fiction. Replace that equipment with strange (but carefully defined) mental powers or with ancient charms and spells and we have moved into the world of supernatural science fiction. In either event, the emphases will be on the alien creatures and on the equipment, not on the people who do the adventuring. (Adult science fiction manifests moral and philosophical and theological concerns and gives greater emphasis to the people in that strange new world, but it is the adolescent variety that interests us.)

What is it in this imagined reality that a certain kind of adolescent finds important? The answer cannot be given in two paragraphs, but a couple of its features are worth remarking. First, science fiction, like Cousteau, shows men working closely with machines. Serious writing (and of course much science fiction too) admits the existence of the machine but treats it as pure menace. There are some notable exceptions to this—Melville's love of the technical apparatus of whaling, Beckett's use of a tape-recorder as a character in *Krapp's Last Tape*—but the serious writer at his most characteristic moments is as bigoted about the technician and machinery as any aging racist could be about blacks. A profound concern about technology is appropriate to our times, but it does seem odd that writers should be so unqualifiedly hostile when, in all probability, they can still remember with great affection the first bicycles they ever owned, when they take pride in their high fidelity sound equipment, when they reach their friends normally by telephone, and when—as they must recognize—they may be kept alive and productive later by heart-pacers. Ursula K. Le Guin spoke truly: "For modern man, nature is technological." The adolescent knows this without knowing that he knows it, and he finds the world in which he meets "slow glass" and "body shields" and "space skimmers" and "hyperdrives" as realistic in its own way as the world of Emile Zola and Frank Norris are in their ways. Science fiction understands the machine intuitively much better than contemporary serious writing does: it, too, often presents the machine as an alien which has invaded our world from within us; it, too, often presents it as irrelevant; but it also presents it as the tool and companion it has come to be. The adolescent is reading a literature which at this moment in our cultural history is unique in its imaginative exploration of man-machine relationships.

Then, there are those exotic intelligences—not just the bug-eyed monsters of the motion picture and the old fashioned science fiction novel (Wyndham's *Day of the Triffids*) but the alien lifeforms, alien intelligences, alien psychologies to which so much of the science fiction writer's imagination is devoted. Whether it be the sorcerer of Tolkien's stories, or a shape-shifting carnivore in Weinbaum's "Martian Odyssey," or the intelligent and benign virus in Clement's *Needle,* or the flame-throwing plants in Aldiss's *Long Afternoon of Earth,* or the bisexual humanoids in Le Guin's *Left Hand of Darkness,* it is the alien which captures most of the reader's attention. Just as *Gulliver's Travels* and the *Odyssey* and Mandeville's *Travels* did in their own day, these stories make manifest the unadmitted uneasiness we have about the obvious. Like us, the adolescent works with categories that usually serve well enough in his dealings with others. He thinks he knows what a high school English teacher is like, what congressmen are like, what career soldiers are like, what actors are like; but the individual teachers and congressmen and soldiers and athletes he actually gets to know have a perverse way of not quite fitting his pigeonholes. He thinks he knows what he himself is; but he finds himself being surprised now and then by something he has done unconsciously—an "accidental" remark that gives someone else pain, his inability to remember somebody's name when he has to introduce him, a sudden spurt of joy when something nice happens to someone he thinks he dislikes. For him (as for us) nothing quite fits that grid his culture and his experience and his reflection has constructed in his brain. In the science fiction aliens, his unadmitted sense of the mysteriousness of others is given the objective correlative, as Grierson and Eliot called it, for feelings that are always inside him. He is in the process of shifting from a world centered upon him to one in which he is just an individual in a crowd of people whose inbuilt purposes are taking them in other directions. He will come to accept this more easily, I suspect, when the otherness is given an unmistakably alien form; he will learn later—as King Lear did—that all the rest of us are aliens too.

Adolescent science fiction shares this interest in the machine and the alien with adult science fiction, but it has other features which repel experienced readers. For one thing, the stories are thickly smeared with sentimental lard. The work of Cordwainer Smith (for instance, "Scanners Live in Vain") offers a fictional universe so bizarre that it is outstanding even within the genre, but the price an adult must pay to share Smith's vision is very heavy: we must swallow a sentimentality of characterization and event that we find almost indigestible. But now we must ask ourselves two questions students of children's literature have no doubt raised many times before. Are we never to say that a book is excellent for adolescents unless it is also a good book for adults? Must we measure adolescent tastes only by their similarity to adult tastes? When I reflect on the long history of my own reading preferences I find that there was no slow evolution but rather a series of abrupt metamorphoses. Perhaps we are butterflies now, but once we were caterpillars and what satisfies us as butterflies was not what we needed then. I am not displeased, today, to recall that I preferred Robert Heinlein's stories to Scott's *Ivanhoe*—a book my own high school teachers forced upon me with only the best intentions.

Science fiction includes some of the many forms the ancient tradition of fantasy is taking today. I suppose no one who has ever looked into the genre has failed to notice this, and yet it does not seem to be generally appreciated. It is a simple fact that the adult reader of science fiction is also interested in Kafka's *Metamorphoses* and Jorge Luis Borges's *Labyrinths* and that the adolescent reads the stories of John Collier and Saki too. *The Lord of the Rings,* a fantasy, might easily be transformed from its subgenre to the other. Put the story into outer space, and have the adventurers move from one planet to another. Make Gandalf a super scientist. Make the different peoples different species found on those different planets. (The thematic content would hardly be affected: no one thinks of Frank Herbert's *Dune* as fantasy per se and yet it presents a more complex fictional universe than Tolkien did, it deals with prescience and the prophet, and it raises ultimate humanistic questions—in, I feel, a more sophisticated and disturbing way.) How different, after all, is a wizard with a magic wand from a scientist with a microminiaturized matter-transformer? The reader does not understand how either gadget works. People who would like to believe for a while in magic will prefer the wizard. People who would like to believe in the unending progress of technology will prefer the scientist. It is a matter of one's willingness to suspend certain kinds of disbelief, and not others, when one chooses between them.

Most of science fiction purports to be about the future, and it is either openly fantastic or a translation of the fantastic into super science. It is, then, a projection into an imagined future of the concerns and wonders of the past, a presentation of that future in the language of the past. "It is a poor sort of memory that only works backwards." For the adolescent, "real" life does lie in the future; it will begin when he is released from school. He finds in even the most technological science fiction an impression of that life in which the ancient worries of man appear once again: love and hate, victory and defeat, honor and shame—and always difficulties, terrors, problems, crises in an unfamiliar world he did not make and will never fully understand. In short, what is implicit in Chaucer and Shakespeare and Austen and Dickens and Shaw and Faulkner is made so explicit in science fiction that even inexperienced readers cannot miss it.

True, most of these science fiction stories the adolescent devours are worth no more than one reading, but this does not argue that the genre itself is not worth his attention. The corpus of the genre—the total of all the stories it has generated—constitutes for him one immense collage; it is a looseleaf book whose chapters are novels and whose subchapters are short stories, which he may enter at any point and explore in whatever sequence interest and chance should suggest. Science fiction is a subliterary genre—*sub*literary because so few, if any, of its stories will sustain the continued attention of thoughtful readers—which closely parallels the junk sculpture of our age. It is not a story-by-story but a story-*with*-story analysis that it requires. The first approach will prove that the whole is composed of junk parts but it will miss the interaction of those parts. It will not see that one flawed story may complement another flawed story and the whole become greater than the sum of its parts.

But one might reply, this argument makes it possible to defend any literary genre that has ever emerged and obliterates distinctions in value. Not so. Of adolescent and adult science fiction I think this is true, but not of most other genres. Spasmodic poetry and the western and the "academic" novel never achieved significance. I do not know enough about children's literary genres to identify the significant among them, but it seems to me that the only other subliterary adult genre for which the same claim can be made is the mystery novel—a web of such subgenres as the novel of detection (Agatha Christie's *And Then There Were None*), the thriller (Eric Ambler's *Coffin for Dimitrios*), police-procedure stories (William P. McGivern's novels), and especially the tradition which emerged from *Black Mask* magazine (Dashiell Hammett's *Red Harvest*). Some genres do not merit the attention of adults or adolescents.

To dismiss books written for children as unimportant because they do not interest adult minds and to dismiss—however regretfully—the children who do prefer them to adult books is, often, to do both an injustice. It fails to recognize that the adolescent mind has its own nonadult requirements and that some adolescent genres have an internal complexity and a pertinence that transcend the limitations of the stories that emerge from them. I think no better example of such an injustice can be found than in the contemporary dismissal of adolescent science fiction by thoughtful readers.

Fantasy, SF, and the Mushroom Planet Books

Eleanor Cameron

Having been asked to put those three names up there in the title together and say something about them, I remember what an innocent I
was about science fiction when I began *The Wonderful Flight to the
Mushroom Planet*[1] for a boy aged eight who was absolutely devoted to
the idea of Doctor Dolittle going to the moon. I was an innocent who
would have agreed heartily that fantasy was one thing and one thing
only: a fanciful work dealing with supernatural events or characters,
and science fiction quite another: a kind of story that draws imaginatively
on scientific knowledge and speculation. I knew nothing then of the
great differings and philosophizings, the setting up and tearing down of
fine lines technically and aesthetically between the two that had been
going on among the devotees of each (in anthologies, science fiction has
been much more apt to raid the fantasy collection than the other way
round) and of the heat of those differings. Fantasy was my love. Science
fiction extrapolated (I'd at least learned *that* word) from the facts of
science, and it was not for me. What I was doing was playing with the
fancies my conception called up, wanting only to tell a story, and having
no notion in the world of "attacking scientific rationalism"[2] or of attacking anything, come to that. Or so I believed then.

And there, as to definitions, if I must think of them, is where I
still am, no doubt, when asked to consider these two genres as separate
categories, while realizing very well that the line between them (if there
is a line) is blurred. Yes, you know it's blurred, says my reasoning.
And, yes, I've read Robert Scholes' *Structural Fabulation* and have to
admit that he has something there.[3] This book, by his own admission on
science fiction, seems to me—much of it—to be in defense of SF. And
is it for this reason that he brings in the Earthsea Trilogy as SF, expli-
cating about *A Wizard of Earthsea* for almost half a chapter in a book
of four chapters, and giving no other novel aside from *The Left Hand*

Reprinted from the *Children's Literature Association Quarterly* 5:1, 5–9 (Winter
1981), by permission of the author and the Children's Literature Association.
Copyright © 1981 by Eleanor Cameron.

of Darkness as much consideration? Surely anyone will admit who has read it, *Wizard* works through magic in revealing Le Guin's philosophy of how a man shall live, rather than through scientific knowledge and speculation. And yet Scholes very acutely, I must confess, asks if Ged's explanation of the sources of power in the universe, "syllables of the great word that is very slowly spoken by the shining of the stars,"[4] is magic, religion, or science. And he replies to his own question that it is Le Guin's gift "to offer us a perspective in which these all merge, in which realism and fantasy are not opposed, because the supernatural is naturalized—not merely postulated but regulated, systematized, made part of the Great Equilibrium itself."[5]

Yes, I see how simplistic it is to try to push a single category into an airtight compartment, when Scholes can draw science fiction and fantasy together under the name of structural fabulation, saying that it "is fiction that offers us a world clearly and radically discontinuous from the one we know, yet returns us to confront that known world in some cognitive way."[6] But why structural, I ask. Because, says Scholes, he is differentiating between tales in which plot is an end in itself, as in so much science fiction, so that what one gets is space opera, and the aesthetically structured work in which the whole organization is meaningful to a degree that gives the reader far more than an exciting read.

All right, then. This is a very useful and fruitful determination, this drawing of science fiction and fantasy together under the term fabulation, enabling Scholes to discuss either and ignoring the old narrow definition of SF. All of Le Guin's worlds—for instance, Earthsea, where magic is an inherent part of life, as well as Anarres, Urras, and the Winter Planet, her science fiction worlds where it is not—are in various details— though by no means all—different from the one we know and yet return us to our own world in some cognitive way, some discerning, reflective way.

But to go back to my ignorant self at the time I began *Wonderful Flight:* I had been devoted to fantasy ever since I had read my first traditional fairy tale, and then gone on to the tales of Andersen and to King Arthur and the myths and legends of the world. Later I fell in love with astronomy when I read Sir James Jeans, and then tried science fiction. Scholes speaks of the popular, uninformed generalizations about SF; that it uses language clumsily, "with neither grace nor wit"; that it is populated by pasteboard characters; that it is, in its plotting, hackneyed and episodic; and that its "subject matter is unreal, escapist, and/or ultimately trivial."[7] Well, these accusations may be uninformed, but in the early 1950s I had found no work of science fiction I could admire for its style, its wit and grace, its characterizations, or its power to capture my emotions and intelligence and imagination all at once. Wells with his time machine had captured my imagination even though I was impatient with the silly machine itself as an unbelievable vehicle in a fiction purporting to be scientific. [See pages 78–82 of *The Green and Burning Tree* for a discussion of *The Time Machine*.] But as for wit and grace of style, or for characterization—no. Scholes would have suggested that I read George R. Stewart's *Earth Abides,* published in 1949, but unfortunately nobody told me about it.

In *The Green and Burning Tree* (written in 1966 and 1967) I asked, concerning the creation of memorable beings, "Who stands out in science fiction compared to the great figures of major literature?" and said that "in science fiction we recall only Captain Nemo, and he is a minor personality indeed."[8] Le Guin later discusses this surprising lack in her essay "Science Fiction and Mrs. Brown," taking off from an essay by Virginia Woolf, "Mr. Bennett and Mrs. Brown."[9]

But, actually, I wasn't thinking of the lack of characterization in science fiction when I began writing *Wonderful Flight,* which immediately involved Tyco Bass. I wasn't thinking of science fiction at all! He came to me overnight, along with the initial conception of the story, and I seemed to know all about him and exactly how he looked as I sat down to write. He is no great character, explored in depth throughout the five books. But he revealed himself to me as imaginative, humorous, serious, inventive, kindly, loving, and good through and through—a wise person because he is who he is and because he has lived for almost 400 years (*Time and Mr. Bass* celebrates his 385th birthday). He is small, no taller than the boys, David and his friend Chuck, who come to be Mr. Bass's confidants. He is fine-boned, light, quick, with a large head covered with wispy hair; he has great round, brown, searching eyes, full of humor, and long, delicate fingers greatly skilled at using a paint brush for aesthetic purposes or searching in the earth for the exact right place to put seeds or tuck in newish plants. He is usually to be seen in a gardening coat, narrow trousers, and elastic-sided boots. These last were provided by Robert Henneberger, the illustrator, and they are so pre-*cise*ly (to use Mr. Bass's word) in keeping with the little man's individuality that I knew they belonged to him.

As for Tyco's goodness, I once said in a seminar apropos of the difference in effect between the fairy tale of "Beauty and the Beast" and the novel *Beauty* by Robin McKinley that the dark side of human nature, personified in the wicked sisters and in the threatening, bitter brooding of the Beast in the fairy tale, is missing from the novel: the sisters in *Beauty* are all good, the father is good, and the Beast is patient and poignant and pitiable rather than threatening. All of this results in a lack of tension, which struck me forcibly on a second reading.

Therefore, without thinking, I ran a risk in letting Tyco emerge, untouched and unmanipulated, just as he had first come to me, and yet he *was* himself. I couldn't have changed him. And there was no evil on the Mushroom Planet, only ignorance and foolishness, and the tension usually resulting from a clash of wills or of personalities, or from a battle between good and evil, is provided in *Wonderful Flight* by the passage of a short period of time in which the two boys must resolve, through their sensitivities and intelligence, the problem of the Basidiumites' illness. In *Stowaway to the Mushroom Planet* it is there by reason of the ego of Horatio Q. Peabody, who desires to make a full public report on Basidium simply in order to gain fame for himself, without a thought for the possible results to the fragile planet and its inhabitants. And in *Mr. Bass's Planetoid* and *A Mystery for Mr. Bass*, it is provided by that facet of Prewytt Brumblydge's character which compels him to focus so narrowly on his own concerns that he loses all perspective. Not until *Time and Mr. Bass* is Tyco pitted against the core of Evil, Narrow Brain, who threatens the creative energies of the Mycetians (the Spore People of earth) and therefore their very existence.

"In your time," writes Tyco's ancestor, Elder Grandfather, in the days of King Arthur, never knowing if his descendant will find these words and be able to translate them, "in your time, our people shall have lessened in numbers, but perhaps this will not matter because, for many generations, they shall have contributed little of value to their different lands in those arts in which, for hundreds of years, they have been most gifted: in the art of song and the creation of great stories, and in the working of metals, the carving of wood and stone, and in aiding those who govern by our quickness of action and wit and perception. . . . Vanity and perfidy and greed shall have defeated our Throngings. . . . Help our people to find strength again. Remind them of the Great Throngings. Encourage them to weave their wordhoards and songs as they used to, to fashion what gives joy and release to the spirit with their skilled fingers, and to find satisfaction in this without thought of gold. *Tell them that only in the act of creation can our people discover themselves again, and regain strength and courage.*"[10]

Time and Mr. Bass, of the five Mushroom Planet books, is most wholly in the realm of fantasy. The others I had written with a twinkle of the eye in the tone. After all, one has only to consider the following curious details within the context of scientific facts and probabilities— or extrapolations. An oxygen urn that goes "pheep, pheep" all through the journey, the sound of which gives the boys a feeling of warm comfort because it reminds them of their friend Tyco, who had invented the urn and whom they trust completely, and which allows them to give their full attention to the unimagined beauty of the constellations, undimmed by atmosphere. Mr. Bass's stroboscopic polarizing filter which he clamps onto the eye of his telescope and which enables him to spot a tiny satellite of earth's on which a race of delicate little beings live. They are Mr. Bass's people (he being a Mycetian), one of a race which began, he explains, when spores from Basidium were carried here to earth in some mysterious fashion across those intervening thousands of miles of space. Mr. Bass's casual inventions: his space fuel atomic tri-tetramethylbenzacarbonethylene, "four drops of which could blow a mountain to smithereens—ten mountains!"[11] And his fluid resinoid silicon sealer (with other ingredients) for the treatment of the exterior of the space ship, which the two boys build. And the space ship itself, put together without help from grownups, and made from old boat ribs, some aluminum sheeting, and a pane of plastiglass. And the little planet, thirty-five miles in diameter ("a little planet just my size," was what David had dreamed of, but this story is no dream), composed of Brumblium, a very heavy element which allows the planet astonishing mass so that the boys need no space suits. And the delicate little race of beings who inhabit it, who reproduce by spores, create exquisite jewelry, make music on maleetles with different tones like recorders, clothe themselves in graceful robes of pressed-out mushroom fibres, and who keep their dead in an enormous, damp, underground cavern where their bodies are naturally preserved to look as if they were still alive.

All of this within the context of fantasy is acceptable, but within the context of science is absurd—yet, of course, notice the various details which appear to take scientific necessities into consideration. Furthermore, the idea of a hole in space came to me while I thought about *Stowaway to the Mushroom Planet,* written in 1954 (see pp. 53 and 100–2 of *Stowaway*) and astronomers did not discover that there are actually Black Holes in space until the early 1970s. Those who see the books as fantasy categorize them as space fantasy, and a friend wrote asking if I were making fun of science fiction, to which I replied that I hadn't intended to. She answered that when a poll had been taken in her corner of the country among young writers of science fiction, asking what books had started them off in childhood as writers of this genre, it turned out that the Mushroom Planet books were mentioned again and again. The joke was on me. Yes! And if they write good science fiction, I am well pleased.

Which brings me to the point that perhaps it doesn't matter whether a story is fantasy or SF, that quite possibly, as my friend would say, it's the wrong question. (To be purely technical, faster-than-light travel, required in all science fiction which takes place in other galaxies and remote planets in our own galaxy, is an impossibility in an Einsteinian universe, so that that kind of SF turns out to be fantasy in any case.) And it is no wonder that the reviewers called the Mr. Bass stories alternately science fiction and space fantasy. "I am rereading *Wonderful Flight,*" my friend writes, "and am I wrong in thinking that you, too, are somewhere in 'the middle ground' (between the Red or SF end of the spectrum and the works with trolls that are likely to be over in the Violet or Fantasy end)? You are playing with and making gentle fun of all space gadgetry, but also you quite soberly present some of the marvelousness and splendor of the universe *as revealed by* physics and astronomy and their technologies—no?"

Yes. I was walking a certain fine line, but in *Mr. Bass's Planetoid* and in *A Mystery for Mr. Bass* (I could see after I'd written them) I failed to maintain quite that middle ground, which had given me pleasure, and that particular tone I was listening for in *Wonderful Flight.* In *Time and Mr. Bass,* in turning from the too scientific tone of the previous two, I went over to Violet, where I was at home and therefore much happier.

But *was* I, unconsciously, underneath, making fun of science fiction in the earlier books? We know not what we are saying in our fictions, something clear to our readers but unseen by us until these revelations are pointed out. Perry Nodelman, in that Winter *Quarterly,* said that "her science fiction attacks scientific rationalism," and that "unlike most science fiction, they [the Mushroom Planet books] describe a world without technology, a romantic's nostalgic dream of a small, soft, misty Eden. Most science fiction heads off into hard-edged Utopian futures into which we could presumably evolve; the Mushroom Planet is more primeval than evolutionary."[12]

But I never desired to paint a picture for children of a kind of Eden because I am a romantic and have the kind of yearning (whether I'm a romantic or not, I don't know—I rather doubt it). I never thought of the little planet as an Eden, but as a fantasy place. The boys did not long to stay on Basidium, but only to visit, nor do David's parents plead to be taken there. And I have nothing against scientific rationalism *itself,* nor against technology *itself,* only a burning resentment of the wickedness men do to their descendants and to all of us and to the natural world in misusing science and technology out of callousness and greed and brutality.

However, is *that* true: that I have nothing against technology and scientific rationalism per se? Perhaps not. Because I recognize that very often scientific rationalism blinds itself, in its dependence upon and respect for intellection alone, to that which may not be able to be turned into equations. "Nature," said Loren Eiseley, "contains that which has no intention of taking us into its confidence." He is speaking of the heart of the mystery which lies beyond equations. And a good many scientists are increasingly willing to admit that our goal could be and will assuredly have to be, not to conquer nature, but to find ways of working in harmony with it, though whether we will ever be satisfied and happy to do this is a question, man being himself.

Ray Bradbury, I was amazed to discover the other evening on television, is just as joyous and eager and full of zest as ever over the idea that if only man can reach out and colonize other planets, we could start all over again and make a decent civilization. But as the fact remains that man must take his own nature with him, I rather wonder at Bradbury's boyish assurance. Why is man going to change the moment he reaches another heavenly body? About man's propensities, David is more than worried in *Wonderful Flight*. "I think it'd be awful to tell people about Basidium," he says intensely. "Why, I'll bet they'd start geological expeditions there, and Basidium'd get all dug up. Then after a while there'd be sightseeing tours, and then hot-dog stands and there'd be pop bottles and paper bags thrown around. And the poor little Basidiumites would be stared at, and people would poke them and point to them and try to get into their houses and maybe want to take some of them back to earth and put them on exhibition, and Ta [the king of the Basidiumites] would be angry and hate us."[13] David couldn't have known at that time what was to happen, but already the moon and space around us are littered with our debris, albeit the debris of our scientific research.

No, the boundary between fantasy and SF is of no moment—except perhaps to the critics—only the absorption of the reader, so that he is compelled to look inward and to ask himself questions which it may never have occurred to him to ask before about our own natures and the infinite desirability of living at peace, so far as is humanly possible, with the natural world.

11 / The Young Adult Novel

The junior novel is junior in its audience and its history. Sarah Trimmer in 1802 began reviewing not only books for children but also for "young persons," but a literature designed for the teenaged market was a 1930s phenomenon. It evolved to rival series fiction or, worse yet, the reading "of the yellow type" that Harriet Barakian in 1923 tried to counter with more commendable books. Except for children's magazines, she could find nothing specifically penned for adolescents. Even confined to adult literature, Barakian's list is highly selective; she recommends several plays of Shakespeare but none of his tragedies.

Barakian was not alone in working against pulp fiction. In the same decade another writer tried to lure boys away from *Police Gazette* to classic adventure stories. A few years earlier, a librarian complained that pulp fiction was capable of "Blowing out the Boy's Brains."[1] In light of all the latter-day concern about stunting the mental and moral growth of teens, a defense of escapist romance, let alone the creation of an industry to supply that literature, seems astonishing.

As several of the selections which follow show, the teen novels of the 1940s and 1950s were hardly realistic. Wish-fulfillment fantasies, they featured prom queens and hot-rod enthusiasts. Teenagers were thus heir to the same escapist formula fiction adults enjoy. Romance will always have some holdings in the kingdom of teenage fiction, but a new realism derived from adult literature eventually made its way into the special literature created for the adolescent. The taboo lifting was inevitable. It often takes a generation for adult trends to migrate to children's books. By the seventies the problems dramatized were of far more import than angling a date to the school dance: abortion, rape, drugs, and so on. So ingrained was the new realism that one author was assured that the book really needed by teens would feature an adolescent unwed father on a Honda.[2]

How much of an improvement the new realism was depends on one's point of view. Dwight L. Burton, who compares it here with the fluff of the forties and fifties, is content that the genre has grown from pap to literary protein. There is now certainly more varied and interesting fare available. The situations presented are more complex with much more frankness in language and in topic, like alcoholism and teenage sexual experimentation.

Topics no longer verboten are still treated, however, with obvious restrictions. As Jane Abrahamson illustrates in her essay, John Donovan's *I'll Get There. It Better Be Worth the Trip* (1969) was able to portray briefly a homosexual incident but without using that or any similar sexual label. Following Donovan's breakthrough, young adult novels did go on to portray avowed gays, as in Isabel Holland's *The Man without a Face* (1973), but however sympathetic the homosexual character, he was usually killed off at novel's end, the way Hollywood movies once dispatched female prostitutes. In Susan Scoppettone's *Trying Hard to Hear You* (1974), the major theme of which is the persecution of gays, one character is killed off in a *deus ex machina* car accident; the other continues his gay lifestyle. Scoppettone broke completely with that stock ending in *Happy Endings Are All Alike* (1978), in which two lesbian teenagers, who go off to separate colleges, continue in their sexual preference. However, because of that ending, the author reports, the book was not well received, and thus remained largely inaccessible to the audience for which it was composed. The author lists some alternative endings that might have been more acceptable to reviewers: "if the girls had grown apart, or found boyfriends and gotten married, or even died! Anything but the continuation of a lesbian relationship!"[3] Realism's ascendancy over its pop romance origins is hard earned and the battle against censorship is hardly won. However expansive, the growth of realism in the young adult novel will never be unlimited.

One critic sees the most significant aspect of adolescent fiction today as the focus on the moment of crisis. Thus young readers learn vicariously how to come to grips with changes, personal or social. This knowledge is crucial to what Erik Erickson terms the identity crisis by which each youth forges a central direction to his or her life. Not only do some teen novels function as informal rite-of-passage manuals for the pubescent, they have quite a readership among pre-teens:

What the novel of crisis has to offer, at its best, is the assurance that one can live through the changes, that they are shared by us all, even though they take on different forms. When poorly handled, the novel of crisis is a clumsy and patronizing medium for crudely constructed stories offering simplistic solutions or rendering misinformation.[4]

But the theme of coming of age can be deftly handled. The most childish thing about *A Wizard of Earthsea,* its author maintains, is its subject—coming of age. Most adults feel rather deeply about the developmental process:

So do most adolescents. It's their main occupation, in fact. . . . [Death] seemed an absolutely suitable subject to me for young readers, since in a way one can say that the hour when a child realizes, not that death exists—children are intensely aware of death—but that he/she, personally, is mortal, will die, is the hour when childhood ends, and the new life begins. Coming of age again, but in a larger context.[5]

The depiction of the adolescent's first confrontation with the death of a loved one can be deftly handled in the young adult novel, for instance, Paul Zindel's *The Pigman* (1968).

Besides the romance versus realism battle, there are limits the young adult novelist must accept to work within that genre. Generally shorter than the adult novel, the novel for teens leaves the writer less room to flesh out characters. For all the trendy talk about tabooless literature, some limits on vocabulary must inevitably remain. Given those limits, the young adult novel, in seriousness of purpose and in effectiveness of techniques, can be, if it chooses, competitive with serious adult fiction. The initiation of youth into adulthood, which appealed thematically to Joyce, Salinger, and Melville, now attracts Zindel, Cormier, and Garner, as well as the adolescent reader whose vulnerable existence is being exposed and, one hopes, not exploited.

The trap in discussing the young adult novel is that it is simpler to discuss situation or plot than artistic intention or theme. It is routinely reviewed and discussed on its extraliterary values. If, beneath all the trendy tabooless literature, there remains a formula fiction, it should be studied as formula, as Marilyn Kaye has attempted.[6]

Frances Duncan, after a self-imposed crash course in the young adult novel (begun when she had inadvertently written one), concludes that it is an "artificial and gratuitous group" in which some excellent writing lies hidden. She urges mainstreaming: opening the locks separating adolescent fiction from general fiction. The adolescent novel, a half-century old at most, is already a commercial habit that would be difficult, if not impossible to break. By the midseventies it was already a viable economic entity, making up one third of the 2,500 new children's books published every year in this country.[7]

Debate about whether there should be a separate teen lit seems quaint, like discussion on the propriety of reading the comics. Barakian claimed that much teen literature was unsuitable or mediocre. Sixty years later, given the strange, sudden growth of the self-conscious and somewhat awkward young adult novel, adolescents have a more suitable and more realistic, but not necessarily mediocre, literature. The young adult novel today is not just a viable industry; it can be, when it chooses, a viable literature.

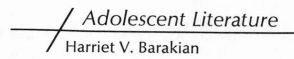

/ Adolescent Literature
/ Harriet V. Barakian

. . . Literature plays a unique part in the life and education of an adolescent. It is one of the greatest opportunities of reaching the child and helping him form ideals from characteristics he already has in his nature. From every point of view, literature reacts upon life and fashions it, as much as life fashions literature. Literature presents accurate pictures of life, and an abundance of material is found from which we can select texts on which to base moral instruction and build admiration, hope, love, ambition, and so on. Men and women through literature express their ideas, their inner selves or souls. There is nothing that makes more strongly for culture than the contact with great personalities. Much of the subject matter in narration, in drama, and lyrics, quite unlike geography and mathematics, stirs the emotions and seems to warrant an appeal to the feelings that otherwise would have remained dormant. It serves as entertainment for our leisure hours, and broadens our outlook on life. Literature, as is true with the art of music, can either demoralize or uplift us to a higher plane; can awaken the good or evil in our natures.

No matter which phase of literature we take, the good or bad, the adolescent is affected ultimately in one of two ways. A farmer planning for his year's crops is pretty careful to select the best seeds to plant, in order that his crops may be of healthy, superior quality. Is it not just as important that we propagate wholesome literature in the minds of our growing boys and girls for the purpose of forming a basis for wholesome thinking and desirable ideals in life? Up to a generation ago the number

Reprinted from *Education* 43:373–80 (Feb. 1923), with permission of Project Innovation, 1362 Santa Cruz Court, Chula Vista, Calif. 92010.

of books written expressly for children was limited, and a girl or boy who had a taste for reading was forced to gratify it by books written for older people. This brought them in contact with good standard works from earliest childhood, so by the time they reached adolescence no pleasure was found in inferior literature. But today there is an unlimited number of books which in all cases are not of superior quality. A great many of them are of low standard, tending to debase, degrade and vulgarize ideals of youth, making vices more attractive than virtues. Many of the cheaper class of magazines and stories that abound in thrilling adventures, exciting moments, and sensational and emotional passages of dialogue only aid to corrupt tastes and ideals and stimulate criminal actions in inexperienced youth. It is a perfectly natural tendency for youth to revel in this sort of reading, since it appeals to their adolescent natures.

On the other hand, the amount of good literature, both English, American and extraneous, is so vast that it never can be exhausted. Why then should not our youth have it? Literature in the form of story, prose, essay, description, and drama is rich in qualities which youth like and possesses something within it that promotes growth as well. The good derived from salubrious literature is so obvious that it leaves all arguments for its justification unnecessary.

The school and the home are the two institutions which come in close contact with children, and which afford excellent opportunities in directing youth toward forming clean habits in reading. It is a common error of some parents to regard this duty of supervising and suggesting proper reading matter as outside their paternal responsibility, believing it to be the purpose of the schools to educate their children, and if they fail to know what and how to read it is through no fault of theirs, but through the school shirking its responsibilities. Other parents, through indifference or ignorance, are unable to perform this duty; still others are poor judges themselves, lacking high standards. It is hardly possible that they can stimulate in youth anything but narrow and uncultivated tastes for reading.

A story I recently read in regard to the subject of reading will illustrate my point. A schoolgirl, in some paper sent up to her teacher, had spoken most enthusiastically of a certain lurid and sensational story by a popular authoress, and her teacher, recognizing the evils of that style of literature, wrote upon the margin of her paper, on returning it, "Not suitable"; to which the girl's father wrote in reply, "Why on earth not?"

Since such is the situation, it remains the high privilege of the teacher to perform this duty of creating a taste for wholesome reading in youth, and to lead them to the various sources where they can make discoveries of their own. In this way their powers of reflection will be exercised properly. The great danger in the use of general reading lies in its selection.

Here again, before a teacher can successfully and intelligently select for her adolescent pupils kinds of literature best suited for them, she should have intimate knowledge of their physical, mental, and social characteristics. Adolescents do not have to be coaxed to read. They are only too eager, as they thirst for the quick glow, touch, and sentiment of life so well delineated in good literature. Literature abounds in interesting personalities that will captivate and enthrall adolescents, and which is a means of molding character. No two individuals are alike in personality; therefore, no two can equally like the same kind of books. Sometimes lack of interest in general reading is because the chords of human appeal have not been touched. If we can discover some one thing or things a youth is really interested in, such as history, geography, nature, the sciences or arts, it is possible to give him books abounding in stories of this type, and so stimulate interest for further reading along these lines. To be able to do this a teacher should be a lover of books, and be eager to share with her pupils the good things which she has herself found in reading. Many children come from homes where good reading material is unknown; here is an enterprising teacher's chance to unfold to them the great treasure and heritage of good books. A desire for a school library can be aroused in the pupils, and the teacher can well cooperate with the librarian of the public library to get other books. I here recall an instance in my teaching experience. The individual was a lover of reading, and read beautifully in class; however, she came from a home where moral character did not exist. She had no father; her mother worked in one of the mills in town, and was not in a position to exert any good influence upon the child. One day, at recess time, I noticed her sitting on the yard settee, reading a book, and six or eight children hovering around her to get within hearing. Interested to know what was going on, I walked up, and with a casual glance took in the situation. Somehow or other the girl had come into possession of a novel of the "yellow type," and was so thrilled by it that she was passing along her thrills to her classmates. Knowing the moral danger of such reading to the girl and those with whom she associated, I thought over this incident during the day, and thought it possible to elicit her interest in the direction of books of more nurturing character. That night after school I had a long chat with her, and discovered the things in which she was interested. The following night I accompanied her to the town library, introduced her to the lady at the desk, procured a card for her, and helped her select a book to take home. Here was a case of redirecting a child's interest for reading into desirable channels. Within a week I had introduced the class to the library —almost every one wanted a card. Besides, every week the librarian sent up to the school fifteen or twenty new books which the children could select from and take home for a certain length of time. This was toward the end of the year. I was amazed at the interested attitude of the children toward the books, and I am sure that having found the source for wholesome reading material they drew from it constantly.

In the magazine and periodical world of literature the same may be said. We want the coming generation of children educated to read the best magazines. Along with the invention of the moving pictures and the rapid development and influence of the speaking stage in the last quarter century, new magazines have been put into circulation for the great mass of people. Many of them are of trashy character, and too many of our young people are reading just this kind of magazine for their pastime.

In my investigation for a full list of juvenile periodicals published in the United States, I was surprised to find something like sixty titles mentioned, both religious and secular. Such a list is found in the American Newspaper Annual and Directory, published annually by N. W. Ayer & Son, Philadelphia, Pa.

Among juvenile (secular) magazines a few are mentioned in the lists below; I give also a short book list of fiction, short stories, essays, autobiographies, poems and plays. To include all good books of value to adolescents is quite impossible, as new ones are being written and published every day; nevertheless, I have endeavored to compile a list which may help adolescent boys and girls to get started in forming the habit, and further encourage them to read worthwhile literature in their leisure hours.

BOOKS / FICTION

	Author		Author
The Little Minister	Barrie	The House of Seven Gables	Hawthorne
A Window in Thrums	Barrie	Adventures of Tom Sawyer	Mark Twain
Romola	Eliot	Adventures of Huckleberry Finn	Mark Twain
Silas Marner	Eliot	The Prince and the Pauper	Mark Twain
Eben Holden	Bacheller		
The Jessamy Bride	Moore		
The Light That Failed	Kipling		
The Virginian	Wister	Little Shepherd of Kingdom Come	Fox
Les Miserables (abridged)	Hugo	The Trail of the Lonesome Pine	Fox
The Blue Flower	Van Dyke		
Treasure Island	Stevenson	Freckles	Porter
Kidnapped	Stevenson	The Girl of the Limberlost	Porter
The Cloister and the Hearth	Reade	Laddie	Porter
Being a Boy	Warner	The Vicar of Wakefield	Goldsmith
Buried Alive	Bennett		
David Harum	Westcott		
Ivanhoe	Scott		

Kenilworth	Scott	The Minister's Charge	Howells
Story of a Bad Boy	Aldrich	The Blazed Trail	White
Armorel of Lyonesse	Besant	An Egyptian Princess	Ebers
Heidi (translation)	Allen	With Fire and Sword	
A Dog of Flanders	Ouida		Sienkiewicz
Ramona	Jackson	Merry Adventures of Robin	
Oliver Twist	Dickens	Hood	Pyle
Our Mutual Friend	Dickens		

MAGAZINES / JUVENILE (SECULAR)

	Address		*Address*
Boy's Chum	Brazil, Indiana	St. Nicholas	New York, N.Y.
Junior Republic Citizen		Riker & King List (for Boys)	
	Litchfield, Conn.		New York, N.Y.
Cook's Trio	Elgin, Ill.	Fame and Fortune Weekly	
Boy's World		Liberty Boys of '76	
Girl's Companion		Pluck and Luck	
Young People's Weekly		Secret Service	
Youth's Companion		Wild West Weekly	
	Boston, Mass.	Work and Win	
Every Girl's Magazine (Camp			
Fire Girls)	New York, N.Y.		

SHORT STORIES

	Author		*Author*
The Happy Prince	Wilde	The Bottle Imp	Stevenson
The Gold Bug	Poe	The Piece of String	
The Purloined Letter	Poe		De Maupassant
The Fall of the House		The Necklace	De Maupassant
of Usher	Poe	The First Christmas Tree	
The Great Stone Face			Van Dyke
	Hawthorne	The Story of the Other Wise	
The Town Pump	Hawthorne	Man	Van Dyke
A New England Nun	Wilkins	Buried Treasure	White
The Three Strangers	Hardy	The Lady or the Tiger	Stockton
The Revolt of Mother		Short Sixes	Bunner
	Wilkins-Freeman	Legend of Sleepy Hollow	Irving
The Jumping Frog	Clemens	Rip Van Winkle	Irving
A Double-Barreled Detective		Man without a Country	Hale
Story	Clemens	Lincoln and the Sleeping	
The Luck of Roaring Camp		Sentinel	Chittenden
	Harte	Wagner's Operas	Wheelock
The Pursuit of the Piano	Howells	Parsifal	
Will o' the Mill	Stevenson	Tannhäuser	
Markheim	Stevenson	Master Singers	
King Arthur Stories	Pyle	Lohengrin	

AUTOBIOGRAPHIES

	Author		Author
Story of My Life	Keller	The Life of Mary Lyon	Gilchrist
The Story of My Boyhood and Youth	Muir	Life of Alice Freeman Palmer	Palmer
The Autobiography of a Super-Tramp	Davies	Life of Edison	Meadowcraft
The Promised Land	Antin	Life of Lincoln	Moore
The Americanization of Edward Bok	Bok	Autobiography	Franklin

ESSAYS

	Author		Author
Travels with a Donkey	Stevenson	A Year in the Fields	Burroughs
Little Rivers	Van Dyke	Birds and Bees	Burroughs
Literary Lapses	Leacock	My Literary Friends and Acquaintances	Howells
Turtle Eggs for Agassiz	Sharp		

POEMS

	Author		Author
Over the Chimney the Night Wind Sang	Harte	Childe Harold's Pilgrimage	Byron
Idylls of the King	Tennyson	The Vision of Sir Launfall	Lowell
Enoch Arden	Tennyson	Mister Hop-Toad	Riley
Tales of the Wayside Inn	Longfellow	A Greeting	Davies
Evangeline	Longfellow	The Devout Highlander	Horne
The Courtship of Miles Standish	Longfellow	The Barrel-Organ	Noyes
Sohrab and Rustum	Arnold	Flanders Fields	McRae
The Prisoner of Chillon	Byron	The Swimming Hole	Riley
		To a Mountain Daisy	Burns
		To a Mouse	Burns

PLAYS

	Author		Author
The Piper	Peabody	The Taming of the Shrew	Shakespeare
The Blue Bird	Maeterlinck	As You Like It	Shakespeare
The Merchant of Venice	Shakespeare	The Servant in the House	Roberts

Pap to Protein?
Two Generations of
Adolescent Fiction

Dwight L. Burton

"Pap" was a favorite label for adolescent fiction when serious attention first was given to it shortly after World War II. An editorial in the
Louisville, Kentucky, *Courier-Journal* in 1951 queried: "But what qualities of mind and taste, alas, can we expect from young people who have
been fed on the pap of the teenage trash reviewed in these columns?"[1]
And Frank D. Jennings followed a few years later with: "The adolescent's
world is fraught with change; its charms 'are wound up,' its horizons are
pulsing with expectancies and actualities. His most heartfelt cry is, as
Sherwood Anderson warned us long ago, 'I want to know why.' The
pastel, gum-drop fiction that has been wrought for him avoids both question and answer."[2]

Whether these writers would agree that the passing of a generation in
adolescent fiction has brought a change from pap to protein, I cannot
guess—but they would not be able to deny great change. My purpose in
this article is to discuss briefly that change from the time that I first became interested in "adolescent literature," the essence of which was, and
still is, fiction—or the "junior novel" as we have come to title it.

THE PREVIOUS GENERATION

A symbolic year of recognition for adolescent fiction was 1951. In
September of that year, the lead article in *English Journal*, the professional magazine for secondary school teachers of English, was on adolescent fiction.[3] The importance of the event was not that I wrote the article.
(There were not many people seriously interested in adolescent literature
in those days!) But for several years, the late W. Wilbur Hatfield, then
editor of *English Journal*, had devoted the lead piece to literary criticism
in which established scholars discussed the greats of past and present.
The article on junior novels, then, was a considerable switch. The junior

Reprinted from *Texas Tech Journal of Education* 7:15–24 (Winter 1980) with
permission of the author and the journal.

novelists I discussed in that long-forgotten essay were Maureen Daly, Paul Annixter, Betty Cavanna, John Tunis, and Madeleine L'Engle. Maureen Daly was included for her *Seventeenth Summer* (alas, the only junior novel she has written), which was the masterpiece of adolescent fiction of that day, a summer vacation love story treating the adolescent characters seriously and perceptively. Paul Annixter also was included for one book, *Swiftwater*, the engrossing story of a boy in the Maine woods whose dream was to establish a refuge for the wild geese he loved. Prolific Betty Cavanna's *Going on Sixteen*, about a shy, sixteen-year-old girl's problems of growing up, was the particular book of hers that I praised; some of her other books deserve the "pap" label. I emphasized John Tunis' books about sports, especially those about the Brooklyn Dodgers. At that time, I had read two books by Madeleine L'Engle, *The Small Rain* and *And Both Were Young*, though she went on to write a number of others, including the Newbery Medal winner *A Wrinkle in Time*. Both of the books I discussed are love stories featuring adolescent girl protagonists.

More evidence of serious critical attention to junior fiction came with the appearance of doctoral dissertations on the genre. One of the earliest, to my knowledge, was that by Stephen Dunning.[4] His careful survey of librarians showed that the thirteen most popular writers of junior novels were Betty Cavanna, Rosamond du Jardin, Henry Felsen, Anne Emery, Mary Stolz, Maureen Daly, James Summers, John Tunis, Amelia Walden, Robert Heinlein, Walter Farley, Sally Benson, and Jessica Lyon. The list indicated that the general area of personal and family problems was the forte of adolescent fiction and that girls were more avid readers than boys, although a wide range of stories of adventure, animals, and sports was available for boys to supplement the few about adolescent problems by such writers as Felsen and Summers. Walter Farley made the list with *The Black Stallion*, which was the beginning of a famous series, and Robert Heinlein with a science fiction piece, *The Red Planet*. Maureen Daly's *Seventeenth Summer* was still popular as was Sally Benson's *Junior Miss*. There was a considerable amount of the fluff that was the object of criticism concerning dates, parties, and new dresses in the books of Betty Cavanna, Rosamond du Jardin, Anne Emery, Amelia Walden, and Jessica Lyon. Some of the most popular titles of these writers are themselves revealing: *A Date for Diane, Practically Seventeen, Going Steady, Wait for Marcy,* and *Sorority Girl*. Definite exceptions to the fluff tradition in girls' stories were those by Mary Stolz, whose books were serious-toned, probing, and sometimes painful.

Dunning's judgments of the literary quality of the novels he analyzed put *Seventeenth Summer* and Mary Stolz's *To Tell Your Love* and *Sea-*

gulls Woke Me at the top of the ratings with a considerable gulf between them and the next-rated books. Dunning's study revealed that the major popularity of junior novels was with younger adolescents, those of junior high school age, although older students read some titles, especially those by John Tunis and Mary Stolz.

Also in 1959, I published *Literature Study in the High Schools*, a book that included a section on junior novels.[5] (These references to my own publications may be risking charges of narcissism, but I need them to build my comparisons of generations!) In discussing the anatomy of the junior novel, I made the following observations. First, more junior novels were about personal problems of adolescents, including family problems, than about anything else, though there was a broad spectrum of subject matter—sports, animals, adventure, social problems, and vocations. The most competent novels about personal problems were those that were fundamentally serious, presenting adolescent characters of complexity and dignity. At that time, I was more impressed, like Dunning, with Mary Stolz than with any other writer of adolescent fiction.

Second, though the distinction between the junior novel and the adult novel was occasionally hard to make, in general, junior novels were shorter and easier to read than were adult novels and were governed by some rather rigid conventions of content and form. The rigorous enforcement of certain taboos, likewise enforced in secondary school literature programs, was a major characteristic. The seamy side of life and the dark side of human nature largely were avoided. Erotic drives, to say nothing of explicit sex or deviant sexual behavior, were ignored; cool kisses were as far as writers would go. Smoking and drinking were seldom alluded to. This over-insistence on a certain concept of "wholesomeness" was very likely a major basis for the pap allegations. From the point of view of literary experience, however, an even greater shortcoming of most adolescent fiction of twenty years ago was its superficiality in dealing with adolescent characters. One critic referred to the "sugar-puff story of what adolescents should do and should believe rather than what adolescents may or will do and believe."[6]

This criticism is a way of phrasing my third observation, that another dominant characteristic of the junior novel of the former generation was a persistent didacticism. Mother or father (or another adult) is right was a familiar theme. Revolt and unconventionality on the part of the adolescents inevitably were chastised. The implied idea was that adolescents should play down differences, not capitalize on them.

Fourth, this celebration of conformity was natural in the junior novel of the time because it was almost completely white middle-class oriented. There were a few books about minority characters, such as Jesse Jack-

son's *Call Me Charley* and *Anchor Man*, about a black boy in a white
school, and Florence Means' *Shuttered Windows*, about a black northern
girl who goes to visit her grandmother in the South. But for the most
part, the books were about families that lived in houses in medium-small
towns or pleasant suburbs (two of Anne Emery's locales were Hickory
Hill and Juniper Lane) and in which the fathers were rather vague characters who went to offices and at home spent much time behind newspapers, and mothers who were youngish, attractive, and intelligent. The
girls often dated the well-scrubbed boys who lived in the neighborhood,
and their parents played bridge together. Usually there were impish, but
basically lovable, younger brothers or sisters.

Fifth, in technique, too, the junior novel of the earlier day was, in general, rigidly patterned. Narrated usually from the omniscient point of
view, the plots built to climaxes near the end, leaving the need for only
a brief wrap-up. Changes in point of view through the narrative were
absent, flashbacks rare, subplots uncommon.

Despite all its shortcomings, though, particularly from the vantage
point of two decades of hindsight, all was not pap in the junior novel of
the past generation. I already have cited the books of Mary Stolz in which
adolescent love could be tempestuous and anguished. James Summers'
stories of less-than-average boys treated school life authentically. Henry
Felsen occasionally found serious drama in adolescent life. Individual
books dipped below the superficialities of adolescent culture. The junior
novel of the time was reaching a wide audience, particularly adolescents
in the twelve- to fifteen-year-old range. It was an important form of vicari-
ous experience at a time when television was not as pervasive as it is
now. If adolescents were encountering pap, their adult counterparts were
not reading anything better in adult literature.

Those seriously interested in adolescent fiction in the earlier years, as
now, were primarily people in English education, interested in preparing
teachers of English and in developing English curricula in the schools.
The obvious reason for this was that we saw in the junior novel a valuable
vehicle for furthering literary education. We talked of the transitional
function of the junior novel, referring to the transition from children's
tales to mature works of literature. This transitional role was the one
Dunning found for the junior novel in the study cited previously. Just as
there must be a continuum from simple arithmetic to higher mathematics, so must there be a continuum in literary education, and at the early
adolescent point in that continuum, the junior novel is a valuable link.

One of the essentials to a mature experience with fiction is the ability
to make abstract identifications with characters and situations in the
work. A fourteen-year-old American girl does not identify automatically

with the fundamental emotional experiences of the old Cuban fisherman in Hemingway's *The Old Man and the Sea,* but the emotional correlatives of her experience with his are undoubtedly there. What is needed to provide her with the ability to make such abstract identifications is experience with works in which more literal identifications are possible —for instance, a book, say about a fourteen-year-old girl whose school, family, and problems are similar to hers. Similarly, with technique in fiction, dealing with the symbolism of Annixter's *Swiftwater*—the wolverine as symbol of evil or wild geese as symbol of aspiration—is necessary training for later dealing with the symbolism of a Joseph Conrad.

THE PRESENT GENERATION

Stephen Dunning's (1959) study of the junior novel was more or less replicated fourteen years later by Alfred P. Muller, whose listing of the most popular junior novels, derived also from a survey of librarians, showed that a few of the "old" popular writers were still holding their own: Betty Cavanna, Rosamond du Jardin, and Zoa Sherburne.[7] But mostly, there were new names: Frank Bonham, Nat Hentoff, Jeannette Eyerly, S. E. Hinton, John Neufeld, Maia Wojciechowska, and Paul Zindel. Two of these latter authors, S. E. Hinton and Paul Zindel, literally have taken the adolescent audience by storm. Hinton's *The Outsiders,* a brief and poignant story of teenage gang warfare in a large southwestern city, featuring a male protagonist, probably has been the most popular junior novel since *Seventeenth Summer.* Hinton has followed with similar books such as *That Was Then, This Is Now* and *Rumble Fish.* It is striking that a young woman can write so tellingly of adolescent boys and teenage gangland.

Zindel, also a Pulitzer Prize-winning playwright and a former high school teacher, writes basically of adolescents in conflict with parents and the adult establishment. Perhaps his best book is *The Pigman,* the story of the strange relationship of an adolescent boy and girl with an old man and the bittersweet consequence of that relationship. His *My Darling, My Hamburger*—of teenage love, pregnancy, and abortion—is unusual both in substance and technique, and strikes hard, though with an almost poetic ending. In Zindel's work, adults often are not admirable and are not models for the young. Freakish teachers seem to abound in his books.

Frank Bonham, turning from his earlier adventure themes, is on Muller's list for *Durango Street,* the story of a black boy in a western city ghetto; Nat Hentoff's books grew from the youth rebellion and unrest of the 1960s. *I'm Really Dragged but Nothing Gets Me Down* presents the dilemma of a boy who opposes the Vietnam War, but who is faced with the possibility of being drafted. *In the Country of Ourselves* is set in a high school disrupted by young revolutionaries incited by a teacher. Jeannette Eyerly, in books such as *Bonnie Jo, Go Home* and *Escape from Nowhere,* deals with the currently vogue themes of teenage pregnancy and drug abuse. John Neufeld brought mental and physical handicaps to the fore in adolescent fiction in such books as *Lisa, Bright and Dark,* the story of a mentally ill sixteen-year-old girl, and *Touching,* about a boy's relationship with his stepsister who has cerebral palsy. The prolific Maia Wojciechowska, who is on Muller's list because of *Tuned Out,* a drug abuse piece, has picked up most of the trendy themes, although her best book, in my opinion, is her early *Shadow of a Bull,* about a Spanish boy who is expected to be, but does not want to be, a famous bullfighter.

From my study of recent junior fiction, I am impressed by two obvious (to me) facts. First, there are many more good junior novelists than there were in the 1940s and 1950s. Second, the junior novel, like the adult best-seller, has been trendy, responding closely to events and trends of the times. Regarding the first point, if I were to write today an article parallel to the one I published in 1951, I would be hard pressed to pick only four or five authors to feature as I did then; and it was fairly easy then. For excellence in the junior novel today I certainly would choose Hinton, Neufeld, and Zindel among those just commented on from Muller's study. Bonham (for *Durango Street*), Hentoff, and Eyerly would be close behind. In addition, I would have to include at least Judy Blume, Norma Klein, E. L. Konigsburg, M. E. Kerr, John Donovan, Robert Peck, and the indefatigable Mary Stolz, the star of the earlier period. All of these have contributed importantly to the junior novel with several books.

Blume, who writes for younger children as well as for adolescents, usually presents precocious girl protagonists in middle-class, suburban settings, though she has run a broad gamut of timely themes. *It's Not the End of the World* is based on the secret journal of a twelve-year-old whose parents are getting a divorce. *Deenie* is about an adolescent girl with scoliosis. *Forever* is a love story with a good bit of explicit sex. Blume's popular books, though positive and relatively lighthearted, are far from superficial, and she is a fine stylist.

Whereas Blume basically treats "normalcy," Norma Klein is an iconoclast, though her protagonists, like Blume's, are middle-class girls. In *Mom, the Wolfman & Me,* for example, the mother is unwed and living with a boyfriend. *What It's All About* is an unusual, episodic story involving a Jewish mother and a Japanese father. Other books treat divorce, abortion, and, lightly, lesbianism. Klein is more experimental in technique than are most of her peers. M. E. Kerr, whose settings are also middle class, presents a world where adult characters, like those of Zindel, are definitely not good models. In *If I Love You, Am I Trapped Forever?* an adolescent boy lives with his divorced, partly crippled mother and has an alcoholic father. The central character of *Dinky Hocker Shoots Smack!* is an overweight girl with a preoccupied mother and an offbeat father. E. L. Konigsburg is unique among the group of writers I have chosen: she is a storyteller unconcerned with problem themes. *From the Mixed Up Files of Mrs. Basil E. Frankweiler* is a sophisticated mystery, a story within a story, of two young people who run away from their suburban home. *Jennifer, Hecate, Macbeth, William McKinley, and Me, Elizabeth* is about a New York City girl's adventure with a young witch. John Donovan writes of boys who have difficulties with parental relationships. *I'll Get There. It Better Be Worth the Trip* has a homosexual theme, handled at low key. Of Robert Peck's several supple stories, the one most popular with adolescents, and most admired by adults, is *A Day No Pigs Would Die,* of a farm boy who has to come to grips early with the fundamentals of life. Though I believe that Mary Stolz's best books are among her earlier ones, she still sets a high standard in such recent books as *By the Highway Home,* about a young girl adjusting to her brother's death in Vietnam and her father's losing his job.

In writing the hypothetical parallel to the article of 1951, I would have to take note, too, of a number of writers who have made "one-shot" efforts or who have somehow triumphed with a single book though their work generally may not be extraordinary. Among the one-shot books, I would select Robert Lipsyte's *The Contender,* the story of how boxing helped a Harlem teenager to find himself; Robert McKay's *Dave's Song,* about how a small-town girl's life is enriched by her relationship with an unusual boy; and Alice Childress' hard-hitting *A Hero Ain't Nothin' but a Sandwich,* a story of a black thirteen-year-old's drug addiction, cure, and his tempestuous relationship with his stepfather. In the category of single triumphs among several books, examples are Ann Head's *Mr. and Mrs. Bo Jo Jones,* about teenage marriage, and Betsy Byars' *Summer of the Swans,* a sensitive, symbol-driven story of a girl and her ten-year-old brother who has brain damage.

Support for my second general observation about the current junior novel—that it has been highly responsive to events and trends of the times—really rests in the comments just made on selected writers and their themes: drug abuse, alcoholism, teenage pregnancy and abortion, the Vietnam War and the draft, youth unrest and revolt, divorce, problems of minorities, ghetto life, problems of mentally and physically handicapped persons, and sexual permissiveness. All of these things have been largely phenomena or discoveries of the 1960s and 1970s.

Although the changes a generation has wrought in junior fiction may be obvious, and a summary of them somewhat superfluous, I cannot resist returning to the anatomy of the junior novel as I described it in 1959, summarized earlier in this article, and as it is today. The forte of the junior novel today as in the earlier time is the *sturm und drang* of the adolescent period, the personal problems of the young person in his or her "rites of passage" to adulthood, natural in books directed to the adolescent. But gone, for the most part, is the fluff of beach parties and slumber parties and fixing hotrods. In the recent books, emotional trauma often runs deep. The cool kissing of yesteryear has given way often to explicit sex with pregnancy and either abortion or early marriage sometimes resulting. Teenagers in the books today are "older" and more sophisticated people, as they are in life, than those of a generation ago. Some of the old categories of junior books virtually have disappeared— sports, animals, vocational stories, and general adventure tales such as the sea stories of Howard Pease and the wood adventures of Jim Kjelgaard.

Junior novels are still generally shorter and easier to read than adult novels, but the rigid conventions of content and form of the earlier works have largely dissolved. The new realism in adolescent fiction has done away with most of the taboos of content, including profane language, drinking, sex, homosexuality, and the like. The dark side of human experience is explored thoroughly, though the junior novel remains basically hopeful and positive. The keys to this change, of course, lie in American society's willingness to be much more permissive in all the media, print and nonprint alike, as well as in a changed view of the nature of the adolescent and the time of his or her induction into adulthood.

The junior novel of this generation is much less didactic than was its predecessor. At least the often obtrusive didacticism of the earlier books is gone. Certainly the "parents are right" theme is not only not prevalent any longer, but it has been reversed in a number of recent junior novels. Adults are not models for the young in junior fiction today. Problems, serious ones of adolescent-parent relationships and communication, are at the heart of many books.

Conformity no longer is celebrated in the junior novel. Revolt, unconventionality, and iconoclasm often are features and do not necessarily result in unhappiness or disaster.

Technique in junior fiction, too, is not nearly so restrictive today. The range in structure and style is nearly as wide as in popular adult fiction. Switching of point of view, for example, is common. Zindel, in *My Darling, My Hamburger,* alternates point of view among four major characters, and each of the chapters in Childress's *A Hero Ain't Nothin' but a Sandwich* is a monologue by one of the characters. Plotting is frequently loose and episodic in works by authors such as Judy Blume and Norma Klein. One of Konigsburg's books features a story within a story. Diaries, letters, diagrams, and graffiti occasionally are used to further narration as they are used in contemporary adult fiction.

The changes in the junior novel over a generation are great. But is the junior novel better—has it passed from pap to protein? I think that the answer, in general, is yes. The dissolving of most of the taboos of content and rigidities of technique has given the junior novel a maturity that, in turn, gives it greater potential for a rich experience for the youthful readers who still read it in vast numbers. The junior novel today is much more like the adult novel than it was twenty years ago, but the authentic junior novel, with the particular tempo and attuning of adolescence, is still easily distinguishable (though adults may enjoy reading it) and offers a special experience for the adolescent reader. For that reason, the junior novel today is even more important in its role of transition to mature literary experience than it was earlier.

I fondly, and I hope not fatuously, believe, albeit without systematic proof, that people today, especially young people, read at least as much and at a somewhat better level than did the previous generation, despite the grip that television has on the time of people, young and old. And I believe that this may be true because an increasing number of teachers have come to believe in the transitional function of junior fiction. The junior novel today penetrates more tellingly than it did earlier to "the perilous stuff that weighs upon the heart." And it is this perilous stuff that leads people to books.

Still Playing It Safe: Restricted Realism in Teen Novels

Jane Abrahamson

There has been a lot of hoopla over the hard-hitting realism of juvenile fiction for older readers. Certainly there has been a dramatic change since the days when the gravest problem faced in teen fiction was whether the freshman heroine would get asked to the sock hop by the dreamy (sigh!) upperclassman. Now each new edition of *The Subject Guide to Children's Books in Print* boasts ever longer listings on death, drugs, divorce, while publishers' catalogs attest to the latest inroads into teenage alcoholism, rape, homosexuality, *et relevant al.*

And yet, to borrow from the French maxim, the more realistic fiction changes, the more it stays the same. Taboos are lifted; restrictions still remain. The word "fuck" is now printable; scenes of lovemaking evidently are not. Judy Blume's *Forever*, a tame mapping of first love charted strictly for adolescents, was nevertheless issued as an adult title, presumably because of the semi-explicit but decidedly soft-core sex scenes.[1]

The restrictions on teen fiction result in books that succeed only in mirroring a slick surface realism that too often acts as a cover-up. It diverts readers. It disguises the fact that, at their core, most realistic novels are unrealistic and, far worse, dishonest. Books that seem to explore social change (alternate life styles, for example) end up reaffirming traditional mores. Books that set out to tackle painful experiences turn into weak testimonies to life's essential goodness.

There is plenty of evidence that conventional morality is still at work in teen novels that pretend otherwise. Besides bans on describing sex, attitudes about sex continue to be frighteningly unenlightened at times.

Throughout Dizenzo's *Why Me? The Story of Jenny,* there is an oddly ambivalent attitude toward Jenny, a teenage rape victim, as if the author were wagging a reproachful finger at her for breaking the code

Reprinted from *School Library Journal* 22:38–39 (May 1976), with permission of R. R. Bowker Company/A Xerox Corporation.

of all good girls—never to take a ride from a stranger.[2] The implication is that perhaps Jenny deserved what she got.

Far more disturbing is Fritzhand's *Life Is a Lonely Place,* a truly nasty-minded exploitation of homosexuality.[3] For reasons too ridiculous to recount, an unwarranted smear campaign is mounted accusing a young boy and his older writer friend of being "queer." Throughout the first person narrative, teenaged Tink constantly assures readers that he is a normal red-blooded boy, and just for good measure, the writer's wife, never before mentioned, is trotted out in the final chapter as if to quell any lingering doubts readers might have. The inference here is that, had the accusations been true, Tink would have deserved all the abuse heaped on him—making this nothing more than a vindication of antiquated prejudices in twentieth-century drag.

In these days of divorce run rampant, the traditional roles of the family and of women (especially as mothers) are quite naturally called into question; the trouble is that the answers, as supplied in realistic books for teens, too often hedge the issues.

When her newly divorced mother skips off to pursue a college career, Jennifer Noel is prompted *To Live a Lie;* she tells new school friends her mother is dead.[4] Mom, clearly the villain of the piece, is resurrected, however, when the ultimate, maternal purpose of her education is made known: she wants her degree so she can take back the kids and support them properly.

In Perl's *The Tell-Tale Summer of Tina C.* again it is Mom who has left the nest following the divorce, this time to shack up with a younger guy who does the cooking and cleaning.[5] Terribly *au courant?* Not really, since Mom has married Peter, who, far from being a contented *hausfrau,* has ambitious plans for opening a gourmet cooking school.

Chester Aaron in *Hello to Bodega* is another author who merely pays lip service to alternate life styles (here a California commune run by a Vietnam veteran).[6] Although it's stated that Gil and Joanna "were, without ever having said the word or passed through the ritual, married," nevertheless, the book ends with them tying the knot—in a double ceremony, no less, with the commune's only other couple. The commune also conveniently folds before the wedding day so Joanna (pregnant) and Gil can set up house as a traditional nuclear family.

The gravest shortcoming of realistic fiction for older readers, however, is not its veiled support of conventional morality, but its failure to respect its audience. Two crucial facts are ignored. First of all, teenagers, even if their reading skills are limited, know if a book is trying to sell them a phony bill of goods. Secondly, adolescents are emotionally resilient: they can accept books about death or divorce—or whatever—

without the reassurances and consolations offered in "problem fiction" for younger readers.

Yet the lion's share of realistic teen novels—even ones which specifically set out to deal with painful or problematic situations—persists in coddling readers with glib assurances.

For example, of all the recent titles on divorce Kin Platt's *Chloris and the Freaks* is the only one where the breakup is not "for the best"[7]; the only one without the facile optimism and tidy solutions that mark lesser efforts (Pfeffer's *Marly the Kid* runs away from her "Lucretia Borgia" mother straight into the welcoming arms of Dad and new wife who doesn't blink twice at the prospect of a permanent stepchild[8]).

Platt's heroine, astrology-nut Jenny, has no such easy out. During the course of a summer she finds herself watching helplessly while her worst fears about a family breakup are fulfilled. Her stepfather Fidel—the one bright star in Jenny's universe—is handed his walking papers; and Jenny is stuck with her childish mother and disturbed sister Chloris.

Platt honestly and compellingly addresses the feelings of powerlessness that are common to all adolescents; the frustrations of still being dependent upon adults, who, often as not, are undependable.

The mainstream of realistic fiction, however, continues to deny these facts. Instead, teenaged characters are shown as sure masters of their fates; authors look solely on the bright side of life and human nature; stories finish on a positive note. Witness the following statements: "Realism in (juvenile) fiction does not mean a story . . . ending unhappily. Relevant natural subjects . . . can perhaps provide a measure of hope or reassurance,"[9] and ". . . librarians and others evaluating YA literature should demand more than a cold rendering of reality. Honesty must be combined with hope, a hope that is life-affirming. . . . "[10]

Unfortunately, these guidelines only serve to enforce the pervading blandness of realistic fiction and to foster a cockeyed optimism in stories whose happy endings do not jibe with anything that's gone before in the book. As evidence are the following two examples of supposedly realistic novels for preteen and teen readers.

Kaye's *Joanna All Alone* is just that—an only child whose upwardly mobile parents can't see past the next cocktail party.[11] As a glimpse at loneliness this is fairly effective—until the sunny-side-up ending when Mummy and Daddy rush home from a country weekend to announce that Jojo's dearest wish (for a baby brother or sister) is going to come true. Fade out on a happy family scene. . . .

In Shaw's *Call Me Al Raft* the hero spends a summer tracking down his father.[12] All Al knows is that Dad was one of the many flings in the long and checkered career of exstripper Amanda L'Amour. Written in a flip-hip style and set in the familiar landscape of California freeways and roadside hangouts, this fudges any claim to realism by its ultra-goopy finale: Al, reunited with his dad, literally sails off into the sunset.

In contrast to these stories, which conclude on such false notes of uplift, stand a few recent books, consistent and uncompromising, whose endings—downbeat to be sure—flow inexorably from characterization and events. They are all strong and jolting and do not condescend by offering bibliotherapeutic crutches to help readers "cope."

On balance, the critical reception of these novels has been hearteningly favorable, yet there exists a countercurrent of wariness as to their appropriateness for a teenaged audience.

George Woods, for example, in the *New York Times* list of the best of the year's novels for older children bypasses S. E. Hinton's *Rumble Fish,* a powerful, raw portrait of a born loser.[13] Fourteen-year-old Rusty James' hero worship of his older brother (the enigmatic, semipsycho Motorcycle Boy) steers him straight into an emotional crack-up from which he never recovers. Although Rusty James recounts the events that led up to his brother's death, it is actually his own post-mortem that he's delivering. Readers can certainly handle the dead-end pessimism (they'll either empathize or feel lucky); yet Woods dismisses the book because it is about "death and disfiguration" and opts, instead for a "calm, placid story." Likewise, the cautious tagline for the review appearing in *The Bulletin of the Center for Children's Books* reads less like an evaluation than a warning that the book must be handled with extreme care: "Memorable but with no relief from depression, no note of hope. . . ."[14]

Two other provocative novels, Platt's *Headman*[15] and Cormier's *The Chocolate War*[16] are also examples of what *Booklist* has cited as a trend towards "didactic negativity." Indeed, both heroes are caught in a "heads you win, tails I lose" setup. Each tries to buck the system only to be beaten down by it.

For Platt's Owen, the system is an ultraviolent section of Los Angeles where there's only safety in numbers, that is, gangs. All his efforts to stay straight are futile (for example, his first pay check from his job at a body shop is immediately stolen), and Owen eventually winds up on the wrong end of a switchblade.

For Jerry in *The Chocolate War*, the system is the tyranny of a boys' prep school run by a power-mad teacher and bullying secret society. He launches a one-man protest by refusing to participate in the school fundraising drive. His crusade, however, is crushed and, as Jerry is carted off to the hospital, he realizes it was useless to try to "disturb the universe."

Both books are startling and stark looks at powerlessness. They do not shy away from the fact that there are situations where virtue does not have its reward and nice guys finish last. They qualify as good literature, because philosophy and plot have been dramatically welded together.

Both titles certainly have flaws: Platt overstates his theme of individual helplessness so that Owen can't seem to turn a corner without getting jumped or mugged; and Cormier underdevelops his characters (they're either lipsmacking villains or ineffectual wimps), but the books should not be faulted for the reasons listed in Betsy Hearne's attack on *The Chocolate War* in a *Booklist* editorial.

Hearne charges that Cormier "manipulates readers into believing how rotten things are" and chides the book for not presenting "the whole truth."[17] This dangerous criticism not only assumes that there *is* a "whole truth," a formula world vision with which all readers would agree and which all juvenile books should reflect, but that young readers are easily manipulated; they are essentially *tabulae rasae* upon which the stamp of every book is indelibly printed. Rubbish! Adolescents are by nature questioning and this extends into their reading as well. They are quite capable of disagreeing with and discarding a book's message.

Adolescents are also manic: by turns ecstatic and desperate. They live at extremes; yet so few books written for them touch either emotional pole. Of course, there have never been any edicts against writing joyful books, and still there are as few truly exhilarating novels as there are ones which are deeply painful.

Oddly enough, the restrictions on teen fiction can occasionally work to the publisher's advantage. For example, Ann Moody's short stories, *Mr. Death,* interesting only in their grisliness and clearly aimed at adult sensibilities, received an undue amount of fanfare and critical attention when released as a juvenile title.[18]

Unfortunately, the restrictions on teen fiction never work to the advantage of the readers. They result ultimately in books that are verisimilar but not truthful.

The pass-fail test for fiction of the realistic mode is not whether a picture of life has been duplicated which is superficially recognizable or falsely reassuring, but whether a vision of life has been created that is real in the sense of universal; a vision that *is* disturbing in the sense that it will arouse and move readers. And isn't that, after all, the purpose of literature?

The Young Adult Novel:
One Author's Response

Frances Duncan

The existence of places, ideas, and objects does not become personally significant until some event gives them emotional loading: For most people Iran became important when Khomeini seized both power and hostages; Mount St. Helens, when it erupted. For me the concept of the young adult novel was interesting but not emotionally charged until last fall, when I was told that my new book, *Guest Soloist* [published by Avon in 1982, as *Finding Home*] was neither an adult nor a young adult book and, as a result, would be difficult to publish.

If the book was neither an adult nor a young adult, what was it? What were the distinguishing differences between the "neither" and the "nor"? As far as I knew, young adult was some branch of juvenilia beloved by librarians and by my agent. I knew this novel was not a juvenile—at least I thought I did. I'd recently been told, "When you were writing *Kap-Sung Ferris* you must have known you were writing a juvenile." I'd listened to myself reply, "Not necessarily," and then was left considering this negation and the eyebrows it had raised. How could I be so naive as not to know I was writing a children's book when that was obviously what I was doing? And where did this leave *Guest Soloist*— in the neither or the nor?

It was my fifth novel. I had lived with the idea and the characters for three years. I had lived intensely with them for the year it took to write the first draft. I knew the book existed. I had mentally pigeon-holed it as "Books: fiction," along with my four other novels, a category which did not include short stories, articles, poems, or book reviews. Now I had to break "Books: fiction" into subsets—adult, young adult, juvenile; or should young adult be a further subset, and if so, of juvenile or of adult?

Reprinted from *The Horn Book Magazine* 57:221–28 (April 1981), with permission of the author. Copyright © 1981 by Frances Duncan. Based on a speech given at the twelfth Loughborough International Seminar on Children's Literature at the University of British Columbia, Vancouver, Canada, on Aug. 19, 1980.

To classify is to compare similarities and differences, to separate oranges from apples. Now I began to feel I was separating Winesaps from Spartans or mandarins from tangerines. The subsets were too discrete to be useful to me, and in disgust I lumped all five novels back into my large mental pigeonhole—"Books: fiction."

When I considered the actual process of writing the novels—a process I tend to describe either as barging through a foggy quicksand swamp grabbing at branches which break off in my hand, all filmed with a slightly out-of-focus camera, or as hanging my soul on a clothesline where five people will ignore it, two brush it out of their way, one tear it down and trample on it, and one, perhaps, stop and examine it— when I considered this process, I could find no differences. Five times I had repeated the process. Maybe the novels were all tangerines or all Spartans. None had been easier or less compelling to write than any of the others. And I had written them all in the same way—that is, oblivious of the potential reader.

For me, writing fiction means telling stories in the way the protagonists direct me to, checking constantly with them to see if they are satisfied; so the who-I-am-writing-for becomes the protagonist. This process creates a closed, secretive space between me and my characters, and it is not until the end of the first draft that I open this space enough to allow the intrusion of the so-called ideal reader—who is, of course, another bit of me broken off, distorted, heightened, and externalized, as is the protagonist. Whether they are thirteen or forty, male or female, the characters—the central ingredient of any book—live off the writer's viscera. Whether in a juvenile, an adult, or a neither/nor, a novel's characters are the tapeworms of literature.

Although I could find no justification for dividing "Books: fiction" into subsets on the basis of the writing process, I had discovered why I'd denied knowing *Kap-Sung Ferris* was a juvenile while I was writing it; then I had been totally concerned with telling Michelle's story of her friend Kim. The fact that the characters were teenagers and so would interest teenage readers had been irrelevant to me. If the process of writing a juvenile, an adult, or a neither/nor felt the same, I had to look elsewhere for criteria for classification. I began reading quantities of young adult novels to see what they were like. I told librarians what I was doing and was inundated with titles.

At the same time I was giving workshops and judging contests on writing for children; and after being hit with this nomenclature for the third or fourth time, I realized that this kind of writing is the only kind in which the emphasis is removed from the creation and placed on the recipient. Writing for adults is described by the product: novel, short story, poem, biography, article. Writing for children, however, includes all of the above and whatever else can be thrown in. Not just apples and oranges but also bananas, cherries, grapes, and the occasional mango. This giant fruit bowl seemed to indicate that the category was too big. It required the sorting expertise of a super-writer to compare picture books, poems, novels, and articles. This was distinctly unfair to the different genres: a comparison of *Where the Wild Things Are* with *A Wrinkle in Time* with *Now We Are Six*. Not only ridiculous, but a disservice to all three.

My discomfort with the category of writing for children continued to grow, and I realized there was a more dangerous aspect to it than just unfairness to the writing or the competence of contest judges. When the emphasis is removed from the product and placed on the consumer—in this case the child-reader—the focus changes from that of a writer trying to create the best, most honest writing he is capable of to that of trying to communicate a message to a specific audience. The creation becomes a vehicle for—in its broadest sense—proselytizing.

I have asked people why they want to write for children, and invariably their first answer is, "I've something to say to them" or "I think I can teach them something." In both answers the implicit something they want to say or teach is their values. Not only does this demean the audience, but it condemns the creation to failure before it is written. A poet writing a poem and a novelist writing a novel do not want to teach. They want something more—to communicate their views on life, certainly, but a whole life view; they create a poem or a novel in which the themes are implicit and indigenous (frequently unrecognized by the writer), a poem or a novel which says to the reader, this is the way I see it, do you? The communication in a novel or a poem becomes more a sharing of writer with reader than is often the case in writing for children. The children who are being written for are considered passive recipients of whatever the writer offers—lumps in desks—and it is a fact that what we learn, we remember much longer than what we are taught.

In its extreme form writing for children spawns what I've called revolutionary tract literature in which the overt, pasted-on message—usually a value judgment—is its reason for having been written; for example, those small books published by feminist presses for the sole purpose of showing Mommy out in the work world and Daddy in an apron. There is nothing wrong with teaching people, but literature is not the vehicle. There is nothing wrong with portraying alternate lifestyles, but books written for this purpose should not be considered literature. Taking the emphasis off the writing and placing it on the reader is the origin of the old chestnuts which still hurt when thrown: "Writing for children? Someday you'll be good enough to write for adults." And the rejoinder from defensive authors: "It's harder to write for children." Both statements are nonsense when the emphasis is put back where it belongs and the poem, novel, or story is written from the only place that allows a living literature: the writer's heart, blood, and guts.

This shift in emphasis from process to product, from book to reader, tied into my original "neither/nor" problem and was illuminated even more through the young adult books I was reading. I learned two things. The first was that if *Guest Soloist* did not fit into a category, it was not my problem. My problem was to create the best novel I could; categorization was a problem for the publisher. (I thought that after my previous novel, *Dragonhunt,* I had in *Guest Soloist* written a nonexperimental book, all surrealism tied to dreams and imaginings. I did not consider that to jump twenty years in alternating sections between the points of view of a thirty-five-year-old woman and a fifteen-year-old girl would be unusual. I learned that there is more than one way to experiment.) Of course, if *Guest Soloist* could not be labeled and therefore not published, it was going to become my problem; and I would have to decide if I wanted the book published badly enough to rewrite it to fit a category. But I've never been in favor of perpetuating systems for their own sakes.

The second thing I learned from my reading of about thirty young adult novels was that we have created an artificial and gratuitous group in which to hide some excellent writing: Jill Paton Walsh's *Unleaving,* Robert Cormier's *After the First Death* and *I Am the Cheese,* Ivan Southall's *What about Tomorrow?*[10] *and Josh,*[11] William Corlett's *The Gate of Eden,*[12] Ruth Nichols's *Song of the Pearl,*[13] Alan Garner's *Red Shift.*[14] If these books were intentionally written to be read by people around the age of the protagonists—fourteen to seventeen—some of them are not being read frequently enough because they are too complex. Many teenagers of the age and ability to read them prefer to read perceived adult books, including mass-market escapism and novelized versions of movies. And because these books are identified as young adult, they are lost to a majority of adults who would not consider reading a juvenile.

It seemed to me that some of the very best contemporary writing had been siphoned out of the mainstream and made accessible primarily to librarians, who had, in effect, become Robertson Davies's literate "clerisy." I was left wondering what Hemingway would have been called if the young adult category had existed in the twenties; and what would the next category be? Now that there were picture books and adult picture books, would there soon be young adult picture books? Or would we move on to old adult books published expressly for the mildly senile?

Eventually, I convinced myself I didn't believe in something as silly as the YA classification, but disbelieving didn't help, for it still existed. The category seemed to have been conceived to accommodate anything not a ponderous tome or an obvious juvenile. I thought this incessant grouping was an outgrowth of the computer age—bytes of information, nothing exists if unnumbered, FORTRAN, BASIC, PASCAL—which had been exploited with great enthusiasm by promotion and marketing people. As I continued my personal battle with the young adult classification, part of me was afraid I was being too simplistic and was ignoring apples and oranges in favor of sour grapes. I continued to ask questions. Why are so many young adult books being written? What kind of books are they? What is different about teenagers? Who is writing these books? Where do writers write from?

I could answer "what kind of books?" first. They are fairly short books; they are fast-moving; they frequently, though not always, have a forward-moving and/or a linear plot; most of them have teenage protagonists; they are dense with implied thought, but pages are not devoted to developing ruminations, so they can seem stylistically thin or superficial. These books reflect the world as it has evolved since mid-century—smaller, more crowded, moving more quickly, with an undertone of fear and desperation because of nuclear warheads, starvation, economic and ecological disasters. People are more physically crowded together in urban centers yet more individually isolated. They are forced through satellite communication to be aware of everyone else in the world, so that as privacy increases in one way, it is destroyed in another. Two kinds of people emerge—the haves and have-nots; the guilty and the starving.

The information boom, which makes facts obsolete before they can be printed, along with our improved communication systems, have encouraged the expectation that if people need to know something they can have the answers fast, simplistically, and in small digestible bits. Information in headlines, grade six reading level; change your life in sixty seconds with Mr. Clean or Reynolds Wrap; solutions to your problems in half an hour. The difficult we do today; the impossible takes a little longer.

Another feature of the young adult novel which misled me for a long time was the age of the protagonist. Adults in this century have not been accustomed to reading about teenagers and expect that books about adolescents must be for adolescents, specifically those slightly younger than the protagonists, for we know children read a few years ahead of their age. We have forgotten that some early novels about teenagers—*Joseph*

Andrews, Kidnapped, and several of Dickens's works—were originally published for adults and only later were adopted by teenagers.

Today's young adult novels are adopted by teenagers who want to know how others live at a time when people don't stay still long enough for them to observe. It used to be that in small, stable communities everyone knew everyone else's business; children grew into adulthood with more directly observable examples of human behavior. They knew that Mr. Jones drank and beat his wife every Saturday, that Sally was slow-witted, that both the cow and Mrs. Brown were pregnant; they had seen how the cow got into that state and could extrapolate to Mrs. Brown. Social-problem novels are avidly read today because they are fulfilling the same purpose—providing information, often superficially, about how others deal with problems.

The cult of the adolescent has predominated since the Second World War. Before then we had created the teenager—a spinoff of society's specialization in the face of more complicated technology, increasing wealth, and child labor laws—and having created teenagers, we began studying them as psychologists and educators; began catering to them as marketers; began justifying, rationalizing, and excusing them as apologists.

Although G. Stanley Hall published a thirteen-hundred-page, two-volume work, *Adolescence in 1904,* it was primarily descriptive, not analytical, as was most of the writing about adolescence until midcentury. Even Freud considered adolescence a time of extended childhood through which the important early stages of ego development continued until they were fully integrated in the adult. It was not until the thirties left the vulnerable jobless and the post-World War II baby boom coincided with increasing technological development that an expendable group of people was created. They were the least experienced, the least trained, and present everywhere—teenagers. There was no place for them in adult society, yet they were too old to be treated as children; so they were put in a social holding pattern. Society suddenly felt their presence, realized that in such numbers they were a new phenomenon, and began examining them like guinea pigs. John E. Horrocks in his revision of *The Psychology of Adolescence* observes:

Since mid-century the interest [in adolescence] has accelerated and is often accompanied by a concern only rarely present in previous generations. . . . Today's adolescent is growing up in a transitional period of great uncertainty and unresolved new directions. . . . The culture seems to offer more inconsistencies . . . [which] are routinely brought to the attention of youth. . . . The adolescent is being reared in a culture that worships youth.

Adolescence is a time of increasing self-awareness, of testing reality, and of seeking status and emancipation as an individual—which usually involves some struggle against adult authorities; it also is a time of great physical change, of developing abstract thought patterns, and of working out a personal value system. Adolescence is a time of potential pain and stress. Not only have we put a group of contemporaries in a social holding pattern and examined them like guinea pigs, but we have done it during their time of possibly greatest physical and emotional stress. We intensified their personal pain and explained it to them. The children of the baby boom which began in the forties reached adolescence in the fifties and sixties. Thus, in *Guest Soloist* I wrote about "the time bomb feeling of the generation which had grown up since Hiroshima: the affluence which was its right could be annihilated momentarily."

The other major question, "where do writers write from?" I answered by saying, "inside themselves." Writers write from what they have experienced, from what is important to them, from how they feel. Writers write out of pain, the pain of what has happened to them or of what they perceive they have missed. As John Fowles stated in *Daniel Martin,* "You create out of what you lack. Not what you have." Then if writers are writing from inside themselves, they are always writing historically. For something to come out of a writer uniquely his own, it has to have gestated a long time.

People in their twenties, thirties, and forties, who are writing the excellent books for young adults, are writing out of their strongest feelings —from their own adolescence. Consequently, many of these good writers are using teenage protagonists not solely because of the emotional load of their personal adolescence but also because teenagers are the people who have dominated my generation's view of society. Teenagers have been the bulge in the population curve, and not considering them manifest enough, our culture flattered them, catered to them, and sought their opinion.

Ultimately, I concluded that all these young adult novels are being written not for today's young adults but about yesterday's adolescents, by yesterday's adolescents; and Fowles should not have to feel apologetic about writing as a "retarded adolescent." Given his time and place in society, there is little else he can do. As more of these fifties and sixties teenagers-turned-writers are published, we can expect more of the so-called YA style of writing. The young adult category will be flooded. Do we have to wait until the dam bursts and spills these books into their rightful place—the mainstream of modern fiction? Or can we recognize that they have been wrongly classified and let them flow out gently?

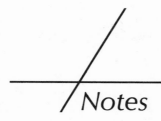

Notes

PREFACE

1. Lillian H. Smith, *The Unreluctant Years* (Chicago: American Library Assn., 1953), p. 7.

INTRODUCTION

1. Ellen E. M. Roberts, *The Children's Picture Book: How to Write It, How to Sell It* (Cincinnati: Writer's Digest Books, 1981), p. 14.

2. *A Fine Anger: A Critical Introduction to the Work of Alan Garner* (New York: Philomel, 1981), preface, p. 7.

3. Walter Lorraine, "An Interview with Maurice Sendak," *Wilson Library Bulletin* 52:156 (1977).

4. Two major categories, the informational book and biography are not represented here because *Beyond Fact*, edited by Jo Carr (Chicago: American Library Assn., 1982) should provide the extensive coverage they deserve. While I thus bypass nonfiction, I am glad to see nonfiction, the neglected stepsister in children's literary criticism, receive book-length analysis.

CHAPTER 1. DEFINITION

1. Julian Hawthorne, "Literature for Children," *The North American Review* 138:384 (1884); Leone Garvey, "What Is Children's Literature?" *Elementary English* 41:475 (May 1964).

2. *Children's Books in England and America in the Seventeenth Century: A History and a Checklist* (New York: Columbia Univ. Pr., 1955), p. 121.

3. F. J. Harvey Darton, *Children's Books in England: Five Centuries of Social Life,* 2nd ed. (Cambridge: Cambridge Univ. Pr., 1958), p. 1; *Cambridge Bibliography of English Literature,* ed. F. W. Bateson (Cambridge: Cambridge Univ. Pr., 1941), vol. 2, p. 553.

4. *New Cambridge Bibliography of English Literature,* ed. George Watson (Cambridge: Cambridge Univ. Pr., 1971), vol. 2, pp. 1013–14.

5. 6 July 1981, p. 75.

6. Gillian McMahon-Hill, "A Narrow Pavement Says 'Walk Alone': The

Books of Russell Hoban," *Children's Literature in Education* no. 20:41 (Spring 1976).

7. Roger Sale, *Fairy Tales and After: From Snow White to E. B. White* (Cambridge, Mass.: Harvard Univ. Pr., 1978), p. 1.

8. John Rowe Townsend, "An Elusive Border," *The Horn Book Magazine* 50:33 (Oct. 1974).

9. Sheila Egoff, *One Ocean Touching: Papers from the First Pacific Rim Conference on Children's Literature* (Metuchen, N.J.: Scarecrow, 1979), p. vi.

10. Elizabeth A. Cripps, "Kenneth Grahame: Children's Author?" *Children's Literature in Education* no. 40:17 (Spring 1981).

11. Elaine Moss, "The Seventies in British Children's Books," in *The Signal Approach to Children's Books*, Nancy Chambers, ed. (Harmondsworth, Eng.: Kestrel, 1980), p. 58.

12. Anita Moss, "MLA Sessions on Children's Literature," *ChLA Quarterly* 5:8 (Spring 1980).

13. Naomi Lewis, Preface, *Twentieth-Century Children's Writers*, ed. D. L. Kirkpatrick (New York: St. Martin's, 1978), p. x.

CHAPTER 2. STATUS

1. Susan Cooper, "Newbery Acceptance Speech," *Top of the News* 33:40 (Fall 1976).

2. Originally a preface to *Dealings with the Fairies* (1891); rptd. in Lance Salway, ed., *A Peculiar Gift* (Harmondsworth, Eng.: Kestrel, 1976), p. 164; Arthur Ransome, "A Letter to the Editor," *The Junior Bookshelf* 1:4 (July 1937).

3. "Writing for Children: A Social Engagement?" *Children Literature in Education* no. 6:18 (Nov. 1971); "A Discussion with William Mayne," *Children's Literature in Education* no. 2:48 (July 1970).

4. Joan Blos, "Forum: On Children's Literature: Some Heuristic Considerations," *Children's Literature in Education* no. 29:104 (Summer 1978).

5. "Books Remembered," Children's Book Council *Calendar*, 36:2 (1977).

6. Otfried Preussler, "What You Write for Children . . . Diversity and Limitations of Children's Literature," *Bookbird* 13, no. 4:3 (1975).

7. Ursula K. Le Guin, "A Response to the Le Guin Issue," *Science-Fiction Studies* 3, no. 8:45 (March 1979).

8. Haskel Frankel, "A Rose for Mary Poppins," *Saturday Review* 47:57 (7 Nov. 1964).

9. Le Guin, "A Response to the Le Guin Issue," p. 45.

10. Roni Natov and Geraldine DeLuca, "An Interview with Arnold Lobel," *The Lion and the Unicorn* 1:82 (Spring 1977).

11. Aidan Chambers, *The Reluctant Reader* (Oxford: Pergamon, 1969), p. 105; based on correspondence conducted in 1967. Garner's statement here antedates the London *Times* article. (Alan Garner, "A Bit More Practice," London *Times Literary Supplement*, 6 June 1968, p. 577). Eleanor Cameron,

"The Owl Service: A Study," *Wilson Library Bulletin* 44:428 (1969) sees Garner's going through a "private tussle" with the problem of writing for the young at the time of the London *Times* article mentioned above.

12. David E. White, "A Conversation with Maurice Sendak," *The Horn Book* 56:146–47 (April 1980); interview recorded Oct. 1979.

13. Joseph Krumgold, "Why Write Books for Children?" Children's Book World, *Chicago Tribune* 5 Nov. 1967.

14. Ellen Raskin, "Newbery Medal Acceptance," *The Horn Book Magazine* 55:383 (1979); E. L. H., "I Do Write for Children," *ibid.,* p. 386.

15. Virginia Haviland, *The Openhearted Audience: Ten Authors Talk about Writing for Children* (Washington, D.C.: Library of Congress, 1980), p. 28 (Cf. "children are the most critical audience on earth," in James Playsted Wood, "The Honest Audience," *The Horn Book* 43:615 [1967]); Isaac B. Singer, "Are Children the Ultimate Literary Critics?" Chicago *Sun-Times,* 12 March 1972, rptd. in *Top of the News* 29:32–36 (1972); Richard R. Lingeman, "Talks with Men in the Field," *New York Times Book Review,* pt. 2, 4 May 1969, p. 32; and Claude Rawson, "The Exaltation of Childhood," London *Times Literary Supplement,* 27 July 1981, p. 837.

16. C. S. Lewis, "On Three Ways of Writing for Children," in Sheila Egoff et al., eds. *Only Connect,* 2nd ed. (New York: Oxford Univ. Pr., 1980), p. 210.

17. Perry Nodelman, "Defining Children's Literature," *Children's Literature* 8:189–90 (1980).

18. James E. Higgins, "A Letter from C. S. Lewis," in *Horn Book Reflections,* Elinor Whitney Field, ed. (Boston: Horn Book, 1969), p. 23.

19. Aidan Chambers, "An Interview with Alan Garner," *The Signal Approach to Children's Books,* p. 289; Nat Hentoff, "Tell It as It Is," *New York Times Book Review,* pt. 2, 7 May 1967, p. 3; Jane Yolen, "It's Not All Peter Rabbit," *Writer* 88:12 (April 1975).

20. *Gates of Excellence* (New York: Elsevier/Nelson Books, 1981), p. 33.

21. Peter Neumeyer, "The Creation of Charlotte's Web: From Drafts to Book: Part 1," *The Horn Book Magazine* 57:489–97 (October 1982).

22. Cited in D. L. Kirkpatrick, *Twentieth-Century Children's Writers* (New York: St. Martin's Pr., 1978), p. 951.

CHILDREN'S LITERATURE, PART 1

1. Donald David Stone, *Novelists in a Changing World* (Cambridge, Mass.: Harvard Univ. Pr., 1972), p. 1.

2. John Goode, "The Art of Fiction: Walter Besant and Henry James" in David Howard, John Lucas, John Goode, eds., *Tradition and Tolerance in Nineteenth-Century Fiction: Critical Essays on Some English and American Novels* (London: Routledge & Kegan Paul, 1966), p. 245.

3. Walter Allen, *The English Novel: A Short Critical History* (London: Phoenix House, 1954), p. 249.

4. Ioan Williams, *Novel and Romance: 1700–1800* (London: Routledge & Kegan Paul, 1970).

5. George Moore, *Literature at Nurse; or, Circulating Morals* (London, 1885), p. 18.

6. Allen Tate, "Techniques of Fiction," *Sewanee Review,* 53:225 (1944).

7. First published 1884. From Henry James, *Selected Literary Criticism,* ed. Morris Shapiro (London: Heinemann, 1963), p. 49.

8. "A Humble Remonstrance," first published 1884. In *Works,* Swanson, ed. (London, 1911–12), IX, 148.

9. First published 1882. In *Works,* IX, 134.

10. S. Colvin, ed., *Letters of Robert Louis Stevenson* (London: Methuen, 1901), II, 20.

11. This essay was discovered "long buried" by Leon Edel and given pride of place in *Henry James: The Future of the Novel. Essays on the Art of Fiction* (New York: 1956). It was not completely unknown before that time, however, and seems to have influenced Walter Allen. See below n. 19.

12. Moore, *Literature at Nurse,* p. 21.

13. F. J. Coleman, Introduction, *Contemporary Essays in Aesthetics* (New York: McGraw-Hill, 1968), p. 17.

14. Wayne Booth, *The Rhetoric of Fiction* (Chicago: Univ. of Chicago Pr., 1961), p. 284.

15. Cornelia Meigs et al., *A Critical History of Children's Literature* (New York: Macmillan, 1969), p. 3 (Hughes' emphasis).

16. Dated May 5, 1925. Quoted in Morton Cohen, *Rider Haggard, His Life and Work,* 2nd ed. (London: Macmillan, 1968) p. 281.

17. H. Rider Haggard, *The Days of My Life,* ed. C. J. Longman (London: Longman, Green, 1926), II, 92. Quoted in Cohen, pp. 284–85.

18. John Rowe Townsend, *A Sense of Story: Essays on Contemporary Writers for Children* (London: Longman, 1971). The book however advocates and offers proper, serious criticism.

19. Allen, *The English Novel,* p. 249.

CHAPTER 3. APPROACHES

1. See "At Critical Cross-Purposes," in *Crosscurrents of Criticism* (Boston: Horn Book, 1977), Paul Heins, ed., for an interchange between Eleanor Cameron and Roald Dahl.

2. Eric A. Kimmel, "Children's Literature Without Children," *Children's Literature in Education* 13:40 (1982).

3. See Brian Alderson, "The Irrelevance of Children to the Children's Book Reviewer," *Children's Book Notes* 4:10–11 (Jan. 1965).

4. See Arthur N. Applebee, *The Child's Concept of Story* (Chicago: Univ. of Chicago Pr., 1978) and G. Robert Carlsen, "Literature Is," *English Journal* 63:23–27 (Feb. 1974). "Interpretive community" is Stanley Fish's key term. See *Is There a Text in This Class?: The Authority of Interpretive Communities* (Cambridge, Mass.: Harvard Univ. Pr., 1980).

5. From *British Journal of Aesthetics,* Jan. 1967, cited in Aidan Chambers, "The Reader in the Book: Notes from Work in Progress," *Signal: Approaches to Children's Books* no. 23:65 (May 1977).

6. See "Literature and Child Readers," Peggy Whalen-Levitt, ed., *ChLA Quarterly* 4:9–28 (Winter 1980).

7. "The Function of Criticism in Children's Literature," *Children's Literature in Education* 13:17 (1982).

8. Bennett A. Brockman, "Robin Hood and the Invention of Children's Literature," *Children's Literature* 10:1–17 (1982).

9. "On Three Ways of Writing for Children," *Only Connect,* Sheila Egoff et al., eds., 2nd ed. (New York: Oxford Univ. Pr., 1980), p. 210.

JUVENILE BOOKS OF THE PAST

1. *Aunt Sally's Life* is also by Margaret Gatty; *Melchior's Dream* (1862), edited by Mrs. Gatty, was written by her daughter Juliana Ewing; *Lightsome . . .* is by Charles Henry Bennett; and *The Fairchild Family* is by Mrs. Sherwood. In the sections deleted (about forty percent of the original review) the author discusses the school story and "a new school of juvenile writers," foremost of whom he finds Mrs. Gatty.—Ed.

LITERARY CRITICISM AND CHILDREN'S BOOKS

1. C. S. Lewis, *An Experiment in Criticism* (Cambridge: Cambridge Univ. Pr., 1965), p. 123.

2. *Ibid.,* p. 1.

3. Elias Bredsdorff, *Hans Christian Andersen: The Story of His Life and Work, 1805–1875* (New York: Scribner's, 1975), p. 255.

4. Bruno Bettelheim, *The Uses of Enchantment: The Meaning and Importance of Fairy Tales* (New York: Vintage Books, 1977), p. 4.

5. Kenneth A. Telford, *Aristotle's Poetics: Translation and Analysis* (Chicago: Henry Regnery, 1965), pp. 59–60.

6. Elizabeth Enright, *The Saturdays* (New York: Dell, 1941), p. 104.

7. Sheila Egoff, "Beyond the Garden Wall: Some Observations on Current Trends in Children's Literature," *The Arbuthnot Lectures, 1970–1979,* Zena Sutherland, ed. (Chicago: American Library Assn., 1980), p. 196.

8. *Ibid.,* p. 197.

9. Eleanor Cameron, "The Art of Elizabeth Enright," *The Horn Book Magazine* (December 1969), p. 644.

10. Norma Bagnall, "Realism: How Realistic It Is?" *Top of the News* (Fall 1980), p. 80.

11. Jay Daly, "The New Repression," *Top of the News* (Fall 1980), p. 81.

12. Flannery O'Connor, *The Habit of Being* (New York: Farrar, Straus & Giroux, 1979), p. 173.

13. John Rowe Townsend, *Written for Children: An Outline of English-Language Children's Literature* (Philadelphia: Lippincott, 1975), pp. 158–59.

CRITICISM AND CHILDREN'S LITERATURE

1. Gillian Avery, "The Children's Writer," in *Rudyard Kipling, the Man, His Work and His World* (London: Weidenfeld & Nicolson, 1972), p. 115.

2. Marcus Crouch, *The Nesbit Tradition* (London: Benn, 1972), p. 8.

3. See the Introduction to Frank Eyre, *Children's Books in the Twentieth Century* (London: Longman, 1971) on the age ranges of books for children.

4. It is not entirely irrelevant to observe that the only other time that I have come across the murder method used by "BB" in *The Little Grey Men*— that of blocking the bore of a shotgun—was in Spillane's *The Girl Hunters*.

5. D. H. Lawrence, *Selected Essays* (London: Penguin, 1950) p. 218. Note that Lawrence partly contradicts himself in the following paragraphs.

6. Erich Heller, *The Disinherited Mind* (London: Penguin, 1961), p. ix.

7. See, for example, F. R. Leavis, *The Common Pursuit* (London: Chatto & Windus, 1952).

8. See, for example, C. B. Cox's "Editorial," *Critical Quarterly* 14:1 (Spring 1972) for a discussion of this problem.

9. Robert Liddell, *A Treatise on the Novel* (London: Cape, 1965), pp. 20–21.

10. This outline was based initially on Guerin, Labor, Morgan, and Willingham, *A Handbook of Critical Approaches to Literature* (New York: Harper & Row, 1966). A similar approach to the problem of criticism and judgement can be found in Yvor Winters, "Preliminary Problems" in *In Defence of Reason*, 3rd ed. (London: Routledge & Kegan Paul, 1960).

11. Northrop Frye, *The Anatomy of Criticism* (Princeton, N.J.: Princeton Univ. Pr., 1957), pp. 247–8.

12. See, for example, Cleanth Brooks, *The Well-Wrought Urn*, 2nd ed. (London: Dobson, 1968).

13. For some of the more unlikely examples of prescriptions, see Wallace Hildick, *Children and Fiction* (London: Evans, 1970).

14. See, for example, *Swallows and Amazons*, p. 17, and *We Didn't Mean to Go to Sea*, p. 190 (Cape editions).

15. John Rowe Townsend. *A Sense of Story* (London: Longman, 1971), p. 9.

16. J. M. S. Tompkins, *The Art of Rudyard Kipling* (London: Methuen, 1959), p. 55.

17. F. R. Crews, *The Pooh Perplex* (London: Barker, 1964).

18. See, for example, William Walsh, *The Use of Imagination* (London: Chatto & Windus, 1959).

THE READER IN THE BOOK

1. Wolfgang Iser, *The Implied Reader* (Baltimore: Johns Hopkins Univ. Pr., 1974), p. 57.

2. Wayne C. Booth, *The Rhetoric of Fiction* (Chicago: Univ. of Chicago Pr., 1961), p. 138.

3. The term was revived by Kathleen Tillotson in her inaugural lecture at the University of London, published under the title *The Tale and the Teller* (London, 1959): "Writing on George Eliot in 1877 Dowden said that the form that most persists in the mind after reading her novels is not any of the characters, but 'one who, if not the real George Eliot, is that second self who writes her books, and lives and speaks through them.' The 'second self,' he goes on, is 'more substantial than any mere human personality' and has 'fewer reserves'; while 'behind it, lurks well pleased the veritable historical self secure from impertinent observation and criticism.' "

4. The original essay goes on to analyze a juvenile work of Lucy Boston as contrasted with one of her adult works. Also included in the original is "Intermission: What the Writers Say." It has been omitted here because many of the ideas there are discussed at length in chapter 2 of this anthology.—Ed.

PURSUING "THE READER IN THE BOOK"

1. W. K. Wimsatt, *The Verbal Icon* (New York: Noonday Pr., 1958), pp. 5–18, 21.

2. Aidan Chambers, "The Reader in the Book: Notes from Work in Progress," *Signal: Approaches to Children's Books* 23:64–87 (May 1977).

3. Reinbert Tabbert, "The Impact of Children's Books: Cases and Concepts (Part I)," *Children's Literature in Education* 10:92–102 (Summer 1979).

4. Wolfgang Iser, *The Act of Reading: A Theory of Aesthetic Response* (Baltimore: Johns Hopkins Univ. Pr., 1978).

5. Louise Rosenblatt, *The Reader, the Text, the Poem: The Transactional Theory of the Literary Work* (Carbondale: Southern Illinois Univ. Pr., 1978).

6. Iser, *The Act of Reading*, pp. 20–21, 135.

7. Rosenblatt, *The Reader*, p. 140.

8. Iser, *The Act of Reading*, p. x.

9. *Ibid.*, 63, 64.

10. Rosenblatt, *The Reader*, pp. 23, 173.

11. Iser, *The Act of Reading*, p. 132.

12. Rosenblatt, *The Reader*, pp. 162, 153, 154, 148.

13. Iser, *The Act of Reading*, pp. 34, 18.

14. *Ibid.*, pp. ix–x, 18–19.

15. Rosenblatt, *The Reader*, p. 122.

16. Iser, *The Act of Reading*, p. 135.

CHAPTER 4. PICTURE BOOKS

1. Uri Shulevitz, "What Is a Picture Book?" *Wilson Library Bulletin* 55:100 (1980). A facsimile of *The Birth-Day Gift* was printed for the Friends of the Osborne and Lillian H. Smith Collections (Toronto, 1969) and as one volume in the Osborne Collection Facsimiles (London: The Bodley Head, 1981).

2. Introduction, *Looking at Picture Books: An Exhibition* (London: National Book League, 1973), p. 6.

3. Brian Alderson, "The American Tradition," London *Times Literary Supplement*, 12 Dec. 1976, p. 1546.

4. Shulevitz, "What Is a Picture Book?" p. 101.

5. Selma G. Lanes, *The Art of Maurice Sendak* (New York: Abrams, 1980), p. 185 and *passim*.

6. "Picture Books: What Do Reviews Review?" *Top of the News* 37:83–84 (1980).

7. Elaine Moss, "Protecting the Innocent," London *Times Literary Supplement*, 1 Oct. 1976, pp. 1244–45.

8. See her selection in part 1, chapter 3 of this anthology.

9. Lance Salway, *A Peculiar Gift* (Harmondsworth, Eng.: Kestrel, 1976), p. 231.

10. See Joseph H. Schwarcz, *Ways of the Illustrator: Visual Communication in Children's Literature* (Chicago: American Library Assn., 1982), for an in-depth study of the genre.

11. Selma G. Lanes, "Sendak at 50," *New York Times Book Review*, 29 April 1979, p. 49.

THE PICTURE BOOK AS ART OBJECT

1. Marjorie Lewis, "Back to Basics: Re-evaluating Picture Books," *School Library Journal* March 1976, pp. 82–83.

2. "Questions to an Artist Who Is Also an Author," *Library of Congress Quarterly* 28:263–80 (Oct. 1971).

LOUDER THAN A THOUSAND WORDS

1. Bette J. Peltola, "Newbery and Caldecott Medals: Authorization and Terms," *Top of the News*, Fall 1979, p. 36.

2. *The Horn Book Magazine*, August 1973, p. 367.

3. *The Horn Book Magazine*, August 1976, p. 151.

4. Rebecca Lukens, *A Critical Handbook of Children's Literature* (Glenview, Ill.: Scott, Foresman, 1976).

5. *Ibid.*, p. 7.

6. *Ibid.*, p. 115.

CHAPTER 5. FAIRY TALES

1. F. J. Harvey Darton, *Children's Books in England*, 2nd ed. (Cambridge: Cambridge Univ. Pr., 1958), p. 85. For more on the background of this period, see Robert Bator, "Eighteenth-Century England Versus the Fairy Tale," *Research Studies* 39:1–10 (March 1971).

2. "Sometimes Fairy Stories May Say Best What's to Be Said," *New York Times Book Review*, pt. 2, 18 Nov. 1956, p. 3.

3. Iona and Peter Opie, eds., *The Classic Fairy Tales* (New York: Oxford Univ. Pr., 1980), p. 18.

4. Barbara Herrnstein Smith, "Narrative Versions, Narrative Theories," *Critical Inquiry* 7:215–22 (Autumn 1980).

5. For a rebuttal to Bettelheim and a Marxist slant on fairy tales, see Jack Zipes, *Breaking the Magic Spell: Radical Theories of Folk and Fairy Tales* (Austin: Univ. of Texas Pr., 1979).

CHAPTER 6. POETRY

1. See Iona and Peter Opie, eds., *The Oxford Dictionary of Nursery Rhymes* (Oxford: Clarendon Pr., 1951).

2. "Poetry for Pleasure," London *Times Literary Supplement,* Children's Book Section, 5 Nov. 1956, p. ix; "This Way Delight," *ibid.,* 15 Nov. 1957, p. vi.

3. "Poetry Books for Children," ed. and introduction by Alethea Helbig, *ChLA Quarterly* 5:9 (Summer 1980); Agnes Perkins, "Critical Summary of Recent Journal Articles on Poetry for Children," *ibid.,* pp. 35–38.

4. Margaret Meek and Peter Hunt, "The Signal Poetry Award," *Signal* no. 35:67 (May 1981).

HOW TO TELL A SHEEP FROM A GOAT

1. Eve Merriam, "Inside a Poem," in *It Doesn't Always Have to Rhyme* (New York: Atheneum, 1964).

2. Marjorie Seymour Watts, "New Shoes," in *I Like Poems and Poems Like Me,* ed. Penny Pagliaro (Press Pacifica, 1977).

3. Richard Munkittrick, "Unsatisfied Yearning," in *Reflections on a Gift of Watermelon Pickle and Other Modern Verse,* Stephen Dunning, ed. (New York: Lothrop, 1967).

4. Dorothy Aldis, "On a Snowy Day," in *All Together* (New York: Putnam, 1952).

5. Marie Louis Allen, "First Snow," in *A Pocketful of Rhymes* (New York: Harper, 1939).

6. Walter de la Mare, "The Snowflake," in *Bells and Grass* (New York: Viking, 1963).

7. Shel Silverstein, "Beware, My Child," in *Piping Down the Valleys Wild,* ed. Nancy Larrick (New York: Delacorte, 1968).

8. Aileen Fisher, "Raccoons," in *Going Barefoot* (New York: Crowell, 1960).

9. Karla Kuskin, "The Witches' Ride," in *The Rose on My Cake* (New York: Harper, 1964).

10. Dorothy Baruch, "Merry-Go-Round," in *Time for Poetry,* May Hill Arbuthnot, ed. (Chicago: Scott, Foresman, 1952).

11. May Hill Arbuthnot, ed., *Time for Poetry.*

12. Mark Van Doren, "Merry-Go-Round," in *Good Morning: Last Poems by Mark Van Doren* (New York: Hill & Wang, 1973).

SOME AFTERTHOUGHTS ON POETRY

1. Francelia Butler, "The Editor's High Chair," in *Children's Literature,* vol. I (Philadelphia: Temple Univ. Pr., 1972), pp. 7, 8.
2. A. E. Housman, *The Name and Nature of Poetry* (New York: Macmillan, 1936), p. 3.
3. John Ciardi, "Manner of Speaking," *Saturday Review,* May 20, 1972.
4. Isaac Watts, "The Sluggard," in *Divine and Moral Songs for Children* (1715).
5. Rebecca J. Lukens, *A Critical Handbook of Children's Literature* (Glenview, Ill.: Scott, Foresman, 1976), p. 163.
6. *Ibid.,* p. 177.
7. David McCord, "Castor Oil," in *One at a Time* (Boston: Little, Brown, 1977), p. 160.

CHAPTER 7. FICTION

1. *From Primer to Pleasure in Reading* (Boston: Horn Book, 1972), p. 50.
2. Pelorus, "Notebook," *Signal* no. 9:129 (Sept. 1972).
3. "The Great American Novel for Children—and Why Not," *The Horn Book Magazine* 50:176–85 (April 1974).
4. "Fiction for Children and Adults: Some Essential Differences," in *Writers, Critics, and Children,* Geoff Fox, ed. (New York: Agathon Pr., 1976), pp. 140–43.
5. London: Evans Bros., 1970; pp. 29, 142.
6. *The Child and the Book: A Psychological and Literary Exploration* (Cambridge: Cambridge Univ. Pr., 1981), pp. 1, 9, 13, 14–15.

CHAPTER 8. FANTASY

1. Anita Moss, review of *Fantasy Literature, a Core Collection and Reference Guide* by Marshall B. Tymn, Kenneth J. Zahorski and Robert H. Boyer (New York: Bowker, 1979) in *Phaedrus* 7:36 (Winter 1980).
2. Neil Philip, "Fantasy: Double Cream or Instant Whip?" *Signal* no. 35:83 (May 1981).
3. Jane Yolen, *Touch Magic: Fantasy, Faerie and Folklore in the Literature of Childhood* (New York: Philomel, 1981), p. 77; Lloyd Alexander, "The Flat-Heeled Muse," *The Horn Book Magazine* 41:143 (April 1965).

CHILDREN'S LITERATURE, PART 2

1. E. M. Forster, *Aspects of the Novel* (London: Arnold, 1927), chapters 6 and 7.
2. E. Nesbit, *Five Children—and It* (London, 1902), p. 18.
3. George Moore, *Literature at Nurse or Circulating Morals* (London, 1885).

4. Robert Scholes and Robert Kellogg, *The Nature of Narrative* (New York: Oxford Univ. Pr., 1966), p. 232.

5. Lillian Smith, *The Unreluctant Years* (Chicago: American Library Assn., 1953), p. 65.

6. Elizabeth Cook, *The Ordinary and the Fabulous* (Cambridge: Cambridge Univ. Pr., 1969), p. 7.

7. W. J. Scott, quoted in Geoffrey Trease, *Tales Out of School*, 2nd ed. (London: 1964), p. 73.

8. Smith, *Unreluctant Years*, p. 152.

TOWARD A DEFINITION OF FANTASY FICTION

1. Examples in this paper are from Peter Beagle, *The Last Unicorn* (New York: Viking, 1968).

2. Austin Warren, "Nature and Modes of Narrative Fiction," *Approaches to the Novel,* ed. Robert Scholes (San Francisco: Chandler, 1961), p. 192.

3. D. O. Hebb, "The Psychology of Fear," *Psychology Review* 53:259–76 (1946).

4. H. P. Lovecraft, quoted by Lin Carter, *Lovecraft: A Look behind the Clhuthu Mythos* (New York: Ballantine, 1972), p. xv.

5. J. R. R. Tolkien, "On Fairy Stories," *The Tolkien Reader* (New York: Ballantine, 1966), p. 10.

6. Ernst Cassirer, *Language and Myth* (New York: Dover, 1946), p. 60.

7. Hutton Webster, *Magic: A Sociological Study* (Stanford, Calif.: Stanford Univ. Pr., 1948), p. 36.

8. Cassirer, *Language and Myth,* p. 45.

9. Beagle, *The Last Unicorn.*

10. Joseph Campbell, *The Flight of the Wild Gander* (Chicago: Regnery, 1972), p. 171.

11. Tolkien, *The Tolkien Reader,* p. 23.

12. Andrew Lytle, "The Working Novelist and the Mythmaking Process," in *Myth and Mythmaking,* Henry A. Murray, ed. (Boston: Beacon, 1968), p. 152.

13. Richard Chase, "Notes on the Study of Myth," in *Myth and Literature,* ed. John B. Vickery (Lincoln: Univ. of Nebraska Pr., 1966), p. 73.

14. Cassirer, *Language and Myth,* p. 14.

ENCHANTMENT REVISITED

1. Virginia Woolf, *Granite and Rainbow* (New York, Harcourt, 1958), p. 64.

2. Lillian Smith, *The Unreluctant Years* (Chicago: American Library Assn., 1953), p. 153.

3. C. S. Lewis, "On Three Ways of Writing for Children," in *Of Other Worlds,* Walter Hooper, ed. (New York, Harcourt, 1966), p. 25.

4. Smith, *The Unreluctant Years,* p. 150.

5. Lewis, "On Three Ways of Writing for Children," p. 34.

6. James E. Higgins, *Beyond Words* (New York: Teachers College Pr., 1970), p. 103.

7. John S. Morris, "Fantasy in a Mythless Age," *Children's Literature: The Great Excluded* 2:80 (1973).

8. G. K. Chesterton, "The Dragon's Grandmother," in *Tremendous Trifles* (New York: Sheed & Ward, 1955), p. 83.

CHAPTER 9. HISTORICAL FICTION

1. Edwin M. Eigner, *Robert Louis Stevenson and Romantic Tradition* (Princeton, N.J.: Princeton Univ. Pr., 1966), 43; Dennis Butts, *R. L. Stevenson* (London: Bodley Head, 1966), p. 31.

2. Martin Green, *Dreams of Adventure, Deeds of Empire* (New York: Basic Books, 1979), p. 220.

3. Robert Leeson, "The Spirit of What Age? *Children's Literature in Education* no. 23:173–75 (Winter 1976).

4. Geoffrey Trease, "The Historical Novelist at Work," *Children's Literature in Education* no. 7:6 (March 1972).

5. "Shoulder the Sky: On the Writing of Historical Fiction for Children." New York Public Library *Bulletin* 79:124–38 (Winter 1976).

6. Leeson, "The Spirit of What Age?" p. 177.

7. Linda Kauffman Peterson and Marilyn Leather Solt, "The Newbery Medal and Honor Books: 1922–1981," *ChLA Quarterly* 6:24 (Fall 1981).

8. *Thursday's Child: Trends and Patterns in Contemporary Children's Literature* (Chicago: American Library Assn., 1981), p. 160.

SOME OBSERVATIONS ON CHILDREN'S HISTORICAL FICTION

1. Alfred Tresidder Sheppard, *The Art and Practice of Historical Fiction* (London: Humphrey Toulmin, 1930), p. 15.

2. *Ibid.*, p. 17.

3. Herbert Butterfield, *The Historical Novel* (Cambridge: Cambridge Univ. Pr., 1924), p. 1.

4. Brander Matthews, *The Historical Novel and Other Essays* (New York: Scribner's, 1901), p. 23.

CHAPTER 10. SCIENCE FICTION

1. "Ray Guns and Rocket Ships," in *Readings about Children's Literature*, p. 368; M. Jean Greenlaw, "Science Fiction: Impossible! Improbable! or Prophetic?" *Elementary English* 48:196 (April 1971); Darko Suvin, "On What Is Not an SF Narration . . . ," *Science-Fiction Studies* 5:45 (March 1978).

2. "Writing for the 'Electric Boy': Notes on the Origins of Children's SF," *ChLA Quarterly* 5:9–12 (Winter 1981).

3. That guidebook may already exist. According to Neal-Schuman Pub-

lishers, *Science Fiction: The Mythos of a New Romance* by Janice Antczak (in press) will focus on science fiction as a subgenre of children's literature.

CHILDREN'S SCIENCE FICTION

1. *Anatomy of Wonder: Science Fiction*, Neil Barron, ed. (New York: Bowker, 1976), pp. 302–7.

FANTASY, SF, AND THE MUSHROOM PLANET BOOKS

1. Eleanor Cameron, *The Wonderful Flight to the Mushroom Planet* (Boston: Atlantic/Little, Brown, 1954).
2. Perry Nodelman, "The Depths of All She Is: Eleanor Cameron," *Children's Literature Association Quarterly*, Winter 1980, p. 6.
3. Robert Scholes, *Structural Fabulation* (Notre Dame, Indiana: Univ. of Notre Dame Pr., 1975).
4. Ursula K. Le Guin, *A Wizard of Earthsea* (Berkeley, Calif.: Parnassus, 1968), p. 185.
5. Scholes, *Structural Fabulation*, pp. 86–87.
6. *Ibid.*, p. 29.
7. *Ibid.*, p. 47.
8. Eleanor Cameron, *The Green and Burning Tree: On the Writing and Enjoyment of Children's Books* (Boston: Atlantic/Little, Brown, 1969), pp. 77–78.
9. Ursula K. Le Guin, *The Language of the Night: Essays on Fantasy and Science Fiction*, ed. and with introduction by Susan Wood (New York: Putnam, 1979), pp. 101–19.
10. Eleanor Cameron, *Time and Mr. Bass* (Boston: Atlantic/Little, Brown, 1967), pp. 214–16.
11. Cameron, *The Wonderful Flight*, p. 15.
12. Nodelman, "The Depths of All She Is," p. 7.
13. Cameron, *The Wonderful Flight*, p. 153.

CHAPTER 11. YOUNG ADULT NOVEL

1. Ruth A. Barnes, "What Book Shall I Buy for My Boy?" *Elementary English* 5:307–8 (Dec. 1928); Franklin K. Mathiews, "Blowing Out the Boy's Brains," *Outlook* 108:652–54 (18 Nov. 1914).
2. Richard Peck, "In the Country of Teenage Fiction," *American Libraries* 4:204–7 (April 1973).
3. Catherine E. Studier, "An Interview with Sandra Scoppettone," *The ALAN Review* 8:10 (Winter 1981).
4. Steve Roxburgh, "The Novel of Crisis: Contemporary Adolescent Fiction," *Children's Literature* 7:254 (1978).
5. "Dreams Must Explain Themselves," *The Language of the Night: Essays on Fantasy and Science Fiction*, Susan Wood, ed. (New York: Berkeley Books, 1982), pp. 45–46. This is an extremely important collection of criticism by Le Guin.

6. Marilyn Kaye, "In Defense of Formula Fiction; or, They Don't Write Schlock the Way They Used To," *Top of the News* 37:87–90 (Fall 1980).

7. "Peck, "In the Country of Teenage Fiction," p. 205; Kenneth L. Donelson and Alleen Pace Nilsen, *Literature for Today's Young Adults* (Glenview, Ill.: Scott, Foresman, 1981), p. 8.

PAP TO PROTEIN

1. "Trash for Teen-agers: Or Escape from Thackeray, the Brontes, and the Incomparable Jane," *Courier-Journal* (Louisville, Kentucky), 17 June 1951.

2. Frank G. Jennings, "Literature for Adolescents—Pap or Protein?" *English Journal* 45:526–31 (Dec. 1956).

3. Dwight L. Burton, "The Novel for the Adolescent," *English Journal* 40:363–69 (Sept. 1951).

4. Stephen Dunning, "A Definition of the Role of the Junior Novel Based on Analysis of Thirty Selected Novels," Ph.D. diss., Florida State Univ., 1959.

5. Dwight L. Burton, *Literature Study in the High Schools* (New York: Holt, 1959).

6. Richard S. Alm, "The Glitter and the Gold," *English Journal* 44:315–20 (Sept. 1955).

7. Alfred P. Muller, "The Currently Popular Adolescent Novel as Transitional Literature," Ph.D. diss., Florida State Univ., 1973.

STILL PLAYING IT SAFE

1. Judy Blume, *Forever* (Scarsdale, N.Y.: Bradbury, 1975).

2. Patricia Dizenzo, *Why Me? The Story of Jenny* (New York: Avon, 1976).

3. James Fritzhand, *Life Is a Lonely Place* (New York: Evans, 1975).

4. Anne Alexander, *To Live a Lie* (New York: Atheneum, 1975).

5. Lila Perl, *The Tell-Tale Summer of Tina C.* (New York: Seabury, 1975).

6. Chester Aaron, *Hello to Bodega* (New York: Atheneum, 1976).

7. Kin Platt, *Chloris and the Freaks* (Scarsdale, N.Y.: Bradbury, 1975).

8. Susan Pfeffer, *Marly the Kid* (Garden City, N.Y.: Doubleday, 1975).

9. M. C. Brei and M. A. Timms, "Realism: Honesty and Hope; Its Value in Books for Children and Young People," *Wisconsin Library Bulletin*, Jan. 1974, p. 46.

10. Frances Hanckel and John Cunningham, "Can Young Gays Find Happiness in YA Books?" *Wilson Library Bulletin*, Jan. 1976, p. 528.

11. Geraldine Kay, *Joanna All Alone* (Nashville: Nelson, 1974).

12. Richard Shaw, *Call Me Al Raft* (Nashville: Nelson, 1975).

13. S. E. Hinton, *Rumble Fish* (New York: Delacorte, 1975).

14. Kin Platt, *Headman* (New York: Greenwillow/Morrow, 1975).

15. *The Bulletin for the Center for Children's Books*, Dec. 1975.

16. Robert Cormier, *The Chocolate War* (New York: Pantheon, 1974).

17. Betsy Hearne, *Booklist*, July 1, 1974, p. 1199.

18. Ann Moody, *Mr. Death* (New York: Harper, 1975).

Bibliography

The following bibliography is limited to anthologies of critical readings, interviews, conference proceedings, and bibliographies. For some additional critical studies, see the notes for each chapter as well as the Rahn and Smith bibliographies. Names listed refer to editors and compilers.

Blishen, Edward. *The Thorny Paradise: Writers on Writing for Children*. London: Kestrel; Boston: Horn Book, 1975. 175p.

Cameron, Eleanor. *The Green and Burning Tree: On the Writing and Enjoyment of Children's Books*. Boston: Atlantic/Little, Brown, 1969. 377p.

Chambers, Nancy. *The Signal Approach to Children's Books*. Harmondsworth England: Kestrel, 1980; Metuchen, N.J.: Scarecrow, 1981, 352p.

Egoff, Sheila A. *One Ocean Touching: Papers from the First Pacific Rim Conference on Children's Literature*. Metuchen, N.J.: Scarecrow, 1979. 252p.

_____, G. T. Stubbs, and L. F. Ashley. *Only Connect: Readings on Children's Literature*. 2nd ed. New York: Oxford Univ. Pr., 1980. 457p.

Esmonde, Margaret P. and Priscilla A. Ord. *Proceedings of the Fifth Annual Conference of the Children's Literature Association*. Harvard University, March, 1978. Villanova, Pa.: Villanova Univ. for the Association, 1979. 122p.

Fenwick, Sarah Innis. *A Critical Approach to Children's Literature*. Chicago: Univ. of Chicago Pr., 1967. 129p.

Field, Elinor Whitney. *Horn Book Reflections: On Children's Books and Reading: Selected from Eighteen Years of the Horn Book Magazine, 1948–1966*. Boston: Horn Book, 1969. 367p.

Fox, Geoff and Graham Hammond, with Stuart Amor. *Responses to Children's Literature*: Proceedings of the Fourth Symposium of the International Research Society for Children's Literature Held at the University of Exeter, Sept. 9, 1978. New York: K. G. Saur for the Society, 1979. 141p.

_____ and others. *Writers, Critics, and Children: Articles from Children's Literature in Education*. New York: Agathon Pr., 1976. 245p.

Fryatt, Norma R. *A Horn Book Sampler on Children's Books and Reading: Selected from Twenty-five Years of the Horn Book Magazine, 1924–1948.* Boston: Horn Book, 1959. 261p.

Haviland, Virginia. *Children and Literature: Views and Reviews.* Glenview, Ill.: Scott, Foresman, 1973, 461p.

_____. *The Openhearted Audience: Ten Authors Talk about Writing for Children.* Washington, D.C.: Library of Congress, 1980. 198p.

Hearne, Betsy and Marilyn Kaye. *Celebrating Children's Books: Essays on Children's Literature in Honor of Zena Sutherland.* New York: Lothrop, 1981. 244p.

Heins, Paul. *Crosscurrents of Criticism: Horn Book Essays: 1968–1977.* Boston: Horn Book, 1977. 359p.

Jones, Cornelia and Olivia R. Way. *British Children's Authors: Interviews at Home.* Chicago: American Library Assn., 1976. 176p.

Kirkpatrick, D. L. *Twentieth-Century Children's Writers.* New York: St. Martin's, 1978. 1507p.

Koefoed, Ingerlise. *Children's Literature and the Child*: Lectures and Debates from the International Course on Children's Literature, Loughborough Summer School, 1972, Hingsgavl, Denmark. Copenhagen: The Danish Library Assn., 1975. 70p.

Lenz, Millicent and Ramona M. Mahood. *Young Adult Literature: Background and Criticism.* Chicago: American Library Assn., 1980. 516p.

Meek, Margaret, Aidan Warlow, and Griselda Barton. *The Cool Web: The Pattern of Children's Reading.* New York: Atheneum, 1978. 427p.

Rahn, Suzanne. *Children's Literature: An Annotated Bibliography of the History and Criticism.* New York: Garland Publishing, 1981. 451p.

Richardson, Selma K. *Research about Nineteenth-Century Children and Books: Portrait Studies.* Monograph No. 17. Urbana, Ill.: Univ. of Illinois Graduate School of Library Science, 1980. 142p.

Robinson, Evelyn R. *Readings about Children's Literature.* New York: McKay, 1966. 431p.

Salway, Lance. *A Peculiar Gift: Nineteenth-Century Writings on Books for Children.* Harmondsworth, England: Kestrel, 1976. 573p.

Smith, Elva S. *The History of Children's Literature.* 2nd ed. Rev. and enlarged by Margaret Hodges and Susan Steinfirst. Chicago: American Library Assn., 1980. 304p.

Sutherland, Zena. *The Arbuthnot Lectures: 1970–1979.* Chicago: American Library Assn., 1980. 203p.

Townsend, John Rowe. *A Sense of Story: Essays on Contemporary Writers for Children.* Philadelphia: Lippincott, 1971. 213p.

_____. *A Sounding of Storytellers: New and Revised Essays on Contemporary Writers for Children.* Philadelphia: Lippincott, 1979. 218p.

Varlejs, Jana. *Young Adult Literature in the Seventies: A Selection of Readings.* Metuchen, N.J.: Scarecrow, 1978. 452p.

Wintle, Justin and Emma Fisher. *The Pied Piper: Interviews with the Influential Creators of Children's Literature.* New York: Paddington Pr., 1974. 320p.